AF804913

30.

19.

2

-4.

-4. MAR.

2

22.

24.

OXFORD
POLYTECHNIC
LIBRARY

Ox
Lib

711

0038904206

TRANSPORTATION PLANNING IN A CHANGING WORLD

EUROPEAN SCIENCE FOUNDATION

The European Science Foundation is an international non-governmental organisation with its seat in Strasbourg (France). Its members are academies and research councils with national responsibility for supporting scientific research, and which are funded largely from governmental sources. The term 'science' is used in its broadest sense to include the humanities, social sciences, biomedical sciences, the natural sciences and mathematics. The ESF currently has 48 members from 18 European countries.

The tasks of the ESF are:

to assist its Member Organisations to coordinate research programmes;

to identify areas in need of stimulation, particularly those of an inter-disciplinary nature;

to further cooperation between researchers by facilitating their movement between laboratories, holding workshops, managing supporting schemes approved by the Member Organisations, and arranging for the joint use of special equipment;

to harmonise and assemble data useful to the Member Organisations;

to foster the efficient dissemination of information;

to respond to initiatives which are aimed at advancing European science;

to maintain constructive relations with the European Communities and other relevant organisations.

The ESF is funded through a general budget to which all Member Organisations contribute (according to a scale assessed in relation to each country's net national income), and a series of special budgets covering additional activities, funded by those organisations which choose to participate. The programmes of the ESF are determined by the Assembly of all Member Organisations. Their implementation is supervised by an elected Executive Council, assisted by the office of the Foundation which consists of an international staff directed by the Secretary General.

Transportation Planning in a Changing World

Edited by
P. Nijkamp
and
S. Reichman

Gower in association with
the European Science Foundation

© European Science Foundation, 1987
All rights reserved. No part of this publication may be reproduced, stored in a retrieval system, or transmitted in any form or by any means, electronic, mechanical, photocopying, recording, or otherwise without the prior permission of Gower Publishing Company Limited.

Published by
Gower Publishing Company Limited
Gower House
Croft Road
Aldershot
Hants GU11 3HR
England

Gower Publishing Company
Old Post Road
Brookfield
Vermont 05036
USA

ACC. No. 389042
CATEGORY PRICE
HN SL £25.00
711.7 TRA
TECHNIC
LIBRARY

British Library Cataloguing in Publication Data
Transportation planning in a changing world.
1. Transportation — Planning
I. Nijkamp, Peter II. Reichman S.
711'.7 HE193

Library of Congress Cataloging-in-Publication Data
Transportation planning in a changing world
Includes index.
1. Transportation — Planning. I. Nijkamp, Peter.
II. Reichman, Shalom, 1935–
HE193.T68 1986 380.5'068 86-14835

ISBN 0 566 05250 4

Printed and bound in Great Britain by
Biddles Ltd, Guildford and King's Lynn

Contents

Contributors

P. Bauchet
Greco Transpace
CNRS
27 rue Paul-Bert
F-94204 Ivry Cedex
France

P.H. Bly
Transport and Road Research Laboratory
Old Workingham Road
Crowthorne
Berkshire RG11 6AU
England

F. le Clercq
Physical Planning Dept
City of Amsterdam
Wibautstraat 3
NL-1091 GH Amsterdam
The Netherlands

E. Fanara
Centro Universitario di Studi sui Trasporti
Via del Bufalo 9
I-98100 Messina
Italy

M.M. Fischer
Institut für Geographie
Universität Wien
Universitätsstrasse 7
A-1010 Wien
Austria

T. Hägerstrand
Dept of Social and Economic Geography
University of Lund
Sölvegatan 13
S-223 69 Lund
Sweden

A.A.I. Holtgrefe
Netherlands' Railways Ltd
Moreelsepark 1
NL-3500 EP Utrecht
The Netherlands

P.M. Jones
Transport Studies Unit
Oxford University
11 Bevington Road
Oxford OX2 6NB
England

E. Kutter
Technical University Berlin
Hardenbergstrasse 29c
D-1000 Berlin 12
Germany

A. La Bella
Istituto di Analisi dei Sistemi ed Informatica
Viale Manzoni 30
I-00185 Roma
Italy

I. Masser
Dept of Town and Regional Planning
University of Sheffield
6 Claremont Place
Sheffield S10 2TB
England

V. Masset
Greco Transpace
CNRS
27 rue Paul-Bert
F-94204 Ivry Cedex
France

P. Nijkamp
Dept of Economics
Free University
P.O. Box 7161
NL-1007 MC Amsterdam
The Netherlands

C.E. Norrbom
The Swedish Board of Transport
P.O. Box 1339
S-171 26 Solna
Sweden

P.O. Pedersen
Sydjysk Universitetscenter
Glentevej 7
DK-6705 Esbjerg
Denmark

S. Reichman
Dept of Geography
Hebrew University
Mount Scopus
Jerusalem
Israel

C.J. Ruijgrok
Traffic and Transport Unit TNO
P.O. Box 215
NL-2600 AE Delft
The Netherlands

I. Salomon
Dept of Geography
Hebrew University
Mount Scopus
Jerusalem
Israel

F. Snickars
Dept of Regional Planning
Royal Institute of Technology
S-10044 Stockholm
Sweden

D. Starkie
Institute for Fiscal Studies
180/182 Tottenham Court Road
London WIP 9LE
England

M. Wegener
Institut für Raumplanung
Universität Dortmund
P.O. Box 500500
D-4600 Dortmund 50
Germany

H.C.W.L. Williams
Institute for Transport Studies
University of Leeds
Leeds LS2 9JT
England

Preface

The present volume is the final outcome of a series of three international workshops on transportation, sponsored by the European Science Foundation (ESF) between June 1984 and April 1985. Each workshop was devoted to a different aspect of transportation, and consisted of an introductory statement, four to five major presentations with individual discussants, a general debate and a summary statement by a rapporteur. The guidelines underlying the workshops were broadly defined according to the general philosophy of the ESF that science and technology cannot be isolated from their societal consequences. Transportation is a case in point: despite its noted technological orientation, it ought to be considered within a context which includes normative precepts on both societal and public policy bases. Given such a philosophy, it was also expected that an analysis of the societal aspects of transportation would reach some definite research and policy recommendations, though not necessarily of a concrete or immediate nature, but rather of a more detached and reflective character.

In retrospect, it turned out that these general guidelines regarding the content of the contributions, coupled with the procedure of convening small and interrelated workshops, actually shaped the form of the present publication. It has grown to a work that is more than a refereed conference proceedings, owing to its internal coherence in content and presentation. This coherence was achieved by two different means: first, by asking contributors to address themselves, whenever appropriate, in their revised papers to issues that appeared to pervade the debates in the workshops; some of these issues will be listed in Chapter 1. Secondly, by calling upon a number of participants, discussants and rapporteurs to contribute more elaborate comments in the form of short papers, to be included in the volume, particularly in order to cover subjects that contributed to a more comprehensive outlook.

Various institutions and persons have to be thanked for their continuing support for this endeavour beginning with the European Science Foundation and in particular its Standing Committee for the Social Sciences. We also gratefully acknowledge the support provided by the national science foundations in the host countries where the various workshops were held, namely Sweden, Austria and the Netherlands.

The book would not have been come into being without the intellectual contributions given by the authors of this book, by the workshop rapporteurs (Peter Jones, Michael Wegener, Henry Zoller, and Ian Masser), and by the workshop participants. Finally we want to express our appreciation for the assistance provided by our home institutions, the Free University, Amsterdam and the Hebrew University, Jerusalem, and our home organisations, the Dutch Foundation for Pure Scientific Research (ZWO) and the Israeli National Academy of Sciences.

Peter Nijkamp, Amsterdam
Shalom Reichman, Jerusalem
1985

1 Transportation Planning in a Social Context

P. Nijkamp and S. Reichman

1. Issues in contemporary transport research

In most Western European countries the first three decades after World War II were a period of sustained economic growth. However, since the end of the 1970s it has become apparent that such a growth pattern cannot continue for ever. Global imbalances such as perturbations in the world economy, ecological disasters, depletion of resources, and the shock of technological innovations, as well as 'domestic' problems such as ageing populations, outdated industrial structures and rigid institutional frameworks, have all contributed to a reversal of the economic expansion. Different countries have adjusted to this new situation with varying degrees of success, but all had to learn how to live with massive unemployment, declining incomes, and stagnating consumption. Moreover, in many countries attitudes towards technological progress and economic growth have undergone a fundamental change from a positive to a more sceptical view, while at the same time other values such as the quality of the environment, the neighbourhood, the family and other aspects of the immaterial quality of life have received more attention. Such fundamental changes of economic conditions and public attitudes could not fail to have serious effects on transport. In the 1960s and 1970s, transport was one of the most dynamic sectors of the economy. Transport policy was mostly concerned with the expansion of transport facilities to cope with the growing demand for mobility of an ever more prosperous society, and demand for it seemed to be insatiable. With each increase in income, people were able to buy more cars and settle in areas further from the city centres, with work trips becoming longer, and more trips for other purposes becoming desirable and possible.

Transport planning, with its goal system, its professional standards and its methodology, was strongly orientated towards serving this demand. The typical transport study extrapolated demand for trips from observed mobility trends and postulated the system expansion ('number of lanes') required to satisfy it. The sophistication with which this was done stood in strange contrast to the limited perspective under which transport was seen; deeply rooted in its engineering tradition, transport planning was for a long time incapable of encompassing the less direct interactions between transport and other aspects of society such as energy and ecology, location and land use, or human lifestyles and activity patterns. Such questions as the relationship of physical mobility to broader issues of urban and regional planning and policy were not treated systematically, nor was much attention paid to the negative effects of car use on social interaction and the reorientation of opportunity sets from nearby to more distant destinations.

Not surprisingly, with the end of the growth period and the accompanying change in public attitudes, this kind of transport planning was severely criticised. In the face of an environment-conscious and always watchful constituency, it has become more and more difficult to implement large-scale transport infrastructure projects such as new motorways, rapid transit lines or airports based on transport studies mainly addressing narrowly defined transport objectives (the 'internal' transportation analysis in a conventional sense). So in a sense the 'crisis' of transport planning was also one of its methodology. Because of the restricted perspective of its analytical tools, transport planning came to be thought of as being 'technocratic' and was made responsible for much of the physical and aesthetic degradation of the urban and rural environment. In response to this widening credibility gap of the discipline, recent approaches to transport analysis have drawn from other disciplines such as geography, spatial economics, sociology and ecology to develop a more comprehensive methodological framework for transport planning (the so-called 'external' transportation analysis in a modern sense).

This new orientation in transportation and mobility research has emphasised the importance of a strong theoretical base as a foundation for the models and analytical methods used. The fast rate of change of the social, economic and technological environment of transport decision makes 'descriptive' methods relying predominantly on the existence of statistical covariation of observables likely to produce erroneous forecasts, except for very short forecasting periods. Thus, theories used should be as 'behavioural' as possible, that is to say, they should as far as possible address the concrete decision situation of individual or collective actors, taking account not only of the choice set itself, but also of actor-specific preferences and constraints and their mutual interactions.

This requires, *inter alia*, the adoption of more sophisticated concepts of rationality than that conventionally applied in transport planning. It needs to be recognised that in day-to-day decisions there is hardly room for comprehensive rational decision-making, but that actors apply simple substitute decision rules such as 'elimination by aspects' or 'satisficing', or follow intuitive or habitual patterns of behaviour. Moreover, it is not altogether clear whether people have more than a rather diffuse perception of their preferences. However, people are known to adjust their aspiration levels with respect to their goals in response to external stimuli, for instance, when constraints such as budget or time restrictions become too dominant.

Because of this interaction between preferences and constraints in the decision process, studying the constraints governing transport decisions becomes of utmost importance. In real life the decision situation is often so restricted by constraints that the choice set contains only one alternative (for example, only one mode as in the case of the captive rider). It is obvious that in that case it is much more important to model the constraints (for example, car availability) realistically than to model the preferences or the choice act itself. Behavioural modelling of preferences and constraints seems to be more easily achieved in disaggregate or micro models. With appropriate sampling and aggregation techniques these can be as efficient as aggregate models and more economical in terms of data requirements. However, in a forecasting framework, these savings may be lost by the extra effort needed to forecast the population of actors in the required disaggregation. In addition, recent advances in utility theory allowing for consistent aggregation of utility over decision-makers or alternatives have reduced the gap between micro and macro approaches and have made the choice of aggregation level a matter of research convenience rather than one of fundamental theoretical relevance.

In this context, it is worth addressing the question of which analytical methods would correspond most to the new behavioural orientation in transport analysis. It is becoming increasingly accepted that 'descriptive' statistical techniques should as much as possible be replaced by more social-science-based methods offering a richer potential for gaining insights into human preferences and motives, but also into the factual constraints of decisions and their influence on the decision outcome. Such methods are, among others, panel and longitudinal studies, in-depth interviews, stated (rather than revealed) preference analyses, scenarios or other semi-quantitative or qualitative techniques, the potential of which for transport analysis still has to be explored. Undoubtedly, these less rigorous ('soft') methods will pose problems of representativeness, estimation, and empirical validation; to overcome these difficulties will be a methodological challenge of a new dimension.

Another important observation is that transport analysis not only has to change its theoretical and methodological orientation, but also its scope, by extending its domain beyond transport itself into those subsystems of the social system that directly or indirectly interact with transport. Those subsystems include, in the first place, the population and household subsystem which — through its demographic and household formation processes, but also through changing lifestyles, work, consumption and leisure patterns — largely determine the demand for passenger transport. In a similar way the freight transport sector is determined by the evolution of the economic subsystem, its changing location and relocation patterns, and the emergence of new production, storage and distribution technologies. New information and communications technologies may also have profound effects both on passenger and on freight transport, and it is urgently necessary to predict and evaluate these. A last point which has to be mentioned here is the relation between transport analysis on the one hand and policy and implementation in a practical planning context on the other. There exists a gap between the increasing technical sophistication of transport planning studies and their practical usefulness in the planning process, and this gap is likely to increase in the future. Policy has not addressed itself so far to such fundamental questions as the legitimation of minimal levels of accessibility, the effect of the concentration of public facilities and the districting of their service area on the supply of public transport, and indeed, the most important question of all, what the role of planning should be in society. One way out of this dilemma would be to increase the information-processing capacity of the planning system by installing computerised transport planning and management information systems. Complementary to this 'high-tech' approach, there is the 'low-tech' alternative of making the methods used more transparent and understandable to planners, politicians and the public at large. Another possible approach which has recently been suggested is to use non-transport solutions to alleviate transport problems.

Finally, mobility and transportation have multiple dimensions, of which the physical (or spatial) dimension represents only one aspect. The needs and interests of individuals and groups are clearly reflected in geographical space, but also in alternative 'spaces', like social space (focusing on social mobility), economic space (focusing on dynamics in production activities and production factors) or information space (focusing on transfer of ideas and thoughts). This multidimensional projection once more emphasises our main point that analysis and planning of transportation and mobility behaviour will only provide meaningful insights and fruitful results if actual trends, planning problems, models and techniques and policy issues are placed in a coherent broad social context.

We have arrived as a society at a point of self-realisation of the consequences of mobility and the choices we are faced with. The revolution in information systems provides opportunities to deal with complex and ever-changing issues in a way that has not been possible hitherto. What is required is a thorough reflection on the future of mobility, taking account not only of economic and environmental requirements, but also the need to cater for social well-being and the quality of life.

2. The scope of the present study

The book is divided into four main sections. Part A is devoted to identifying some of the main concerns and dilemmas facing present-day transport in industrial economies. These are examined in terms of societal values, individual roles and behaviour, incompatibilities in urban environments and readjustments in the production system. Finally, the problem of devising adequate conceptual frameworks so as to enable a meaningful analysis of complex short-term and long-term processes is being considered.

In Part B, transportation as an institutionalised procedure in a number of countries is discussed, with examples from the Netherlands, Sweden and the UK. The main emphasis here is on the justification and operating principles of transportation as a public utility, and whether these coincide with changes in the observed reality. Concluding this section is a paper discussing the need to anchor transport planning in public policy methodology and framework.

Methodological considerations are at the core of Part C, presenting a wide scope of models, ranging from mobility modelling to integrated freight models, and from joint land-use and transport models in urban areas to interregional trade modelling. The concluding contribution here briefly reviews some of the recent modifications in modelling methodology with the reappearance of supply-side models.

Part D discusses policy-making in transportation from different aspects: conceptual problems in identifying policy cycles and their turning-points, some of the issues related to the adoption of deregulation practices in Europe, and finally an outlook on the potential relationships between transport policy and evaluation and that of related fields, such as urban and regional development.

As can be seen from this brief description of the structure of the volume, transportation has been defined in broad terms, ranging from individual activity patterns in urban environments to macro-freight and person movements on an international scale, as in the case of deregulation policies. More specifically, though, mobility is defined here mostly in terms of physical mobility, rather than social and economic mobility or the mobility of thought.

For all its flexibility, a word of caution should be added with respect to this internal structure: the temporal dimension in the future-orientated contributions has purposely been left fairly loosely defined. In other words, no attempt is made to identify definite target dates as to when some foreseen trends or outcomes are expected to materialise. There are two main reasons for this prudence. In certain areas the expected outcomes of discernible trends are not independent of institutional interventions which may well affect their future evolution. In addition, there are other areas where it is felt that there are obvious gaps in our knowledge of cause-and-effect relationships. In general, however, it may be said that most of the studies dealing with future trends presented below have a short- to medium-term horizon, rarely exceeding the late 1980s.

Three main areas of concern are more specifically reflected in the present volume: the image, the performance and the accountability of the transportation system.

The image of transportation in the 1980s seems to have become tarnished on several, sometimes conflicting, grounds. On the one hand, in an evolutionary perspective, it has become evident that the quest for ever greater mobility can no longer be acceptable as an implicit societal choice, or, for that matter, as an explicit societal goal. On the other hand, from a contemporary perspective, given the many stagnation phenomena that can be observed, transport has not only lost some of its lustre, but also appears to show some difficulties in adjusting to the changing circumstances. Finally, the study of transport phenomena as an endeavour of scientific inquiry has also developed a problem of image, in the sense that it is sometimes regarded by mainstream social scientists as an arbitrary carving-out on a subject-matter continuum, and is consequently in need of determining its conceptual coherence.

As for the performance of the system, concern is voiced regarding a lack of effectiveness noticeable at several levels. There is the question whether the analytical apparatus currently used in the formulation of transport plans is equipped to handle the complex planning issues of the 1980s. Next, it is suggested that transport no longer possesses effective self-regulating processes, as used to be the case in the past. As a result, people who managed to improve their well-being following a transportation improvement are bound to lose it sooner or later to others who follow their example. Hence the so-called 'tiptoe' effect, otherwise known as the paradox of universality. This reaction is particularly apparent in car-orientated urban environments, where some people are always trying to improve their well-being and are later followed by others who take away the benefits they had gained — suggesting that there is an inherent dynamic to mobility which means that change is a self-fuelling process.

Another basic question concerns the relationship between transport supply and land-use patterns: is the concentration into smaller numbers of larger schools, hospitals, post offices, government offices, factories, warehouses, and so on, a response to a transport technology that has permitted these economies of scale to be realised, or have transport improvements merely helped to mitigate what would have occurred anyway and otherwise would have led to a general reduction in well-being? These are difficult questions, but central to an understanding of how society is changing — and hence what could be done to modify or accentuate undesirable or desirable trends, respectively.

In the third area of concern, that related to accountability, the greatest divergences appear. Assuming that there are legitimate differences of opinion, from an ideological viewpoint, as to the role of planning in society, it is shown that in this area there are many deficiencies in dealing with some of the most important issues that practitioners and planners should be responsible for.

The above-mentioned notions lead necessarily to a discussion of the role and effectiveness of planning in society. Are we following an inevitable path of development, with planners merely reacting to change and 'fire-fighting' where necessary, or is there a more positive role for planners? It can be argued that development is responsive to certain changes in circumstances both outside (for example, the oil crisis) and inside (for example, a change in public attitudes to bicycle use) each country, and that regulation and incentives have some effect; but exactly how much is not clear. However, since countries differ in their practices regarding speed limits, tax concessions for commuting or company car-ownership, and so on, this is an area where new insights based on inter-country comparisons could be gathered.

Many of the points are made in connection with the role of public transport in society, reflecting the existence of a real problem in assessing the benefit of public transport, owing to its 'permissive' function in enabling access to public facilities. This is related to the growing problem of financing such access, particularly when the social services themselves become less dispersed as part of deregulation policies.

Following the various contributions that address themselves to these central concerns, a concluding chapter discusses some of the main conceptual frameworks that are needed to assess present-day transportation research, and suggests the main lines of such a research agenda.

3. Concluding remarks

Mobility and transportation are essentially the spatial representation of dynamics in our complex society. They are at the same time a multi-dimensional projection of various underlying forces, such as economic objectives, safety considerations, environmental standards, energy use, land-use compatibility and maintenance of community lifestyle.

In industrial economies mobility and transport have become a major sector in their own right and have come to be regarded as an end in themselves, rather than as a means to an end. This isolationist view runs the risk of giving an incomplete and unbalanced view of the role of transport in society. Social sciences can help to redress this balance by providing a framework for looking at positive and negative aspects of mobility, and for assessing its value in relation to social life and human well-being in changing industrial societies.

Scientific analyses focusing on the societal aspects of mobility in relation to transport cover a wide range of issues. An important issue is physical mobility in relation to urban and regional policy and planning in the broader contexts of social, economic and psychological mobility. So far, however, a coherent methodology which is wide-ranging in nature and which aims at developing concepts and thought-structures for bridging the gap between technological and social perspectives on transport and at establishing a socially-orientated framework for assessing and evaluating alternative transport futures is lacking. It is clear that mobility is a very complex phenomenon, which cannot be understood outside the social, economic and political systems within which it exists.

PART A: EMERGING TRENDS

2 Human Interaction and Spatial Mobility: Retrospect and Prospect

T. Hägerstrand

1. Mobility and its limits

Mobility is a concept employed in a variety of contexts. In an economic context the reallocation of factors of production in general and of labour in particular is referred to as mobility. The social scientist tends to understand mobility as the movement of individuals and groups either between social positions or between places of residence (migration). Physical planners and engineers associate mobility with locomotion and travel. On the purely abstract level we may even speak of the mobility of thought as a precondition for cultural development and an essential aspect of political freedom. It is evident that no sharp boundaries can be drawn between these different meanings. They overlap, and they partly condition each other. As a general concept, mobility is viewed in a positive light and connected with progress and growth.

A dominating force behind the transformation of all forms of mobility during the past century and a half has been the explosive expansion of our ability to move people, information and goods in geographic space. The train, the motor ship, the motor car, the aeroplane and the various types of telecommunications have in a short period of time changed the patterns of economic and social interaction locally as well as globally in ways without parallel earlier in history, with the possible exception of the effects of printing. Every aspect of mobility has been more or less reshaped by our liberation from the immediate present which the new technologies for transportation and communication have provided. In the industrial world, at least, friction of space seems to be a problem of the past.

The facts of the revolutionary increase in spatial mobility are well known. But the full societal consequences are oddly enough only partially investigated and understood. It is, for example, only quite recently that the social impact of the telephone has been thoroughly examined (Pool 1976).

In general, the social sciences have considered technological developments as a somewhat trivial issue at the periphery of the dominating conceptual systems. Engineers, industry and the leading actors on the market, on the other hand, have adhered to the simple philosophy that more and more and faster and faster unquestionably made things better and better. In this situation mobility became a goal in itself. That a more complete evaluation would have been in order long ago is evident from the very visible problems related to physical mobility which politicians and planners encounter today, such as deaths and injuries, pollution and the seemingly limitless pressure for new investments. No doubt there are also less visible negative consequences of mobility to take into account, for example inequality of access to jobs, services and amenities. To say this is not to deny the tremendous benefits that have accrued from the mobility transition; it is only to underline that the future poses the problem of counteracting the negative aspects while retaining the positive ones.

When considering a balancing act of this kind it is sometimes useful to make a thought-experiment which takes matters to their extremes in both the minimum and the maximum direction. There can be no disagreement about the fact that a society without mobility is unthinkable. To be immobilised is a disaster also for the individual.

The other extreme is more interesting to consider. The absolute contrast to immobility is provided by the fantastic means of transportation we read about in ancient tales — the flying carpet — which in no time takes its passenger to any desired point. I suppose that many people would think that to own such a device would be the height of quality of life. Telecommunications have come close to having removed the friction of space in that way. Technologies for passenger transportation are undoubtedly pressed in the same direction.

Now, if we assume that the flying carpet is a real possibility, it would be a wonderful asset as long as only a few people owned one. If it became generally available — in the way the motor car has become — the aggregate outcome would be absurd. This would be so even if the limitations of space and energy could be overcome. Mobility beyond a certain limit is in all probability destructive for human society. One does not have to believe in criminal intentions in order to see that the mere possibility for great masses of people to turn up unexpectedly at attractive destinations would cause unmanageable situations. If all constraints on mobility were removed, one would have to recreate protection by other devices, probably more difficult to tolerate and certainly more difficult to put into practice. The constraints we accept today as unavoidable because of the nature of the world and the limitations of technology would have to be substituted for in the controversial realm of police interference.

Clearly, this imagined case of maximum mobility is in itself of little interest, since the flying carpet will for ever remain in the world of tales. But what is interesting to think about is how far we can move in the direction of more and more mobility before we come across still more unacceptable side-effects than there are today. I am confident that not only travel but also migration must have its upper limits. Beyond them we would not be able to create and maintain habitable places and regions. The sad thing is that objects and capabilities which are good in themselves for the individual or the small group lose much of their value for everybody as soon as they become adopted by great numbers.

Thus it is by no means self-evident that more and more and faster and faster is also better and better. But in order to find out about societal gains and losses related to different patterns of mobility we have to improve the bridges between the realms of the social and the engineering sciences. The beginning of true progress in the understanding of mobility lies in the realisation of its place in the total fabric of social and economic life.

Before proceeding further with reflections on these matters I will briefly indicate some basic features of the conceptual model which lies behind the various observations I am going to make later on.[1]

2. Mobility and human interaction

2.1 A conceptual model

The most straightforward way of placing physical mobility in its context is in terms of time use. Time — being equally available to everybody as a resource and a constraint — is more easily applicable than money as a common denominator for everything that is going on. Movement, for example, takes time just as do sleeping, eating, working, shopping, playing or merely sitting idle. But the time perspective alone is too limited. The purpose of movement is to overcome distance. Thus we have to try to see it as a space–time phenomenon. Now, stationary activities (or inactivities, for that matter) not only have a duration: they are also bound to locations and occupy space. In other words, they are likewise space–time phenomena. A set of graphs (Figures 2.1–2.5) will indicate how movement and stationary preoccupations can be fitted together in a space–time conceptualisation.

Figure 2.1a, read from the bottom plane and upwards, describes the space–time trajectories of the members of a family over a 24-hour day. In the morning the members move out to fixed 'stations', that is to places of work, schools, day-care centres, and so on, in the environment. Some return home for lunch. The whole group assembles again in the afternoon. In addition to these major moves out and back again, some minor errands are performed at destinations close to workplaces or home. For most families in urban-industrial environments the pattern of trajectories is very repetitive. Day after day turns out almost the same with the exception of weekends and longer holidays. But these less routinised situations can also be depicted in the same fashion.

In Figure 2.1b the human trajectories are viewed from the vantage point of a school which draws in teachers and pupils from the environment in the morning and sends them back in the afternoon. A factory or an office would not come out much different except in cases of shift-work. A service establishment, on the other hand, would be a combination of two different sets of trajectories, one set produced by the stationary employees and a second set by the visiting customers.

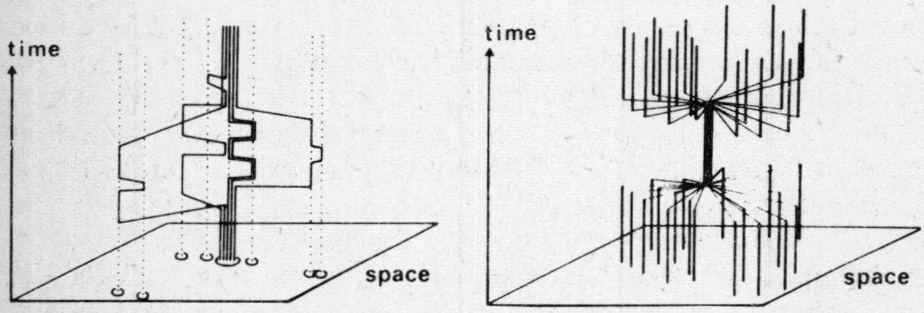

Source: Carlstein (1983, p. 42).

Figure 2.1 24-hour trajectories generated by a household (left) and a school (right)

In principle, if not in practice, it is possible to depict the days and weeks of whole populations in the same manner. One can at least try to keep such an image in mind. One may also think of adding the flow of tools, materials and messages, although in these cases the resulting patterns would be different, in particular because such items can be stored away unserved in ways human beings cannot. Since the focus here is on the social value of mobility and not on human ecology as a whole, further discussion of non-human matters will be omitted. An attractive side of the suggested kind of notation is that it is independent of scale. One can easily describe both industrial work at a machine by the minute and long-distance migration seen over lifetimes. Of course, the larger the scale, the more one has to abstract from minor movements.

Already the simple examples given in Figure 2.1 show traces of how a hierarchy of programmes, emanating from decision–makers at various levels and by actors with various powers, gives rise to movements. Daily household decisions about shopping and recreation are reflected in short excursions performed in time-windows left open in those schedules that are determined by institutions. On the other hand, once a contract has been concluded with an employer, the corresponding movements by the employee have to be performed day after day as long as the contract is in force. Movements generated by compulsory schooling are totally unavoidable parts of the national educational programme and are defined from above for years ahead. Thus the generation of movements in a population is always a mix of free choice, necessity and compulsion. Movements differ a lot from those commodities we either buy or abstain from buying. Movements have only partially a 'free value' (for example, as entertainment and recreation). Predominantly they are intermediate links of either short-term activities, like going out to buy a newspaper, or, more important, of rather fixed long-term activity sequences. One can apply a similar reasoning to the flow of materials and messages. In these cases the orderly realisation of these longer programmes requires that opportunities to move are such that the internal logic of series of tasks to perform can be maintained in terms of sequences, durations and deadlines.

The trajectories of people, messages, tools and materials in a society make up an interwoven and extremely complex network. Figure 2.2 illustrates in a very simplified fashion such interconnections, which were already implied in Figure 2.1. It is clear how, for example, the time schedules defined for work-places and schools and the opening hours of service establishments determine which programmes can be carried out and which cannot. Even if movements were instantaneous we would still have to face simultaneity conflicts. We are unable to be at more than one place at a time, even if we want to be everywhere, which seems to be the case in the present restless world.

The graph does not define a particular spatial scale. We may think of facilities located in only one big building or on a campus with few steps between them or else located in a region with miles between them. In the first cases it would be convenient enough to walk. In the second case a demand for transportation facilities would arise. Thus, given a system of activities, we ought to make a distinction between the *movements* that are required and the *distances* that have to be covered. The number and timings of movements are a direct result of

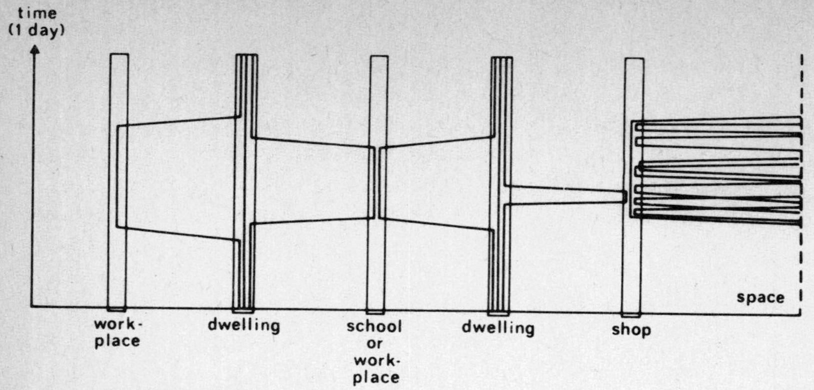

Source: Carlstein (1983, p. 43).

Figure 2.2 Couplings during a weekday between individual trajectories at dwellings, work-places, schools and shops. The entire trajectories of individuals visiting the shop are not included except in one case

how activity sequences are split up into separate tasks between locations. The distances to cover, on the other hand, depend on the spatial structure of locations and on what activity sequences individual people want to or have to join and are able to join.

When thinking about people's ability to join activity sequences it is less revealing to consider observable behaviour than to try to uncover the limits of what is possible. I have already pointed out the trivial — but normally overlooked — circumstance that we can only be at one place at a time. And in order to achieve something we have to stay on for various durations. Therefore, not even the flying carpet would remove the upper boundary of what can be achieved simultaneously in terms of human cooperation in a society. The more we remove the bottle-necks of space the stronger we begin to feel the bottle-necks of time.

The second boundary for participation is defined by the speed with which a person is able to move between locations. Figure 2.3 illustrates in the simplest possible manner what this means under normal everyday conditions and under the assumption that the road network is dense. A, B, C, and so on, represent habitats in which people have the base-points from which they can move out in the morning and to which they have to return in the evening. The set of destinations in space and time which are within potential reach when the day begins is then defined by the maximum velocity available plus the timing of return to the home. The resulting space–time 'volume'

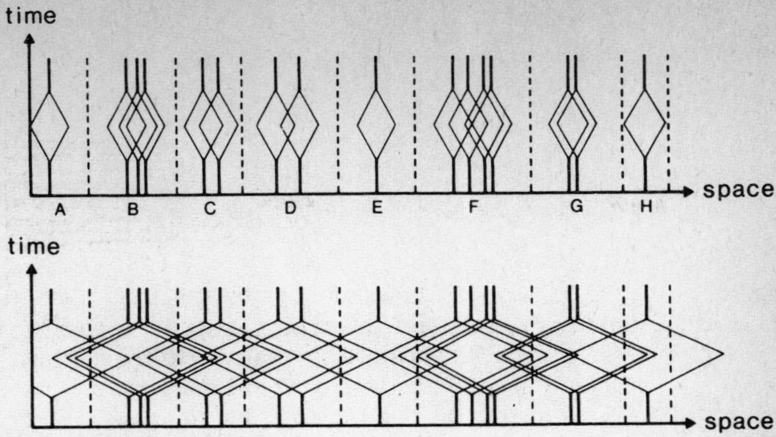

Source: Carlstein (1983, p. 101).

Figure 2.3 The relation between speed of movement and daily space-times ('prisms') available for action and interaction given the same spatial distribution of base-points

assumes the shape of two cones. The individual is, so to speak, contained in this 'prism', unless the travel is extended over several days. But even then the necessity of returning makes similar outer boundaries unavoidable.

Under pedestrian conditions (Figure 2.3a) daily social interaction is confined to the narrow realm of one's own habitat. Most children and many old people still live under these restricted conditions. With the advent of more speedy means of movement, for example horses or bicycles (Figure 2.3b), the daily prisms cut into each other over wider ranges. The opportunities for interaction are much increased. But the space–time confinement is still there. The same holds true even with the high velocity of the automobile.

Compared to practice, these illustrations exaggerate the potential for interaction. As was said before, most trips lead to destinations where tasks with a certain duration have to be performed. Consequently, the residual prism is deformed, approximately as illustrated in Figure 2.4. When the need to remain at stations is taken into account it is clear that the remote parts of potential prisms at any speed are of little use because they admit only short stays before the return journey has to begin. So even in a wholly motorised society the more distant destinations are of little daily value as long as we adhere to the habit of having a home to return to for sleep and protection of our belongings. This kind of conceptualisation makes clear that access to jobs, services, and so on, is not only a function of location and

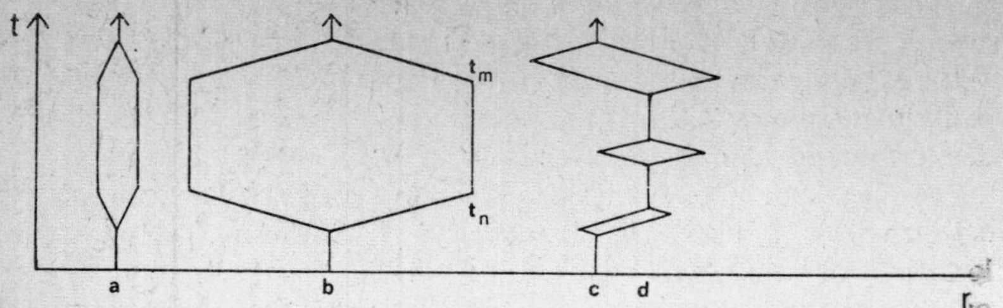

Source: Hägerstrand (1970, p. 21).

Figure 2.4 a and b illustrate the maximum spatial range of choice of stationary activity of duration $t_n - t_m$ available to a person with low capability to move (a) compared to one with high capability $t_n - t_m$ located at maximum distance in either case removes all freedom to do anything but commute.
c–d illustrates the remaining prisms available to a person with working time $t_n - t_m$ (including break in the middle of the day) at a shorter distance (d) from base-point (c) than maximum

mobility but also of the timing of work and opening hours of establishments. What lies beyond the open prisms in terms of locations and durations does not exist in practice.

2.2 Mobility and social communication

Face-to-face interaction between humans requires that trajectories come together in bundles at places, remain together for various durations and depart in different directions in order to join new combinations. As was said before, we find partly a repetitive pattern in the bundling of trajectories (at homes and at places of work) and partly groupings of a more individual nature.

When one looks more closely at these bundles of trajectories one finds that some represent real social interaction. In other cases we have to do with mere coincidences as between people on a pavement, in a waiting hall or in a queue. Goffman (1959) calls the latter situation a 'traffic relationship' (cf. Hannerz 1983). It should be noted that some bundles are mixtures of the two types just mentioned. A market-place, a shop or a bank contain both strong social interaction (mutually among employees and between employees and customers) and weak traffic relationships (between customers who happen to be present simultaneously).

The emphasis laid on bundles of human trajectories does not imply that all human interaction can be exhaustively described in these terms. Books, letters and telephone calls are left out, as well as the media and the signals issued from the man-made environment. These are all important vehicles of social communication. They interact in various ways with the physical movement of people. But I find it most convenient conceptually to link these other aspects to the frame which the unbroken human trajectories form as they meet and part.

The development of physical mobility has gradually changed the spectrum of bundles that people form with respect to number, location, duration, size and type. Also an unceasing redistribution of opportunities to participate has taken place among members of the population. One must bear in mind that as innovations in transport technology spread they not only break through earlier constraints; they also put up new barriers. But all this is an aspect of social reality which has not been systematically studied to any larger extent. It is therefore not possible in a discussion about change to reach deeper than to the fairly obvious.

Even in medieval times the tiny literate part of society maintained surprisingly wide social networks. But contacts were kept alive mainly by letter and by oral messages transferred by the few travellers. Opportunities to meet in person were not frequent. When they came about, visitors tended to stay with friends for days and weeks. This general pattern remained until the advent of the railway. Diaries and collections of letters from the eighteenth century and onwards give rich information about the travels abroad that educated people made a few times in a lifetime.

Ordinary people were bound to their localities and regions. Around 1840 70 per cent of migrations in rural areas were shorter than 20 miles and 95 per cent shorter than 70 miles (Hägerstrand 1974). One must assume that travel and social networks had the same modest spatial dimensions.

A rather unexpected observation is that the railway and the motor car do not seem to have led to any dramatic expansion of the migration fields, up to the 1960s in any case. 51 per cent of the urban and 72 per cent of rural migrations in Sweden were still shorter than 70 miles (Jakobsson 1969). A similar observation is made by Moline (1971) with respect to marriage relations between people in small towns in America. Clearly, more distant migrations have grown in number. But this fact is naturally explained by growing occupational differentiation rather than by the new means of transportation. Specialisation gradually tends to make corresponding vacancies more widely spread geographically. One must conclude, however, that one major effect of the transportation revolution has been that personal contacts can be maintained in quite a new fashion. No longer does a long-distance migration of a family member need to mean a farewell for years or for life.

The attractiveness of the means of private transportation (walking, horse and carriage, bicycle, motor car) in the local and regional scales has always come from the temporal and spatial freedom it provides. Travellers can move out and return at will without the straight-jacket of a timetable. They can also choose the routes they want in the surrounding road network. Mobility is available with a minimum of planning. This makes it very easy to calculate during the day the shape of the remaining prisms of potential future destinations.

It is consistent with this situation that, for example, universities, in which immediate human interaction is essential, most frequently are planned according to the campus principle with pedestrian movement as the totally dominating internal mode. This form of layout makes the flow of people between buildings very smooth. It also gives rise to unplanned encounters along the pathways, important for access to mixed types of information and for social cohesion.

Public transportation on the other hand (bus, train, aeroplane) as known today is bound to timetables and to predefined routes. The space–time prism — if that is the best word to use in this case — within reach of the traveller has a complicated topology. Timetable information and planning is needed and occasional inability to be punctual can cause great problems, in particular if the trip involves a change of vehicle. A car-owner today — and even a cyclist — can permute daily programmes — and so handle unforeseen events — in many more ways than somebody who is travelling by bus or train. By that they are much less sensitive to the location of facilities, opening hours and logistic problems at home or at the work-place (Lenntorp 1976). Figure 2.5 illustrates how trajectories differ between a person who can rely on private transportation and another person who is bound to bus or train as they carry out exactly the same sequence of tasks.

A different way of comparing modes of movement is to calculate in how many ways the same programme in terms of tasks and kinds of destination can be carried out from the same base-point in the same environment. Lenntorp (1974) has made some estimates by way of simulation for a medium-sized Swedish city (*c.* 100,000 inhabitants).[2] Of course, the outcome varies according to location of base-point. But on average the bus system could not provide more than two to three times more permutations than walking, whereas the car made all potential permutations possible. The bicycle came rather close to the same.

It is beyond doubt that private transportation increases the autonomy of the individual tremendously compared to timetabled public modes of movement. It is no surprise that car drivers do not want to go over to public transportation, even if it costs nothing, as

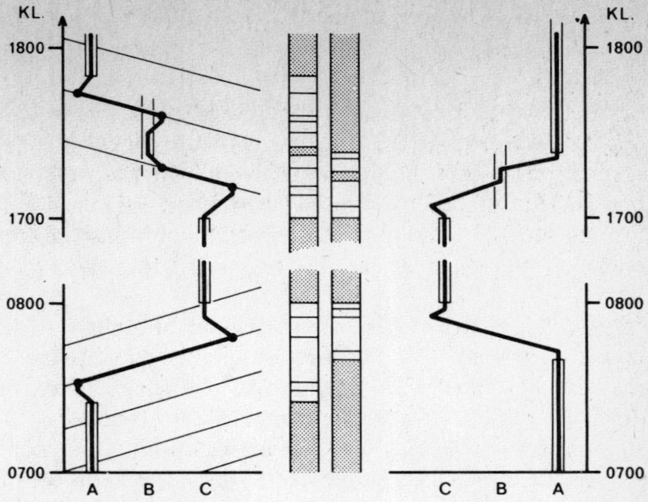

Source: Lenntorp (1974, p. 280).

Figure 2.5 Trajectories representing the same morning and evening programme carried out with the aid of public transport (left) and individual movement (right). Speed makes little difference compared to location of stops and waiting times

long as they can find parking space close to their points of destination.

It is interesting to note that neither states nor industrialists to begin with seemed to be interested in trying to make people independently mobile. The bicycle, the car and even the aeroplane grew out of the efforts of scattered creative wizards and engineers during the later part of the nineteenth century. To begin with in any case, all three means of transportation were viewed as sport articles rather than as vehicles of general economic value or of practical interest to consumers. Racing events were organised from the very beginning.

Both from a technological and a psychological point of view the bicycle occupies a central position in the development. Many of the early motor-car factories developed out of bicycle manufacture. The Wright brothers, pioneer producers and pilots of flying machines, were originally bicycle-makers (Wilson 1973). The bicycle also created a taste for mobility among broad strata of the population who had never experienced that feeling before and by doing so prepared the market for the general use of motor vehicles.

Commuting by car began in the 1920s (Moline 1971) in the United States. In Europe the expansion of commuting by car developed only after World War II. An intensification took place over several decades. It is possible that a limit may have been reached by now in terms of both spatial range and frequency but this is difficult to bear out.

The increase of daily mobility has had advantages as well as costs with respect to working life. The car, but also the bus and rapid transit, have considerably enlarged the area in which a person can seek employment without moving from his or her home. Thus mobility has helped to maintain residential stability in times of industrial structural change and has also helped people to choose a home away from their place of work.

So far the positive sides of individual mobility have been emphasised. There are also more questionable consequences of an economic and a social nature in the wake of such mobility. In areas where urban settlements are within commuting distance of each other, individual decisions have made the aggregate situation somewhat paradoxical. Settlements exchange every day large numbers of commuters in identical occupations. From the point of view of society the situation gives rise to a cost of transportation which hardly has anything positively to do with productivity at the places of work. There is reason to suspect that the high mobility level in modern society, not just with respect to commuting to work, hides a lot of corresponding carrying of coals to Newcastle.

The present separation of home and place of work, made possible by the motor car, seems also to have added a new dimension to social segregation. Spatial vicinity in pedestrian society never *per se* prevented social segregation between status groups, as is evident from the strict hierarchies found in factory towns or on big estates. But spatial vicinity at least conveyed a certain mutual knowledge of day-to-day life across social boundaries and a certain common sense of place.

When new means of transportation are put at our disposal, new ways of being *present* with respect to each other are made possible. But this side of the matter is only half of the full set of consequences. An equally important social fact is that specific patterns of presences at locations and on roads between these by necessity generate specific patterns of *absences*, because of the indivisibility of the human trajectories. Since we are predisposed to focus on what we gain by innovations and to turn a blind eye to those options which get lost, technological development related to physical mobility has been guided by desires to enlarge our potential for becoming present as fast as possible further and further away from our base-points. The generated shadow patterns of absences have not been equally visible. As things now tend to develop, social groups disappear out of each other's sight and consciousness. This is so not only because of the distances between housing areas of different quality, but also because the street has ceased to be the kind of meeting-place it used to be. A striking new feature of modern society is the way in which the motor car and television between them have made people absent with respect to each other. It is hard to believe that the conditions of the poor in many big cities of the world would be as easily neglected as they are if it were not as easy as it is for the better off to stay away from problem areas physically and therefore also mentally. In addition to this, mobility has made possible a remarkable absence of people in all kinds of housing areas during the day and in urban centres after work. Spontaneous social control is weakened by this and protection has had to become institutionalised by police and television surveillance.

On the national and international scene the style of social communication has changed considerably in line with increasing opportunities for fast long-distance travel. Instead of the classic combination of business and private visiting we have quick return trips rather like commuting. Those who participate meet many more times than ever before, but mostly only for the short time-span when they are playing their role. No deeper mutual knowledge about the general circumstances and interests of participants is gained.

Tourism in its commercial forms is quite certainly overestimated as a means of establishing contacts between people in different countries and cultures. In contrast to the standardised package tour private excursions abroad are clearly a positive feature of motorism.

The history of social communication is still to be written before the consequences of the revolution in transportation can be judged. But, taken together, the general impression is that mobility in its present forms has caused rather impersonal — sometimes even hostile — traffic relationships to expand at the expense of more permanent and deeper social ties.

Once people met on the road and frequently stopped for a conversation. The car driver is isolated in his shell, most often alone. The immense number of hours devoted to commuting is almost as many hours deducted from social intercourse. At a different level of mobility, we once had a culture of travel developed on the big trans-oceanic ships. The flight passenger of today is first treated as a possible criminal before entering the vehicle and then during the journey is virtually a prisoner in his seat.

3. The social distribution of mobility

Ever since the domestication of the horse, transport technology has created differences in mobility between population categories, differences which sometimes have been reflected in the class structure. It is, for example, no accidental circumstance that chivalry is an ancient word for knighthood. Also in the farming villages some had access to the mobility provided by horses whereas others had to rely on slow oxen or had no draught-animals at all.

The railway caused first of all *spatial* differences. People living close to the stations could suddenly climb many steps up the mobility ladder. Stations became points of strong attraction for in-migrants and the rail network came to restructure the pre-existing pattern of urban settlements, or — as in America — to a certain extent to lead the colonisation movement. Railways also came to reinforce urban segregation by permitting upper- and middle-class people to move out from central areas and establish peripheral suburbs at attractive locations. But the train *per se* was an equalising means of transportation. The passengers in the first and in the third class moved at the same speed and arrived at their destination simultaneously.

The train widened the range of access, but choices were constrained by the timetable. The bicycle, on the other hand, gave its users — within a more modest range — autonomy with respect to both space and time of a kind which before had been available only to horse-owners. Mass-production of bicycles began a hundred years ago. The bicycle, with its very low energy requirement and easy handling, became the most evenly distributed vehicle throughout age groups and social classes which has ever been invented. After Queen Victoria had made cycling respectable it became possible also for young ladies to get out on the roads and simultaneously reach the freedom of a 'rational dress' (Wilson 1973). The bicycle era is an overlooked episode in the history of female liberation.

During its first half-century motorism gave rise to quite a dense network of bus services, which reached its maximum while the railway still served the small villages. Both trains and buses transported bicycles along with the passengers. The still relatively few private cars had not yet been able to erode the market for public transport. In my opinion, this short period offered the most widely distributed mobility throughout the population that we have ever had. The speed, of course, was low, and the range gave emphasis to local and regional integration.

The subsequent growth of car-ownership again divided the population into very mobile and very immobile strata. This is not just a question of social class any more. It is frequently overlooked that in one-car families — which are the most frequent — the person who keeps the car parked at his work-place puts the rest of the family in the low mobility group. Nevertheless, public transport lost ground in local and regional relations. Settlements became reorganised in order to suit the dominating car-borne population. Even in areas where subsidised public transport remains, the difference in mobility between car drivers and the rest is considerable. Until recently in any case road-building has favoured motor traffic and neglected the cyclist and also the pedestrian, in spite of the fact that the overwhelming number of all movements are made on foot.

Today the low mobility group is made up of low-income people, the young, the elderly, the handicapped, single women in low-paid occupations and many wives during the day. Their access to jobs as well as to services, recreation, relatives and friends is many times more limited than the range open to the car driver. The degree of isolation is highest in rural regions but can also be considerable in parts of metropolitan areas.

Because of the great advantages of individual mobility this is not likely to be given up once the majority of a population has adopted it. Individual mobility is now seen as an essential aspect of personal freedom. It is also deeply ingrained in the physical and institutional structure of society. So what about that part of the population which cannot or does not want to drive a car? I think it can be shown by the model presented earlier that the internal interaction potential of a population is at its optimum when everybody has the same capability to move (as is approximately the case on a campus). This equality cannot be restored. But public transport can at least move things in that direction. It is not just benefiting those who use it but the population as a whole. It saves time and effort, for example, when somebody is coming to see you, if you do not have to move out and pick him up. Work, consumption and social life get a larger population base to draw upon when nobody is cut off from participation. A minimum mobility is not just a question of fairness. It is a matter which indirectly concerns also the very mobile.

The period of motorisation has also been marked by increasing large-scale spatial inequalities. Air transportation and express trains favour the big agglomerations and a restricted category of passengers. Scattered investigations indicate that centre-to-centre mobility is rather limited to a small population of businesspeople and officials. The same individuals travel repeatedly on the same route, some weekly or more frequently. Thus the large number of registered passengers does not signify a broad participation. The division of the transportation system into an individual sector, dominated by automobiles, and a long-distance collective sector made up of airlines and fast trains tends to leave out a middle zone of relations where, on the one hand, the distance is too long to be conveniently covered by car and, on the other, too short for flights.

The spatial inequalities in access created by fast long-distance modes of transport have also been a pre-requisite for the re-organisation of the lines of command in industry and public administration. On the whole it is probably correct to say that the major centres have gained in power and influence.

4. Threatened values and future tasks

Mobility as we know it today is not only a positive phenomenon. Some of the questionable consequences have already been mentioned. It is now rather generally agreed, at least in Europe, that there exists a whole range of values to care about, values which are threatened by too much mobility: human lives, social cohesion, the beauty and habitability of urban and rural landscapes, clean air, even silence. It is remarkable how little attention is given to the fact that about 250,000 individuals in the world are killed on the roads each year and about 10 million injured. Traffic is presently our biggest war. The motor car has also had a destructive effect on built-up environments. It has behaved like 'an elephant in a china-shop', as somebody put it. In other words, some limits have to be set. But where and how?

Politically, the problem of finding the proper amount of mobility is difficult to handle. We have only partly to do with distinct population groups, representing opposite interests. Even the environmentalists take their cars when they move out to demonstrate against some new road-construction. Most of us are equally schizophrenic about the matter. We shift values with the role we happen to be in and the place we happen to be at. In addition there is a lack of knowledge of in what ways mobility is important and how it interacts with other values.

We have no doubt to continue to live with a high degree of individual motorised mobility. Some seem to believe that the new information technology may reduce the amount of physical movement. It is rather more likely that the demand will increase. The shorter working hours which are foreseen will in any case make wider time-windows available which might come to be used for travel.

Mobility in itself is beyond the direct reach of the politician and the planner. Such influence as is deemed necessary must be achieved by indirect means. Yet the variables one could work on are probably many more than have been seriously touched on so far. As was argued before, the need to change location and the need to cover distances of various lengths represent different facets of mobility. The first reflects the successive bundling of trajectories, the second the relative location of stations at which the bundlings take place. These two aspects, of course, are mutually dependent. Nevertheless, transportation planning has paid attention almost exclusively to the art of covering distances, whereas the organisation of human interaction has largely disappeared out of sight. Hence the pedestrian realm (to which even motorists have to belong most of the time) has not been much taken into account. Economic calculations have tended to aggregate chunks of time as if it were money-like and have abstracted from its existential logic. They have also consistently concentrated attention on the value of being present without deducting the cost of being absent.

The above examples are put forward only to indicate the need to place mobility in its full context before one can draw conclusions about what is sound policy and about where and how to intervene. This is no easy task to perform, since mobility is linked to almost everything else. The improved conceptual clarification and simplification is now the first challenge we have to tackle.

Notes

1. The literature concerned with the 'time-geographic' model is very scattered in books and papers and deals with many aspects other than mobility. Particularly relevant in the latter connection are Lenntorp (1976), Burns (1979) and Carlstein (1983), in particular Chapter 2 ('Life paths and living possibility boundaries') and Chapter 8 ('Time allocation and the carrying capacity of a population time-budget').
2. Lenntorp's investigation is reported in a preliminary fashion in Hägerstrand (1974), pp. 25–37.

References

Andreasson, Rune (1978). 'Traffic Accidents' in *Health and Society I. Accidents and Violent Death.* Stockholm: Committee for Future Oriented Research.

Bauer, R.A. (1969). *Second-Order Consequences.* Cambridge, MA: MIT Press.

Burns, Lawrence D. (1979). *Transportation, Temporal and Spatial Components of Accessibility.* Lexington, Mass.: Lexington Books.

Carlstein, Tommy (1983). *Time Resources, Society and Ecology. On the Capacity for Human Interaction in Space and Time.* London: Allen & Unwin.

Dilsaver, Larry Michael (1979). 'Some Notes on the Negative Impacts of International Tourism', *Association of Pacific Coast Geographers*, **41**, 109–18.

Goffman, Erving (1959). *The Presentation of Self in Everyday Life.* New York.

Hägerstrand, Torsten (1970). *Tidsanvändning och omgivningsstruktur.* SOU 1970:14.

Hägerstrand, Torsten (1973). 'The Impact of Transport on the Quality of Life'. Paper presented at the Fifth International Symposium on Theory and Practice in Transport Economics arranged by the European Conference of Ministers of Transport, Athens.

Hägerstrand, Torsten (1974). 'En landsbygdsbefolknings flyttningsrörelser', *Svensk Geografisk Årsbok.*

Hannertz, Ulf (1983). *Över gränser. Studier i dagens socialantropologi.* Lund.

Hildred, William P. (1959). 'International Air Transport Problems', *The Advancement of Science* **XVI** (63).

Jakobsson, Arne (1969). *Omflyttningen i Sverige 1950*–1960. Lund.

Lenntorp, Bo (1974). 'Transporter i dygnsprogrammet' in *Ortsbundna levnadsvillkor*. SOU 1974:2, pp. 265–82.

Lenntorp, Bo (1976). 'Paths in Space–Time Environments: A Time-Geographic Study of Movement Possibilities of Individuals', *Lund Studies in Geography*, series B, no. 44, Lund.

Masefield, Peter G. (1955). 'Recent Progress in British Air Transport', *The Advancement of Science*, **XII** (47).

Moline, N.T. (1971). 'Mobility and the Small Town 1900–1930'. University of Chicago, research paper.

Pool, Ithiel, ed. (1976). *The Social Impact of the Telephone*. Cambridge, MA: MIT Press.

Wilson, S.S. (1973). 'Bicycle Technology', *Scientific American*, **228** (3).

3 Mobility and the Individual in Western Industrial Society

P.M. Jones

1. Introduction

The concept of mobility in its various forms is an important feature of Western society, and is reflected in its social, political and economic systems. Freedom of thought, action and movement are considered to be basic rights in democratic societies, and it has been suggested by several analysts that without this flexibility modern technological society could not have developed so rapidly nor have become so diversified in its products and services. Travel and transport are but one facet of mobility, but they are very much in the public eye, since movement takes place in public spaces using shared tracks and sometimes shared vehicles. Transport policy and investment are often the subject of public debate, at both national and local levels, and transport has a symbolic as well as a functional significance as the lifeline of a nation's productive systems.

One of the most significant transport developments in the Western world since World War II has been the phenomenal growth in private vehicle ownership, especially cars. Taking the United Kingdom as an example, between 1948 and 1978 the number of registered private cars and vans rose from 1.4 million to 14.4 million, and by 1978 over 80 per cent of motorised passenger movement (that is, excluding walking and cycling) was by private vehicle. The increase in private vehicle ownership has resulted in people travelling both further and more often than hitherto. Over the 20 years to 1975, travel by private transport increased by 243,000 million passenger-kilometres in Great Britain, but this was matched by a decline of only 29,000 million passenger-kilometres in travel by bus and rail (Maltby and White 1982).

This transport revolution has had fundamental effects on mobility, lifestyles, land-use patterns and the environment (Allsop 1980), and is now recognised to have brought both considerable gains and losses (see especially Chapter 2 and 4 of this volume). Modern society faces something of a dilemma, with transport being a valued and indeed integral aspect of modern life, yet one which is perceived to cause considerable social and environmental hardship. To compound the issue, many people adopt a schizophrenic attitude in which new roads are welcomed, indeed demanded — as long as they don't affect the individual's property — and congestion and pollution are seen by motorists as being caused by other people's vehicles, not their own. At the same time, governments find it increasingly costly to maintain the transport infrastructure and services on which people have come to depend. The problem is unlikely to go away, with continual increases in travel in many countries and a growing gulf between those with and those without private transport, coupled with an awareness of future problems relating to energy shortages and environmental issues.

At the core of the problem are questions concerning the nature of mobility, its relation to transport provision, its value to society and implications for well-being. This paper attempts to contribute to the debate by discussing the nature and measurement of mobility, as seen from the perspective of the individual. It begins by looking at some problems relating to mobility and ways in which they might be resolved. This is followed by a review of some quantitative measures defining mobility or the consequences of mobility. The paper then outlines an activity-based framework within which many of the aspects can be related, and discusses its strengths and weaknesses. The final section draws some conclusions from the work that has been reviewed.

2. Mobility: problems and solutions

The nature and effects of mobility can perhaps best be understood by first considering some mobility-related problems and the ways in which society has sought to deal with them.

2.1 Problems faced by specific groups of travellers

Providers of transport services for many years tended to view their market as a homogeneous one, comprising motorists, bus travellers, rail users, and so on. Only relatively recently have governments and transport operators looked specifically at the travel requirements of different population groups — often to discover that their apparent mobility problems are as much due to non-transport as to transport causes. There is now an extensive literature dealing with the travel needs of different groups, and only a few studies are cited here, for illustrative purposes.

[? private vehicles may be more comfortable + efficient for these groups

The elderly and handicapped have received particular attention in recent years, both from researchers and from government agencies and politicians. In the United States, legislation has been introduced to make public transport systems more accessible to handicapped people (for example, through provision of lifts at underground stations, or buses with low step heights). While this has undoubtedly benefited some elderly and handicapped people, many have questioned whether the money has been well spent and whether such action has enhanced the mobility of these groups significantly. Improved physical accessibility may be a necessary but not a sufficient condition.

The complex relationships between level of trip-making, desire for trip-making and physical disability are illustrated in a study by Bailey (1981) among groups of elderly and disabled people in the South and Midlands of England. Two activities were selected for analysis — food shopping and social and recreation activities — and respondents were grouped according to whether or not they participated in the activity at present and whether they would like to participate more. Bailey then defined a personal mobility index, using each respondent's own perception of the physical difficulty he or she incurred in travelling. When relationships were examined between the mobility groups and the activity participation groups, the desire for more activity participation seemed to be unrelated to the degree of restriction in mobility — other factors seemed to be involved.

Evidence that mobility is related to more than simply the provision of a suitable transport system is confirmed by a study of disabled people in Canberra, where a gaming simulation approach was used to explore likely reaction to the introduction of a mobility allowance. Findings are reported in Faulkner (1982). The study identified four groups of disabled people, with different attitudes and constraints. About 40 per cent of the sample had access to a car or were able to use other forms of transport without assistance, and so had little inclination to travel more; another 16 per cent were more physically restricted, but reported themselves satisfied with their lower trip rates and did not increase their travel when provided with resources to do so. Among those who expressed a desire to travel more, the gaming simulation distinguished between people who were restricted by the cost or configuration of the transport system (27 per cent) and those whose mobility was restricted primarily by socio-psychological barriers (17 per cent), such as requiring someone to accompany them on outings from home. Thus, only approximately a quarter of those interviewed would be helped directly by further government initiatives to improve the accessibility of the transport system, through financial, organisational or physical means — although policy-makers often see this as essentially a transport problem.

A similar recent interest in women's travel issues (for example, Rosenbloom 1978) has demonstrated the wide-ranging nature of changes in society that would be involved in removing the frustrations felt by many women with children who would like to obtain work. Inadequate transport provision may be one facet of the problem, but provision of child-care centres, changes in role definition and more flexible attitudes of employers to working hours are all required if women are to become more mobile.

2.2 Psychological and physiological aspects of transport provision

In addition to the psychological and physiological benefits which people in Western society enjoy through the provision of transport and potential for movement, there is also evidence of considerable disbenefits associated with mobility. For example, Cullen and Phelps (1975) found that workers who had long or difficult journeys to work in the morning by public transport were showing relatively high levels of stress at work by mid-afternoon. It seems, therefore, that travel conditions can have a general effect on health and well-being.

Another concern in several industrial countries, including Britain, is a growing fear of travelling at night, particularly on foot, but affecting all modes of transport. In a recent exploratory study of non-work travel in Oxford, Jones and Kilvington (1983) found evidence of this concern among people of all ages. It affected not only pedestrians, but bus and car users as well — the latter particularly when they were using a multi-storey car-park near the centre of Oxford. People reported five responses to this fear of travel at night:

- Travel less and spend more leisure time at home.
- Reschedule journeys, so they take place in daylight hours.
- Change trip destination, to places where people felt safer.
- Increase chauffeuring by car of people unable to drive — thus making such people dependent on others.
- Adjust psychologically to the concern and 'take a chance'.

This is clearly a symptom of a much more general malaise in society and strikes at the very heart of the concept of mobility as illustrated here: a restriction on freedom, both of action and potential for action.

2.3 The problem of congestion

The existence of congestion at certain points on the transport network at particular times of day is a very obvious transport 'problem' faced by all groups of travellers, but concentration of demand in time and space has benefits as well as costs. To some extent it is desirable that there is a concentration of people at the same times and places, in order to make use of an existing mass-transit system, for example.

This is also true for many other types of activity, whether it be gatherings for entertainment purposes (such as attending a football match or the theatre), or for the efficient functioning of an industrial or office complex. The concomitant peaking of demand for other facilities which do not benefit from joint utilisation follows naturally from this. This mass movement forms part of the resulting ebb and flow of daily life. Thus, although traffic congestion may appear to be inefficient, wasteful or harmful in its own right, these disbenefits may be considerably outweighed in a broader context by the economic and social benefits which arise from people assembling in large groups for other activities — it may be a price worth paying.

In the early days of urban transport planning there were concerns that places like London would literally 'grind to a halt' unless improvements were made to the road network (Hart 1976). In most cases this has not happened, because traffic finds its own level and the social and economic systems adapt to the prevailing conditions; transport improvements can stimulate demand and a deterioration in service can suppress it.

A dramatic illustration of the ability of an economy to adapt to changes in transport provision is afforded by the collapse of the Tasman Bridge in 1975. This connected the city centre of Hobart in Tasmania with the growing eastern suburbs, and it collapsed after one of its pillars was struck by a ship. The 30 per cent of the city's residents living on the eastern side had to face a detour by road of more than one hour, or use a ferry service which was augmented during the period of the collapse. The study provides an opportunity to examine the effects of a very sudden and dramatic reduction in accessibility by road. Lee and Wood (1982) carried out a series of monitoring studies and identified two forms of adjustment. 'Operational' adjustments to travel patterns involved changes in mode and route, the timing of travel, the destination of journeys and the consolidation and chaining of trips, as well as an increase in telephone calls. The volume of cross-river travel dropped by nearly 50 per cent in the period immediately after the bridge collapsed. The second kind of response was 'structural' adjustments, which affected more basic aspects of behavioural orientation and lifestyles and were often associated with pressures for land-use change. The authors identified four changes: redirection of patronage for shopping and services (leading to a build-up of facilities on the east bank); structural adjustments in social networks; changes in job location (helped by internal transfers between large organisations); and relocation of residence, or making arrangements to stay in the city centre overnight. Other forms of response were also reported to a more limited extent, such as purchasing a second car for use on the west bank and using the passenger ferry as a link between the two vehicles.

The evidence of adaptability of motorists and other travellers to travel restrictions suggests a converse policy to relieve transport congestion. Instead of providing more capacity at peak periods, make it easier for people to use the existing capacity more efficiently; for example, in order to spread the peak, give workers greater freedom in the times at which they work. The effects can be quite dramatic: the introduction of flexible working hours at government offices in Ottawa led to a reduction of nearly 50 per cent in peak traffic levels (Teply 1982). The evidence from this and other studies suggests that a sizeable proportion of travellers would be prepared to bring forward their work arrival and departure times by up to one hour, given suitable opportunities or incentives. A British study (Shapcott and Steadman 1977) indicates that the amount of flexibility would be greater still among workers with children if it were not for the fixed hours operated by British schools.

The lessons to be drawn from this work are that congestion is not simply a transport problem, demanding a transport solution. Both the causes and the solutions may be outside the conventional domain of the traffic engineer or traffic operator. Clearly, there will be occasions when it will be worth while to invest in order to alleviate congestion, but this requires a much broader assessment of the consequences and options than is carried out at present. As society moves towards new styles of work and leisure, the need to understand, evaluate and implement transport and mobility-related policies within a broader framework will become even more apparent.

2.4 Assessment: the nature of mobility

In this section the concept of mobility has been restricted to transport and the everyday behaviour of individuals. Again, it should be stressed that this is only part of a wider concept of mobility, which encompasses residential and industrial relocation, social mobility, and so on — all of which form part of a continuous process of development and adjustment in modern industrial societies.

Even at this restricted, day-to-day level, however, mobility is clearly a complex concept, including notions of:

(a) individual action, in the form of observed movement, or travel;
(b) potential action, in terms of journeys which people would like to

make, but are unable to, because of limitations in the transport system and/or their own commitments restricting them in time and space, or financial restraints; and

(c) freedom of action, which may never manifest in action, but gives the individual options from which to select and the knowledge that he *could* do something, if he so desired.

In the next section we review a number of measures of behaviour which have been or could be used to describe these aspects of mobility, as well as the *consequence* of restricted or enhanced mobility for the individual. These are grouped under six headings, and some advantage and limitations of each group are briefly outlined.

3. Measures of mobility

3.1 Travel-based measures

The first group of measures records the amount of travel that is observed in an area, using up to three types of indicator:

(a) trip rates;
(b) trip length (or total distance covered in a period of time);
(c) proportion of the population who are travellers on a given day.

Examples of ways in which these measures have been used as indicators of mobility are provided in Cerwenka (1982).

Although such measures can be obtained with a reasonable degree of accuracy and precision — though judgements are involved about which person, mode and purpose categories to use — there is no unambiguous way of interpreting the data or assessing trends over time. From the point of view of well-being, is more or less travel a good thing? At least implicitly, most writers have assumed that an increase is preferable to a decrease, but the previous section has identified several cases where this is not so.

At the level of the individual, higher levels of travel may be an indicator of a decrease rather than an increase in well-being. For example:

(a) Increased risk of road accident or physical assault may encourage households to escort children on more outings from home: this can lead to a significant increase in trip rates (since one trip by a child may generate two adult passenger trips) and in the proportion of travellers in the population.
(b) The concentration of education, medical and shopping facilities

into a smaller number of larger units leads to a higher average trip length for consumers wishing to use such facilities, and an overall increase in the volume of travel — through necessity rather than choice.

(c) Among teenagers, increased levels of trip-making may reflect poor social and environmental conditions in their home neighbourhood, or a lack of purpose in life, rather than a desire for travel *per se*.

Of course, there are instances where a reduction in travel is associated with a deterioration in mobility and well-being (for example, elderly people who are afraid to go out at night), but the point is that, a priori, measures of travel do not serve as a proxy for mobility in their own right — they have to be interpreted within a wider context.

3.2 Measures of transport-system performance

A second approach to gauging the level of mobility in an area is to record the amount and type of transport provision. Car-ownership, for example, has been used in several studies of social well-being as an indicator of freedom of movement, but we should attach at least two caveats to the measure. First, studies by Hillman *et al.* (1973) and other writers have shown that car availability is a better measure of the value derived from owning a car, and that in this respect household car-ownership statistics can be misleading. Secondly, in areas of low service provision (notably rural areas) there may be an important element of 'forced' car-ownership among poorer households who have to make major sacrifices in order to meet car-ownership and running costs; in this latter instance, there is likely to be an *inverse* relationship between car-ownership level and social well-being.

With regard to public transport services, statistics are available on factors such as numbers of vehicles operating, total vehicle-miles and average headway. These can provide one dimension of an overall picture of mobility, but are only of limited value, for three reasons:

(a) They are often too broad to be very useful; for example, a given total of vehicle-miles operated could be in the form of a high-frequency coarse network or a low-frequency fine network.
(b) Aspects of service which are of interest to the potential traveller are often not recorded, notably the reliability of the service and the variability in travel and waiting times.
(c) The usefulness of a transport network depends on the density and configuration of land uses which it serves, and so cannot be assessed in isolation from this.

3.3 Measures of accessibility

Accessibility attempts to bring together measures of transport system and land-use supply, to provide an indication of ease of physical movement among activity facilities. It is thus more complete than measures of transport-system performance, and less ambiguous than measures of travel, since it is more likely, a priori, that better accessibility is to be preferred to worse[1] — although the marginal value of improvements may approach zero.

A wide range of measures of accessibility has been proposed in the literature, using both comparative approaches (for example, percentage of opportunities within *t* minutes of home — see Sherman *et al.* (1974)) and composite indices (for example, Hanson 1959). Early studies tended to emphasise accessibility among places, but more recently attention has switched to a concern with various forms of personal accessibility, which accord more with notions of mobility.

Essentially, personal accessibility is concerned with the ease with which people can use a range of facilities, as part of which travel *may* have an important role to play. Unlike travel-based measures, accessibility recognises the derived nature of most travel demand and may lead to an assessment of well-being which is significantly at variance with that inferred from the former. This distinction is emphasised by the Independent Commission on Transport (1974, p. 120):

> In a well-endowed town a person may have access to a vast range of facilities with very little travelling. While possibly less mobile in the ordinary sense of the word than someone who travels greater distances to work, school, and recreation or to visit friends, he may nevertheless be better placed, since the act of travel, with the time, cost and personal effort involved, is something which he usually would prefer to avoid.

One of the strengths and weaknesses of this work is that it provides a measure of potential rather than a measure of behaviour: that is, it shows the opportunity surface, available to a population group in an area, and does not usually relate this to the level of usage. To the extent that poor accessibility may prevent people from using facilities, the ability to highlight such problems is an important advantage of the approach, but on the other hand some improvements in accessibility may be perceived as irrelevant or unnecessary and therefore not very effective at enhancing well-being.

3.4 Measures of choice

This approach, pioneered by the Department of Geography at Lund under Professor Hägerstrand, takes the accessibility work one stage further, by looking at the flexibility which people have in organising their behaviour within a given space–time environment. It is thus concerned with potential rather than actual behaviour, but is more specific than the accessibility work in that it itemises the range of choice, and incorporates a continuous time dimension.

A number of practical applications have been carried out using the PESASP simulation model (for example, Lenntorp 1977) to look at how activity-travel patterns are restricted by transport and land-use provision. The model measures the number of possible ways in which a person could accomplish an existing activity programme, given certain timing, sequencing and duration constraints on activity participation. A conceptually similar approach has been used at Groningen University (based on the CARLA model developed at the Transport Studies Unit (TSU)) to examine the scope for reducing rural bus service levels with minimum disruption to household activity patterns; this work is reported in Clarke *et al.* (1984).

The approach has much to commend it in terms of its ability to examine the detailed social impact of transport policies from the viewpoint of daily life, and to take account of intra-household constraints on mobility. However, there are many important value judgements involved both in the method itself and in the interpretation of the results, which have an important influence on the conclusions that can be drawn from such a study. For example, do we assume that more choice is necessarily a good thing, and are all behaviour options equally desirable?

3.5 Measures of lifestyle

In many anthropological or sociological studies the time budget (that is, the time devoted to an exhaustive set of activities over a given time period) has been used as a general comparative measure of the quality of life (for example, Szalai and Andrews 1980), both between cultures and over time. In a planning context Meier (1959) has argued for the use of time rather than money as a social unit of account, and has suggested indices such as the amount of uncommitted time or the variety of activity participation as a basis for assessing social benefits.

This presupposes, however, that benefits can be defined unambiguously — a person who becomes unemployed may register a higher score on both these measures, and yet feel worse off in social terms. More generally, there is no clear evidence to suggest that satisfaction with activity participation correlates closely with the frequency or duration of participation. Robinson (1977), for example, cites evidence to suggest that satisfaction with activity participation correlates well with time spent on the activity, but Kelly (1973) found only a very low correlation between time and perceived value of the activity — and none between time and money expenditure.

Another limitation of the time budget measure is that it provides a very specific definition of behaviour that may not reflect the effects of a policy on lifestyles, either because changes that are perceived to be important appear to be insignificant when judged against total time allocation, or because they are not captured at all by this measure. The latter was evident in one study of the effects of school-hour and school-transport changes on family life (Heggie and Jones 1978), where the significant effects were at the level of changes in activity timing and location, and in joint activity participation.

Writers such as Pirie (1979) have attempted to formalise the impacts on lifestyle by proposing that measures should be developed to assess the amount of *disruption* to an activity pattern caused by a policy change. This could be done either through surveys, or by using the types of model described in Section 3.4. Although it is possible to devise such 'objective' measures of impact — given suitable data on household activity patterns — there are again no reasons to suppose that this correlates highly with 'subjective' measures of change. In some instances small adjustments to behaviour may be perceived as very undesirable, or certain types of major change as very desirable.

3.6 Travel need and hardship

Another way of dealing with mobility-related issues is to focus directly on problem areas, through attempts to measure hardship and needs for travel. The danger here is that we are likely to find what we look for: that is, the answer will be influenced by the way in which we set up the problem.

Unlike the earlier measures, which represented alternative ways of defining observed or potential action, need and hardship are more explicitly concerned with a judgement about the socially acceptable level of provision of services. As such, they can be — and have been — expressed in terms of all the earlier measures. For example, they may be defined in terms of

(a) differences in trip rates between 'disadvantaged' and other groups;
(b) the setting of minimum accessibility standards;
(c) an assessment of the minimum degree of choice which people should be able to enjoy;
(d) a judgement about the degree of disruption which people should be expected to face in their daily lives before serious hardship occurs.

Each of these measures in turn is likely to suggest different kinds of policy option to tackle the problem. Concern with trip rates, for example, may lead to higher transport-service provision, whereas an accessibility- or activity-pattern analysis may suggest the need for mobile services, or the retiming of land-use or transport-service provision, respectively.

4. A framework for studying issues relating to mobility and the individual

One theme to emerge strongly from the review of mobility-related problems in Section 2 is that mobility is really about everyday behaviour rather than travel *per se*, and that in many instances non-transport measures can do more to increase mobility for individuals than transport-related ones, or can achieve the same objective more efficiently. Here we outline a framework for examining travel in the context of daily behaviour, and then discuss how it and the various mobility-related measures in Section 3 might be used to explore the issues raised in this paper.

4.1 Travel in the context of household activity patterns

The framework outlined here represents an approach to studying personal travel and transport-related problems which has formed the basis of several projects carried out by the TSU. It incorporates and builds on several concepts described in Hägerstrand (1970) and Kutter (1973) and is outlined in Jones *et al.* (1983) and described more fully in Jones (1983).

Instead of focusing on travel directly, as a series of independent 'trips', we begin with a measure of daily behaviour, characterised as a series of activities that people undertake in order to satisfy basic physiological needs (such as sleeping or eating), role commitments (such as work, educational and domestic activities), or other personal preferences (leisure activities). Most activities make use of facilities that are only available at a few locations in space and which may only be open during certain hours of the day (or certain days of the week). By convention or necessity, participation in certain activities may be subject to space–time constraints on their timing, duration and/or location (such as sleep, work, or meals), or be complementary to other activities (for example, personal care and sleep, or meal preparation, eating and clearing away).

Together, the activities in which a person participates make up his activity programme and activity time budget (that is, the allocation of time to individual activities within the programme), structured in terms of a daily *activity pattern*. This results from a process of activity scheduling, in which an individual attempts to satisfy his activity needs and preferences, subject to their timing and sequencing requirements, the availability of facilities in space and time and to any constraints imposed by others. In doing so he or she has to recognise that it is not usually possible to undertake two major activities at once, nor to be in two places at once, and also has to allow sufficient time to travel between sites (taking account of public transport schedules and reliability, or the need for a margin for delays if travelling by private transport). An individual's spatial opportunity set can be enlarged by using a faster or more frequent mode of travel, or by a reduction in the timing constraints of activities (Burns 1979).

Most people live in multi-person households, or interact socially with family and friends and so have to take account of constraints imposed through interpersonal linkages. These affect which activities are undertaken (joint leisure activities, chauffeuring of children, and so on), as well as when and where they are to be carried out. An individual's or a household's activity needs, resources and constraints are strongly influenced by life-cycle stage, which is thus an important determinant of activity patterns.

The observed daily travel pattern becomes a subset of the activity pattern. Within this framework travel plays a unique role in daily life; it acts both as an integrative process — a lubricant to the scheduling of behaviour which facilitates the transition from one activity to another — and to some extent as a desirable activity in its own right. Indeed, the provision of facilities for movement has more than a passive influence on behaviour, as such facilities prescribe opportunities for participation and ultimately influence land-use patterns. Travel is thus a means to an end, an influence on the ends themselves, and an end in its own right.

These activity-based concepts are particularly useful when we examine individual and household *adaptation* in response to changes in the environment, household resources or personal needs or wants. Because all major aspects of behaviour are included it becomes possible to trace the secondary effects of changes (for example, a non-transport policy may have indirect travel repercussions) and to see how adjustments to travel behaviour may be affected and constrained by other factors. Most conventional forecasting models assume that people can make marginal adaptations along a continuous response curve as conditions gradually change, but this is not always the case. Absolute timing constraints and the operation of interpersonal linkages between household members (and others), and space–time linkages between events, lead to the emergence of threshold points that result in discontinuous response patterns.

Further, by knowing the activities that people undertake over a day and the various constraints associated with participation and scheduling, it becomes possible to identify those decisions which involve perceived choices and to investigate the trade-offs people make between options and activities. Thus, when people choose to save money and accept a longer journey time they are also foregoing time that could be spent on some other (non-travel) activity. The approach also identifies those situations in which time is at a premium because of timing or scheduling problems.

It is also possible to examine ways in which travellers might link or consolidate trips as transport costs increase, or find alternatives to travel, such as telecommunications, or substitute at-home activities. In this way it becomes possible to explore a wide range of mobility-related issues within a common framework.

4.2 Application to the study of mobility-related issues

An example of one family's behaviour where the husband works different shifts is shown in terms of a daily activity pattern in Figure 3.1. The blocks represent time spent on different types of activity, differentiated according to whether the activity was travel, or took place inside or outside the home; linkages among household members are also shown. This type of representation helps to highlight the role that travel plays, as a link between successive activities at different locations.

The diagram shows two patterns: one with the husband working an early shift (6a.m.–2p.m.) and the other when he works a late shift (2p.m.–10p.m.), and illustrates some repercussions of this on the rest of the family.

(a) Expressed in *trips*, there is a net increase in mobility at the household level when the husband switches from early to late shift; he and his daughter both increase their travelling (the latter because she is able to come home for lunch), while the wife has to curtail evening journeys to be with the daughter (and because her husband has taken their car to work).

(b) In terms of *choice* there appears to be a direct trade-off between husband and wife: when on early shift, the husband's day is heavily constrained by work and child-care, while the wife has considerable freedom of timing and activity in later afternoon and evening. On late shift, the husband has a free choice of activity in the morning, while the wife becomes heavily constrained in the evening.

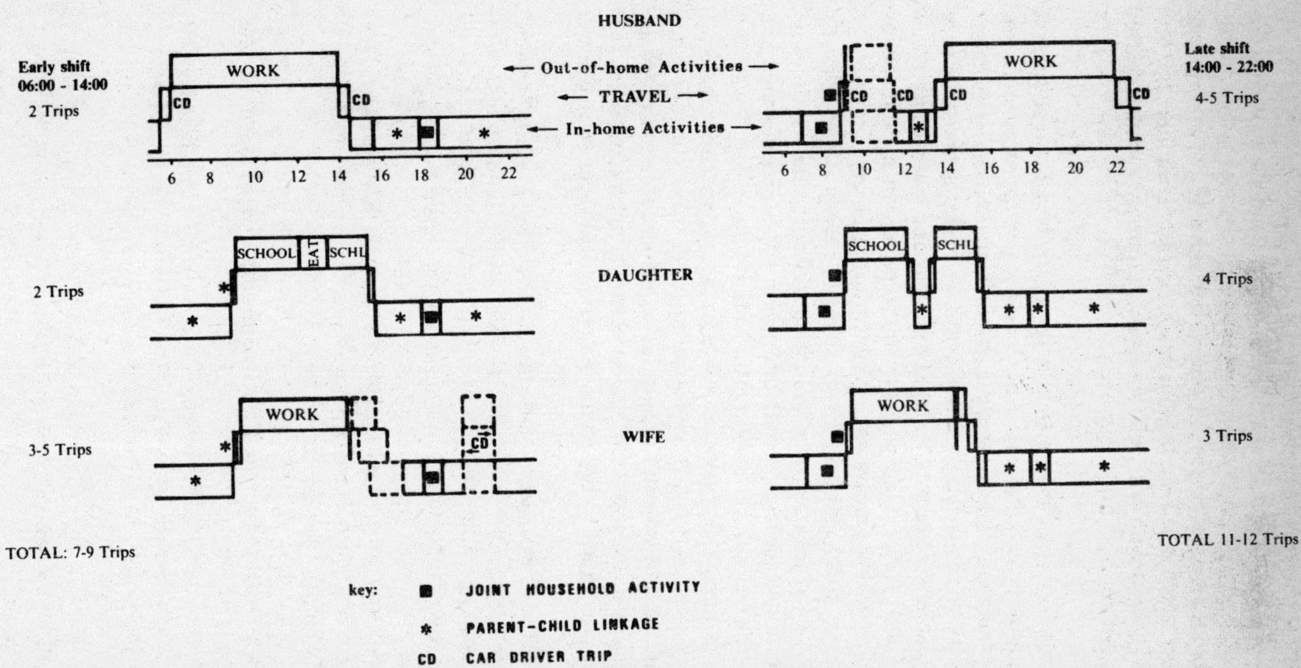

Source: Jones *et al*. (1983, Figure 9.6)

Figure 3.1 Some effects on family mobility of a two-shift work pattern

(c) Looked at in terms of lifestyle and *time budgets*, we see a mixed pattern. More time in total is spent away from home when the husband is on early shift (although the total trip rate is less), while the daughter spends more time with her parents if he is on late shift. The joint meal switches from breakfast to dinner and the prime responsibility for child-care also alternates with the shift being worked.

This simple example shows that it is possible to look at several aspects of mobility simultaneously and that it is important to do so, because the various measures are each saying something different about mobility and its effects on family life. Further, even at this very detailed level, we can see that there are gainers and losers, and trade-offs to be made in deciding whether mobility has been reduced or enhanced by some technological or institutional change.

By developing this approach, it is possible to derive — and relate to one another — a number of consistent indicators of mobility. In terms of the three dimensions identified in Section 2.4 we could measure

(a) movement using quantities such as trip rates, trip durations, and so on;
(b) potential for movement, through some of the transport system performance measures, and the accessibility measures; and
(c) freedom of action, by looking at the range of choices people have.

It is also possible to take account of some of the other mobility-related aspects, such as time pressures, or the behavioural consequences of fear of travel at night.

There are two important limitations to the approach, however. First, it cannot of itself provide judgements about the importance of different indicators, nor, second, does it provide a framework for developing an exhaustive set of measures. In terms of the first limitation the approach does not directly

(a) give an indication of the relative importance of each of the measures;
(b) give guidance as to whether well-being would be enhanced by an increase, decrease or stabilisation of the particular indicator;
(c) indicate the value people place on changes in the level of any of the indicators.

It thus needs to be augmented by attitudinally based or socio-politically derived information.

Also, comprehensive as they are, the activity-related measures do not provide a complete basis for measuring mobility or the effects of changes in the level of mobility. In particular, indicators of psychological well-being or physical health are outside this paradigm. What is encouraging, though, is that some of the latter measures can be related to aspects of behaviour recorded within the activity approach; Kam (1982) cites several studies which point to a relationship between social roles and depression and mental illness, which could be explored further using activity-based measures.

5. Conclusions

From the limited material which has been presented here, it is clear that mobility is a very important constituent of individual well-being, although a rather complex concept which is multifaceted and not fully understood in analytical terms. It is evident that we need to understand mobility as relating to travel and non-travel aspects of behaviour, both in order to gain a full understanding of the concept and to be able to set it in the context of the individual's daily life. A number of measures have been outlined which deal with some aspects of mobility, and it is argued that most can usefully be related and developed within an activity-based framework for studying human behaviour.

The ability to relate travel and non-travel aspects of behaviour is particularly important when we speculate on the future role of mobility in the post-industrial societies of the twenty-first century. From current developments, it is clear that we will need to take account of a wide range of effects of the telecommunications revolution (see, for example, Wigan 1983), and major social and economic changes such as a significant reduction in working hours or a smaller proportion of the population in gainful employment. Not only will these developments affect the various dimensions of mobility that we have considered, but they may also modify the basic notion of mobility itself, raising issues such as freedom of entry to computer networks and information systems.

The proposition that travel-related mobility problems need to be studied in the broader context of household activity patterns parallels a similar concern in many other subject areas to broaden the context in which topics are examined. Capra (1982) outlines similar developments in the fields of physics, medicine and economics, as workers in these areas also come to grips with the notion of society and life as much more interconnected phenomena than was appreciated within the Newtonian–Cartesian mode of thought.

A number of basic areas are not adequately addressed by the material presented here: these include the importance we should attach to different measures of mobility — even, in some cases, whether more or less of a certain indicator is to be preferred — and the relationship between mobility at the level of the individual and that experienced by society as a whole. The latter can partly be dealt with through a process of aggregation (e.g. by looking at the effects of changes on different socio-economic or life-cycle groups). But broader issues such as how institutions other than the family are affected by changes in mobility, or to what extent in the longer term constraints become choices, requires that this approach be related more explicitly to other frameworks dealing with the economic, environmental, social and political aspects of mobility. In short, approaches for examining mobility and the individual should be seen as one facet of a much more comprehensive study of mobility and society; the challenge lies in bringing together the insights which the various disciplines have to offer, to deal with the mobility problems of the twenty-first century.

Notes

1. There are exceptions, however, where we wish to protect an area from overuse, or in the case of people who do not like to be 'on top of' their work; or the possibility that accessibility improvements might lead to higher noise levels, and so on.

References

Allsop, R.E. (1980). 'Transport Studies and the Quality of Life', *Environment and Planning A*, **12**, 339–56.

Bailey, J.M. (1981). 'Application of the Concept of Social Need in the Planning of Transport Services for Elderly and Disabled people'. Oxford: Transport Studies Unit, Oxford University, ref. 159/CP.

Burns, L. (1979). *Transportation, Temporal and Spatial Components of Accessibility*. Lexington, Mass.: Lexington Books.

Capra, F. (1982). *The Turning Point: Science, Society and the Rising Culture*. London: Wildwood House.

Cerwenka, P. (1982). 'Assessment of Society's Transport Needs: Mobility of Persons'. Paper presented at ECMT Conference, November.

Clarke, M., C. van Knippenberg and J. Splinter (1984). 'Analysing the Effects of Rural Bus Service Reductions on Lifestyles'. Paper presented to the Transportation Research Board Meeting, Washington DC, January.

Cullen, I. and E. Phelps (1975). 'Diary Techniques and the Problems of Urban Life'. Final Report to the Social Science Research Council, Grant no. HR2336, February.

Faulkner, H.W. (1982). 'Simulation Games as a Technique for Information Collection: A Case Study of Disabled Person Transport Use in Canberra' in T. Beed and R. Stimson, eds, *The Theory and Techniques of Interviewing. Proceedings of an Advanced Training Workshop*. Sydney: Hale and Iremonger.

Hägerstrand, T. (1970). 'What about People in Regional Science?', *Papers of the Regional Science Association*, **24**, 7–21.

Hanson, W.G. (1959). 'How Accessibility Shapes Land Use', *Journal of the American Institute of Planners*, **25**, 73–6.

Hart, D.A. (1976). *Strategic Planning in London: The Rise and Fall of the Strategic Road Network*. Oxford: Pergamon Press, Urban and Regional Planning Series, Volume 12.

Heggie, I.G. and P.M. Jones (1978). 'Defining Domains for Models of Travel Demand', *Transportation*, **7**, 119–35.

Hillman, M., I. Henderson and A. Whalley (1973). 'Personal Mobility and Transport Policy'. PEP Broadsheet no. 542.

Independent Commission on Transport (1974). *Changing Directions*. London: Coronet Books.

Jones, P.M. (1983). 'A New Approach to Understanding Travel Behaviour and its Implications for Transportation Planning'. PhD thesis, London University.

Jones, P.M., M.C. Dix, M.I. Clarke and I.G. Heggie (1983). *Understanding Travel Behaviour*, Aldershot: Gower.

Jones, P.M. and R.P. Kilvington (1983). 'Exploratory Study of Private Travel — Value of Time Study, Phase II'. Oxford: TSU (unpublished).

Kam, B.H. (1982). 'Role Situations and Activity Scheduling: An Empirical Analysis'. PhD thesis, Urban Planning Department, University of California at Los Angeles.

Kelly, J.R. (1973). 'Three Measures of Leisure Activity: A Note on the Continued Incommensurability of Oranges, Apples and Artichokes', *Journal of Leisure Research*, **5** (2), 56–65.

Kutter, E. (1973). 'A Model for Individual Travel Behaviour', *Urban Studies*, **10**, 233–56.

Lee, T.R. and L.J. Wood (1982). 'Adjustment in the Urban System: The Tasman Bridge Collapse and its Effects on Metropolitan Hobart', *Progress in Planning*, **15** (2), 63–150.

Lenntorp, B. (1977). 'A Time-Geographic Simulation Model of Individual Activity Programmes' in T. Carlstein, D. Parkes and N. Thrift, eds, *Human Activity and Time Geography*. London: Arnold.

Maltby, D. and H.P. White (1982). *Transport in the United Kingdom*. London: Macmillan.

Meier, R.L. (1959). 'Human Time Allocation: A Basis for Social Accounts', *Journal of the American Institute of Planners*, **25**, 27–33.

Pirie, G.H. (1979). 'Measuring Accessibility: A Review and a Proposal', *Environment and Planning A*, **11**, 299–312.

Robinson, J.P. (1977). *How Americans Use Time. A Social-Psychological Analysis of Everyday Behaviour*. New York and London: Praegar Publishers.

Rosenbloom, S., ed. (1978). *Women's Travel Issues: Research Needs and Priorities. Conference Papers and Proceedings*. US DoT Research and Special Programs Administration.

Shapcott, M. and P. Steadman (1977). 'A Study of the Introduction of Flexible Working Hours in Reading'. Cambridge: The Martin Centre for Architectural and Urban Studies, Cambridge University (unpublished).

Sherman, L., B. Barber and W. Kondo (1974). 'Method for Evaluating Metropolitan Accessibility', *Transportation Research Record*, **499**, 70–82.

Szalai, A. and F.M. Andrews (1980). *The Quality of Life: Comparative Studies*. London and Berkeley, Sage Studies in International Sociology, Volume 10.

Teply, S. (1982). 'Network Travel Behaviour, "Levels of Choice" and Urban Transportation Management', *Traffic Engineering and Control*, February, 71–6.

Wigan, M.R. (1983). 'Transport and Communications Interactions'. Australian Road Research Board (unpublished).

4 Dilemmas in Car Mobility — The Disenchantment of Speed

E. Kutter

1. The automotive society

In Hägerstrand's thought experiment (in Chapter 2 of this volume), the flying carpet would be a wonderful asset as long as only a few people owned one. If it became generally available, in the way of the motor car, the aggregate outcome would be absurd. If we transfer this thought experiment to car mobility the greatest enemy of the attractiveness of the motor car is its own success (Sachs 1984, p. 47). Consequently we detect a decrease in the percentage of car drivers who regard car driving as a pleasure from 63 per cent in 1960 to only 41 per cent in 1981 (Aral 1982–3).

In spite of the broad consensus regarding the day-to-day use of the car, we begin to realise that the communication problems of our settlement system cannot be covered by the automotive system alone. The evolution from the 'period of promotorism' to the functionally subdivided and suburbanised town of today with its hierarchical transportation networks took place over a long period; it seems to be a development along the lines of the stereotype of the 'structures which have developed over the years'. But, analysing this development with regard to cause–effect relationships, we detect enormous influences of transportation technology. Only the outstanding possibilities of car mobility enabled the urban dweller to move beyond the city boundaries.

This dependency on car mobility characterises the present situation of the settlement system generally: when the communication function of public transport was partially taken over by the car the transportation sector acquired an uncontrolled dynamism of its own. As an outcome of possibilities brought about by the car, settlement structures changed drastically and are now difficult to serve by public transport. This in turn results in increasing car-ownership and in the end car traffic, owing to its space requirements and its disturbance potential, is accepted as an autonomous activity. Today we are confronted with a large measure of social consensus concerning the division of functions in transport: the car receives its own infrastructure, and car traffic establishes yardsticks (speed level). Finally, car traffic becomes an economic factor and loses its function as a means to an end.

On the other hand, it is quite clear that in European settlements only half of all movement needs can be covered by the car system; by confining our planning considerations to car mobility we produce great spatial differences between car drivers and carless people. Car traffic also has other consequences which must be seen more critically today: the speeds are out of proportion to the existing safety components and constitute an unacceptable nuisance to other modes of transport, and in the environmental-ecological system, as well as in the driving system itself, car traffic creates incredible problems merely because of the massive occurrence of vehicles.

Car mobility induces many follow-up problems in the area of safety, traffic noise, air pollution and environmental and social acceptability. Therefore, we should ask whether we can continue to demand monofunctional facilities along the lines of the Charta of Athens; whether we can try to cope with the necessary physical movement by even more self-regulation. Should our settlement system continue to be tailored to only one transport system, a system to which, in addition, the maximum possible freedom of movement is granted?

2. Mobility-orientated transportation planning

As an outcome of planning processes during the 'suburbanisation era' — which was also an era of car mobility — infrastructural facilities were precisely tailored to specific activities. Transport facilities, for example, were broken down hierarchically and designed for subproblems of communication only. Transportation planners acquire their information on today's traffic needs on the basis of an uncritical analysis of the status quo. Forecasts regarding future developments or regarding the effects of certain policies thus depart from self-regulation and from the assumption that the present mechanisms of traffic generation are maintained. The transport sub-specialist accepts transport requirements, characteristic data of the vehicle fleet and even the characteristics of movement behaviour. On the whole, we find that the transport planner is usually doing a 'repair job': when answering pressing questions, such as how to reduce the negative consequences of today's traffic, he replies with a high degree of special competence, but constant transport policy premises are his point of departure. And this so-called planning ultimately results in noise-abatement walls, more concentration of traffic, more monofunctionality such as residential 'reservations' and finally even more transportation needs.

As we have seen, car mobility enabled the citizen to move beyond the city boundaries, thus starting the suburbanisation processes. But the application of current traffic-engineering measures, taken as corrective measures, only results in excessively expensive and hardly effective projects. In the area of public transport, for example, competition with the car, absolutely necessary when starting from current premises, is only possible at high speeds and over long distances, and therefore rapid transport takes priority everywhere (Hall 1985). But to make public transport competitive with the overwhelming advantages of the motor car we would have to make virtually unfundable investments to approximate the transit speed to car speeds in order to gain a further percentage of the overall traffic volume (see, for example, Kutter 1985a, p. 28). This fast-transit strategy causes only a small improvement in the modal-split area, and the quality of public transport in the short-distance area must deteriorate because of economic considerations. This in turn fosters the concentration of economic facilities in only a few places and induces new transportation requirements. Thus the transportation planner, taking the quality of car mobility as a point of departure, is caught in a vicious circle (see Figure 4.1). The outstanding feature of this vicious circle is the parallelism of mobility-induced deconcentration of housing areas and antagonistic processes in the area of economic land uses; this combination makes faster transportation systems necessary and inevitably induces more consequential functionalism.

Another absurdity of our conventional wisdom becomes obvious if we take the time-of-day-related increases in passengers into consideration: the increases occur mainly during peak hours, for routine activities which could quite easily be shifted. As Wachs (1985) reported, the ratio of peak vehicle-miles to off-peak vehicle-miles increased from 1:8 in 1960 to 2:1 in 1975. But off-peak transit services normally recover much more of their operating costs from fares than do rush-hour services. This means that increases in passenger volume normally tend to worsen operating results, and this leads to the conclusion among the transport authorities that higher fares must be charged during peak hours; this may make sense from the operational point of view but it is nothing short of absurd from the point of view

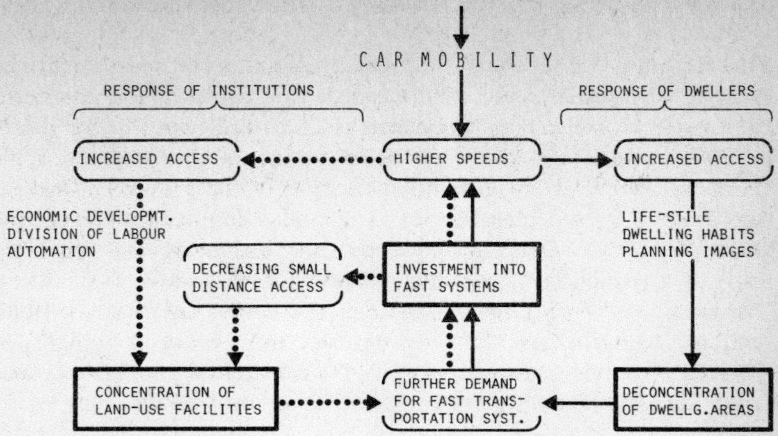

Source: Kutter (1983), p. 180

Figure 4.1 Vicious circle of the settlement–transportation system introduced by car mobility

of transport policy. The present structure of transportation services, furthermore, contains some social incompatibility, as already pointed out by Wachs (1985): 'those riding less than one mile paid fares $0.17 more than operational costs, while 25-mile-trip riders, the high-income classes in the suburbs, paid fares which averaged $3.17 less than the costs'.

But even a concept of public transport which is radically different from the outlined conventional wisdom has no chance at all in a society which equates the unhampered satisfaction of communication needs with a 'free social order': if we slow down public transport and change over to high-density networks, served by buses or a dial-a-ride system, we cannot adequately serve the existing long-distance network, and this will lead to increasing the effects of disurbanisation, once more leaving a higher share of all movements to car traffic. Besides, when implementing high-density and low-speed public transport, the operating results may even worsen because public transport, in the near-distance area, is now challenged by increased walking and cycling.

By and large, car-mobility orientated transportation planning is unable to deviate from the above-mentioned vicious circle because the motor car has set the yardstick for mobility. Therefore the European planner should have every reason to rethink the conventional wisdom in transportation planning.

3. Why should we aim at mobility-behaviour modifications?

The uncontrolled evolution of the transportation sector may be described by some trends of the last decade which in the long-term lead to a horror scenario. Model calculations for Berlin (Kutter 1985a, p. 30) showed that the very development of socio-demographic characteristics leads to enormous changes in the movement system (see Table 4.1). A decreasing percentage of young people reduces the share of captive riders; at the same time increasing car-ownership leads to a reduction of the share of pedestrians as well as of riders. Increasing car travel now will cause an increasing nuisance potential. And, as a consequence, the necessity of subsidy will become higher in the area of public transport as well as in the area of maintenance and repair of a permanently widening infrastructural sector.

Table 4.1 Changes in the movement system (Berlin) caused by socio-demographic changes (1976–83)

MODE OF TRANSPORT	PERSON MOVEMENTS/DAY (THOUSANDS)*)			RESULTING SPLIT	
	POP. 76	POP. 83	VARIATION	1976	1983
WALKING	1502	1483	- 19	29.6%	29.2%
DRIVING	1634	1790	+156	32.2%	35.3%
RIDING	1934	1797	-137	38.2%	35.5%
ALL MODES	5070	5070			

*) 1.93 MIO. INHABITANTS (≥6 YEARS) IN 1976

Source: Kutter (1985a, p. 30)

If we ask how the problem of the transportation sector should be managed with regard to these changing boundary conditions we have to recognise that our policies are aimed at highly inconsistent goals:

- The postulate of free mobility implies the supply of adequate capacities and has to accept the numerous follow-up problems brought about by car-induced developments in the settlement system.
- The available resources, especially space for land uses and infrastructure, are strictly limited in European countries; and therefore we have to restrict the ecological effects of traffic, or, much more expensive, we have to perform a 'repair job'.

- As European policies are starting from social acceptability when handling problems of transportation infrastructure, we have to compensate for the disadvantages of the carless by some kind of social transport system.

Analysing the life cycle of urban development, the stage of suburbanisation and disurbanisation is equated with a kind of throw-away ideology. As a consequence, the high follow-up costs of investment in the meantime take the main share of the total funds; in Berlin, for example, the cost of repair and maintenance in the transport sector already amounts to 83 per cent of all available funds. Other examples, such as London Transport and the New York subway, show that for years it has not been possible to meet maintenance and repair expenses. And from this derives the fact, taking the present economic stagnation into consideration, that it is no longer possible to avail of throw-away ideologies. This in turn leads to the question of how the transportation sector can be dealt with in the face of diminishing public funds. Evidently, under these circumstances, we can at best satisfy a single sector of the above-defined duties (see Figure 4.2):

- If we follow the American example and choose self-regulation and free mobility, the total funds are needed for the provision of more capacity and for maintenance and repair; but our money will not run to providing social public transport and environmental compatibility.
- The moderation of the negative effects of car mobility in the status quo is only possible by means of more monofunctionality and more 'reservations'; our infrastructural system will become even more tailored to the car, it will become more inconsistent and unpayable in the end.
- A reduction in subsidy for social public transport does not fit into our market system and, if we nevertheless continue to favour the car-mobility yardsticks, it will not guarantee a change of movement habits and therefore could lead to an intolerable situation in the transportation system as a whole.

So in the end we have a free choice between a system which is socially unacceptable and unacceptable too in the ecological area, and insolvency in the transportation sector or the economically inconsistent sector which, in the end, will come tumbling down. If we want to take into account all three above-mentioned goals we obviously

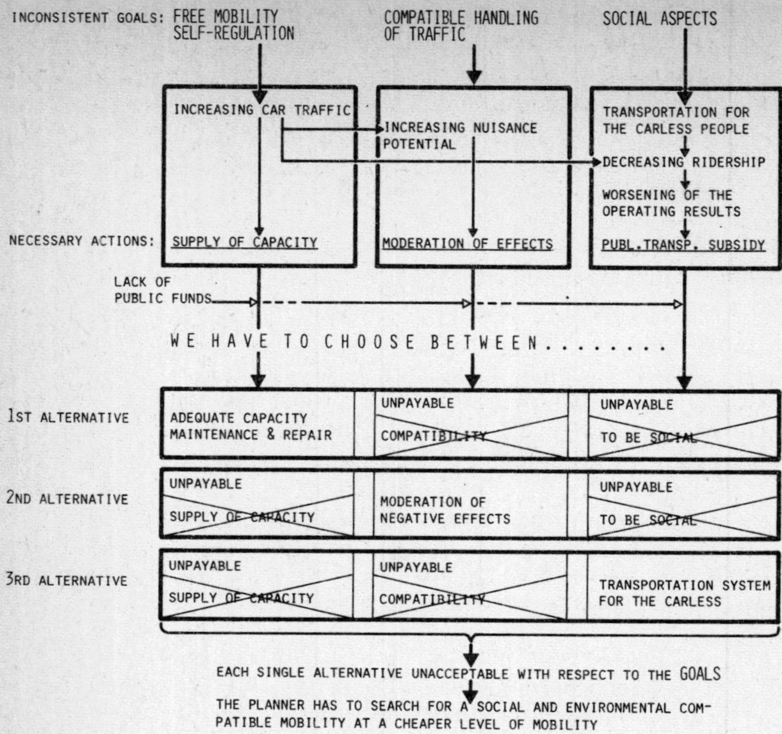

Figure 4.2 Different goals and possible alternatives in European transportation policy

have to search for socially and environmentally acceptable mobility at a cheaper rate, and this could only mean a slower level of mobility.

4. Are mobility-induced processes reversible?

In a society that considers itself automobile there arise some doubts whether there is any chance of a reversal of current trends and mobility habits. The outstanding issue here is the split between the modes of movement. And the connected main question, how these shares of different transport modes are determined, has so far been considered starting from the status quo, especially from the point of view of the loser, public transport: planners have very often tried to substantiate the effects of faster rapid transport under the magic notion of attractiveness, which in reality causes only a very small change from car to public transport — if other determinants, such as parking restrictions, are excluded. But even this car-orientated status quo supplies other information too: information upon the restrictions on car traffic, characteristic measures to promote 'non-traffic'. But it is necessary to start a more objective analysis of the causes and effects of today's transportation situation. Examples for research results in this sense of a better understanding of cause–effect relationships are outlined below.

Effects of accessibility. Considerations of the quality of access have in the past, for the most part, been introduced to split models only. But this access has a decisive share in determining the selection of destinations. Calculations carried out in Berlin showed that an increase in the speed of public transport induces pedestrians to choose more distant destinations, thus having much greater effects in the area of settlement structure, from a long-term perspective, than with regard to the classic objective of reduction in car traffic (see Table 4.2).

Table 4.2 Changes in the movement system in Berlin caused by increasing speed of the public transport system

MODE OF TRANSPORT	PERSON MOVEMENTS/DAY (THOUSANDS)*)			RESULTING SPLIT	
	100KM RAPID TRANSIT NETW.	170KM RAPID TRANSIT NETW.	VARIATION	(100KM)	(170KM)
WALKING	1446	1391	- 55	29.2%	28.1%
DRIVING	1745	1726	- 19	35.3%	34.9%
RIDING	1753	1827	+ 74	35.5%	37.0%
ALLMODES	4944	4944			

*) 1.88 MIO. INHABITANTS (≥6 YEARS) IN 1983

Source: Kutter (1985a, p. 28)

On the other hand, we may draw the conclusion from these negative effects that the use of vehicle transportation in a real situation is strongly influenced by local accessibility in the near neighbourhood. In this context the strategies in land-use planning, typical structures of new towns versus the nineteenth-century structures, determine the share of non-traffic (pedestrians and cyclists). Moreover, these conditions for non-traffic activities are an important point of departure for the quality of the day-to-day life of all those categories with strong social ties within the dwelling area (e.g. lower car availability, little children, etc.).

Effects of tax policy. It is usually stated (see, for example Bly 1982, p. 34) that rising fuel prices have a very small influence on traffic volume. But contrary to this, an analysis of traffic development in Denmark (Golob *et al.* 1983, p. 14) draws a totally different picture of possible developments. Taxes and duties, first of all, are three to four times higher for the medium-sized car in Denmark than for a similar car in other European countries. From 1971 to 1976 expenditure on cars rose sharply, by 60 per cent, while fares on public transport became cheaper. Because of this, private car traffic decreased by about 10 per cent, while public transport increased by about 50 per cent.

Speed reductions and the vehicle fleet. The current discussion of transportation-policy effects is usually reduced to the mode of conveyance. Input variables belonging to other sub-areas, such as the technical equipment of the vehicles in transportation, are treated as constants. When arguing about speed limits, the technological data of the vehicle fleet are, unfortunately, time and again taken as the point of departure. This distorts the argument because in the event of drastic speed reduction a completely different design of the vehicles is possible — and probable, as the Japanese example has shown (small cars sharply increasing). And this will lead to much higher energy savings than stated in current research.

From the results of cause–effect analyses, as outlined above, there derive some reasonable ideas about the probable effects of partially new targets in transportation planning. If, for example, speeds are lowered generally, new starting conditions for the division of functions in traffic emerge. The existing speed differences, hitherto the cause of the high car usage, would be considerably reduced. Thus the relative quality of the non-car traffic would be improved and this, in turn, would have consequences concerning the modal choice. As a by-product, the speed reduction would have consequences for the choice of destination: the distances covered would be shortened and the short-distance area would be strengthened which, in turn, would probably foster a tendency towards reurbanisation. From a long-term perspective we could rethink principles like structuring networks in stages or protected residential reservations and the street could, in the end, regain its multifunctionality.

5. Conditions of mobility-behaviour modifications

Since the majority of Europeans equate the satisfaction of enormous mobility wishes with a free social order, there is not much chance of a consensus on policies which cut down free mobility by regulation. So the crucial problem would be to work out a conclusive argument. One of the opinion-forming components, in this context, is the basic attitude towards the notion of provision for vital needs. Applied to transportation, what we really need is not provision of transportation processes but rather a plan for how to make activities possible. Instead of ensuring the optimal handling of an externally determined transportation demand we should ask: how can the necessary activities and the connected movements be handled in a manner which is as environmentally and socially acceptable as possible?

Such a concept for a viable settlement structure must start from the fact that the built-up structures of our urban regions contain long-lived facilities in all land-use and transportation areas. And therefore we must start our considerations upon a politically willed building backwards from the current structure and the currently necessary transportation processes. In this area the crucial problem is the socially acceptable handling of the necessary car traffic which has so far been a nuisance, excessively expensive, and characterised by intolerable speeds. But with respect to the existing settlement structures we can't get rid of the automotive traffic in the short term. Building backwards towards reurbanisation therefore must start with a combined concept for the integration of car mobility and public transport.

Within this comprehensive concept the adequate division of duties between the different modes of transportation, including non-traffic, would take a key position. But in this context, planning should make a contribution to making possible a substantially more objective process of weighing up the systems. Current evaluations are often falsified by the fact that the different systems are measured with entirely different yardsticks:

- railways and air traffic are subject to strict regulation; safety regulations are mostly established deductively and cause considerable costs in operation;
- contrary to this, in car mobility, an effort is made to derive safety standards from today's driving habits.

This, of course, leads to prejudiced results when comparing the public and the private systems.

Taking another glance at the present transportation system, the rivalry situation, for example, in Berlin, is characterised by a two-and-a-half times higher accessibility for the car driver; and this finding indeed leads to the question why there is anyone still using public transport. Starting from this status quo, we undoubtedly have to develop new ideas concerning settlement–transportation systems (better: space–time concepts) that are viable by means of tolerable and lower speeds and a more acceptable split between the different transport modes.

One of the main shortcomings when analysing the transportation phenomenon in the past was to focus only on vehicle movement which resulted in an overestimation of the distances to be covered. Movement which, taken as a whole, is conducted in the context of day-to-day life covers much shorter distances than we reported in the past. In Berlin, for example, the average distances covered in overall traffic are 5.14km for work and 2.23km for shopping; within the shopping movements 50 per cent cover less than 1km, and 50 per cent of car users make trips of less than 1.3km (see Table 4.3).

Table 4.3 Distances/time expenditure to be covered in everyday life

		CORE AREA			SUBURBAN AREA		
DISTANCE TO CBD		3 KM			15 KM		
WORK TRIPS	MODAL SPLIT	WALKING 12%	DRIVING 46%	RIDING 42%	WALKING 4%	DRIVING 50%	RIDING 46%
	AVERAGE DIST.<KM>	-	3.2	3.7	-	9.0	9.6
	TRAVEL TIME <MIN>	-	8	23	-	18	48
SHOPPING TRIPS	MODAL SPLIT	WALKING 60%	DRIVING 17%	RIDING 23%	WALKING 40%	DRIVING 27%	RIDING 33%
	AVERAGE DIST.<KM>	<1.0	1.6	2.6	>1.0	4.0	7.0
	TRAVEL TIME <MIN>	10	4	16	15	8	35

Source: Kutter (1985b, p. 5)

Taking such findings as a point of departure, concepts for tolerable speeds using a reasonable expenditure of time can be developed. Computations for Berlin in this context draw the following picture when starting from a speed reduction to 30km/h all over the town (Kutter, 1985b):

- within the core area the daily time expenditure (for an average of 2.5 movements) increases from 32 minutes to 40 minutes.
- for dwellers in the new towns, the time expenditure increases from 81 to 93 minutes per day, and
- the average town dweller must add 9 minutes to his present time expenditure of 57 minutes.

It stands to reason that this increase is much less than usually expected or used when arguing against speed reduction. Considerations as outlined above could be completed by environmental aspects and safety considerations and, at a more objective level, finally result in indicative values concerning a tolerable speed level.

6. Epilogue

Meaningful person-movement concepts can only be drawn up by settlement planning and transport planning working in co-operation. This co-operation should certainly be understood as a mutual relationship: no land-use planning without consequential movements, and no fixing of transport concepts without an analysis of settlement-structure effects. An implementation of new (actually 'old') space–time-structures would be no self-regulation and no development along the lines of the stereotype of the 'structures which have developed over the years', but a politically willed organisation of the environment. While this could be quite normal in the categories of planning, it has never been practised in this form so far. Acquired rights would be affected, habits we have grown fond of would be restricted. Consequently, it is to be expected that even the planning preparations of such concepts will entail polemic controversies in a society that considers itself automobile.

But if the viability of European towns is to be maintained there can hardly be an alternative to a general reorganisation of the urban structure towards reurbanisation and a disenchantment with speed. The American town can certainly not serve as a model, all the more so since the structures fixed there will no longer be affordable for European post-industrial societies with their social and environmental/ecological goals. As far as this aspect is concerned, Europeans are clearly better off, since their towns have not yet been tailored to high-speed transportation to such an extent that a real reurbanisation would no longer be possible.

References

Aral, A.G. (1982–3). *Aral-Verkehrstaschenbuch.*

Bly, P.H. (1982). 'Effect of the Recession on Travel Expenditure and Travel Patterns'. Paper presented at the OECD symposium on the impact of the economic situation on travel in urban areas, Paris.

Golob, J.M., B. van der Hee and S. Prahl (1983). 'Travel behaviour in Denmark in a Period of Economic Recession'. Paper presented at the Tenth Planning Research Colloquium, Zandfoort, the Netherlands.

Hall, P. (1985). 'Urban Transportation: Paradoxes for the 1980s', in G.R.M. Jansen, P. Nijkamp and C. Ruijgrok, eds, *Transportation and Mobility in an Era of Transition.* Amsterdam: North Holland Publishing Co., pp. 367–76.

Kutter, E. (1983). 'Brauchen wir überhaupt noch öffentlichen Personennahverkehr?', *Nahverkehrspraxis*, **31**, 179–81.

Kutter (1985a). 'Ist Selbstregulierung im Verkehrsbereich heute noch ausreichend?', *Verkehr und Technik* **38**, 27–31.

Kutter, E. (1985b). 'New Targets for Transport Facilities Planning' in G.R.M. Jansen, P. Nijkamp and C. Ruijgrok, eds, *Transportation and Mobility in an Era of Transition*. Amsterdam: North Holland Publishing Co., pp. 377–87.

Sachs, W. (1984). 'Die Liebe zur Geschwindigkeit' in *Scenario Autoverkehr 2000*, Volume 24 of the Schriftenreihe Energie und Gesellschaft. Berlin: Technische Universtät.

Wachs, M. (1985). 'The Politicization of Transit Subsidy Policy in America' in G.R.M. Jansen, P. Nijkamp and C. Ruijgrok, eds, *Transport and Mobility in an Era of Transition*. Amsterdam: North Holland Publishing Co., pp. 353–66.

5 Impacts of Advanced Technology in the Production Sector on Freight Transport and Communications

P.O. Pedersen

1. Industrial development trends

Until the mid-1960s most manufacturing industries produced goods for the final consumer market on the basis of inputs of raw materials, and the most important locational factor was nearness to the large urban regions, where a large part of the consumers are concentrated and where the large harbours and railway terminals are located.

During the 1960s and the early 1970s a division took place in many firms between, on the one hand, administration and management functions, which stayed in the centre, and, on the other hand, the simpler parts of the production, which were often moved out of the metropolitan areas, basically to exploit cheap labour on the periphery. For instance, Thorngren (1970) and Törnquist (1970) argue that this pattern developed owing to the developments in telecommunications which made it possible to send over long distances routinised information as it is communicated between branches of a concern, but which is insufficient to replace more complicated face-to-face contacts breaking ground for new innovations and developments. Therefore, the management and administrative functions as well as the more innovative industries stayed behind in the metropolitan regions.

However, over the last ten years the structural rationalisation of manufacturing industries increasingly seems to have led to a further division of production into systems of firms producing intermediate goods and services to each other, rather than to the final consumer, firms which are knotted together by commodity flows and sometimes also by common ownership.

This process of division does not only take place in the traditional consumer industries, but to an even larger extent in the machinery industry, which has become more and more important as the levels of mechanisation and automation have increased, and in administration and management, where different types of specialised consultancy firm are created.

The basic reason for the functional division of production is the economies of scale which can be obtained by specialisation. However, there are other reasons which strengthen the tendency to divide production into different firms. Firstly, it can be advantageous for a firm, both for market and technical reasons, to separate out a sub-product if the optimal size of production of the sub-product is much larger than the firm's own demand for the sub-product. Secondly, it may for financial reasons be easier to expand production if the less profitable parts of a production are handed over to other firms. Thirdly, a company may, by spreading the production to smaller firms, be able to locate the different parts of the production where their production factors are best or cheapest. Especially with regard to wages, it may, by a divide-and-rule policy, reduce the efficiency of labour unions and thus the wage level. Fourthly, it will often be advantageous for a larger capital-intensive firm to hand over cyclical, seasonal or other peaks in the production to other firms, in order to utilise its own production capacity more smoothly and spread the risk of overexpansion from itself to other firms.

The process of division results in the creation of a hierarchial system of interrelated firms which will often be centred either on large factories mass-producing standardised consumer goods, machinery or intermediate goods or on factories producing large machinery, ships or turnkey production units.

Many of the larger firms in such a system will be linked together by ownership because the dominating firms in the system will often try to buy technically more advanced subcontractors on which they are dependent and other firms operating in their market.

These large firms at the top of the system often have a large fixed capital and many white-collar workers (human capital). Therefore it is important for them to have a stable workforce and a relatively stable demand, which can secure an efficient utilisation of capital. To achieve this, first, they will often attempt to hand over the simpler parts of the production and the larger fluctuations in demand to a set of usually relatively small independent subcontractors, which will function as buffers for the fluctuations. Second, standardised production in the large firms often leaves room for smaller firms to operate in small specialised markets, where the standardised products cannot be used. Thirdly, the need for firms specialising in service and maintenance of the production system becomes larger and larger as the capital intensity increases. Finally, the need for diverse management services increases as production becomes more complex and markets more internationalised.

Under the network of larger firms, therefore, there exists an undergrowth of small firms which are often formally independent, but in reality depend indirectly on the larger firms. These small firms will often be exposed to a very fluctuating market. If they want to survive they must try to establish a very flexible production system which can absorb the fluctuations. Therefore, they are usually not very capital-intensive. They will often try to employ skilled labour, which is itself flexible. Otherwise they are based on unskilled labour, which is easy to hire and easy to fire. The turnover of these firms is rapid because many are forced to close at the same time as low capital intensity makes it relatively easy to start new firms.

The large production firms at the top of the system today seem not to be very distance-dependent. They are no longer bound to the market of the large towns and they trade raw materials and intermediate goods with each other over long distances. Distance does not seem to mean much to them, and some studies describe modern industry as enclaves which have no contact with their region of location. Their regional multiplier is said to consist practically only of the wage multiplier, and even that is becoming smaller and smaller as the labour force in the standardised production units is rationalised away. (See, for instance, O'Farrell and O'Loughlin 1980, Perrons 1981 and Christensen 1981.)

For the smaller firms, distance seems to be much more important. They are often dependent both on the larger and on other small firms in the region. However, this dependency between the large and the small firms seems to be reciprocal, not in the sense that the large firms are dependent on any one of the small firms, but in the sense that their high productivity depends on the existence of an undergrowth of small firms, which at short notice are able to solve many different, small, but acute tasks.

This close interdependence between the firms in a region was documented by Grøn (1983, 1984) in a recent study of the metal products and machinery industry in two counties in Jutland, Denmark. The study was carried out as a two-phase interview analysis. In the first phase, about 50 firms with more than 50 employees were interviewed. In the second phase their local suppliers and customers were interviewed. The study showed that there was a close network of contacts between the local firms, much closer than expected (see Figure 5.1). The study also explains why many studies find the larger producers of standardised goods to be enclave industries. This is because these studies have been interested in the largest flows of raw materials and intermediate goods, and these are not usually local. But the modern factory depends not only on a few large input flows, but also on hundreds or thousands of small inputs, each of which may not be important, but which together are necessary; and many of these inputs will be provided by small local firms. It is typical of these inputs that they are not produced and delivered at regular intervals, and that the service element in them is high.

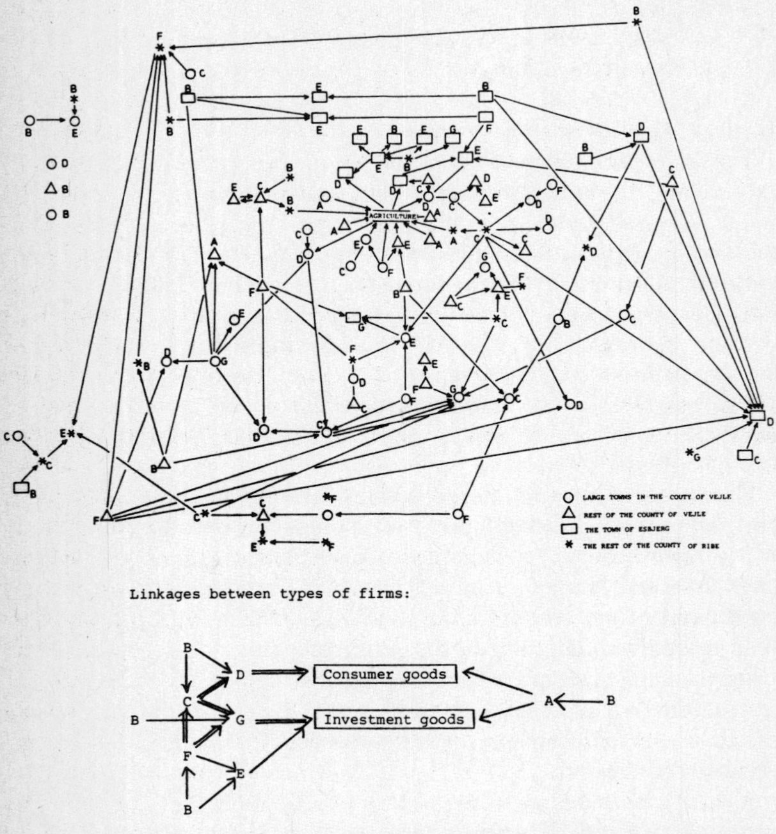

Figure 5.1 The pattern of trade linkages between firms in two Danish counties (Ribe and Vejle)

When the larger production firms are no longer bound to the large cities one of the reasons is probably that the undergrowth of small specialised firms, which earlier existed in the metropolitan regions only, today exists also in many of the provincial regions of Europe.

A closer look at the network of firms shows that the firms play very different roles in the production system. Grøn (1984) identified seven such different roles (shown in Figure 5.1):

(A) small independent firms producing a simple product in small series or to order
(B) simple subcontractors producing simple products to order and often in relatively large series — often used by other firms as buffer
(C) subcontractors producing mass-produced components
(D) producers of standardised final products in mass production or large series
(E) firms producing a technically complex product to order
(F) technically advanced subcontractors
(G) firms producing large complex capital goods.

Of these D and G will be the large dominating firms producing for the consumer and the investment markets respectively. C and F are often large, advanced subcontractors. Together with D and G they make up the core of the industry, which will often be integrated by ownership. E will typically be smaller niche industries, usually producing investment goods in small series. B are simple, often small, independent subcontractors and A are small, simple independent firms producing a product of their own for the final consumer or for investment markets.

The different types of firm have very different labour requirements. C and D are mass-producing, capital-intensive firms operating on the vertical labour market, using partly highly educated functionaries and partly specially trained unskilled labour. E, F and G operate especially on the horizontal labour market, using skilled labour to increase flexibility. Finally, A and B use more unskilled labour and to some extent operate on the unstructured labour markets.

The different types of firm also require very different inputs of raw materials and intermediate goods, and therefore may have different optimal locations.

Unfortunately Grøn's study did not focus specifically on the transport and communication pattern of the firms, but his results are precise enough to indicate the existence of two different contact networks, a network of long-distance flows between the larger, often mass-producing firms and local networks of relatively short distance flows between the smaller firms and between the smaller and the larger firms.

The flows between the larger firms often consist of large flows of standardised products or bulk ware with very little content of information, while the local flows to a large extent consist of flows of small quantities of goods, where transportation of goods, persons and information are integrated in a service delivery.

2. Transport, communication and production networks

The division of the production system into an integrated/internationalised network of larger firms and local/regional undergrowth of smaller firms is primarily the result of the larger firms' attempt to utilise specialisation and scale economies in production, reduce labour costs and spread the risk caused by fluctuations in demand. But the specific shape of the system and its locational pattern is probably to a large degree determined by the development of transport and communications systems during the 1970s.

What has specifically characterised the development of transport and communications systems during the last 10–15 years is service improvements and cost reductions over long distances. Inter-city flight and railway systems are much more developed than they were in the 1960s, and also telephone and telex systems are used much more widely for long-distance calls.

In the goods transport sector containerisation and the establishment of specialised systems for bulk transportation have reduced transport costs, especially of standardised goods and bulk ware over long distances. This has especially been the case in the energy sector where pipelines, specialised rail connections and revived barge traffic has taken over large parts of fuel transport.

Over short distances, on the other hand, improvements have been few, and in the central cities transport may even have deteriorated. Only in the field of internal transportation, communications and storage planning in the large firms have improvements taken place.

However, improvements in the goods transport sector especially have benefited the large regular commodity flows, which can utilise the container system or pay for specialised transport systems. For those, transport costs have been drastically reduced. At the same time, a larger part of the costs has been moved from distance-dependent costs to terminal costs, so that transport costs no longer depend very much on distance. Also reloadings, which used to be prohibitively expensive, play a minor role when a container chain is first established. This has made it possible to integrate the different transport systems and use different means of transport on different parts of a transport route depending on which is cheapest.

Thus it is especially the larger firms which have been able to benefit from improvements in the goods transport sector during the last 10–15 years. Advantages have especially been obtained on large regular flows of standardised commodity flows, and costs have been reduced mostly over long distances.

However, as we saw above the large capital-intensive firms typically depend on a very large number of different commodities and services, which they will buy in small quantities and often at irregular intervals. The delivery of these commodities and services at the right moment will often be critical for the productivity of the firm. For these deliveries the transport system has hardly been improved. Therefore, short distance is still an advantage here. One of the difficulties of rationalising these transports is that the service content is high, so that commodities, persons and information often have to be transported together.

The one-sided development of only the long distance transport networks thus naturally supports the development of the hierarchial industrial structure presented above, and leads to a polarisation of the transport and communication systems partly around the heavy, long-distance specialised transport networks and partly around the small, short-distance distributive transports.

An indication of this polarisation can be seen by looking at the development in the number of vans and trucks with different carrying capacity (shown in Table 5.1). The table shows that only the largest trucks and the smaller vans between one and two tons have increased their share of the truck fleet.

Table 5.1 The van and truck fleet in Denmark, distributed according to carrying capacity

	< 1000 kg	1000-2000 kg	2000-4000 kg	4000-8000 kg	> 8000 kg	total
1960	115530(69,7%)	14347(8,7%)	12002(7,2%)	18340(14,1%)	453(0,3%)	165672(100%)
1965	160865(69,3%)	30320(13,1%)	8701(3,7%)	30594(13,2%)	1562(0,7%)	232042(100%)
1970	144451(59,0%)	55643(22,8%)	7616(3,1%)	32060(13,1%)	4875(2,0%)	244645(100%)
1975	106803(47,8%)	72433(32,5%)	8974(4,0%)	27586(12,4%)	7664(3,4%)	223460(100%)
1980	125565(50,7%)	80407(32,5%)	10600(4,3%)	19512(7,9%)	11723(4,7%)	247807(100%)
1983	111867(48,4%)	81324(35,2%)	9471(4,1%)	16519(7,2%)	12021(5,2%)	231202(100%)

Source: Statistiske Meddelelser og Statistiske Efterretninger. Danmarks Statistik.

At the same time as improvements in the transportation system during the last 10–15 years have paved the way for important changes in the industrial structure, changes in the industrial structure will have consequences for the future demand for transport.

3. Future trends in demand for transport

If the hypotheses stated above hold true, the production system is developing into a hierarchical system of firms and the transport and communications systems into a polarised system, centred:

- partly on a system of highly specialised long-distance transport and communication networks, especially fit for transport of highly standardised goods and bulk ware, and where freight, persons and information are transported in different networks;
- partly on local short-distance transport and communications systems designed to transport smaller and less standardised consignments of goods and where freight, persons and information often have to be transported together.

Changes in this polarised system take place either through rationalisation of the transport or communications systems or through structural changes in the production system, which lead to a changed demand for transport and communications.

The specialisation and spatial division of production by themselves lead to increased demand for transport. On the other hand, there are technical changes taking place in the production system which tend to reduce the demand for transport, either by standardising the freight so that cheaper modes of transport can be used, or by substituting person transport with freight or information flows or by substituting freight flows with information flows.

In the literature on the influence of telecommunications on the demand for transport most interest has been focused on the possibilities of reducing commuting through the use of home computers and terminals (Jeppesen 1984). Though this is no doubt a possibility, or may be rather a risk, I think it may be overestimated. At the turn of the twentieth century, when the small electro-motor was introduced, similar prophecies were made about increases in the number of home workers in, for instance, the textile industry (Lindberg 1906). The prophecy was never realised to any large extent and it might be interesting to compare that situation with the present one.

Here, where the focus is more on goods transport, we shall rather be interested in the possibilities for substituting person transport with goods transport or goods transport with data communication. Such substitutions would usually be made possible by a standardisation in the production process. In his study of structural changes in the manufacturing industry, Grøn (1983; 1984) found a number of examples of standardisation processes which may lead to such a substitution.

For instance, some firms which used to produce and store their products in a limited number of variants now instead have decomposed their product into standardised components, which are easier to store and transport and which can be rapidly combined into a large number of variants of the final product. Assembly of the components is now done only to customer order and according to customer specifications.

With such a production system the components may be produced on a large scale in a few factories and sent to and stored at decentralised assembly plants close to the potential customers. In this way long-distance transport of both the unstandardised final product and of the fitter are substituted by short-distance transport and only the standardised components, which are usually cheaper to transport, will have to be transported over long distances.

Such a standardisation of components may also make repair and maintenance easier. In ideal cases the repairer may not need to show up at all, because the customer can exchange the defective component and send it to the factory for repair or exchange. In this case the importance of transport time might also be reduced. Thus the combined transport of the repairer and spare parts have been substituted by the transport for standardised goods.

With the introduction of computer assisted (CAD/CAM) and automated production systems the process of standardisation may be carried even further, to a point where you only store the product specifications and the raw materials and produce the total product to order in production plants close to the customer, in extreme cases even on the customer's own machinery. Also some maintenance and repair may be done by data transmission. Here both person and goods transport are substituted by data transmission.

As these examples show, the changes in production structure will lead to a certain substitution between persons and goods transport and between goods transport and data transmission. However, the most important effect will probably be an increased standardisation of the transported goods, which will make long-distance transport economic in cases where it is not today. This will make further spatial division of production possible and thus lead to increased demand for transport.

4. New technology and the transportation sector

Rationalisation of goods transport can take place by

- rationalisation of the individual modes of transport;
- integration of the different modes;

- integration between the transport system and other service functions attached to the origin and/or destination of the freight.

Rationalisation of a transport mode is done by reducing the terminal cost, increasing the degree of utilisation of transport material and personnel, and increasing speed and regularity. The most important means to achieve this has in recent times been the introduction of different forms of containers. This has reduced the time for loading and unloading and thus reduced the terminal costs. At the same time it has given the transport user freedom to load and unload at any time which is convenient. It also has made it possible for the transport company to pick up and deliver freight outside normal opening hours and thus extend the hours of utilisation of trucks. This increased flexibility also increases the probability of obtaining return freight.

Finally, the container system makes it much cheaper to change transport mode and thus opens up the possibility of using different modes on a single trip, depending on which is cheapest. This is likely to lead to an increasing integration of the transport modes, which may give back to the railways and to short- and intermediate-distance shipping some of the market share that they have lost over the last decades.

Such an integration of transport modes will be further supported by the introduction of so-called paperless transportation, where all information on a consignment for customs offices and shippers is processed and transmitted by electronic media. Ideally, such a system of paperless transportation might be extended to consist of an unbroken chain of information linking the production and storage system of the producer to the storage and production system of the buyer. This would open up new possibilities for rationalisation especially of local short-distance transports, which today are often relatively inefficient, by extending the principles of internal transport and storage systems, as they are used within firms, to the whole urban area.

It also opens up the possibilities that a number of service functions at the origin or destination of the freight trip may be integrated into the transport system. Storage facilities are already integrated in the activities of many forwarding agents. But there seems to be an increasing tendency for transport companies also to try to establish different purchasing or marketing functions at the terminals of their freight routes. The advantage of such integration is that the shippers' knowledge of terminal regions may be used for as many different administrative processes as possible. Purchasing functions are probably easier to integrate in the transport system than marketing functions, especially if shippers organise transport for competing firms.

These tendencies in the transport sector may favour large transport companies for whom it is easier to realise the advantages of using data processing and transmission in transport planning. However, it may also favour the development of large independent forwarding and shipping agents, who buy transport services from road hauliers and shipping companies, but do not have transport means of their own. Such a structure of the transport sector would be in line with the functional division which is taking place in other parts of the production system, and such independent forwarding agents will be better able to integrate the different transport modes than firms which are both transporters and forwarding agents.

Most of the innovations in the transport sector discussed have benefited long-distance transportation of large standardised quantities. However, many transport costs are still due to short-distance transport of small unstandardised quantities, which today are much less efficient than long-distance transport.

One strategy to reduce these costs is, as we saw above, to standardise the services and commodities produced so that they can be transported by a cheaper mode of transport. Another strategy would be to increase the efficiency of the local transport networks, which is not usually very high. One possibility for doing this would be to extend the principles known from internal transport and storage systems to a whole sector or region. In South Jutland the agricultural sector has attempted to set up such a common distribution system, which should serve all the supermarkets in the region. However, because of internal competition in the sector this attempt has so far not been very successful.

5. Conclusion

Most transport planners have been especially concerned about person transport. In the period of rapidly increasing car density this was reasonable because the number of cars was decisive for the capacity problem.

Recently, the focus has been more on freight, because road maintenance is in focus and it is trucks which are decisive for maintenance costs. At the same time the transport of goods is growing rapidly as production becomes more and more specialised and internationalised. Therefore, there is good reason to be more interested in the goods transport sector.

Traditionally goods transport studies have been based either on simple extrapolations or on input–output models. Such studies tend to assume that technology is fixed. Therefore, they cannot help us when we want to look at the effect of new technology on the transport sector.

This becomes especially problematic because of the apparently increasing mutual interdependence of the development of the transport sector and of the production sectors. I have in this paper tried to show that the structural changes taking place in the production sectors are at least as important for development in the transport sector as new technology in the sector itself.

During the last 10–15 years the technological changes in the transport and communications sector have benefited the long-distance transportation of large quantities of standardised products. The response to that in the production sectors has been, firstly, both a functional and a spatial division of production, which makes it possible to locate the different parts of the production where the production factors are best or cheapest, and has led to an increasing demand for long-distance transport and communication. Secondly, there has been a standardisation of both intermediate and final products, which makes it possible to utilise more standardised and cheaper modes of transport and communication.

The next logical step would be to make innovations in local short-distance networks, but this is still ahead of us.

References

Christensen, Poul Rind (1981). *Den nordjyske industri. En undersøgelse af arbejdsdeling, arbejdsmarkedsforhold og filialproblemer.* Aalborg: Institut for Produktion, Aalborg Universitetscenter.

Grøn, Jens (1983). 'New Technology, Production Linkages and the Labour Market'. Paper presented at an OECD workshop on Research, Technology and Regional Policy, 24–27 October.

Grøn, Jens (1984). 'Produktionskæder og det regionale arbejdsmarked' in Sven Illeris and Poul Ove Pedersen, eds, *Industrien — Koncentration eller spredning.* Copenhagen: AKF and SUC.

Jeppesen, Sven Erik (1984). 'Telecommunication — Transport Interaction — and Spatial Structure'. Paper presented to the ITTI workshop, Telematic, Stuttgart, June.

Lindberg, Jak. Kr. (1906). 'Elektroteknikken og det lille haandværk', *Det nye Aarhundrede*, **4** (1), 169–71.

O'Farrell, P.N. and B. O'Loughlin (1980). An Analysis of New Industrial Linkages in Ireland. Dublin: The Industrial Development Authority. Publication series, paper 6.

Pedersen, Poul Ove (1983). *Vandringerne og den regionale udvikling — i et langsigtet perspektiv.* Esbjerg: Sydjysk Universitetsforlag.

Perrons, D.C. (1981). 'The Role of Ireland in the New International Division of Labour: A Proposed Framework for Regional Analysis', *Regional Studies*, **15** (2), 81–100.

Thorngren, Bertil (1970). 'How Do Contact Systems Affect Regional Development?', *Environment and Planning*, **2**, 409–27.

Törnquist, Gunnar (1970). *Contact Systems and Regional Development.* Lund Studies of Geography, Series B, no. 35, university of Lund.

6 Mobility as a Societal Value: Problems and Paradoxes

P. Nijkamp

ΠANTA REI
(Heraclitos)

1. Introduction

Spatial mobility in a modern society has two faces: increased access to many facilities brought about by advanced transportation technology (reflected *inter alia* in Concorde, the Hovercraft, the TGV and the Shinkansen) and increased decay in quality of life due to congestion, environmental pollution and noise pollution. These contrasting (and sometimes paradoxical) developments have placed the mobility of man and society at the centre of scientific and political interest (see also the contributions of Hägerstrand (Chapter 2), Jones (Chapter 3) and Kutter (Chapter 4) in the present volume).

The control of this mobility process is also fraught with difficulties: it is as if mobility acts like an avalanche which cannot be stopped. '*Homo mobilis*' is apparently a spatial actor whose spatial behaviour is hard to influence. Market solutions and/or institutional solutions (for example, regulations) may be helpful to bring about a marginal change in the mobility pattern, but mobility itself appears to have a very firm position in the hierarchy of needs of individuals, households or groups.

The integral rise in spatial mobility in the past decades is marked by various characteristics:

- Mobility is an integrated process in which multiple actors with multiple motives (consumers, entrepreneurs and government agencies) play a joint role: residential mobility, job mobility, recreation, commuting, shopping, entrepreneurial relocation and geographical decentralisation reflect the same tendency.

- Mobility is — according to Say's Law — usually a derivative of the supply of physical communication infrastructure (such as road and railway infrastructure): the 'hardware' determines the rise in 'software'.
- The mobility pattern reflects structural changes in modern societies: increased interaction patterns, increased leisure time, simultaneous occurrence of geographical concentration and deconcentration, increased participation by women in the labour force and differential dynamics (fast dynamics versus slow dynamics, or different adjustment speeds) between the components of an interwoven spatial system (cf. Johansson and Nijkamp 1984).

Mobility has become the medium through which a modern society generates and enjoys its welfare, so that it is no surprise that mobility trends are hard to influence.

Clearly, mobility processes in the past decades have also had a significant impact on the subject matter of such disciplines as geography and regional science. In the period before the 1960s much attention was focused on location analysis, while in more recent decades the analysis of spatial interactions and processes has come to the fore (see Masser and Brown 1977). Especially in the 1970s the 'geography of movement' opened up a rich field of scientific research (see Lowe and Moryades 1975). So far, two new analytical 'movements' can be observed in the 1980s, namely the analysis of individual spatial choice processes (see Nijkamp, Leitner and Wrigley 1985) and the analysis of structural spatial changes (see Nijkamp, Rima and van Wissen 1985). It is clear that both trends have a profound effect on research directions in the field of geographical mobility (including the judgement of the societal relevance, or social costs and benefits, of the 'mobility movement').

The first formal contributions to spatio-temporal aspects of choice behaviour can be found in traditional space–time geography (see, for instance, Hägerstrand 1970). In a modelling framework, location–allocation models based on programming theory have played an important role in aggregate spatial choice and interaction analysis. In the 1970s, categorical spatial choice models focusing on distinct alternative choices came to the fore. Categorical spatial choice models aim at describing, explaining and forecasting disaggregate choice behaviour in a spatial context (for instance, in housing-market, transportation and labour-market analysis). At a later stage, panel studies and longitudinal data analysis have drawn a great deal of attention in spatial choice research, while simultaneously the spatial activity-based approach came into existence. Very recently, event-history analysis has demonstrated its potential in discrete spatial choice analysis (for a review, see also Fischer and Nijkamp 1985 and Jansen *et al.* 1985). It is increasingly realised, however, that spatial mobility is a multi-dimensional phenomenon, which has to be studied in the context of broader socio-economic and technological developments (see Pickup and Town 1983).

2. A typology of locational mobility

In the past century, human settlement patterns have exhibited significant changes. Approximately a century ago only 1 per cent of the total world population was living in cities of more than a million inhabitants, while nowadays more than 10 per cent is living in such metropolises (cf. Button, 1976). To take another example: São Paolo had in the year 1900 some 250,000 inhabitants, while according to United Nations forecasts this city will have more than 25 million inhabitants by the year 2000: an increase by a factor of 100 in 100 years!

This tendency towards a higher spatial concentration has led to many diseconomies: congestion, criminality, segregation, pollution and decline in residential quality. These agglomeration disadvantages have acted as a new stimulus for spatial mobility, as many people have made an attempt to avoid these diseconomies by moving to suburban and rural areas, thus causing again environmental deterioration and energy consumption. Thus we see here again one of the most striking paradoxical aspects of mobility: mobility causes negative externalities, which evoke new mobility in order to avoid such external effects; this new mobility causes further social costs, and so on. Altogether the spatial mobility pattern exhibits a cyclical pattern, both in space and in time.

Such a cyclical pattern has been identified in many European countries (see van den Berg *et al.* 1982). The spatial development phases of many cities in Europe can be characterised by the following sequence of spatial urban processes: urbanisation, suburbanisation, disurbanisation and reurbanisation. It should be added, however, that this is only a superficial representation of complex spatial developments. First of all, many of these processes have been highly selective: high- and medium-income people act as trend-setters for the spatial dynamics in modern societies; less wealthy people and specific groups (immigrant workers, ethnic minorities, one- and two-person households) tend to stay within the city (or move into the city). Consequently, the spatial distribution of people reflects at the same time a socio-economic segregation. Such drastic spatial movements of people are not only caused by quality-of-life factors, but also by major changes in our industrial societies, which reflect simultaneously concentration and deconcentration tendencies and hence lead to complex settlement patterns.

In the second place, it should be noted that locational mobility may exhibit complex spatial movements. Suppose we make a distinction between the core of a city, a surburban ring, an intermediate area and a rural area (see Figure 6.1). Then a wide variety of spatial and urban development processes can be distinguished. Table 6.1 makes an attempt at representing these processes by examining the combinatorial possibilities of the net spatial flows to all four areas concerned. For instance, case 1 is a situation where the core of a city is growing to the detriment of its ring, its surrounding intermediate area and the rural areas, so that this is the purest form of urbanisation. Analogously, case 2 is a pure form of a combined urbanisation–suburbanisation, while case 13 is a pure form of suburbanisation. All kinds of pure, intermediate and mixed configurations can be distinguished by means of Table 6.1.

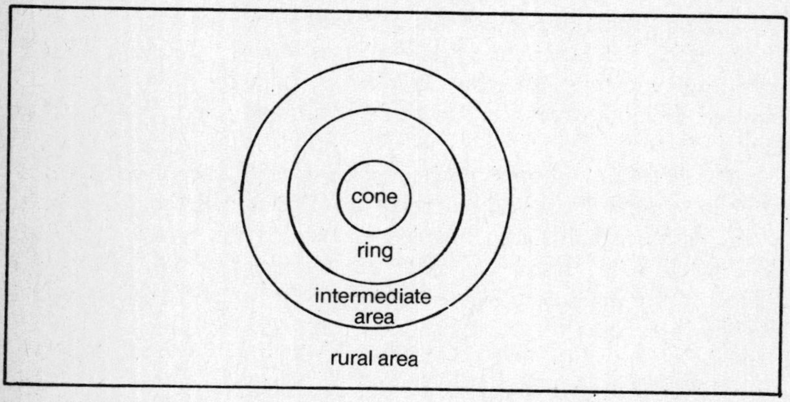

Figure 6.1 Configuration of a spatial system

Several cities in Western countries (for example, Berlin, Amsterdam) exhibit a decline in the population share of the whole agglomeration, while intermediate areas are growing; this situation corresponds to case 6 or case 14. On the other hand, a policy of urban renewal and of compact city design which aims at revitalising the whole urban agglomeration can be represented by means of case 2 or case 11.

It should be noted that a similar table can be designed for entrepreneurial mobility. Cities have lost many industrial activities owing

Table 6.1 Combinations of locational movements in a spatial system

	1	2	3	4	5	6	7	8	9	10	11	12	13	14
core	+	+	+	+	–	–	–	–	+	+	+	–	–	–
ring	–	+	+	–	–	–	+	+	–	–	+	+	+	–
intermediate area	–	–	+	+	–	+	+	–	–	+	–	+	–	+
rural area	–	–	–	–	+	+	+	+	+	+	+	–	–	–

Legend: + net increase of population share
– net decrease of population share.

to entrepreneurial movements to suburban (or sometimes intermediate) industrial areas. On the other hand, nowadays there is also an increased tendency for small-scale business activities to flourish again in the cities. For instance, Naisbitt (1984) claims that about 70 per cent of current economic activity is related to the information sector, which does not necessarily require a location in urban centres. In addition to this 'high tech', however, there is also a trend towards 'high touch' (small-scale activities based on face-to-face contacts), which needs the city as a 'breeding place' (the so-called 'incubator hypothesis'). Altogether, the present mobility patterns of entrepreneurs are highly complex and exhibit mutually contrasting developments.

It is clear that a superimposed pattern of household and entrepreneurial mobility processes based on Tables 6.1 and 6.2 (below, p. 79) would provide an adequate picture of the actual locational movements in a dynamic spatial system. A research agenda for analysing in a more detailed way these mobility processes would have to include at least the following two important items:

- a more adequate analysis of the individual behavioural backgrounds and driving forces of mobility; and
- a more appropriate impact analysis of public policy instruments upon mobility patterns.

The first issue is extensively discussed in Part C of the present volume, while the second issue is further taken up in the following section of this chapter.

3. Impact analysis of public policies

It has already been mentioned that people tend to have a love–hate relationship with mobility. Mobility opens the way to a wide variety of personal and professional contacts, to participation in various amenities and to an increase in the stock of knowledge. Mobility leads to an increase in the efficiency of production factors and to a rise in the utility of goods. Beside these positive aspects, a wide variety of negative externalities have to be mentioned: congestion, decrease in safety, environmental degradation, exhaustion of energy, noise nuisance, land use, destruction of valuable monuments, etc. A city like Athens has become a glaring example of the negative effects of spatial mobility.

It is conceivable that several policy measures have been proposed and implemented in order to keep mobility processes under control. In several cases, fairly unrealistic policy goals have been advocated, such as a reduction in mobility. Even apart from the fact that mobility is closely connected with the economic performance of a country and is thus hardly controllable, it has to be mentioned that mobility does not exist in a single mode. Mobility is made up of a wide spectrum of possibilities, such as professional mobility, entrepreneurial mobility, residential mobility, recreational mobility, social mobility, shopping mobility, etc., each of these options having its own specific driving forces. Crude measures which do not discriminate between these various mobility modes may do more harm than good. Moreover, spatial mobility may have a multi-purpose character and also a selective socio-economic distributional character. These considerations lead to the conclusion that mobility policy is necessarily multidimensional in nature and needs fine tuning.

An impact analysis of policy measures on spatial mobility is hampered by many limitations:

- the aims of a mobility policy may be in conflict with other aims of a socio-economic policy;
- various elements of a mobility policy (infrastructure policy, compact city design) may require a very long time, while mobility patterns themselves may exhibit rapid changes and adjustments to new circumstances;
- the constraints within which a mobility policy has to be implemented are often fuzzy or uncertain in nature (cf. the uncertainty regarding the stock of oil reserves);
- mobility policy is in general a meso- or macro-policy which is unable to discriminate between the individual motives of '*homo mobilis*'.

Consequently, assessment of the integral — rather than partial —

effects of a mobility policy is very problematic, especially because various counter-intuitive results may emerge. For instance, a reduction in private transport might lead to a reduction in daily mobility, but might consequently on the other hand also lead to a greater interest in residential quality, which might in turn cause higher priority to be given to a more spacious living environment. Such substitution processes are hard to trace, although it is necessary to make an attempt to assess all direct and indirect impacts of policy measures regarding mobility behaviour.

In this regard, an integrated systems approach based on a qualitative impact assessment may be extremely meaningful. This qualitative impact analysis is based on a 'qualitative model' of a complex system (made up of edges, nodes and dynamics) represented by means of an arrow scheme (cf. Nijkamp and van Pelt 1984). The arrow is constructed so that all linkages that exist between variables are represented (see Figure 6.2).

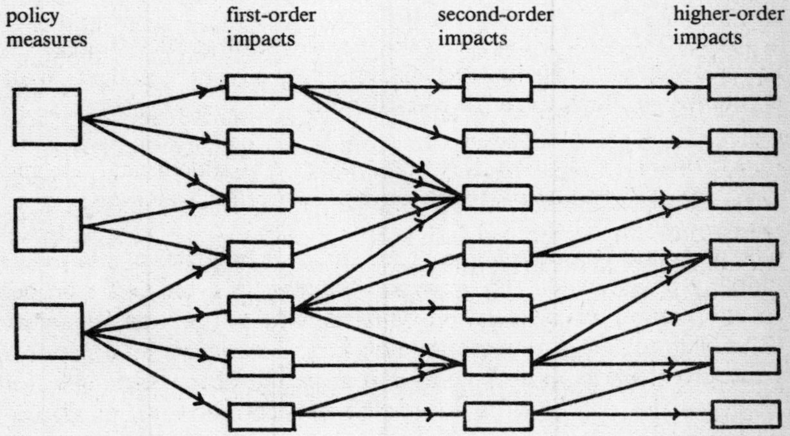

Figure 6.2 A qualitative systems representation for impact analysis

The logic of this approach is very simple: given the intuitive qualitative model, the direct impacts of policy measures upon certain variables have to be assessed as accurately as possible. If no formal model exists, *ad hoc* procedures and heuristics have to be used. Then the second-order impacts related to the first-order impacts can be assessed along similar lines; if no quantitative information is available, qualitative information (rankings, binary codings) can be used as well. The procedures will be continued through all stages of the qualitative model until the reliability of the sequence of impacts becomes almost zero. Several applications have demonstrated the feasibility of this approach (see also Nijkamp 1982). The results can be included in a qualitative impact table (see Table 6.2), which represents all direct and indirect effects of policy measures.

Table 6.2 An impact table of policy measures

Policy measures	*First-order effects*	*Second-order effects*	*Higher-order effects*
Price policy Supply policy Regulations etc.			

It has to be added that the evaluation of various policy strategies is the next step of the analysis. In this respect, two types of evaluation for alternative strategies can be carried out:

a monetary evaluation based on a social cost-benefit analysis; and
an integral evaluation based on multiple criteria analysis.

A monetary evaluation of the pros and cons of effects of alternative mobility policies is an almost impossible task, as it requires a proper transformation of all relevant impacts into a common monetary denominator. So far, integrated monetary assessments on a national basis have never been made; only partial attempts have been made, for instance, the net benefits of spatial concentration *versus* deconcentration, or the net benefits of private transport versus public transport.

A multiple criteria evaluation of alternative policy strategies is also fraught with many difficulties owing to lack of insight into political priorities, though it has to be added that on a partial basis (for instance, a regional or urban scale) several attempts have been made to evaluate the effects of mobility policies.

4. Selective mobility

It has already been indicated that mobility is always a selective process: it discriminates according to age, income, race and many other attributes. In migration analyses these attributes are often included as explanatory variables. In this respect, locational mobility appears to be a mirror of the age, socio-economic and ethnic composition of society (see Burright 1984).

In recent years, the issue of selective transportation mobility has come to the fore (see, for instance, Maggied 1982). In an earlier article, Koutsopoulos and Schmidt (1976) tried to make a systematic listing of all constraints that hamper individual mobility. They made a distinction between trip-making constraints (physical constraints, psychological and informational constraints and socio-economic constraints) and environmental constraints (locational constraints, administrative constraints and demand-response constraints). The specific weight exerted by each constraint will then determine the transportation mobility pattern of people (both car-owners and carless people).

Alternative studies in the area of selective transportation mobility have been carried out by Paaswell and Recker (1978) and Webber (1973). The common conclusion in many empirical case studies is that mobility (for instance, total travel time of daily activities or number of migration movements per year per individual) is an increasing function of income (see Figure 6.3), though this curve has evidently a saturation level. The relationship between location, sex and travel mode choice for journey-to-work decisions exhibits also a high degree of selectivity, as is also reflected by Figure 6.4.

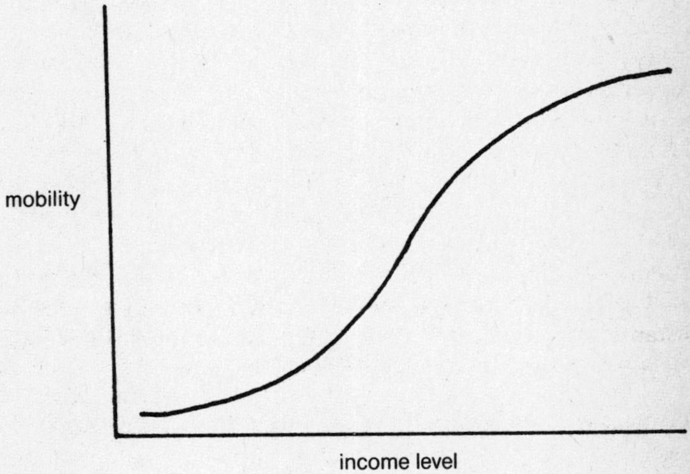

Figure 6.3 Mobility as a function of income

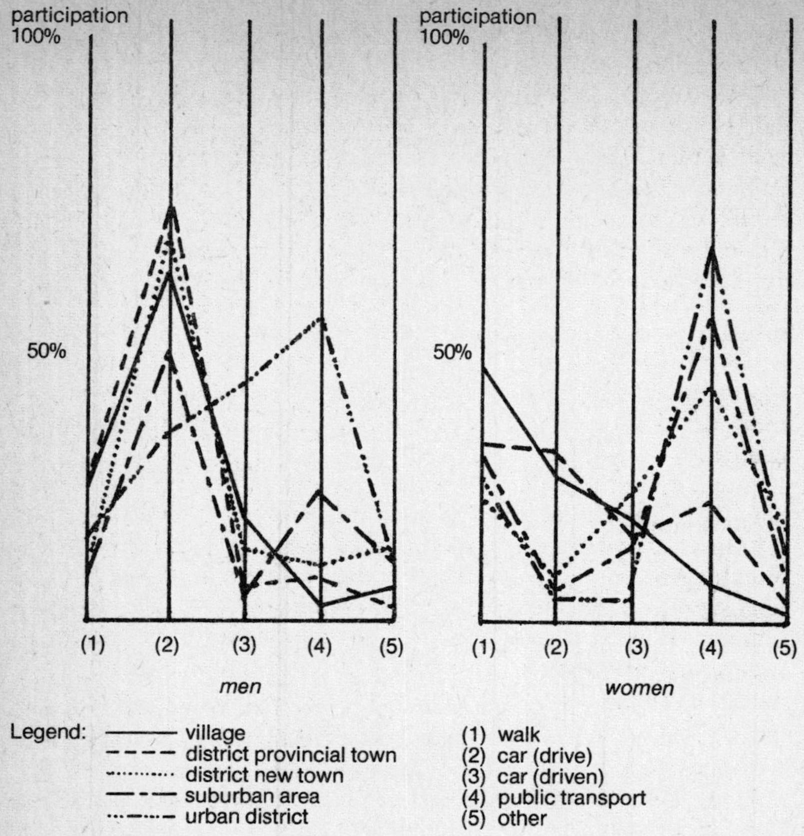

Figure 6.4 Travel-to-work, by sex and by area (adjusted from Hillman *et al.*, quoted in De Boer, 1980)

In a recent paper, Kutter (1985) questions the trends in physical planning to design and selective spatial layout that supports the current status quo: settlement and town planning fulfils the needs of an 'automotive' society, based on a segregation of functions (working, shopping, living, recreation, and so on) and the transportation sector has gained an important societal power. He states that in the recession period of our post-industrial society a critical re-evaluation of current planning modes is necessary, with particular emphasis on the assessment criteria which today favour the car in an extreme fashion.

Instead of 'planning for transport' he makes a plea for 'planning to enable societal activities'.

The obvious conclusion can be drawn from this section that, if (1) mobility is so closely connected with income, age and location and (2) structural changes in our society continue to affect the socio-economic, demographic and locational pattern, profound changes in mobility patterns are to be expected (see also Section 6), while it will also become increasingly difficult to pursue a mobility policy that will have a structural balancing effect on selective mobility.

5. Mobility and recession

Since the oil crisis in 1973, various intriguing questions confront us. How much mobility do we need in order to maintain a growing economy? And how much is mobility affected by the economic recession?

Many countries exhibited a fairly sharp rise in oil prices after the first and second energy crises in the 1970s. Altogether, however, the net average increase of oil prices over the last decade has been fairly modest: the general costs of car driving have on average in most countries kept pace with the general rise in consumer prices. Yet, psychologically, the oil crises have had a profound impact on technology and mobility, which is also reflected in increased attempts at constructing more energy-efficient equipment, designing more fuel-saving cars and building more energy-efficient, compact cities.

At the same time, because of the economic recession, locational mobility in many countries has drastically decreased (see Jansen *et al.* 1985). Two factors especially favoured this reduction in mobility: the poor perspectives on the labour market, so that people tend to become less willing to take risks regarding the choice of a new job and a new residence, and the collapse of the housing market, so that house-owners can only sell their property at a considerable loss. Though reliable figures for most countries are still lacking, there is some empirical evidence that the locational mobility trend of the 1960s and the 1970s has not continued into the 1980s.

More empirical research has already been done in the area of transport mobility. It appears that in many countries ownership and use of cars is stagnating. Whether or not these new circumstances herald a change in the direction of transport planning, however, is difficult to say, as the answer to this question requires a far-reaching analysis of the features of the car market, of transport mobility and of household expenditure patterns (see also Allanson 1982, Bates *et al.* 1981, Button *et al.* 1982 and Ferguson and Mogridge 1985).

Bly (1985) has reviewed the available evidence showing how travel has been affected by the fuel price rises and recurrent economic difficulties that have followed from the first oil crisis in 1973–4. Clear empirical results are hard to achieve, as the most severe effects of the recession have been felt only fairly recently. It turns out that, thus far, rising fuel prices have caused a measurable fall in road traffic, but the short-term elasticity is small and in the longer term the effect may be even smaller, as people shift to more fuel-efficient vehicles and continue to cover much the same distance by private car while still spending much the same proportion of their budget as they did previously. Car-ownership has continued to increase in most countries, although at a much slower rate than before. Some countries, however, show a reversal of this trend. For instance, Denmark has exhibited a reduction of 4 per cent in the number of cars registered since 1979, while there is also a slight decline in household car availability in the Netherlands since 1980.

Road traffic in Denmark has fallen even more sharply than car-ownership, by about 10 per cent between 1978 and 1981, while several other countries have also recently shown a reduction in traffic. In some countries there has been a modest shift from cars to public transport. Bly concludes that it seems likely that, unless the future holds a long-lived and sizeable reduction of real disposable incomes, the general tendency will continue towards increased dependency on private cars and dispersing land-use patronage which is difficult to serve by public transport.

The foregoing notions clarify once more that the relationships between spatial mobility, car-ownership and car use, expenditure patterns and economic recession are fairly complex. This is also reflected by a small sample of 79 respondents in the Netherlands. These respondents were classified into car-owners and non-car-owners and were asked which adjustments in expenditure patterns had become necessary in order to cope with the present recession. The results of this survey are included in Table 6.3.

One more problem has to be mentioned. If the economic recession leads to a reduction in car use, a shift towards public transport is a plausible consequence. However, in many countries (if not all) public transport is confronted with deficits. The tendency to shift to public transport would lead to more passenger-kilometres by means of public transport and hence to higher deficits. As a consequence, public transport might have to reduce its service level or to increase its fares in order to stay within its tight budget. This would imply that transportation mobility based on private transport would lead to higher societal benefits.

Table 6.3 Results of a survey on effects of economic recession on expenditure patterns

	Car-owners	Non car-owners		Total
		Never owned car	Previously owned car	
I. Persons not economising at all	9	3	2	14
II. Persons economising, but not on transport	18	6	1	25
III. Persons economising on transport and other things	17	3	7	27
IV. Persons economising only on transport	4	0	1	5
V. Persons who claim not to be economising on transport, but who are doing so	3	2	3	8
Total	51	14	14	79

Source: Baanders *et al.* (1985)

Holtgrefe (1985) has shown that such a pessimistic picture is not realistic. After an analysis of the cost structure of different transport modes, he concludes that the flexibility in changing supply of public transport facilities is high enough to restrict the rise in costs. Thus a careful planning of public transport may avoid the negative effects of economic stagnation.

6. Analyses of structural change

Our mobile societies are facing new developments that may have a profound effect on spatial mobility patterns. Examples of such driving forces are: the transition towards the information society (including advanced telecommunications), increased participation rates of women on the labour market, deindustrialisation tendencies in various countries, compact city design, and so on.

At present the spatial configuration of many countries is in a period of rapid transition. Especially in the developed countries, a shift from a phase of growth to a phase which can be characterised by stagnation and decay of economic functions of the city can be observed. These transitions affect urban systems in a structural way. Not only are some key factors within the system exhibiting drastic changes, but also the interaction pattern between components of complex dynamics. Such structural changes may cause these systems to move to a new equilibrium state or a sequence of bifurcations.

Spatial interaction patterns in a complex system are not an isolated phenomenon *per se*. Their development can only be understood as the result of changes in key components governing that system (such as housing, employment, retailing). In order to explain, predict and evaluate these developments, a dynamic systems approach focusing attention on dynamic trajectories of a spatial system is necessary.

Various models or theories take for granted that urban fluctuations must inevitably occur in a dynamic urban system. Possible causes for such cyclical endogenous patterns in a spatial system are:

1. A functional substitution from residential to other land uses, which are, in themselves, less attractive for the city. This substitution can take place as a result of:

   (a) excessive demand for transportation facilities within the city;
   (b) the rise in land prices, owing to an over-attractiveness of the city (in this competition for available space, only a limited number of land uses can survive).

2. The selective nature of suburbanisation, owing to constraints (for example, political, economic) for certain population groups to move away from the city. In this view, suburbanisation is considered as the outcome of changing housing and environmental preferences of people and is to a large extent autonomous.

3. Ageing and obsolescence of physical stocks in the city. During a period of rapid growth, new construction activities outrun ageing processes. If the city becomes congested, and land becomes unavailable, the city ages and cannot adjust itself to new situations. A possible effect of this is a slow-down of growth, which may eventually turn into a decline.

Clearly, predicting the spatial mobility effects of structural changes in a dynamic system is a complex matter, especially in the long run, and deserves much more attention in our research efforts. The societal value of mobility — from a long-term point of view — can only be assessed if adequate insight is obtained into the endogenous and exogenous dynamics of complex spatial systems and into the differential dynamics of various systems components. This issue will be taken up further in the final section of this paper.

7. Prospects

In a challenging paper, Peter Hall (1985) discusses various paradoxes for the 1980s with regard to spatial mobility. From the 1960s onwards, urban transportation planners almost everywhere forsook the ideal of individual motorised mobility for all and substituted a mix of urban traffic restraint and the promotion of good public transport. This change in policy was fortified in the 1970s after the 'Limits to Growth' discussion, the first and second energy crises, and new ecological awareness. Public transport infrastructure, however, required also heavy investment and reinforced the traditional urban–suburban mobility patterns: outward deconcentration of population coupled with preservation of service employment in the urban core. In addition, city centres were made more attractive for shopping (pedestrian malls, and so on). Hall argues that there is virtually no evidence that such systems could actually generate activity; such systems serve at best a minority of all journeys made within the urban system.

Given the decreased importance of energy scarcity and given the deconcentrated spatial configuration generated *inter alia* by public transport, it is — according to Hall — foreseeable that in the long run the use of the car will increase and that the position of public transport will decrease, at least if economic growth resumes its course. On the other hand, the current recession challenges the subsidies for public transport because of the general pressure on public spending. Thus, while in the 1970s a policy of spatial deconcentration took place, public transport is left with the job of providing a fixed minimum level of service for a diminishing number of people; disproportionately, these people also happen in general to be the least affluent. These are the transportation-poor, who in many cases coincide with the money-poor. Altogether, public transport service is almost bound to be inferior.

Hall's view, however, underestimates some new developments which may have a major impact mobility pattern (see also Brotchie *et al.* 1985). In the first place, many countries have started a policy of urban revitalisation and renewal in order to stimulate the breeding-place function of the city for residential, entrepreneurial and recreational activities. Several cities demonstrate that this policy is going to be successful. The trend towards deconcentration or concentrated deconcentration is not inevitable: many cities are starting to show the first signs of rejuvenation. This (selective) shift in locational mobility patterns caused by more compact city designs will also exert a significant impact on transport mobility (especially care use).

Secondly, the micro-electronics revolution may have a profound impact (cf. Salomon and Salomon (1984) and the contribution of Pedersen (Chapter 5) in the present volume). American experiences especially demonstrate that medium-sized cities appear to provide eminent breeding grounds for innovation and new activities: the traditional centres of innovation (New York, Washington, Chicago) have lost power, while new (smaller) centres are flourishing (Seattle, Houston, Boston). Thus, the spatial pattern that is most likely to emerge is not so much a concentrated versus deconcentrated configuration, but a large cities versus medium-sized cities configuration. A further spatial deconcentration is likely to be hampered by the 'high touch' social contact need that is a consequence of 'high tech' developments.

Undoubtedly, spatial development processes and spatial mobility processes will exhibit wave-like cyclical or fluctuating patterns in the future. Upswings and downswings of cities in a spatial system are almost inevitable (see also Nijkamp and Schubert 1984). This can also be illustrated by using the 'depression trigger' hypothesis, which has recently become very popular in innovation research. Suppose a city as part of a system of cities has a fairly low socio-economic performance relative to other cities (low value added, high unemployment, high criminality rates, and so on). Then the city will try to enhance its

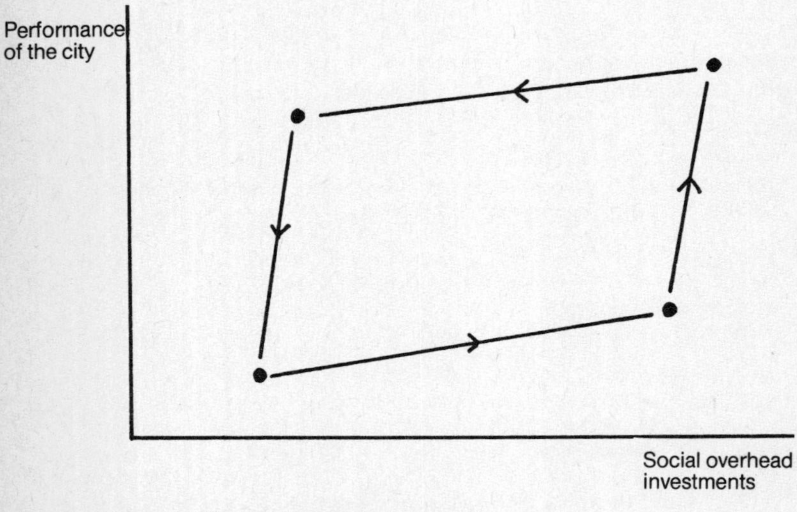

Figure 6.5 Cyclical urban developments

relative performance by increasing its investments in social overhead capital (communication infrastructure, educational facilities, R&D centres). Of course, it will take some time before a critical threshold level of urban improvement has been reached, but then a rapid rise in the urban performance may emerge. However, the city cannot afford to keep its social overhead investments at a very high level, so that in due course they will decline. Because of the inertia of a spatial system, it will take some time before the inevitable decrease in the performance of the city takes place, but beyond a critical threshold value a certain drop in performance may occur. This cyclical development is illustrated in Figure 6.5. The upswing and downswing of the city has of course direct influences upon the mobility pattern of this system. Consequently, the mobility pattern cannot be judged as a value in itself, but is contingent upon the complex mechanism of a dynamic spatial system.

References

Allanson, E.W. (1982). *Car Ownership Forecasting.* New York: Gordon and Breach.

Baanders, A., J. Kremer-Nass and C.J. Ruijgrok (1985). 'Income Decline and Travel Behaviour' in G.R.M. Jansen, P. Nijkamp and C. Ruijgrok, eds, *Transportation and Mobility in an Era of Transition.* Amsterdam: North Holland Publishing Co., pp. 37–54.

Bates, J.J., M. Roberts, S. Lowe and P. Richards (1981). *The Factors Affecting Household Car Ownership.* Aldershot: Gower.

Bly, P.H. (1985). 'Effect of the Recession on Travel Expenditure and Travel Pattern' in G.R.M. Jansen, P. Nijkamp and C. Ruijgrok, eds, *Transportation and Mobility in an Era of Transition.* Amsterdam: North Holland Publishing Co., pp. 15–36.

Brotchie, J., P. Newton, P. Hall and P. Nijkamp, eds (1985). *The Future of Urban Form.* Beckenham: Croom Helm.

Burright, B.K. (1984). *Cities and Travel.* New York: Garland.

Button, K.J. (1976). *Urban Economics.* London: Macmillan.

Button, K.J., A.D. Pearman and A.S. Fowkes (1982). *Car Ownership Modelling and Forecasting.* Aldershot: Gower.

De Boer, E. (1980). *Vervoersongelijkheid, Relevantie en Onderzoekbaarheid.* Delft: Institute for Urban Research, Delft University of Technology.

Ferguson, G.J.W.A. and H.J.H. Mogridge (1985). 'Is Car Ownership and Use Stagnating?' in G.R.M. Jansen, P. Nijkamp and C. Ruijgrok, eds, *Transportation and Mobility in an Era of Transition.* Amsterdam: North Holland Publishing Co., pp. 55–74.

Fischer, M.M. and P. Nijkamp (1985). 'Categorical Data and Choice Analysis in a Spatial Context' in M. Batty, B. Hutchinson and P. Nijkamp, eds, *Optimization and Discrete Choice in Urban System*, pp. 1–30.

Hägerstrand, T. (1970). 'What about People in Regional Science', *Papers of the Regional Science Association*, **24**, 7–21.

Hall, P. (1985). 'Urban Transportation: Paradoxes for the 1980s' in G.R.M. Jansen, P. Nijkamp and C. Ruijgrok, eds, *Transportation and Mobility in an Era of Transition.* Amsterdam: North Holland Publishing Co., pp. 367–76.

Holtgrefe, A.A.I. (1985). 'Stagnation and Public Transport in the Netherlands' in

G.R.M. Jansen, P. Nijkamp and C. Ruijgrok, eds, *Transportation and Mobility in an Era of Transition*. Amsterdam: North Holland Publishing Co., pp. 335–52.

Jansen, G.R.M., P. Nijkamp and C. Ruijgrok, eds (1985). *Transportation and Mobility in an Era of Transition*. Amsterdam: North Holland Publishing Co.

Johansson, B. and P. Nijkamp (1984). 'An Analysis of Episodes of Urban Event Histories'. Research paper. Laxenburg: International Institute for Applied Systems Analysis.

Koutsopoulos, K.C. and C.G. Schmidt (1976). 'Mobility Constraints on the Carless', *Traffic Quarterly* (January), 67–84.

Kutter, E. (1985). 'Is the Functionally Divided Automatic Society Still the "Ultima Ratio" in Planning?' in G.R.M. Jansen, P. Nijkamp and C. Ruijgrok, eds, *Transportation and Mobility in an Era of Transition*. Amsterdam: North Holland Publishing Co., pp. 377–87.

Lowe, J.C. and S. Moryades (1975). *The Geography of Movement*. Boston: Houghton Mifflin.

Maggied, S. (1982). *Transportation for the Poor*. Boston/The Hague: Martinus Nijhoff.

Masser, I. and P. Brown (1977). *Spatial Representation and Spatial Interaction*. The Hague: Martinus Nijhoff.

Naisbitt, J. (1984). *Megatrends*. New York: Warner.

Nijkamp, P. (1981). 'Urban Impact Analysis in a Spatial Context'. Research memorandum 1982–5. Amsterdam: Dept of Economics, Free University.

Nijkamp, P., H. Leitner and N. Wrigley, eds (1985). *Measuring the Unmeasurable: Analysis of Qualitative Spatial Data*. The Hague: Martinus Nijhoff.

Nijkamp, P., A. Rima and L. van Wissen (1985). 'Structural Change in Urban Dynamic Models' in G.R.M. Jansen, P. Nijkamp and C. Ruijgrok, eds, *Spatial Mobility in an Era of Transition*. Amsterdam: North Holland Publishing Co., pp. 121–40.

Nijkamp, P. and U. Schubert (1984). 'Structural Change in Urban Systems'. Collaborative paper CP–83–57. Laxenburg: International Institute for Applied Systems Analysis.

Nijkamp, P. and M. van Pelt (1984). 'Urban and Regional Impact Analysis in Development Planning' in L. Chatterjee and P. Nijkamp, eds, *Urban and Regional Policy Analysis in Developing Countries*. Aldershot: Gower, pp. 171–80.

Paaswell, R.E. and W.W. Recker (1978). *Problems of the Carless*. New York: Praeger.

Pickup, L. and S.W. Town (1983). 'The Role of Social Science Methodologies in Transport Planning' in S. Carpenter and P. Jones, eds, *Recent Advances in Travel Demand Analysis*. Aldershot: Gower, pp. 34–57.

Salomon, I. and M. Salomon (1984). 'Telecommuting: The Employee's Perspective', *Technological Forecasting and Social Change*, **25**, 15–28.

Van den Berg, L., R. Drewett, L.H. Klaassen, A. Rossi and C.H.T. Vijverberg (1982). *Urban Europe*. Oxford: Pergamon.

Van Lierop, W.F.J. and P. Nijkamp (1984). 'Perspective of Disaggregate Spatial Choice Models' in D.A. Pitchfield, ed., *Discrete Spatial Choice Analysis*. London: Pion, pp. 141–62.

PART B: PLANNING ISSUES

7 Policy Cycles and New Planning Issues

F. le Clercq

1. Introduction

This contribution deals with cyclical aspects of policy preparation and policy formulation. In this context, cycles mean that the degree of attention paid to specific issues fluctuates over time. For instance, one often observes that an issue is ignored for some time, then suddenly receives a great deal of attention, and after some time is again neglected. Policy issues often exhibit a pattern of 'upswings' and 'downswings'. At present, the issue of transportation as a whole seems to be in the 'downswing' phase of such a cycle, as, after a time of growing awareness of and political attention to transportation (reflected, *inter alia*, in large infrastructure investments), transportation seems to be disappearing gradually from the public agenda.

Within the transportation sector, similar observations can be made for smaller issues like investments for highways, promotion of public transport, concern about ever growing commuter flows, and so on, to take just some examples from the Dutch situation.

These fluctuations in policy and planning issues deserve closer analysis, because under the surface of the present (overall) stabilisation of mobility many things are changing, which may cause new fluctuations in policy interest. For instance, the introduction of new communications technologies may give rise to a new policy cycle.

Not only do these new developments make policy-cycle analysis necessary, but it also seems useful to make cross-comparisons of such cycles or to characterise a particular situation (or a phase of a cycle) with respect to an adequate policy to be implemented.

For this analysis of policy cycles three distinct points of view will be studied successively:

- the policy preparation and implementation process, often called (as a whole) the '(transportation) planning process';
- the dynamics of transportation as a social and spatial phenomenon; and
- the interpretation of policy as a product in the framework of a product life-cycle approach.

Two examples will also be given which are taken from actual practice, and the paper will end with a prospective view on new planning issues.

2. Policy and Planning

The rational planning process is often characterised as an 'upside-down' process, from goal to implementation (Chadwick 1971). There is a clear parallel to a standard mathematical programming (or optimisation) problem of selecting the most effective instruments given a goal or objective function after which the solution can be implemented.

Actual practice, however, shows another picture. It merely works from the bottom up. Planning does not usually start at a very generic level but mostly at a level at which real problems can be solved by real solutions within an implicit framework of societal priorities. To give an example, traffic congestion is solved by the construction of new lanes. More complex problems are solved by means of sets of measures, for instance, losses in public transport by subsidising systems (or programmes) for improving the competitiveness of public transport with respect to other modes.

At the global and social level of changing attitudes and patterns the supply of new technologies, opinions and ideas may also change. Such changes are usually neither based on nor formulated as well-defined goals, but exist as values or feelings, such as the idea that it is desirable to live in the inner city (urban gentrification), or a positive attitude towards technological innovations. If there are such changes at this general level of attitudes, they are either autonomous changes, or they reflect the bottom-up process of the recognition that small problems can no longer be solved within the existing framework of accepted ideas and related measures. In this way such 'driving forces' in society seem to work from the bottom up. This picture of such 'forces' and the related policy-making process are reflected in Figure 7.1.

'Forces' can enter the policy-making process at several levels. Generally the tendency in planning agencies will be to break down forces into well-defined problems and treat these at the appropriate level of policy implementation. However, this can result in

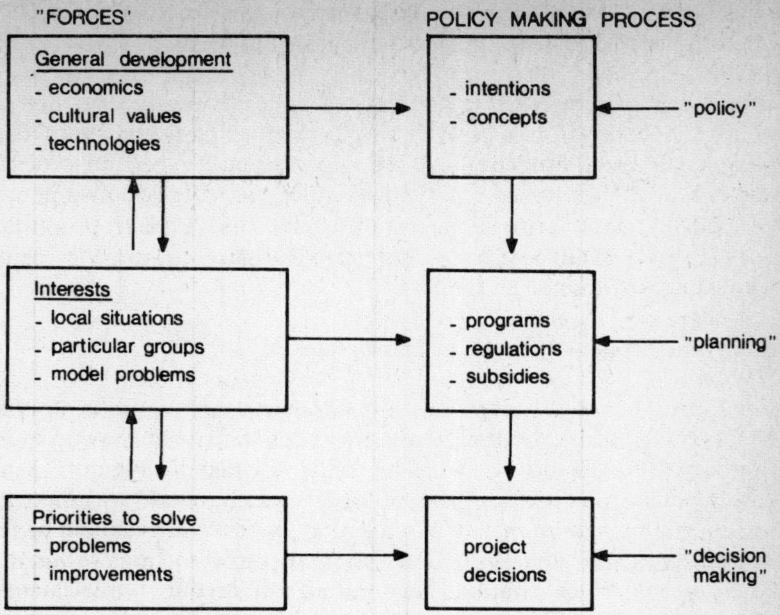

Figure 7.1 Causes and policy-making process

misconceptions. For instance, changes in socio-demographics (different household compositions, higher divorce rates, etc.) can be treated at the technical planning level (lower trip production) or as a derivative of an already known problem (captivity to public transport). It can also cause changes in the interests of particular groups to be acknowledged in planning programmes or it can even be reflected in changes in attitudes and the need for other concepts like less separated places for work and living, and related planning measures.

The meaning of policy (formulation), planning and decision-making is associated with each of the successive levels in the scheme. A policy is a large set of intentions, sometimes formulated as goals, and related planning options. Planning in the strict sense concerns the selection of the appropriate instruments and tools, given the environment in which they have to operate. Decisions on real projects are taken on the basis of priorities and with a view to qualities to be attained. They have to fit a programme or a plan.

A consequence of this way of reasoning is that a policy will only be slightly altered, mainly because it takes time to become aware of the need for change, and because the related planning and decision system is hampered by inertia (see also Section 6 of this contribution for an example, and le Clercq 1985), thus causing waves of policy-makers' interest.

In order to identify either the stage of policy or the need to alter a policy the acting forces as well as the state of performance of the planning levels should be analysed. For instance, when no project decision can be taken, notwithstanding good decision-support methods like multi-criteria analysis, one has to move a level upwards. Is the project really needed or supported by any group? does it fit within a programme? and so on.

3. Transportation dynamics and policy-making

The phenomenon of dynamics in transportation planning in the Netherlands during the last 30 years has been analysed elsewhere (le Clercq 1985). To do so the scheme represented in Figure 7.2 is employed. It expresses the internal mechanism within the transportation system as a demand-supply system which should be in equilibrium (Manheim 1979). The system as such functions within an environment which contains the spatial system but also elements related to non-spatial developments in society (among which is the value system). It is assumed that the role of governments is to maintain or to strive for equilibrium by applying the instruments they have to hand. The more regular instruments are investments, regulations and subsidies.

These governmental tasks coincide with the planning and decision levels of Figure 7.1 and will mostly influence supply. The extent to which a government is prepared to intervene causes dynamics in transportation, for instance when the government decides to withdraw from subsidising public transport.

Changes within the transportation system in equilibrium, or in its immediate environment, also cause dynamic behaviour to which government has to react. These changes are usually caused by shifts in demand.

With respect to a situation of growing demand, it is quite useful to distinguish between 'demand pull' and 'supply push,' that is, the question whether a growing economy creates a demand or whether new technologies create new opportunities. The former has been surely the case in the past, say in the last 20 years, whereas the latter may happen in the near future.

Here we restrict ourselves to possible reaction patterns of (governmental) policy-makers. By extending a simple example the existence of a policy interest cycle and its variations will be

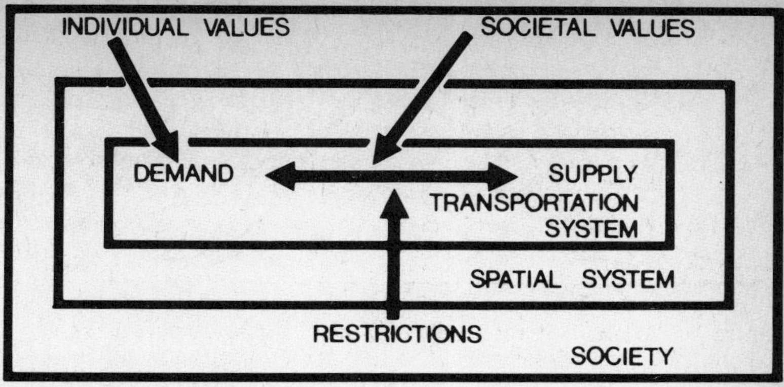

Figure 7.2 An analytical model for the functioning of transportation

demonstrated. Let us assume that transport demand is growing fast, for instance because of increasing car-ownership. When this phenomenon has been observed for some time, government has to react; for instance it may decide to build new roads (create supply) according to levels of service (equilibrium conditions). We can now postulate that the government's reaction is influenced by two characteristics of the problem:

1. The impact the problem will have. This will be greater if the problems grow faster. In this example it is expressed by the marginal rate of change in traffic demand.
2. The effort needed to find a solution (that is, the required level of equilibrium). A government will be interested until the marginal effort exceeds the marginal problem (that is, growth in demand).

So the first order derivative of the cumulative demand function (through time) steers the intensity of the policy interest. Its duration depends on the time needed to find solutions.

Then Figure 7.3 is obtained when taking into account a time-lag before reacting. In this figure a starting stage can be identified in which demand is already growing, but government does not react, because it is not sure whether demand will continue to grow or not. If government decides to react it is assumed that interest and supply (investments) grow as fast as demand is growing. Interest will drop very rapidly when created supply meets demand, although this does not imply that investments will also drop. These will roughly follow growth in demand. In this last stage, discussions at the project level

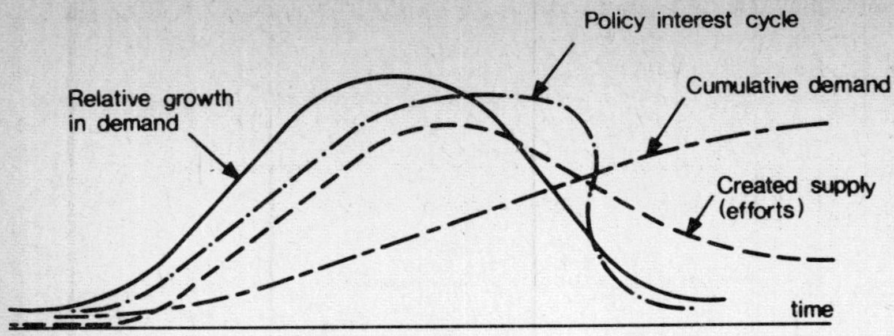

Figure 7.3 Policy interest cycle as a function of transport demand

will be held regularly in which the project's contribution to meet demand have to be proved, because everyone is aware of the decreasing need for provisions. The time periods associated with the various stages depend in this example very much on the growth in demand of the issue in question. It can, however, be imagined that government is not able to react sufficiently, for instance because of a lack of financing. Then policy interest (and public discussions) will also be continued, because people suffer each day because of inadequate facilities.

This is just one example of how to construct a policy cycle. With reference to Fig. 7.1, it is now possible to construct several reaction patterns or policy cycles (Fig. 7.4 and Table 7.1). Two types of reason to react are distinguished: a positive cause and a negative one. By negative is meant a cause which is a failure of the present policy because of inappropriate policy-making, while positive refers to unforeseen developments which cannot be captured by existing policies.

It is assumed that changes in either planning or policy are generated due to substantive problems. Depending either on the magnitude of the problem or the type of the problem it may be necessary to go up to the policy level. For instance the difference between cycles 2 and 2a in Table 7.1 is that real problems of category 2 can be solved at the planning level, whereas there may also be problems which can only be captured by a change at the policy level.

This scheme suggests that only substantive changes within the transport phenomena cause structural interest cycles. They will also cause policy changes. Only temporary policy-makers' interest is mobilised by events which need intervention to assure the application of particular instruments within an already formulated policy. Policy

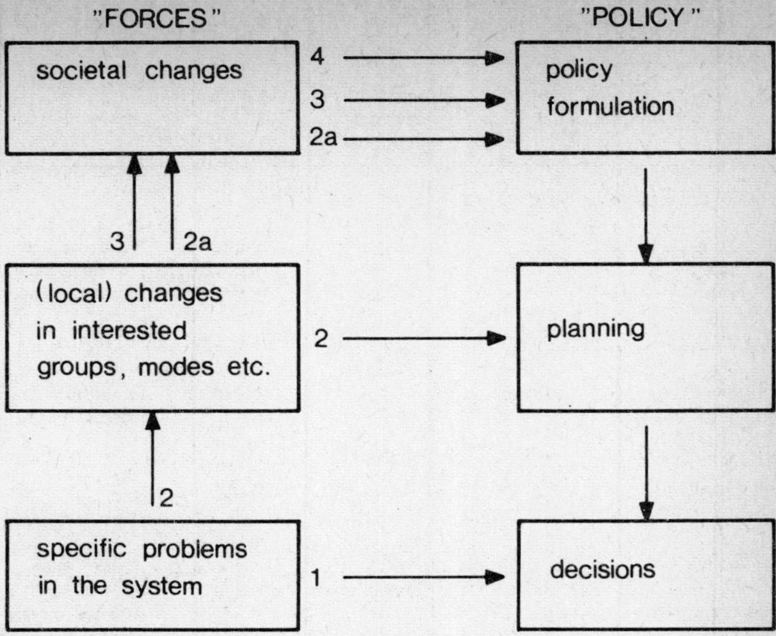

Figure 7.4 Causes of changes in the policy making process

interest (either structural or temporary) is sooner mobilised where real problems are concerned. Whether general changes in society or interest groups will give rise to policy changes and new policies will depend on the extent to which public interest is involved (such as demand for new goods).

4. Policy-making as a life cycle

Recently the Dutch Minister of Housing and Environment introduced the policy life-cycle concept to describe changing interests in policy-making. He distinguished four stages in policy-making:

1. acknowledgement of the need to formulate a new policy;
2. policy formulation;
3. realisation of a solution; and
4. maintenance of the solution system developed.

In a policy cycle the main characteristic of the first stage is the

Table 7.1 Various causes of policy changes, according to Figure 7.2

	Cause of route	Policy of action	Reason for process entrance	Influence on this entrance	policy interest
	Positive cause	Negative cause			
1	Real problems (lack of supply)	—	Decisions	Fit into programme	No continued interest after implementation
2	Real problems caused by local changes (land use, interest groups)	Unforeseen problem	Planning	New planning tools needed (money, network extension, etc.)	Will cause temporary interest
2a	Ditto, problems cannot be isolated	No solutions exist at all	Policy formulation	Structural problem	Policy *change* needed. Interest depends on size of problems.
3	Structural changes in patterns	Conflicting interests with respect to existing plans/ programmes	Policy formulation	Structural changes which cannot be met by existing plans	Policy *change* needed. Whether it will be picked up depends on interest of society.
4	Change of attitudes in society, new technologies	Change in available resources	Policy formulation	Planning goals have to be checked at least	Great, can cause *new* policy cycle

uncertainty whether or not to intervene in a problem. The second stage shows an increasing importance in politics of the issue in question with an ever increasing consensus about the solution. In the third stage, when a solution has been found, the political importance drops very rapidly, and in the fourth stage interest is only latently present.

The first stage is equivalent to the left-hand 'forces' column in

Figure 7.1, the other three to the respective stages of policy formulation, planning and project decision. The preceding section, however, demonstrated that a cycle is not always completely performed. It can start half-way as a correction of an existing cycle, at the end as a reaction to a former (failing) policy or as a completely new policy. In this sense it is probably more valuable to compare policy cycles or rather the management of policy-preparation processes with the management of business concerns, which also has continually to face new facts and new situations.

The idea of an organisational life cycle is to express the degree of maturity of an organisation for dealing with its tasks. The way it reacts to changing conditions would give an indication of the stage an organisation has reached (see, for instance, Adizes 1980).

Descriptions of such life cycles start with an organisation that does not have any rule on how to work but accepts each task it can handle (on the basis of the available persons). Then it moves to an organisational stage in which the work is organised according to efficiency criteria (depersonalised). A third stage is that of internal regulations and a probable fourth stage — negative — that of bureaucracy where not the tasks to be performed, but the rules to be followed, are the main purpose. A positive fourth stage is that of reproduction of the lessons of the past in order to create new initiatives within the already established system of organisational rules.

The importance of this kind of description for our present case of policy cycles lies in the recognition that dealing with a task (a problem, a policy) over a longer period changes the attitude of the organisation while it does this. This changing attitude is characterised in the explanation of innovation changes in industries as a move away from focusing on new product developments to focusing on process optimalisation (Rothwell and Zegveld 1981).

So, with respect to the idea of life cycles as the terms in which to describe policy preparation and implementation processes, two ways of thinking are possible:

1. A policy cycle may be considered analogous with a product cycle. This enables us to characterise the role and degree of interest of the policy-makers for a particular issue.
2. A policy cycle may be considered analogous with an organisational process. This takes into account learning processes about ways of dealing with problems and evolving policies. This description points to the kind of measure which will be selected to reach solutions: in the earlier stages substantive solutions; in

subsequent steps organisational performance (like committees) and more and more regulation will be introduced.

The second approach suggests that some of the changes in the policy process as described in Table 7.1 will lead to organisational and procedural improvements. This is true in particular for changes 2a and 3, which deal either with problems that cannot be met by existing programmes or with new evidence and conflicting interests which were not covered by existing policies. For instance it can be expected that new regulations and/or subsidies will be provided in an attempt to save the policy already agreed on.

5. Characteristics for identifying policy cycles

5.1 Introduction

This section will synthesise the three preceding ways of characterising policy-making processes. For this purpose the four steps introduced in Section 4 are characterised with respect to substantive matters and behaviour of actors involved, Table 7.2.

A distinction is made between policies for new issues and policies which are reformulated. The 'reformulated policy' column shows a much greater interest of the parties involved. They also have more normative behaviour. This is because a previous policy was not successful. This could be either because of the way the policy was formulated, because of counter-effects or because of unforeseen developments; although in the last case behaviour will usually be like that in the case of new policies.

5.2 Inertia in policy-making

At a few stages a lack of interest and action of policy-makers is mentioned. According to Figure 7.3 this can be either at the beginning or at the end of a policy cycle. Such periods of inertia need more attention, because transportation now seems to be in such a period. Inertia in the policy-making process can be defined as 'doing nothing', or 'keeping policies unchanged', although changes occur in transportation.

A period of inertia may occur:

- at the emergence of a new issue when it is still questionable whether the issue will find its way to the political agenda, or
- at the end of a policy cycle, either
  (a) when a policy has been concluded successfully, or
  (b) when a policy has failed to give results (in this case politicians

Table 7.2 Characteristics of policy cycles with respect to substantive actions involved and behaviour of politicians and public

	New Policy	Reformulated policy
		Acknowledgement
Substance	— New demand — New technologies (supply) — Real or perceived problems to be solved	— Existing planning no longer fits with problems or interest groups — New societal values
Actors:	— *Politicians*: latent interest — *Public*: less aware except in cases of public supply	— *Politicians*: great interest — Much public debate — Conflicts between planners (to maintain old strategies) and politicians
		Policy formulation
Substance:	— Forecasts — Alternative strategies — Choice of direction/ 'equilibrium' — Look for solutions	— Choice of new directions either directly (following political debate in preceding stage) or after testing some alternatives
Actors:	— *Politicians*: highly involved, adaptive behaviour — *Public*: less so	— *Politicians*: highly involved, normative behaviour — *Public*: very critical — Lobbies — Strong commitments
		Solutions
Substance:	— Programme for new investments — Priorities — Subsidies	— Focus on precise regulations of role of actors — Investment rules — Subsidy control
Actors:	— *Politicians*: diminishing interest *Public*: even more interested	— *Politicians*: strict control of each project — *Public*: critically following
		Maintenance/implementation
Substance:	— Project decisions	— Project decisions
Actors:	— *Politicians*: depending on public — *Public*: depending on project problems	— *Politicians*: great interest in individual projects — *Public*: great interest in individual projects

are not inert at all, but no decisions can be taken because there is no consensus about what to do).

Particularly when changes in policies are necessary, dramatic situations may occur, as has been indicated in Table 7.2. Taking experiences in Amsterdam as a starting point, such transitions have the following characteristics (see also the levels of Figure 7.2):

1. The public becomes aware of what has really been agreed at the planning level, because of the impact of some projects.
2. They oppose the planning level (try to alter plans), which primarily leads to a conflict with civil servants.
3. Civil servants advising politicians how to act then insist on continuity in the planning agreements.
4. When the public persist in their objections, discussions go back to the level of policy formulation, that is, values are reformulated in the political arena.

Two recent cases demonstrate policy change in Amsterdam. The first one has to do with a starting process, namely the reformulation of the urban renewal process. The other has to do with the final stage of a policy-making process with respect to urban transportation. Both cases are related by their contents, because one project which covered both fields mobilised public particiption. This was the plan to construct an underground system, for which an old neighbourhood had to be demolished.

5.3 Urban renewal

The position of urban renewal on the temporal axis of urban policies is shown in Figure 7.5. Urban renewal started to be a policy issue at the end of the 1960s. The idea was that part of the population would move to the new satellite towns and that the older neighbourhoods would be demolished and reconstructed according to modern standards. This approach was first applied in a neighbourhood through which an underground railway line had to be constructed.

Although everyone agreed on urban renewal as a policy issue, people then became aware of the real plans involved. There was a lot of public opposition. The policies had to be reformulated. This took about eight years, during which time hardly any houses were built. The final result was a separation of urban renewal as a working process to upgrade older neighbourhoods, and spatial planning as a means to upgrade the complete city with all its functions. To promote the latter it was decided to end the satellite town policy, to use sites for

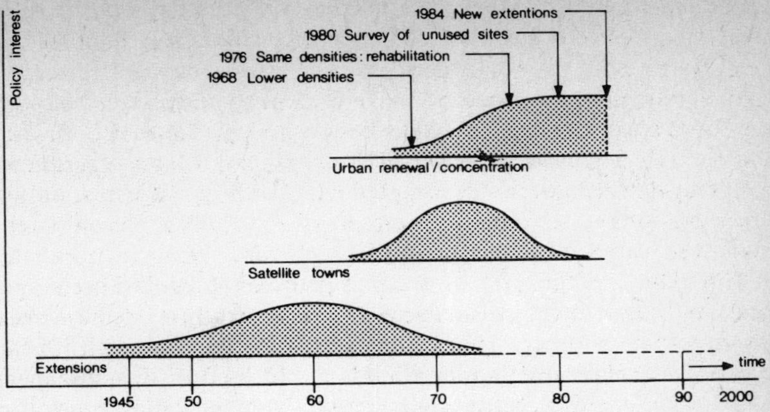

Figure 7.5 Sequence of urban policies with respect to urban and city renewal

house construction, which had until then been reserved for other functions (mainly roads), and to extend the existing city only in those places where consumers can be found for already existing services.

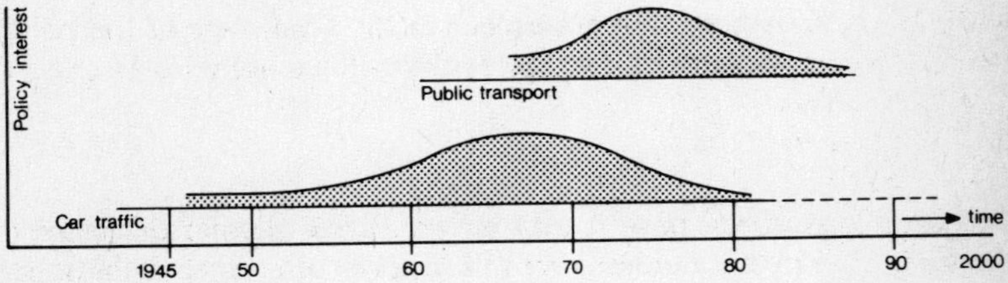

Figure 7.6 Sequence of transportation policies

5.4 Transportation

In the 1960s, when car traffic problems became urgent in the old centre of Amsterdam, the following strategy was developed: car traffic would be given the room it clearly needed, by a number of cuts through bad neighbourhoods surrounding the city centre; more room would also be created by putting the trams underground, that is, by building an underground system. The policy can be characterised as favouring both car and public transport.

In the late 1960s public transport got into the red. Patronage did not continue to grow. The construction costs of the underground system rose rapidly. There was a lot of opposition to the demolition of old neighbourhoods, so it was decided to construct no further underground lines in the older parts of the city. A new policy was introduced for these areas. Preference would be given to public transport. The tram system would be improved. The reverse holds for the periphery of the agglomeration: a new ring road was to be constructed, only a few radial tram lines were to be extended, and reservations only were made for a circular light rail system.

This shift in policy took as much as ten years. Little has been done since towards making the investments that are really needed to create an up-to-date network. Much effort was spent on discussions of the project level about each radial tram line. Much effort was also spent on discussions with central government about regulating control of the deficits of public transport. Central government started to require traffic-management schemes, in order to be informed about public transport priorities, then moved over to a grant system normalised to demand, and finally (or at least up to the present moment) decided for a block grant system combined with decentralisation of executive power.

The outcome of an analysis of these two examples is that the issue of urban renewal demonstrated the starting characteristics of getting under control a new policy which is really needed to solve problems, whereas the transportation example is at the final stage of the policy which tried to keep urban traffic problems manageable.

6. New planning issues

When we look ahead now, it may be wondered whether this stage of inertia in transportation planning will continue. In our contribution, a distinction will be made between substantive matters and planning-process improvements.

As has been explained above, substantive sources for really new policies will be found in new problems, new interest groups or new developments in society. For example, with respect to Amsterdam, a number of these can be foreseen.

- demand: new interest groups will enter the market (increasing number of female workers; shifts in working hours giving rise to new patterns);
- supply: new technologies (information technology, telecommunications):
  (a) additional possibilities or substitutes for trips;

improvements in public transport information and control;
(b) improvements in road and network capacities,

- urban system (a) new demands, the opportunities of the city are to be used to a maximum extent (in accordance with a growing interest in urban life-style);
  (b) requirements for the allocation of new sectors;
- values: (a) increasing economy;
  (b) new population: new ideas.

With respect to transport, only those indicators which cannot be captured by the existing systems, and which will therefore cause serious problems, will give rise to new policies. In Amsterdam, this will probably be the case with respect to the location of new activities and the related population and its demand for transport facilities. Modern work places are at present located on the periphery of the agglomeration. New sources of employment, such as airport-related activities, high-tech activities, and so on, also tend to be concentrated in those areas. The city-orientated, well-educated population, on the other hand, either lives in the central parts of the agglomeration or in the wealthy suburbs outside Amsterdam.

This restructuring of both the urban structure and its users could cause serious traffic problems at the border of the metropolitan area instead of — as in former years — in the city centre. A new urban transportation problem may arise, which will demand new policies to deal with dilemmas, such as whether to reorganise old structures to meet new demands or to create new facilities, leaving older ones unused.

Process improvement will include shortening of time-span and investment strategies for prepared plans as well the involvement of various interest groups in plan preparation. The first two items relate to the change from master planning to incremental planning, which has, of course, a lot to do with the order of magnitude of the issue in question. The bigger the issue, the greater the need for a comprehensive approach. Now it can be supposed that transportation will move to a project-based approach, which will demand investment and financing strategies. The required attitude of government and its officials has to be to manage real-time decisions and create opportunities for project realisation instead of planning for an integrated future. For instance it is not the *plan* for a ring road that is important to create new developments, but the *knowledge* that it will really be constructed.

The latter — involvement of interest groups — relates to the recognition that neither solutions nor resources nor acceptance can be generated by government alone. Bodies such as planning authorities will become more and more important in order to bring parties together which can generate both resources and societal acceptance (Kreukels 1985). Both improvements are directed toward the same objective, namely to respond more adequately to new challenges.

References

Adizes, I. (1980). *How to Solve the Mismanagement Crisis.* Los Angeles: Development and Organizational Research Institute.

Chadwick, G. (1971). *A Systems View of Planning.* Oxford: Pergamon.

Kreukels, A. (1985). 'Planning as a Mirror of Western Societies in the Coming Decades: The Case of the New American Metropolitan Planning'. Paper presented at IPSA World Congress, Paris.

Le Clercq, F. (1985a). 'Dynamics in Transportation Planning: An Overview' in G.R.M. Jansen, P. Nijkamp and C. Ruijgrok, eds, *Transportation and Mobility in an Era of Transition.* Amsterdam: North Holland Publishing Co., pp. 1–11.

Le Clerq, F. (1985b). 'A Policy of Urban Deconcentration — the Amsterdam Case', *Proceedings of PTRC Summer Annual Meeting, 'Planning for Development'.* London, pp. 83–92.

Manheim, M.L. (1979). *Fundamentals of Transportation Systems Analysis,* Vol. 1. Cambridge, MA: MIT Press.

Rothwell R. and W. Zegveld (1981). *Industrial Innovation and Public Policy: Preparing for the 80s and 90s.* London.

8 Planning for Mobility: The Wish and the Reality

*P. H. Bly**

1. Introduction

There is no shortage of people eager to offer their own solutions to some aspect or other of society's failings. On closer inspection, the proferred solution often requires a change in human behaviour. Transport planners, in their own limited field, also strive to improve the common lot. On the whole, they are more realistic than to rely on provoking any fundamental change in human behaviour, but their job nevertheless requires them to predict how people will behave in a variety of new and different situations, and to some degree they must try to modify behaviour.

Given the complexity of people's travel decisions, this is no easy task. Of course, people are well able to decide for themselves where to travel to, and how best to get there. If the demand is strong enough, the commercial market will provide whatever facilities are necessary. However, the justification for central planning is the belief that it is possible to find solutions to social problems which are better overall than the result of leaving everyone to find his own optimal solution. That this is so in some respects is accepted by virtually everyone: especially in the realms of building development, even the most evangelical free marketeer is likely to be grateful for controls which prevent the more remarkable examples of unfettered individual choice being built next door. Such 'negative' planning by means of prohibitive legislation or regulation is generally fairly successful, though it may be evaded and it may discourage some activities which are

*The work described in this paper forms part of the programme of the Transport and Road Research Laboratory, but the views expressed in this paper are not necessarily those of the Department of Transport.

socially desirable. 'Positive' planning aimed at persuading, rather than coercing, people into a course of action which contributes to the overall plan tends to be harder to achieve.

Centralised planning normally involves some conflict between the wishes of the planner and the wishes of the individual, because although the planned solution is intended to make the majority better off than they would be otherwise, it often requires that a minority, possibly a substantial minority, are worse off than under their own optimal solutions. For this reason, even if the planning is wholly successful many people may feel that it is not, and the planner cannot expect to be universally loved. On the other hand, planners share the professional advantage of doctors: most of their clients will survive in spite of them. Within the restrictions applied by planners, people are sufficiently adaptable and flexible to forge a way of life which will make even badly thought-out solutions appear to work. Consequently, the success or failure of planning is often difficult to measure. Given these uncertainties about the efficacy of planning, it is probably prudent to impose restrictive planning on people only when the potential net advantage can be seen very clearly. The trouble is that, although the immediate effects of a planning decision may be predicted reliably, it may produce ripples which spread very much wider through the complex interconnections of human behaviour, so that some of the longer-term results may be quite unforeseen.

2. The aims of transport planning

The broad aim of transport planning is to provide people with the sort of mobility that will enable them to perform all the activities they need and wish to do. In considering how this might best be done, there is a fundamental distinction between people who have a private car available for their travel, and those who do not, because of the enormous difference the private car can make to a person's mobility. For those with a car available, mobility requires the provision of an adequate road network and parking facilities. For those without, attention tends to be concentrated on providing adequate public transport, though for some sections of the population, and for suitable areas, the need might be for better facilities for cycling. For local travel, planning to make walking easier is too often neglected, while it is frequently suggested that, rather than planning to meet the demand for longer-distance, mechanised travel, it might be more profitable (and energy-saving) to reduce the need for travel itself by organising all the necessary destinations (job, shops, services) within easy walking distance for everyone.

Since planning often involves inconveniencing the minority in order to benefit the majority, the notion of trading off one advantage against another is implicit in the approach. At simplest, the trade-off may simply be between money and travel benefit. On the whole, the provision of better public transport is not opposed for its own sake even by people who never use it (though residents not infrequently oppose the introduction of buses into their quiet suburban streets, and not everyone is keen to have a railway at the bottom of the garden), but if the improved services make a substantial demand on public taxes there may well be resistance. Often, the trade-off is between transport advantage and non-transport detriment. New roads are opposed because they spoil the view, or more fervently still by people who live close to the route and who will have to suffer the noise, vibration and pollution (most fervently of all, of course, by those whose homes must be demolished to make way for the road, unless they feel the compensation payment is adequate). But the trade-off may also be between one transport aspect and another. Even in rural areas, transport benefits in terms of new roads and rail routes may be bought at the expense of making other travel less direct: they tend to be particularly disruptive to walking, and to make it less pleasant. In urban areas, this type of conflict can present even more serious problems.

On the whole, the problem of ensuring a satisfactory level of mobility for people in rural or low-density suburban areas tends to be one of money. Some form of public transport service can make a great deal of difference to those who have no car available (though the self-help and ingenuity by which most people manage to cope when there is no public transport should not be underestimated), and the planner's job is largely to decide on what services can be provided, and the most efficient way of doing so, within the inevitable financial constraints.

In urban areas the interactions between one transport mode and another, and between transport and the pattern of activities, are more complex. The Buchanan Report in 1963 pointed out that, given the density of activities in central London, a solution which provided unhindered access by private car would be physically impossible, even if it were desirable. In big cities, there is an obvious conflict between public and private transport, and help for one will often be traded off against disadvantage for the other.

3. The changing city

Although the Industrial Revolution changed virtually every aspect of society, perhaps its most profound effect on our way of life was that it urbanised the great majority of the population. As people moved out of agricultural employment and off the land, industrial towns and cities grew very rapidly, acquiring remarkably high residential densities before the development of mechanised public transport finally enabled the towns to spread over larger areas at rather lower densities. The process of urbanisation has been virtually complete in northern Europe for some decades now, though it is still continuing in southern Europe and on the eastern and western peripheries.

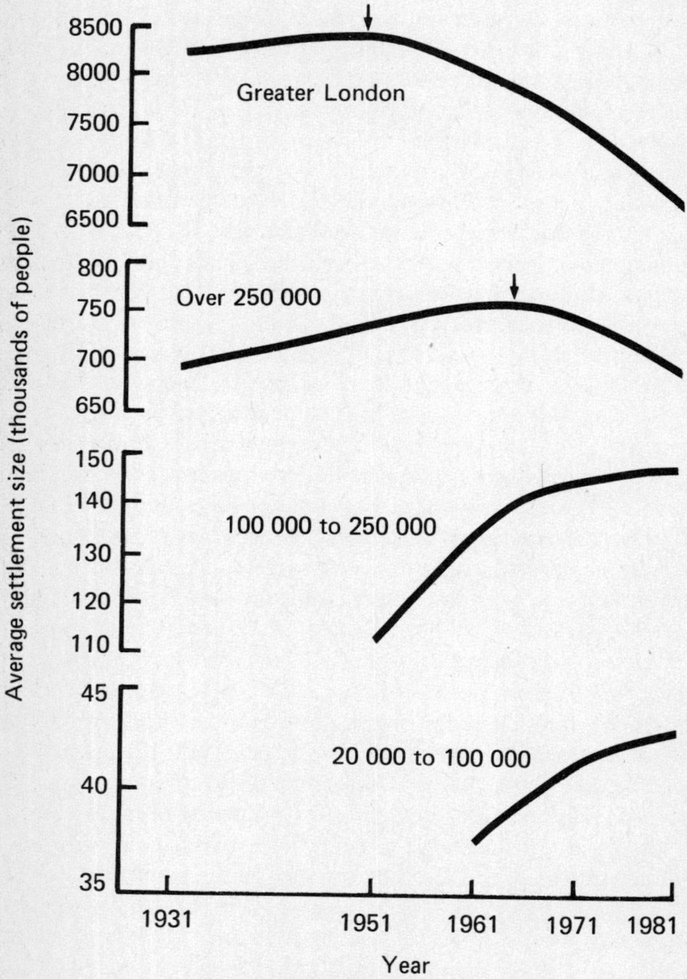

Figure 8.1 Changes in population in towns of different size, England and Wales, 1931 to 1981

After growing steadily for over 150 years, the populations of the largest cities have now begun to decline. Indeed, as Figure 8.1 shows for Britain, the population of London began to decline around 1950. The largest cities other than London continued to grow until the early 1960s, when they too began to decline, leaving the medium-sized towns growing fairly rapidly, but with the growth there flattening off in the 1970s. Presently, the fastest growth is seen in the smaller towns. Thus there is a net movement of population out of the big cities into the smaller towns and rural areas. The process has been described as 'disurbanisation' or 'counterurbanisation' (Berry 1977) and considered as part of an urban 'life cycle' (Drewett 1983), but the people involved remain truly urbanised: this is no move 'back to the land', and many of the people may still work in the city while living in a small town in the peri-urban area, as growing affluence and the mobility conferred by the private car encourage them to seek more space in which to live. The process is furthest advanced in North America and Britain, where there is a long tradition of living in houses as opposed to apartments and where a small garden has long been seen as an ideal even where overall residential densities are high. Nevertheless, material reviewed in a recent Transport and Road Research Laboratory (TRRL) study for the European Conference of Ministers of Transport (Webster *et al.* 1984) shows that the same trends are clearly visible in other European countries.

This growth of smaller towns at the expense of the big cities is a relatively new phenomenon, but the underlying search for more living space has been fuelling a shift of population from the inner areas of towns out to the peripheral areas since the last century. This has been accompanied by, and is in part a consequence of, a consistent fall in average household size: in Britain this has halved since 1900. The extensive low-density suburbs of Britain and North America give their towns a markedly different appearance from the more compact towns of continental Europe, yet, as Figure 8.2 shows, the same decline in inner area densities and spreading outward of the urban areas can be seen in French and German cities. The residential densities in the central areas of both Lyon and Munich are considerably higher than those in Manchester, yet the fall in average density over the past decade or so is very similar in all three cities. Average densities in the outer areas have risen because more of the land is occupied by housing, and not because of any increase in built density. Figure 8.2 also shows that both Lyon and Munich have less of a central crater in the population distribution than does Manchester: this is indicative of an important difference between living habits in Britain and continental Europe: not only are the citizens of mainland Europe more

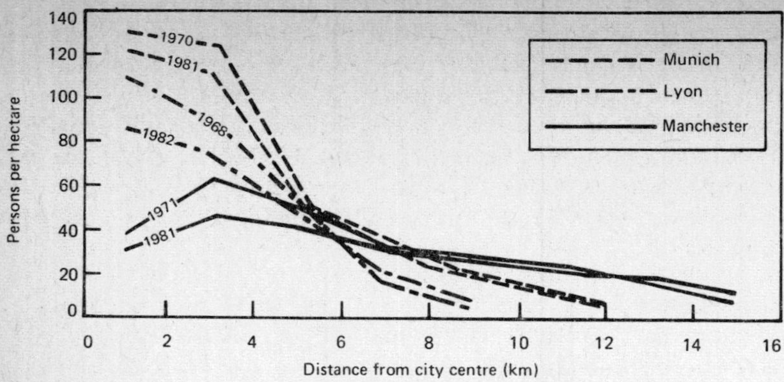

Figure 8.2 Changes in average population density with distance from city centre in Lyon, Manchester and Munich

likely to live in apartments than are those of Britain, but the wealthy are quite satisfied to inhabit apartments close to the city centre (in the more attractive cities at least), whereas high-income families in Britain and North America generally live well away from it, often in rural or semi-rural seclusion. This probably indicates a difference in the quality of city life generally, and the social life of the central city in particular.

In Britain average urban densities have been falling steadily throughout the century: urban land provision in England and Wales has risen from an average of 20.7 hectares per 1,000 population in 1901 to 33.7 in 1971 (Best 1981). Inner-city densities have been falling in London since 1851, and in Paris since at least 1876: it is interesting to note that the trends in the parameters describing the density distributions have been very similar in both cities (Bussière and Stovall 1975), but that Paris's present distribution is similar to that of London 40 years ago.

And it is not only the people who are leaving the cities: employment too, is decentralising. Table 8.1 shows the change in manufacturing, service and total employment between 1959 and 1975 in Great Britain, categorised into different sizes and types of town. Manufacturing employment has declined in the country as a whole, but the loss has been in London and the big city conurbations, while the smaller cities and towns have gained. Service employment has increased everywhere, but it is the smaller cities and towns which show the largest percentage increases. It is not clear whether there has been an absolute decline in the amount of service employment in city centres, though in Manchester, for example, which is a relatively prosperous conurbation, employment in the distributive trades in the central and inner areas declined between 1971 and 1975, and although office employment remained fairly stable in the centre it showed a sizeable increase in the outer areas, so there has been a relative decentralisation (Dasgupta 1983). Whether or not there is absolute decline in the central areas, the tendency to build hypermarkets and shopping malls in suburban areas seems to be well established in all European countries.

Table 8.1 Changes in employment in Great Britain, 1959–75

Type of area	Change in employment, 1959–75, as a percentage of total employment in the area		
	Manufacturing	Services	Total
London	-13.0	+ 1.9	-11.4
Conurbations	- 7.9	+ 5.9	- 4.7
Free-standing cities	+ 1.1	+16.0	+12.5
Industrial towns	+ 6.9	+21.1	+22.0
County towns	+ 7.5	+15.2	+18.0
Rural areas	+11.1	+11.4	+14.3
Whole of Great Britain	- 2.2	+10.8	+ 5.1

Source: Fothergill and Gudgin (1983)

Mobility is not just a question of being able to move about; it also depends on the distribution of destinations which need to be accessed. Consequently, it is clear that these very substantial changes in our towns must have an important impact on mobility. Since the enabling force has been the huge increase in private car-ownership (which has multiplied fivefold, typically, since 1950), it is hardly surprising that these changes should benefit those who have a car: the smaller towns and lower-density developments provide more space for parking and using the car, and the out-of-town shopping malls and industrial estates avoid much of the traffic congestion. Yet even car-owning households contain many people for whom the car is not generally available (except occasionally, or when the need to be ferried as a passenger may be especially great), and for these people the more dispersed pattern of destinations can be inconvenient.

People who live in very compact towns have little need of mechanised transport for their internal travel: after all, in most of the towns there was none until well in this century, and the strongly centralised pattern of jobs, shops and services was suited to walking, on which the great majority of inhabitants had to rely. Before the coming of the private car, one consequence of the spreading outwards of such towns was a rapid rise in the provision and use of public transport. Even where car-ownership is fairly high, the suburbanisation of a highly compact town is likely to lead to more, rather than less, public transport use. This will be especially so where cheap, heavily-subsidised services are operated, but if the density of demand is high enough even commercially provided services will offer high frequencies at relatively low fares.

However, as the towns spread further, and the residential densities continue to fall, there will come a point where potential users are too dispersed for public transport to provide an attractive service. People with no alternative will still use it, because distances to many destinations will be too long to walk, but many people with no car available may take to bicycle or motorcycle, or may favour more local destinations even though they are less attractive, and public transport use will fall. This is especially true if the suburbanisation of the population is accompanied by decentralisation of the destinations, since public transport works well only when it can collect its passengers and take them to a spatial concentration of destinations. Its health therefore depends on city centres retaining a large share of destinations (or, alternatively, local centres becoming sufficiently strong for the city to assume a polycentric structure), so that the public transport network is essentially radial. Pushkarev and Zupan (1977), for example, give estimates of what residential densities and levels of activity in the city centre are necessary to support various levels of public transport service, under American conditions. Public transport can serve non-central developments such as major industrial estates or suburban shopping complexes (in some countries special works buses are an important component of the transport network), but it is unlikely to be effective if the catchment area is large and the travelling population dispersed. Private car, by contrast, is more convenient to use away from the congested centre, and is as convenient for orbital trips as for radial ones, so it tends to encourage shops and jobs on the periphery.

4. Public transport

The urban trends discussed in the preceding section do not augur well for public transport, though it is possible that the spreading of initially very compact towns could at first increase the demand for public transport, before further dispersion either erodes the services or makes them more costly to provide. The trends will tend to make public transport less available, or at least less convenient, between the desired origins and destinations. At the same time, the private car seems set to continue becoming more available: in most countries, the recession and increased fuel prices have had remarkably little effect on car ownership trends, though Denmark and Sweden and, in second-car-ownership at least, the Netherlands show evidence of some stagnation in recent years (see, for example, Bly 1985).

The 1970s saw considerable increases in fuel prices, and fuel forms a third of the cost of operating a private car, but only about 5 per cent of the cost of operating bus services. Of course in many countries the fuel price rises have been largely eroded by inflation, and at the moment oil prices are relatively low, but in the longer term fuel prices will certainly rise in real terms, probably by a factor of two to three excluding tax, which forms a large component of the total cost in most countries (Porter 1979). However, as Ferguson and Mogridge (1985) amongst others have discussed, there is considerable scope for improvement in overall fuel efficiencies so that the real cost per kilometre driven may increase by a relatively small proportion, and it seems unlikely that either ownership or use of private cars will be greatly discouraged by future fuel costs. Public transport's operating costs, by contrast, tend to be governed by labour costs, and labour costs inevitably increase in line with national affluence: recessions apart, they increase in real terms by a few per cent per year. Automation may soften this trend for some rail systems, but for bus services it is unavoidable. Consequently, not only are trends in land-use and travel patterns operating against the interests of public transport, but so are trends in costs. Analysis of national aggregate public transport operating data from 16 countries, and of data from 117 individual towns in ten countries, showed that in most cases there had been some improvement in productivity, measured by the number of vehicle-kilometres operated per employee, but these were far smaller than would be required to offset rising wages and, overall, real cost per vehicle-kilometre had risen by an average of 2.5 per cent per year between 1970 and 1980 (Bly and Oldfield 1984). In the past decade or so, rising costs have been offset by rising subsidies in almost all countries, but the sums of money involved have now grown so large that even the most committed subsidisers are becoming uneasy about whether growth in subsidy can be maintained.

Since the late 1960s, rising subsidies have done more than merely compensate for rising costs. In the data from the 16 countries and 117 towns, real fares were declining in about two-thirds of both countries and towns, while the amount of service provided, as measured by the number of vehicle-kilometres operated, was rising in the vast majority of cases. About two-thirds of the cases showed a rising trend in the number of passengers carried, but it was clear that the extra passengers were quite insufficient to pay for the extra service and to compensate for the reductions in fares. The proportion of costs covered by subsidy rose rapidly everywhere in the late 1960s and the first half of the 1970s, accounting for as much as three-quarters of costs in Belgium, Italy and the Netherlands. In the harsher economic climate of the late 1970s and early 1980s, the growth in subsidy has been at a much slower rate generally, and in several countries the fraction of costs covered by subsidy has actually declined. There is no doubt that, if subsidies were to be held constant as a fraction of cost, the upward trends in public transport use would turn to decline in many countries: estimates of this depend upon the assumptions made, but with plausible values for the demand elasticities it seems that only four of the 16 countries, Italy, France, Finland and the Federal Republic of Germany, would retain an upward trend (Bly and Oldfield 1984). Even so, differences in subsidy do not account for the wide range of variation of the trends, from average declines of almost 4 per cent per year between 1970 and 1980 to average growth of much the same size, a variability which contrasts strikingly with the uniformly upward trend in car use. Much of this variation can be explained in terms of changes in fares charged and the amount of service offered (which do depend on subsidy, of course, but they also depend on changes in operating costs), and changes in car-ownership, population, urbanisation and unemployment.

Year-on-year changes in passengers carried, as observed in the data for the 16 countries and 117 towns, have been estimated on the basis of the model:

$$P = P_o F^{e_f} K^{e_k} N (N - \beta C) U^g J^h$$

where P is the number of passengers carried per year; P_o is a constant; F is the real fair paid per passenger, e_f is the demand elasticity with respect to fare; K is the number of vehicle-kilometres operated; e_k is the demand elasticity with respect to vehicle-kilometres; N is the national population, C is the number of cars owned nationally; U is the percentage of national population living in 'urban areas' (so defined); and J is the proportion of unemployed workers. The various coefficients (e_f, e_k, β, g, h) were estimated by regression analysis of the data to give plausible values in agreement with current knowledge, but for the purpose of explaining the trends it was felt appropriate to use demand elasticities which, at –0.45 and +0.45 for e_f and e_k, were rather larger than the cross-sectional estimates, because the longer-term effects of fares and service can be expected to be greater than the short-term effects. More details of the procedure are given in Webster *et al.* (1984).

Figure 8.3 shows the result of this exercise for the national data, by subtracting from the observed passenger trends between 1970 and 1980 the estimates of the effects each of the component factors would be expected to have on passengers, to leave the 'residual trend', that is
Figure 8.3 shows the result of this exercise for the national data, by subtracting from the observed passenger trends between 1970 and 1980 the estimates of the effects each of the component factors would be expected to have on passengers, to leave the 'residual trend', that is
that part of the trend which remains unexplained by the model. The ranking of the countries by residual trend, which might be considered to represent an innate tendency of conditions in the country to favour or discourage public transport use, perhaps because of social or demographic structure, or policy, differs considerably from ranking by actual trend. The standard deviation of the actual trends has been reduced from 2.03 to 1.39 in the residual trends. The same analysis applied to the data from the 117 towns produces a very similar ranking of countries by residual trend, and the standard deviation of 5.75 in the actual trends is reduced to 3.01 in the residual trends. Thus the model explains about a third of the total variability between countries, and about a half between towns. This may not seem very much, but given the uncertainties in the data, the different definitions and methods of measurement, and the fact that the model assumes that the component mechanisms operate at the same strength in all countries (demand elasticities might be expected to differ in different countries, but statistical estimates of values for the individual countries showed no convincing and systematic differences between them), it is unlikely that any analysis could bring the residual variance very close to zero. Moreover, the residual trends are related in a statistically significant way to the absolute level of use of public transport (per head of population): countries with a higher than average level of use, which presumably have more mature and comprehensive public transport networks, and perhaps a stronger public transport 'habit', tend to have a more positive trend. If this relationship is included as part of the 'explanation', the standard deviation of the national residual trends is reduced to 1.0: thus at least half of the total variability has been accounted for, representing maybe three-quarters of that part of the variation which is likely to be explicable.

For the rest, it seems clear that the strongly positive residual trend

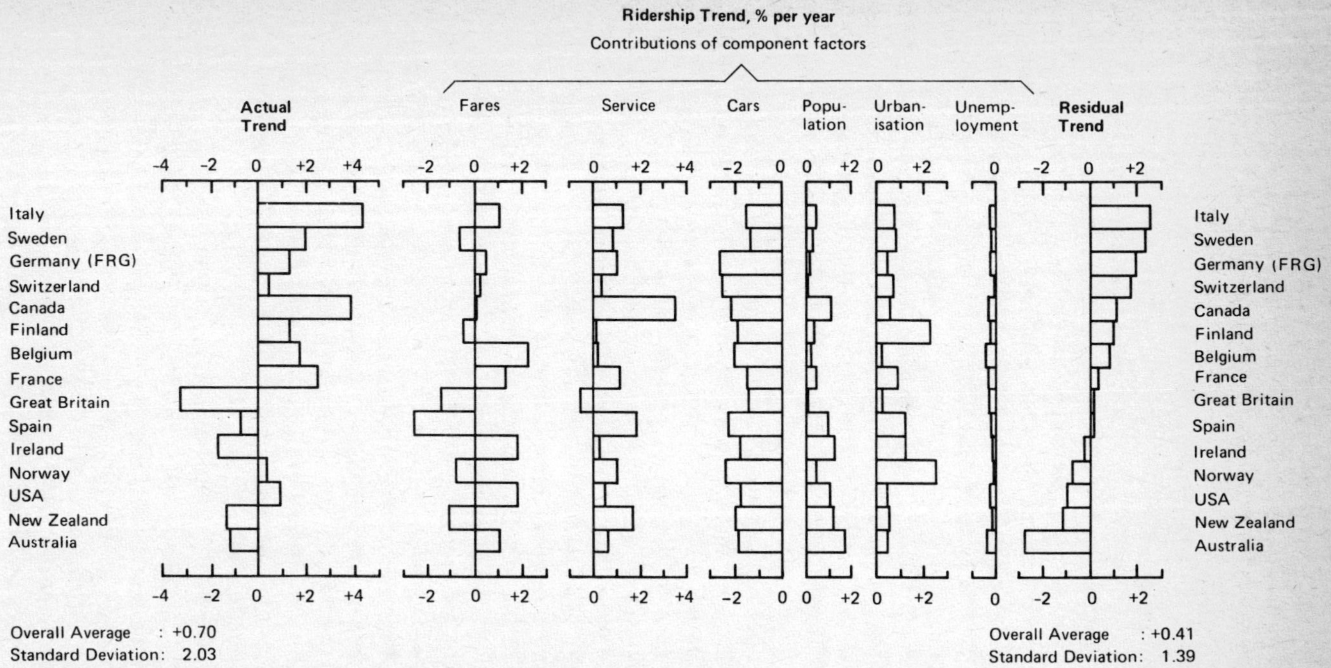

Figure 8.3 Estimated residual trends for national data (assuming fares elasticity of –0.45, vehicle-kilometeres elasticity of 0.45)

in Italy is a result of the fast growth of its big cities: the urbanisation factor used in the analysis could reflect the continuing urbanisation of Italy only at a global level, and it cannot portray the extent to which growth may lie in the bigger cities, where public-transport use is high, rather than in the smaller towns, nor the extent to which the people moving into urban areas for the first time are likely to be poor, and non-car-owners, rather than relatively affluent. Switzerland and Finland might have favourable trends because geographical barriers (mountains and lakes, respectively) tend to channelise travel flows in a way which is convenient for public transport. The negative trends in Australia, New Zealand and the United States are probably connected with the extensive, very low-density suburban development and high car-ownership which is prevalent in those countries. Britain's suburban development is similar in form, but less extreme, and Britain does not show a large negative residual trend. Much suburbanisation in Britain took place before there was appreciable car-ownership, so that travel from the dispersed suburbs to work places and shops depended largely on public transport. The result was that by 1950 public transport use per head was very much higher in Britain than in the rest of Europe; since then mass car-ownership has caused a sharply downward trend, though absolute levels of use are still slightly higher than in the rest of Europe (Webster *et al.* 1984).

Sweden's positive trend might be thought to be associated with urban planning which strongly encourages public transport (Stockholm's high density satellite towns with fast rail connections to the city centre), but in fact results from the national data are probably less reliable than those from the Swedish town data, which give Sweden a negative residual trend overall. Nevertheless, it is possible that the upward trends in the Federal Republic of Germany and Canada are connected with urban planning, and the emphasis on strong city centres fed by high-quality rail systems. Even so, the question remains whether policies and plans which are successful in attracting more people to public transport are genuinely providing a system which can compete with the private car, or whether the extra passengers tend to be those without a car who might otherwise have walked to a closer destination.

The study which TRRL carried out for ECMT paid special attention to the effect of car-ownership on public transport use. The study collected household survey data covering a total of 83 surveys in 61 towns in eight countries. In many cases the data available did not provide everything necessary for analysis, and in many more the data were so incompatible that no reliable comparisons could be made of travel behaviour in different countries. There was, however, a substantial number of surveys in Britain and France which could be compared. One particularly interesting result of this comparison is shown in Figure 8.4, where public transport use by people in households owning no car is compared with that by households owning one car. Naturally, car-owning households make less use of public transport than households which do not have a car, but the surprising aspect of Figure 8.4 is that the relationship is linear across a very wide range of public transport use (generally from high use in big cities, especially in Britain, to low levels in smaller towns) and the relationship applies equally well to both Britain and France. Thus it seems that when a household acquires a car, its use of public transport (per household member) is reduced by about 40 per cent, regardless of whether the household is in an area where public transport use is high (that is, where, presumably, public transport services are good) or an area where it is low (with poor public transport), and whether the household in question is in a French city or a British city. Similarly, households with two or more cars make only 70 per cent of the public transport trips per head made by households with one car, in a relationship which is also stable across a wide range of public transport use, and in both Britain and France. Data from other countries were more sporadic, but on the whole they were consistent with the same interpretation, suggesting that increasing car-ownership will have much the same relative effect in reducing the demand for public transport whether the services provided are good or bad, and whether the towns are dispersed or compact.

Finally, the analysis of the public transport trends described earlier found that there was no statistical relationship between either the level of subsidy paid, or the rate of growth of subsidy, and the residual passenger trend. Thus although subsidy undoubtedly can increase patronage by providing lower fares and better service, there is no evidence here that, once the effects of fares and service have been taken into account, high levels of subsidy have any deeper or more permanent effect. It is still possible, of course, that some countries have a favourable residual trend because of transport (or planning) policies other than subsidy.

5. Implications for planning

The studies and evidence discussed in the previous sections have considered only the very broad trends in transport and urban development. They can say nothing about the effects of planning policies operating at a detailed level. Nevertheless, they suggest that certain global mechanisms are having a profound effect on mobility. The

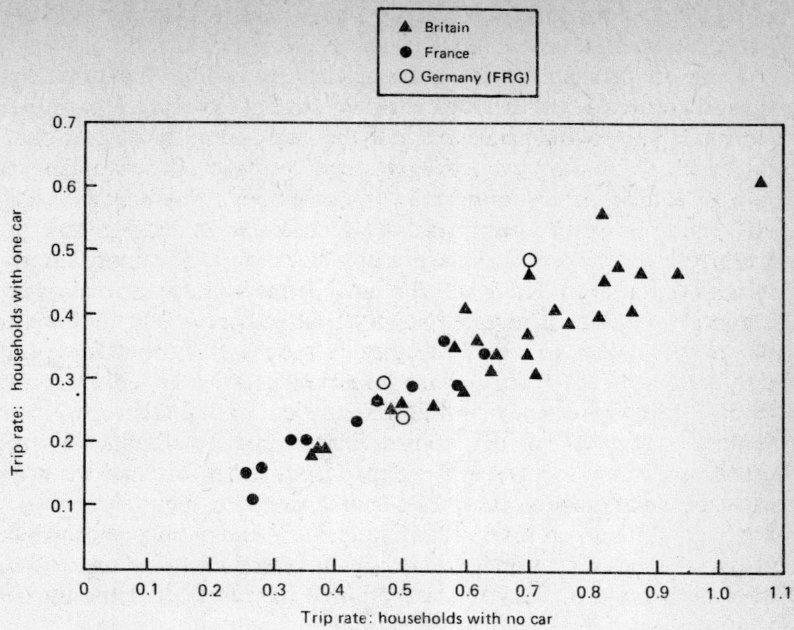

Figure 8.4 Comparison of trip rates for bus and tram between households with and without cars

moral for the planner is that, unless a realistic view is taken of the extent to which such trends can be modified, policies may well fail and resources be wasted. This is especially true where capital investment in infrastructure is involved, since the time-scale is so long that the population and activity pattern of the planned area will certainly change appreciably during its lifetime.

Growing car-ownership will continue to increase the mobility gap between the haves and the have-nots, not simply in the sense that those who have the car, and who are obviously more mobile, will increase in number, but also because those who do not will find that the pattern of desirable destinations becomes increasingly more difficult to access by public transport. Moreover, unless the authorities are willing and able to provide continually increasing subsidies, public transport services are likely to become more expensive as costs increase. Ultimately services seem likely to decline even in those countries where continuing urbanisation is presently boosting their use, because eventually urbanisation will saturate and probably reverse, and even compact towns will see densities falling to the point where public transport is more difficult to sustain, though more necessary than ever for those without a car.

These are problems the planners will have to address. When viewing the difficulties caused by rising car-ownership, there is a temptation to feel that things would be simpler if the clock could be turned back. Given the value those who have it attach to the car this is unlikely to be a defensible proposition, but in any case even if this were a socially optimal solution it would be one which tends to disadvantage the majority for the sake of a (presumably) larger advantage to the minority. True enough, those who have permanent access to a car are a minority (though the United States has already reached a state where the ratio of cars to people is greater than a half), but for many purposes members of car-owning households have a vested interest in the car, whether they have full-time access to it or not: the worst inconveniences of their car-determined lifestyle are ameliorated by the possibility of being given a lift in the family car if their need is great enough. Consequently, schemes aimed at discouraging the private car are likely to be faced with a lot of opposition, and many people will be prepared to go to considerable lengths to avoid whatever restrictions have been applied, because for them the alternative to using the car will be second best by a large margin.

This is not to argue that the car cannot be controlled. In some areas it undoubtedly causes problems which are sufficiently serious for its restraint, or even prohibition, to be beneficial in spite of the inconvenience to its users. For example, modelling by Lynam (1984) and Oldfield (1979) of the effects of imposing charges on private traffic in central London suggested that the policy could raise average road speeds so much that even car users who transferred to public transport would have a door-to-door speed that was higher than prior to restraint. However, the results of restraint are likely to be unpredictable if a large proportion of travellers is affected. The unexpected response may simply reduce the efficacy of the policy. For example, Bailey and Layzell (1982) studied the effect of parking controls in central Oxford which reduced the amount of free public parking by 60 per cent. Over a ten-year period across the introduction of these restrictions, the amount of free private parking (often on land not intentionally provided for this purpose) increased 30-fold, almost exactly compensating for the loss of public parking. Of course, car-ownership had increased over the period, so that even the constancy of parking spaces implied a relative increase in restraint, but the response certainly weakened the measure.

A more serious worry with restraint is that the longer-term effects may actually run counter to the intention of the policy. If restraint is imposed by pricing (parking, area licensing or road pricing) then a high enough price will reduce congestion to whatever level is desired. However, the result is not merely a shift from car to other modes, but restraint will also persuade some car users to go elsewhere. This may be unimportant if the restrained area is a very powerful magnet for jobs, shops and services, and the car already plays a fairly minor role in travel to the area, as in the centres of major cities such as London. But for areas which are inherently less attractive destinations, restraint might drive people away to such an extent that employment, shopping and other facilities decline markedly: certainly, traffic conditions will have been eased considerably but the users of public transport may be left with a much less attractive set of destinations, and although their transport services will be able to run faster, service levels may have to be cut because fewer people are visiting the city centre. Of course, such an unwelcome result depends on the existence of nearby destinations which are almost as attractive as the restrained area. But even if this is not the case in the short term, it is still possible that in the longer term restraint might encourage development of alternative centres.

Indeed, the attractiveness of city centres holds the key to the future health of public transport. Residential dispersion and lower densities will make public transport less convenient and/or more expensive, but if the central area remains a powerful attractor then public transport will remain an important feeder to it. If, on the other hand, city centres lose many of their facilities so that not only the residential origins but also the employment and service destinations become dispersed, fixed route public transport will be severely undermined. New types of transport may then prove more effective, and in some areas deregulation may encourage this (see the contributions of Bauchet and Masset (Chapter 19) and Fanara (Chapter 20) in this volume), but it is difficult to imagine that they will be able to provide a very high level of service at low cost while labour remains such a large component of transport costs. It may be necessary to encourage those who need transport services to concentrate together in some way, so that they can be served more easily. Attention might be paid to making moving house as easy as possible so that people are freer to choose the locations which best suit them, though collecting together particular types of people carries the danger that undesirable social segregations might be reinforced. The housing developments which will cater for the low-density, smaller-town style of living could, with careful design, make some form of public transport provision both cheaper to operate and easier to access than has been the case with most of the new developments in the past (Potter 1984). It would be unrealistic to believe that such measures will go very far towards solving the underlying problems, but they could make a very worthwhile contribution. The suggestion that provision of adequate local facilities could make longer-distance travel unnecessary might also be considered, not because it would actually reduce travel (or save energy, a favourite preoccupation of many proponents), but rather because it might provide an adequate, if limited, set of services for those who do not have access to mechanised travel. The people who have the greater mobility will still prefer to travel longer distances for both work and shopping, because of the greater choice that it gives them, as studies of travel budgets have shown (see, for example, Goodwin 1978).

6. Conclusion

It is inevitable that a discussion of the gap between what transport planners would like to achieve and what can actually be done will sound rather negative. This paper is certainly not intended to be a criticism of planners. Anyone who has to predict human behaviour and then to marshall it into some unifying framework is deserving of sympathy rather than censure, and the tendency to consider one limited aspect at a time, and to concentrate on the short-term response, is quite understandable. But the complexity of the entire system of activity patterns and travel habits means that changes in one item may eventually affect many others, and the secondary and longer-term results may ultimately sum to a more important conclusion than the planned short-term effects. It is true that many of these indirect mechanisms are uncertain and cannot be predicted at all reliably, but they should not be ignored simply because they are unknown. Hopefully, urban modelling will eventually be able to represent realistically the two-way link between transport provision and land-use patterns (see Wegener's paper (Chapter 14) in this volume). Such work is still at a fairly early stage of development, though the International Study Group on Land Use Transport Interaction is trying to compare the behaviour and predictions of a number of the interactive spatial models which have been constructed by researchers around the world (Bly and Webster 1984). But until the longer-term effects can be reliably quantified, it is important that planners at least consider to what extent they might conceivably modify the intended result, and as far as possible adopt policies which can cope with these uncertainties. It is also important that planners take a realistic view of how towns will look in the future, for there is little point in providing long-lived and expensive transport systems (whether they be more roads for private traffic, or rail networks for public transport) which become superfluous because of future changes in the structure of the town. It is essential to determine what sorts of activity, and how much, will remain in the city centres of the future, and to estimate the future distributions and densities of population, with special emphasis on people without access to the car. Planners can then consider what sort of public transport it will be possible to provide within the financial constraints, and to what extent land-use and town planning might improve the access of the transport-deprived to a basic range of activities. The needs-related planning discussed by Reichman and Salomon (Chapter 11) in this volume is likely to become increasingly important.

There is a natural reluctance to accept change, and the social and business activity at the heart of many cities is undoubtedly a valuable ingredient of their inhabitants' lives. Yet it seems clear that the largest cities will eventually lose population, and that people will live at increasingly lower densities. This is not to suggest that all cities in all countries are necessarily converging towards an identical end point: cultural differences will continue to dictate differences in structure and density, but the overall direction of change is clearly similar in all the countries studied, and it is bound to affect the form, and probably the amount, of central area activity. Cities built on heavy industry have been facing the problems of inner-city decline for decades. The solutions lie for the most part outside the transport field, but they will not be achieved without an acceptance that some decline in population and employment is inevitable and that there is therefore no point in trying to rebuild the city as it used to be. Similarly, in tackling transport problems there is no point in trying to turn back the rising tide of car-ownership because, however detrimental it may be to the highly concentrated city, that and more space to live in are what most people want. Even in the most severely environmentally and energy-conscious future, some form of motorised personal transport will surely exist, maintaining the impetus towards a more dispersed way of living. If this transition is inevitable, then planners can ensure that it takes place as smoothly as possible so that city centres, and their attendant transport systems, can adapt rather than decay.

References

Bailey, J.M. and A.D. Layzell (1982). 'Travel Behaviour and Traffic Restraint: A Study of Households in Oxford'. Department of Transport, Department of the Environment, TRRL Report SR 734. Crowthorne, Berks: Transport and Road Research Laboratory.

Berry, B.J.L., ed. (1977). *Urbanization and Counterurbanization.* London: Sage.

Best, R.H. (1981). *Land Use and Living Space*. London: Methuen.

Bly, P.H. (1985). 'Effect of the Recession on Travel Expenditure and Travel Patterns' in

G.R.M. Jansen, P. Nijkamp and C.J. Ruijgrok, eds, *Transportation and Mobility in an Era of Transition*. Amsterdam: North Holland Publishing Co., pp. 15–36.

Bly, P.H. and R.H. Oldfield (1984). 'Where Are Public Transport Subsidies Going?', *Proceedings of the International Conference on Financing Urban Transportation*. Lyon: Laboratoire d'Economie des Transports, September.

Bly, P.H. and F.V. Webster (1984). 'Land Use/Transport Models: How Effective Are They,,' *Ekistics*, **51** (305), 147.

Buchanan, C. (Chairman) (1963). *Traffic in Towns*. Report of the Working Group on Traffic in Urban Areas. London: HMSO.

Bussière, R. and T. Stovall (1975). *Systèmes evolutifs urbains et regionaux à l'état d'equilibre*. Paris: Centre de Recherche et de Rencontres d'Urbanisme.

Dasgupta, M. (1983). *Employment and Work Travel in an Inner Area Context*. Department of the Environment, Department of Transport, TRRL Report SR 780. Crowthorne, Berks: Transport and Road Research Laboratory.

Drewett, R. (1983). 'Towards Reurbanization and Deconcentration: The Duality in European Urban Development Trends in the Decade to 1981'. Tenth Transportation Planning Research Colloquium, December, Zandvoort, Netherlands.

Ferguson, G.J.W.A. and M.J.H. Mogridge (1985). 'Is Car Ownership and Use Stagnating? Fuel Consumption Models and their Implications'. Tenth Transportation Planning Research Colloquium, December, Zandvoort, Netherlands.

Fothergill, S. and G. Gudgin (1983). *Unequal Growth: Urban and Regional Employment Change in the UK*. London: Heinemann.

Goodwin, P.B. (1978). 'Travel Choice and Time Budgets' in Hensher and Dalvi, eds, *Determinants of Travel Choice*. Farnborough: Saxon House.

Lynam, D.A. (1984). *Application of CRISTAL to Evaluate Changes in Travel Charges in London*. Department of the Environment, Department of Transport, TRRL Report SR 40. Crowthorne, Berks: Transport and Road Research Laboratory.

Oldfield, R.H. (1979). *Model for Estimating Effects of Fares, Traffic Restraint and Bus Priority in Central London*. Department of the Environment, Department of Transport, TRRL Report LR 749. Crowthorne, Berks: Transport and Road Research Laboratory.

Porter, J. (1979). *The Transition to Road Transport Fuels from Coal: A Preliminary Study*. Department of the Environment, Department of Transport, TRRL Report SR 519. Crowthorne, Berks: Transport and Road Research Laboratory.

Potter, S. (1984). 'The transport versus land use dilemma'. *Transportation Research Record*, 964. Washington, DC: Transportation Research Board.

Pushkarev, B.S. and J.M. Zupan (1977). *Public Transportation and Land Use Policy*. Bloomington, IN, and London: Indiana University Press.

Webster, F.V., P.H. Bly, R.H. Johnson, N. Paulley and M. Dasgupta (1984). *Changing Patterns of Travel*. Report to the European Conference of Ministers of Transport. Crowthorne, Berks: Transport and Road Research Laboratory.

9 Planning Criteria in the Provision of Public Transport Services

C.E. Norrbom

1. Introduction

1.1 Transport policy

The current guidelines for transport policy in Sweden were laid down by parliament and government in 1979 with the general aim of providing adequate transport facilities at minimum cost throughout the country. Emphasis is placed on creating conditions for the proper economic utilisation of transport and measures taken to promote this policy are based on socio-economic principles. A proper working of the transport services and an effective use of existing transport resources is regarded to be fundamental to a balanced development of industry and employment in different parts of the country.

The feasibility of maintaining free and effective competition varies for different sectors and modes of transport and in different parts of the country. Conditions in the transport market are such that pricing and running of public transport with the aim of covering total expenditure or cost does not automatically lead to a socio-economically desirable development and distribution of traffic. There is also an obvious risk that the allocation of resources to finance investments in the public transport system will be insufficient.

Thus, for social reasons, a certain supply of public transport is considered necessary. Traffic safety, environmental protection, resource conservation and land-use restrictions are other reasons for promoting public transport through community and state subsidies. It is also in accordance with the requirements of fair distribution and in order to ensure a basic standard of transport in different regions.

1.2 Organisation of public transport in Sweden

For reasons of planning and administration public transport is often classified as local, regional and interregional, depending on where and over what distances it is performed. Administration and operation also vary between these categories and between the various modes of transport.

Thus, regional traffic is run by 24 county transport corporations which are responsible for the local transport services as well. However, in densely populated areas a special operating unit often takes care of local transport.

The county boards for public transport were established between 1978 and 1983 after a decision taken by parliament in 1978. This was the starting point for better co-ordination of public transport. The areas within which a single transport co-ordinator can work became considerably larger than before.

Through this reorganisation, responsibility for planning, operating and financing local and regional public transport has accrued to the county councils and local authorities. The county transport boards can in their turn either call in State-owned, municipal or private transport companies as contractors or operate the services themselves.

The State takes considerable responsibility for interregional traffic. As almost the whole infrastructure is State-owned this traffic can be influenced by the State. Subsidies for operation are, however, only given to some unprofitable railway lines and to the ferry service to the island of Gotland. Apart from these exceptions all interregional traffic is run on a commercial basis and operated by either private or State-owned companies. Figure 9.1 illustrates the relation between the different markets and the public transport share of each of them.

2. Transport developments

2.1 Historical background

Before the county transport corporations were formed, the communities — in Sweden about 280 — together with both private and State transport companies had responsibility for public transport. Traffic was to be maintained on a commercial basis and this led to a considerable decrease in public supply from the 1950s onwards, when private motoring started to grow and the urbanisation wave became very intense in Sweden.

This went on with a few exceptions — cases where the community started to subsidise transport — until the beginning of the 1970s when a State bus subsidy system was introduced for regional traffic. Transport planning was, however, still in many hands as several traffic companies provided transport services.

Towns with more than approximately 20,000 inhabitants were

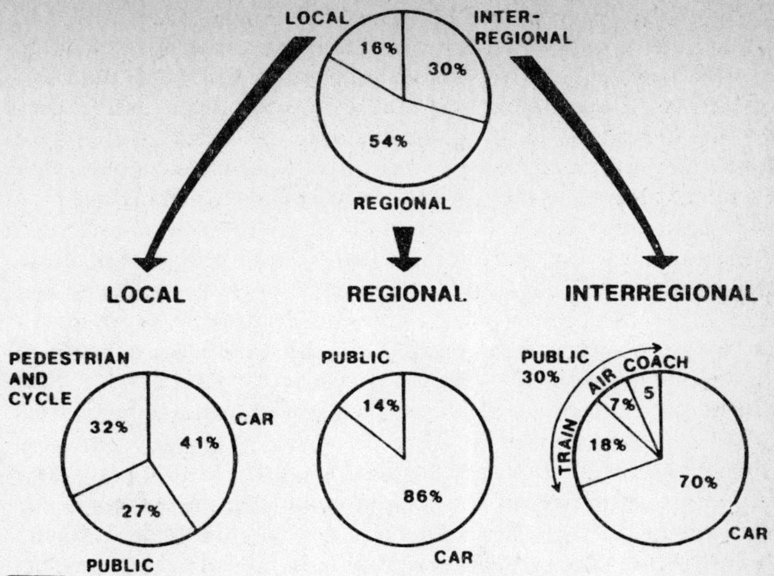

Figure 9.1 Total transport mileage, different markets

responsible for local traffic, which was also carried out by private traffic companies on a commercial basis. This traffic became unprofitable during the 1960s, but most towns started to subsidise it out of their own funds.

The trend of decreasing public transport supply was broken when the 24 county transport corporations were formed. In this context it is also interesting to note the development of various kinds of travelling. Far and away the highest rate of increase is shown by journeys to work. While total transport mileage has increased by 20 per cent, transport mileage for journeys to work has increased by more than 50 per cent.

2.2 Local transport

Since the beginning of the 1980s local public travelling has increased by 5 per cent. This modest growth is partly due to the fact that local transport was already extensive before the county transport corporations were formed. Another explanation is that the possibilities of overall planning, including of dwelling places, services and workplaces as well as of transport, were increased when the responsibility for planning was placed on one and the same county authority.

2.3 Regional transport

Regional public transport showed a tremendous development in the early 1980s, primarily as a result of the reform of the county transport corporations. Thus, regional bus traffic rose by 50 per cent between 1980 and 1983. Some reasons for this were the improved supply of public transport, mainly due to more or less systematic concentration on services adapted to the needs of the work-force. In many cases the provision of information to the public, in the form of co-ordinated timetables, and so on, was improved. School transport was scheduled and opened to the general public. Fare tariffs were co-ordinated and standard monthly season tickets were introduced which were invariably cheaper than previous fares, partly because of the introduction of subsidies. Apart from this, the rising cost of car journeys at a time when household incomes stagnated contributed to the attractiveness of public transport.

Regional train services have grown in importance, too, partly as a consequence of the expansion of the commuter train services in the three large urban areas, Stockholm, Gothenburg and Malmö. Figure 9.2 illustrates the above-mentioned local and regional public transport development.

In connection with the establishment of the country transport corporations more or less thorough investigations were made in different counties. The county transport corporation in *Uppsala*, for instance,

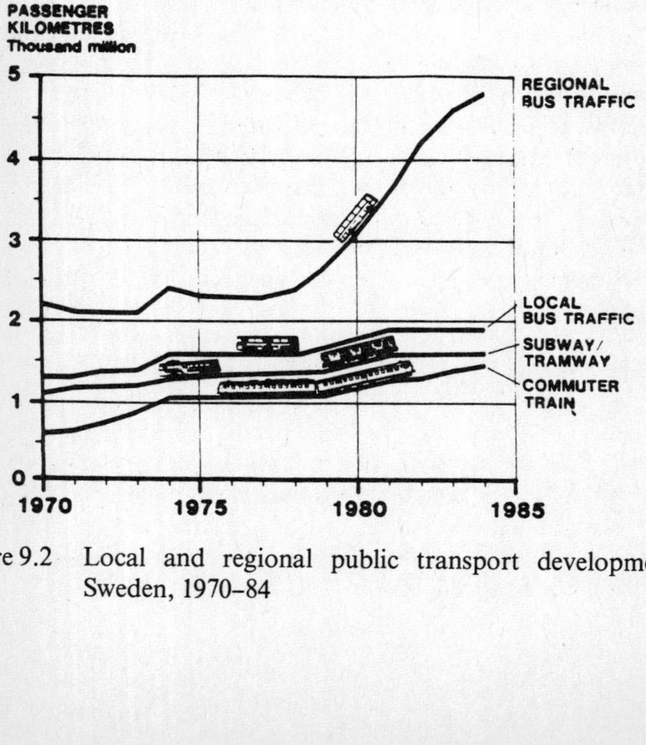

Figure 9.2 Local and regional public transport development in Sweden, 1970–84

paid much attention to building up a transport system that would suit the work-force and also on making it easier for those who lived in areas with poor transportation opportunities to use public transport in order to reach the places where the work-force was needed.

By analysing official statistics and making complementary investigations (for example, questionnaires were sent to all companies with more than ten employees so as to examine their employees' travelling needs, starting and finishing times of the working day, and so on), new routes were planned in accordance with the material gathered.

After these changes had been carried through — which resulted in a doubling of public transport supply — a 200 per cent increase in the number of passengers was reached. Public commuter travelling increased from about 17 per cent to almost 40 per cent. The absolute number of commuters also rose considerably — about fourfold.

A great number of these were new commuters and more than 50 per cent were females. Consequently, improved public transport has had positive effects on the rate of employment in the Uppsala region. This is partly because people who had no suitable private transport could take a job and partly because the possibilities of accepting a job in another place were increased. It is also a fact that improved public transport especially favoured female employment.

Thus, a great deal of improvement has been carried out in recent years, but in spite of this there are still great differences between the supply in different counties and also the fare rates, etc.

2.4 Interregional transport

By the end of the 1970s interregional public transport — civil aviation and long-distance rail journeys in particular — underwent a period of growth. This was partly due to changes in fare determination — low-price fares — and improved services and supply of transport.

Aviation still continues to expand. Rail traffic, however, has been stagnating since the early 1980s. A greater differentiation with regard to both fares and services is therefore promoted. A basic supply of inter-city trains with frequent departures on the main routes is being completed with special trains for business people. Older rolling stock is being used for special low-fare journeys at weekends. Charter trains for travel agents are also being promoted.

Figure 9.3 shows the market shares for interregional journeys of different distances. The market shares vary depending on the availability of transport modes and fares, quality, etc. Naturally railway and air transport increase their market shares with increasing distances, while private car transport decreases and bus transport is the most common alternative in average-length journeys.

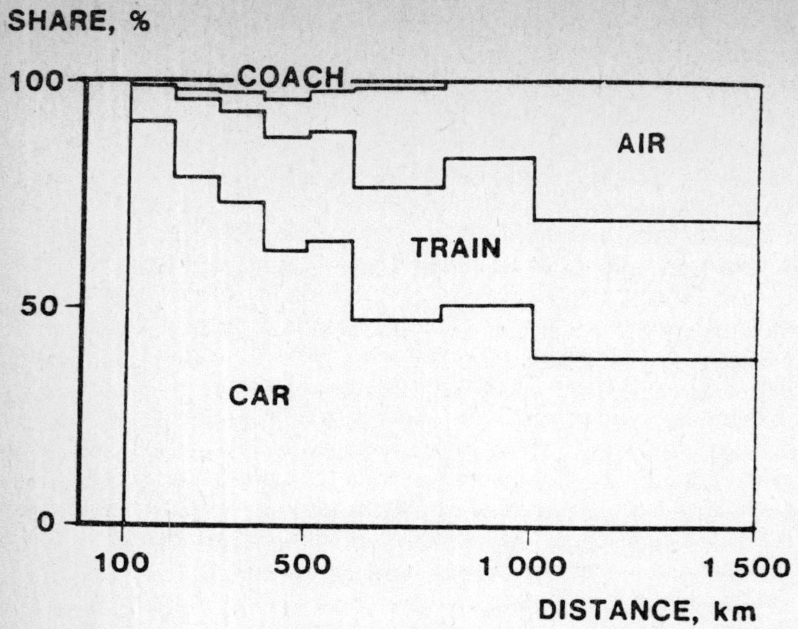

Figure 9.3 Interregional passenger transport — market shares by distance

2.5 Future trends

In the future, total transport mileage is expected to grow, although at a slower rate than up to now. This is mainly due to slower economic growth in consumption and a considerably lower rate of house-building. The continued growth of public transport is foreseen, although no reduction in private motoring is expected. Regional public transport will probably continue to rise but more slowly than at the beginning of the 1980s. Expansion is expected in long-distance aviation and rail transport as well.

Radical changes in rail travel are expected to occur when travelling time is drastically reduced by the introduction of new fast trains. As the number of passengers in Sweden is insufficient to justify the building of completely new lines, the Swedish company, ASEA, and the State railway company are developing a train with an active 'tilting' system. Some prototypes are expected to go into service by the end of the 1980s and they will be introduced on a large scale in the 1990s.

Although private motoring is by far the most used mode of transport the disadvantages become more obvious the more intense traffic grows. These problems are especially serious in densely populated areas. The problems of noise, pollution, energy consumption and traffic accidents cannot be neglected. In this context, public transport plays an important role. Another aspect is that even though car density is quite high there are still many people who have no car and for this group public transport is the only alternative and therefore a necessity.

3. Planning criteria in improving public transport

Measures taken to improve the attractiveness of public transport are therefore very important. In Sweden we try to work according to the following guidelines in planning for a better public transport system.

It is important to *tailor* transport services to people's needs. As in the Uppsala example, it is necessary to carry out surveys in order to determine the most effective route network. Traffic supply has to be adapted to various requirements during different periods and for different travelling purposes. In accordance with recent developments, which show that it is possible to increase the number of journeys to work undertaken by public transport, it is still more urgent to improve transport services for this category of people.

The transport element also has to be placed within the wider context of *social planning*. In order to plan for the most effective route network it is also necessary to identify people's travelling patterns and the level of public transport demanded between living areas, work-places, service centres and recreation areas. The local authorities therefore need to be involved in the allocation of all locally based resources both between sectors (shops, health, schools, industry) and within the transport sector. As an expensive transport supply to, for instance, suburban areas with a dispersed land-use pattern is very extensive, a more systematic and explicit co-ordinaton between transport planning and land-use planning is of great importance.

A *mutual understanding* between different sectors of planning is, however, of great importance at every planning level. In accordance with the kind of transport provision undertaken, not only local authorities and various private and voluntary organisations, but also regional and national authorities have to be involved. At the national level, for instance, it is important to balance different investments in highways, railways, tunnels and air traffic against each other, so that parallel systems, for which the number of travellers will never be sufficient, are avoided. The same criteria can of course be applied for each level of planning.

Priority for public transport. In order to improve the attractiveness of public transport especially in densely populated areas signal priority is introduced and separate lanes are reserved for buses and taxis — at least during peak hours. Certain areas have also been subject to traffic clearance, the result of which is that some streets have been closed to private motoring.

In sparsely populated areas where a regular public bus service is too expensive *special arrangements* are made, for example, complementary taxi services connected to the scheduled bus service, co-ordinated passenger and freight service, and so on. In some areas projects in which a village association is responsible on a voluntary basis for the operation of feeder traffic are carried out.

Improved accessibility. This means that much work is expended on planning routes, timetables and frequency in accordance with people's needs for transport between residential areas, work-places and service centres. Continuous follow-ups in order to make the route network more effective in existing built-up areas are also of vital importance.

Improved comfort. It is important to design bus stops, terminals, waiting rooms, and so on, in such a way that people don't mind waiting for a few minutes. Great attention also has to be paid to travelling comfort not only with regard to seats but also to the design within the vehicles.

Improved information. Much attention is paid to facilitating information in the form of, for instance, easily readable and co-ordinated timetables. The areas within which modern electronic technology is used are continuously extended. Thus, various projects are carried out in order to facilitate not only traffic operation but also traffic information to the public concerning timetables, choice of routes, signs, and so on. Information is broadcast daily on local radio stations about the prevailing situation of the public transport system.

Better co-ordination between various means of transport and transportation tasks. As short a time as possible should be used on walking to bus stops, on travelling and on waiting when making a connection with another route or mode of transport. Co-ordination between public transport within urban areas and public transport which serves routes to and from the cities can be improved in many cases.

Changed tax policy. The principles for peak-load pricing in certain areas and for special groups are under investigation. Practical tests will be carried out in one county in the near future. Projects for the standardisation of fares for journeys that are made across county borders are also being carried out.

Technical improvements. Promotion of better solutions from an energy saving point of view, and the development of alternative fuels and engines will lead to reduced pollution and lower running costs.

Far-reaching automation. Studies have shown that it has not been possible to raise production per employee in public transport at the same rate as in society as a whole. Therefore efforts are being made to promote less personnel and more capital-intensive systems and automation in ticket-handling, for instance.

Development of new transport systems. New systems for urban traffic are tested continuously in co-operation with local and regional organisations, private bus constructors and bus companies. They deal with various forms of public commuting, commuter traffic with only a few stops during peak hours, co-ordinated planning and operation of different public modes of transport, dial-a-bus, the establishment of computer-based order–operation–information centres, etc.

It is also important not to forget the transport needs of those who are *disabled.* Directives for the construction of transport carriers are under continuous discussion and are being set up in agreement with the designers and constructors. A special travel service with both State and municipal subsidies is also provided for people who have difficulties in using the public transport system. This service is run by the local authorities although a national transport service exists for inter-regional travel. The passenger pays on average only 20 per cent of the operating cost.

4. Planning trends

However, the financial side of public transport services with high frequency and comfort is problematic. The need for subsidies has grown tremendously during the 1980s with the extension of public transport in Sweden. Today the national average subsidy for local and regional transport is 59 per cent of operating costs.

Therefore we have to search for solutions to these problems. It is not an easy task. We think, however, that it is at least partly a question of more integrated planning between different sectors of society. There is an obvious connection between the situation of residential areas, work-places, shopping centres and leisure activities.

It is also a question of finding other transportation principles, new transport systems, co-operation and co-ordination between different transport companies and modes of transport. In a country like Sweden, which is sparsely populated and where people have long distances to travel, we cannot afford to have parallel systems: different modes of transport have to be complementary to each other.

However, what we are still lacking is detailed information about people's travelling needs and patterns. Therefore we try to work as closely as possible with the transport research institutions both within the country and internationally. Presently, we are working on a comprehensive forecast of the development of public transport to the year 2000. At the same time as theoretical studies are being made, we also consider it very important to apply different ideas to real-life situations. This means that to a great extent we are involved in and promote different projects in order to bring about improved public transport.

Today there is also a growing tendency to look at public transport more from a socio-economic than from a commercial point of view, as previously. At the same time as an economic view of public transport has grown the systems of planning have become better. It is important to find new methods for measuring the benefits as the degree of market financing decreases. As regards public traffic the most explicit planning systems are developed for local transport — for which the degree of subsidy is also the highest. The development of better systems for the planning of regional transport has also made progress. Recently the government has taken steps to find a comprehensive cost–benefit analysis that can be applicable to comparisons between different modes of interregional transport. A growing interest in finding new sources of income can also be traced. Attention is being focused on special employers' contributions, site charges, traffic licences and other forms of street prices.

All this means that transport planning has to become an integrated part of the planning in other sectors of society to a greater extent than before. Today public transport is also looked upon as part of social services and as a means of implementing dwelling policy and regional policy within an area.

References

Länsstyrelsen i Uppsala län (1983). *Kollektivtrafik och arbetsmarknad i Uppsala län 1975–1981*. Uppsala.

Regeringens proposition 1977/78:92 (1978). *Om åtgärder för att förbättra lokal och regional kollektiv persontrafik*. Stockholm.

Swedish Transport Research Board (1985). 'Swedish Local and Regional Public Transport in 10–20 years' in *Economic Prerequisites and Financing Methods*. Stockholm.

The Swedish Board of Transport (1983). *Directions for Providing Facilities for the Disabled on Public Transport Vehicles*. Stockholm.

The Swedish Board of Transport (1984). 'Economy of Public Transport'. Paper presented at the United Nations Economic Commission for Europe Seminar on the City and its Transportation in Moscow, October.

The Swedish Board of Transport (1985). *Transport in Sweden — Summary in English*. Report no. 1985:3. Stockholm.

The Swedish Institute (1985). *Transport Policy and Traffic Trends in Sweden*. Stockholm.

10 Public Transport Planning between Fictions and Frictions

A.A.I. Holtgrefe

1. Public transport at risk

Literature on public transport is becoming rather negative. It seems to me that many authors are tending to lose courage about the future of public transport. The reasons for this almost world-wide pessimism differ greatly from country to country.

A major cause is the deteriorating financial situation of many subsidised public transport companies, which, in combination with the budgetary problems of many governments, tends to bring about a reconsideration of the need to spend great amounts of money in this sector. Gwilliam (1984) puts a series of question marks over the traditional strongholds in defence of public transport subsidies. His main conclusion is that none of the major categories of market failure, such as monopolistic markets, road congestion, the existence of externalities and decreasing cost industries, implies subsidisation of public transport as the second-best solution. The conclusions of his study support and strengthen the tendency of several European governments to raise fares and to cut the level of service of public transport. Subsidies may result in more staff and higher unit costs (Webster 1984) or will, especially when cross-elasticities between the use of the car and of public transport are low, go to those people who are actually using the system (Gwilliam 1984).

Countries where public transport is considered as a necessary element of economic development face a huge problem in raising funds for their investment plans. Two examples are India (Singh 1985) and Portugal (Cobeira 1985). The latter country is trying to develop and reconstruct the Portuguese railways to achieve a network comparable to those of other European countries.

During the early 1970s, the Spanish railways (RENFE) tried to reduce marginal costs through considerable investments improving the capacity of equipment and manpower. This investment programme was based on the assumption that the demand for passenger transport by rail would increase in the next years. The present situation is considered to be worse than it was 15 years ago (Vázquez Cábezas 1982). The demand forecast levels have not been fulfilled, nor have marginal costs declined. Demographic and spatial development also contributed to the bad performance of RENFE: 'the Spanish railway network, both by its pattern and by its characteristics, fails to match accurately the majority of the trends in the pattern to industrial and urban development'.

Even geographic circumstances can encourage pessimism, as in the situation of Denmark (Andresen 1982). The author states that 'Denmark is and will remain a country which lacks the conditions for a rational and modern railway operation'. He is referring to the eccentric position of Copenhagen, the scarcely populated mainland and the many islands.

Inconsistency in objectives and short-sightedness on the part of governing authorities is another reason for pessimism about the future of public transport. London Transport have shown dramatic changes in levels of fares, in the structure of fares and in the levels of services in 1980, 1981 and 1982 (Cameron 1982). Within a period of six months considerable and dramatic reductions in fares and an increase in the level of service were followed by a doubling of fares and a reduction in services. Public transport planning becomes impossible when it is treated like a yoyo. Another example of a stop-and-go fare policy is the Dutch situation during the 1980s (Holtgrefe 1983). Fare increases with the objective of getting additional revenue did not bring in the expected results because price-elasticity appeared to be high. Recently, on 1 April 1985, a reduction in fares on the Netherlands railways was introduced.

Another source of gloom is the dangerous situation of regional bus transport in many European countries (Glassborow 1982). Governments are generally more concerned about keeping urban transport and railways in existence than about conserving regional transport.

The low and barely increasing productivity of public transport is also fruitful soil for negative or defensive reports. The International Union of Railways (UIC) presents an annual comparison of the performance of a series of European railways. British Rail, showing a relatively poor performance in the UIC statistics, tried to shade this negative picture by means of a thorough and detailed analysis (Gwilliam *et al.* 1980). A recent study of the financial situation of the national Belgian railways (NMBS/SNCB) uncovers the fundamental reasons for its very poor performance (Sobemap 1984). The Belgian situation clearly shows that a mixture of objectives, a majority of which have nothing to do with railways or transport policy in general, can destroy the industrial characteristics of a railway company. In this case sound managerial objectives are subordinated to employment policy and to a policy of maintaining a strict balance with regard to the two main parts of the country, Flanders and Wallonia. The employment policy results in an enormous surplus of staff (20,000 employees), and the balance policy leads to double- and over-investment.

This short survey of bad news about public transport in the 1980s, though far from complete, shows that there is a lot of friction menacing the future of public transport. The examples in this section even indicate that continuity of public transport is not as self-evident as it seems.

2. Friction suffocating public transport

2.1 The absence of a thorough measurement of social value

The negative financial results of public transport companies are clear but their positive effects on society cannot be translated into equally measurable benefits. This absence of a yardstick is a real danger to the future of public transport. Politicians are freely allowed to cut the level of service or to increase fare levels with the irrefutable argument that public transport is important to society, but not at any cost. There are cost-benefit studies on specific projects like new railway lines, and it is also possible to calculate the cost and benefits of marginal changes in the transport system (Beesley *et al.* 1983). Nevertheless, the question of the integral value of the complete public transport system remains unanswered. This question is of paramount importance, because expecting break-even financial results in public transport, as some governments contemplate, is almost equal to demanding the closure of the complete network (see also Section 3.2). The solution to financial problems cannot be found in closing unprofitable lines. The weak lines in rural areas support the main lines of the network. Closure of those rural lines means a truncation of the whole network. Moreover, the financial results of public transport in congested areas are worse than elsewhere, in spite of the intensive use of public transport in those areas.

2.2 Stable productivity ratios

The performance of a public transport company can be measured by a short list of productivity ratios. Three types can be distinguished (Sobemap 1984):

- technical productivity, which measures the production (train-, or bus- or seat-kilometres) per unit of a production factor (labour, rolling stock, infrastructure);
- commercial productivity, measuring the sales volume (passengers or passenger-kilometres) per unit of a production factor; and
- economic productivity, which compares revenue to cost.

According to the UIC statistics, the technical and commercial productivity of railways is, on average, still at the same level as it was ten years ago. Economic productivity has declined in almost all cases. This unfavourable situation will continue unless the railways succeed in increasing technical and commercial productivity at a rate equal to the increase of real national income. Otherwise, the rise in the prices of production factors will not be compensated (Nash 1982). The enormous differences between the production ratios in various countries suggest that improvements are possible in many cases. Figures about urban and regional public transport show the same phenomenon of stable productivity ratios. Even in a rather positive situation with increasing technical productivity, as in the area of Hanover, the cost average declined during the past ten years (Pällmann 1982).

2.3 The use of the private car and public transport

The relationships between the use of the private car and public transport are more complicated than those between other competitive products. The startling growth in the ownership and use of cars during the past decades mainly generated new mobility but also meant stagnation in the use of public transport. The decreasing spiral starts with the decisions of some people to use the car instead of public transport because the generalised costs (a weighted combination of price, time and comfort) of the private car are considered to be lower than those of public transport. These decisions and the autonomous increase in car mobility affect the quality of the public transport system in two ways. First, the level of service of public transport is adapted downwards in order to keep supply and demand in balance. Second, the congestion on the roads also affects the road-using part of public transport, which means a further decline in its quality and an increase in its operating cost (owing to the additional vehicle cycle time). Then, other people decide to change their modal choice in favour of the car, resulting in a further deterioration in the quality of public transport.

A striking result of this really suffocating demand and supply competition between the modes is the average speed of buses and trams without free lanes in congested areas. Many cities offer a mere 10 kilometres per hour public transport system, amounting to an expensive jog (Mogridge 1984).

To many people the initial situation of being without a private car is better than the final situation of congestion for all modes of transport. The result of the individual optimisations of modal choice is in many cases a lower average travel speed than before. This tension between individual choice and social benefit is symptomatic of the transport sector. If individuals are left free to decide on their travel modes, public transport becomes the victim of this 'prisoner's dilemma'.

2.4 State regulations and boundary conditions

The financial results of public transport companies are by no means indications of their managerial level of performance. Many government regulations limit the commercial sector of those companies (except for the case of some private American railways which are not submitted to public service obligations). Many companies have no freedom in fares and have no right to offer a commercially based level of service. Instead, they have to operate unprofitable activities. In some cases public transport is used as an instrument in employment policy (as in Belgium). Wages and working conditions are prescribed. And so are the factories where the rolling stock has to be bought. There are safety regulations and anti-pollution regulations. Investments, sometimes even of small amounts (typewriters!), have to be approved by the governing authorities. In some countries public transport suffers the constant reshuffling of top management posts whenever there are swings in the political situation (Vázquez Cábezas 1982). The result is that the managerial capacity of public transport companies is suffocated by an overwhelming number of regulations.

An attempt was made to split up the financial result of the federal German railways (DB) and of the national French railways (SNCF) into a purely commercial sector without specific State regulations, a social sector with governmental, regional or local regulations and an infrastructural sector (Estival 1985). The commercial sector shows a positive financial result in this analysis.

2.5 Delay of investments in infrastructure

Investments in public transport infrastructure do not keep pace with spatial developments. Many new cities have been built with the intention of connecting them to the public transport network. Unfortunately, administrative and financial problems have generally caused such delays that the population of the new cities was already accustomed to the use of the private car.

Bottle-necks in the capacity of existing networks are not removed owing to the operating results of the companies. This policy is a real threat to the continuity of public transport.

2.6 Lack of international co-operation

The absence of co-operation is traditional in the history of European transport. As for the railways, the differences in gauge, in voltage, in platform construction and in rolling-stock conditions have their roots in the distant past. It would cost billions of gold francs (the European railway currency) to bring the railways to a common standard. But every year it costs many millions of gold francs and a loss of quality of service to bridge the various standards of the countries.

It is true that since World War II there has been an increase in international co-operation among the railways (Cobbett 1982). The international railway organisation (UIC) and the association of technical railway research (ORE) are two examples of this. The timetables of the member countries and the fares for international trips are fairly integrated. However, this does not mean that international co-operation is guaranteed for the future. The protection of national rolling-stock industries and the promotion of a national version of high speed trains may lead to waste of knowledge and money. The different attitudes of European governments towards the value of public transport hamper sound international co-operation.

2.7 The complex organisation of public transport

At least three types of public transport company operate side by side in many urban areas:

- the local transport system (bus, tram and underground railway) under the administrative rule of the authorities of the central town;
- the regional transport system (bus and light rail) with its links to the authorities of the region, district or province; and
- the national system (rail) with its relations to the central government.

This triple (and crippled) organisation is a source of many money-wasting conflicts. The political directions and objectives of the three administrative layers may be entirely different, while the subsidised companies may dispute segments of the market with each other. In the Federal Republic of Germany an umbrella organisation with the participation of at least six organisations and administrations (Hamburg, Rhein-Ruhr) has been created in an attempt to improve co-ordination.

Not only in the cities, but also in the rural areas, there is a tendency for public transport companies to become competitive with each other: the weakest railway lines have to prove continually that their performance is better than that of the alternative of a strong bus line.

The struggle between public transport companies shows a strong resemblance to a wrestling-match in the mud.

3. Fictions about public transport

3.1 Artificial problems

3.1.1. No substitution between private and public transport? The degree of substitution between public and private transport is a very important element in the determination of the welfare benefits of public transport. For example, a combination of a low cross-elasticity of demand between public and private transport, a significant price elasticity of demand for public transport, and high marginal costs of public transport, are not very suitable for subsidies (Gwilliam 1984, p. 26). In such a situation low fares mean high operating costs without substantial social benefit except consumers' surplus. A combination of high marginal costs and significant price elasticities is realistic during peak hours. But is a low or even negligible cross-elasticity also realistic? The statement that private and public transport operate on two separate markets is far too absolute. The degree of substitution depends on the differences in travelling costs, time and comfort between the modes. If these differences are small, cross-elasticity will be high. In many market segments there are opportunities for public transport to stay and become competitive.

3.1.2. Subsidised public transport a road to inefficiency? Sometimes it is argued that subsidisation takes away the incentive to get the best, or at least a fair level of performance because a financial deficit will not be followed by stopping the money-consuming activities. It is also argued that society is a hostage to subsidised, socially beneficial activities. This problem is artificial because it is possible to make strict agreements with management about the amount of money to be paid by governing authorities for a specified level of production: making profits is replaced by meeting contracts.

3.1.3. Does public transport cost more than private (car) transport? Mobility is paid for by passengers per passenger-kilometre. These marginal costs emphasise the appearance that public transport is expensive. Calculated on an integral basis, public transport is a relatively cheap mode for the passengers. The social costs of public transport are clearly far below those of private car transport.

3.1.4. Is the social significance of public transport immeasurable? In spite of the many problems nowadays to indicate the value of the public transport system (see Section 2.1), the answer is in the negative. There is no reason to lose hope of getting the solution to such a crucial problem in transport.

3.1.5. Does public transport meet demand? Each individually intended trip is unique in its combination of time and space. A transport system which can meet this specific combination is the favourite in the eyes of the consumer. The private car pretends to offer such a system, and in many situations — an important exception is transport in congested areas — it really does. At first sight, a public transport system does not fulfil the individual needs of the consumer. However, if it really works as a system, from the framework of the inter-city trains to the rural dial-a-ride bus, public transport can meet individual demand. Moreover, this system has the fundamental advantage to society of converting individual trips to combined parts of trips.

3.2 Facile solutions

3.2.1. Free public transport. A continuously decreasing number of people think that public transport should be free because its social value is so great that it is wrong to handle it as an economic good. This extreme opinion implies that the marginal social costs of travelling by public transport are non-negative in the case of zero fares, which is not true.

When revenues are lower than the bare sales cost, free public transport is sometimes advocated for budgetary reasons. However, in this calculation the additional cost, raised by new demand, is completely neglected.

3.2.2. Subsidy-free public transport. Quite the opposite opinion among a growing number of people is that subsidising public transport is like pouring money down the drain. The best policy to purify the transport sector would be to stop subsidies because they are based on vague socio-economic arguments.

The political impact of this opinion is shown by the Reagan administration which is thinking of stopping subsidies to Amtrak, the federal inter-city railway network. This extreme opinion seems to be based on the idea that what cannot be measured does not exist.

3.2.3. Public transport for everybody everywhere. Many people consider mobility a fundamental right, like freedom, food and housing. The second step in this reasoning is that a lot of people do not have the opportunity to travel by car. Consequently, a complete public transport system needs to be supplied to all those people. The question is if, and to what extent, mobility may be considered as a fundamental right. Which trips are unpayable and also absolutely necessary for sufficient living conditions? It is not likely that many trips fall into that category.

3.2.4. Public transport, an anachronism. Transport by rail started its life cycle in the first half of the nineteenth century. The golden steam-rail monopoly reached its peak in the decades before World War I. Between the wars a real war was going on between omnibus companies in many countries. The monopolistic steam of trains underwent a metamorphosis and turned into competitive diesel and electric buses, trams and trains. After World War II, the car smashed the market share of public transport. And where are we now? At the end of a life cycle of 150 years of the glorious public transport product? Is its network an extensive and expensive museum? Some people affirm the statement that public transport is an anachronism. They forget that the sole target of *laissez faire, laissez aller* is the real anachronism in modern society (the 'invisible hand' is 210 years old). Planning will be necessary between frictions and fictions.

4. Some promising planning directions

4.1. Integration and co-operation

The consumers of transport services are users of a system. They are not interested in the separate suppliers of transport facilities. The use of the railway network depends on the quality of service of rural bus lines. They are the essential capillary vessels of the public transport systems. Railway officers have to defend the quality of these lines as well as that of their own network.

The service to the consumers cannot end at the exit gate of the station or at the stop where people leave the tram or bus. The quality of the connection, which is an essential part of the trip of many passengers, has to be improved. The total cost of the trip is what counts to the consumers, not the fare of a specific part of the trip. The supplying companies, not the customers, have to solve the problem of integration of fares.

The number of executive organisations and levels of governing authority in transport has to be small. An umbrella organisation will be necessary in urban areas, where local, regional and national institutions compete with each other.

Many governments consider public transport and private transport as two separate sectors of society. This attitude is fundamentally incorrect, for these two types of transport are linked to each other on the demand and on the supply side. They compete for the favour of the consumer and use the same scarce space in the cities (Lefèvre 1985). Public transport planning has to be integrated with transport planning in general.

The European Council of Ministers (ECMT), at its meeting in May 1984, decided on a concrete working plan for improving passenger traffic by rail and for action to be undertaken at the European level in favour of this traffic (De Waele 1985). Many of the recommendations concern standardisation and harmonisation of composition of international trains, of interval-service timetable systems and of seeking optimum patterns of connections. It is a requisite for a future adequate high-speed railway network between the large city centres in Europe that an agreement be achieved on standards.

International co-operation in research is an important access road to standardisation. (Examples are international organisations like ECMT, ORE and UIC, and international studies like those of Gwilliam *et al.* (1980) and of the Transport and Road Research Laboratory (1980).)

4.2. Quality improvement

The consumer of the public transport system is using the products of the system while he is in the middle of the production process. He consumes at the very moment of production. Intermediate and final quality control checks before the products find their way to the 'shops' are generally impossible in transport.

Moreover, the products of the public transport system are very complex and the number of quality aspects is numerous. Such various things as the availability of information before the trip, the presence of telephone boxes (in working order) in the station hall, the kindness of the staff and their willingness to help, the punctuality of the timetable, the availability of a seat, the cleanliness of the coach and the comprehensibility of information are all aspects of the passengers' total impression of quality. There are at least 70 of these aspects. Even if each aspect is good in 95 per cent of cases (under the assumption of independent distributions) then the product always has defective aspects. A product that has no stable high quality standard, but is a risk to the customers, can hardly be considered as competitive.

Quality is not another word for luxury; quality is producing what has been planned to be produced. A lack of quality also means additional costs in order to repair the defective situation. Planning in public transport has to be directed towards high quality standards.

4.3. Productivity improvement

As mentioned in Section 2.2, productivity in public transport is disturbingly stable in relation to other transport sectors (Tefra 1984–1985). It is an absolute necessity to increase the commercial productivity (the number of passenger-kilometres per unit of production factor). By raising the quality standard of the products and by integration and co-ordination of public transport, productivity can be increased when both the planning process and the management information system are improved (Reid 1985). Future possibilities to increase labour, rolling-stock and infrastructure productivity are network information systems to improve the daily planning process.

4.4. Deregulation

The planning effort of public transport companies can only be effective when they are free, within certain limits, to determine the size and the scale of their operations, their sales policy (including the fare level and structure), their wage and employment policy and the composition of their board of directors. The price of this regulated freedom is a medium-term contract with the governing authorities indicating the amount of money government is prepared to pay for a specific performance of the company. This amount may be fixed, which will be preferred by the governing authorities, or may vary with the sales volume. A well-defined concept of social benefit of public transport is of paramount importance during the negotiations about this contract.

4.5. Pricing based on social costs

Compensating public transport for its social benefit is not the only way to smooth out the unequal competitive conditions between public and private transport. It is in some cases also possible to internalise the relatively high social cost of private transport. The concept of road pricing, intended to ask a price for causing congestion to other road users, is well known. Use-dependent levies as a compensation for pollution is another example. Effective internalisations of external effects reduce the need for governing authorities to subsidise public transport, because continuation would imply double counting in favour of public transport.

5. Important directions of research in the area of public transport

The need to find yardsticks for the social valuation of public transport has been stressed before in this paper. The world-wide problem of justification (in the positive, not in the normative sense of the word) of budgetary support by governments is a major area of research.

Close to this problem of valuation and rationalisation is the question of financing the deficits of public transport. It is worth the effort to analyse what type of contract between government and public transport companies is both budgetarily acceptable to the government and will stimulate the transport companies towards efficiency.

The extent of independency of management is another interesting aspect of the relationship between authorities and companies to be studied.

Governments and administrations try to achieve goals in the transport sector by taking measures. They have a fare and price policy, they limit or stimulate the construction of infrastructure, they restrict traffic in town centres, they build new towns, they stimulate regions or make living in the old towns more attractive. Based on the experiences of the past decades the effectiveness of government actions may be questioned. Do governments really have the influence and power to change the transport consumption of people? Getting the answer to this question might lead to deregulation.

The organisation of public transport, especially in urban areas, and the structure of international railway lines, deserve objective and cool analysis. Sensitive decisions about the most effective type of organisation or the best high-speed railway system need to be prepared by thorough analysis.

Substitution, as is mentioned in Section 3.1, between public and private transport does exist, but the degree of substitution determines the effect of measures influencing the modal choice of people. The determination and analysis of cross-elasticities of demand are useful activities.

International comparison between public transport companies by means of a series of productivity ratios is a contribution to the control of performance of the co-operating companies. A study on the collection and analysis of these ratios is highly recommended.

Naturally, the series of research topics is almost infinite. The list mentioned in this section is directed to the continuity of public transport, its threats and opportunities, and is meant as a support to planning between frictions and fictions.

References

Andresen, O. (1982). 'Railways'. Paper presented to the Ninth International Symposium on Theory and Practice in Transport Economics, Madrid.

Beesley, M.E., P. Gist and S.E. Glaister (1983). 'Cost Benefit Analysis and London's Transport Policies,' *Progress in Planning*, **19** (3). Oxford: Pergamon.

Cameron, J.C.F. (1982). 'Urban and Regional Passenger Transport'. Paper presented to the International Symposium on Theory and Practice in Transport Economics, Madrid.

Cobbett, D.J. (1982). 'Railways'. Paper presented to the Ninth International Symposium on Theory and Practice in Transport Economics, Madrid.

Cobeira, A. (1985). 'The Objectives and Strategies To Be Developed by a Railway Undertaking in an Environment with Serious Structural Constraints', *Rail International* (February), pp. 47–51.

De Waele, A. (1985). 'Action to Promote International Traffic by Rail between the Countries of the ECMT', *Rail International* (February), pp. 43–46.

Estival, J.P. (1985). 'Les entreprises ferroviaires européennes à la recherche de critères de gestion spécifiques', *Transports*, **300** (January), pp. 9–17.

Glassborow, D.W. (1982). 'Urban and Regional Passenger Transport'. Paper presented to the Ninth International Symposium on Theory and Practice in Transport Economics, Madrid.

Gwilliam, K.M. *et al.* (1980). *A Comparative Study of European Rail Performance.* London: British Rail.

Gwilliam, K.M. (1984). 'Aims and Effects of Public Financial Support for Passenger Transport'. European Conference of Ministers of Transport. Round Table 67, Paris.

Holtgrefe, A.A.I. (1983). 'Stagnation and Public Transport in the Netherlands. Demand, Cost, Supply and Planning'. Paper presented to the Tenth Colloquium on Transportation Planning Research, Zandvoort, the Netherlands, December.

International Union of Railways. *Annual statistics.*

Lefèvre, C. (1985). 'Transports collectifs et croissance urbaine: l'example des métros américains', *Transports*, **300** (January), pp. 18–24.

Mogridge, M.J.H. (1984). 'Transport in the Conurbations: Some Lessons from the Last Decade' *International Colloquium on Financing Urban Transportation.* Lyon: Laboratoire d'Économie des Transports, pp. 94–109.

Nash, C.A. (1982). *Economics of Public Transport.* London: Longman.

Pällmann, W. (1982). 'Urban and regional passenger transport'. Paper presented to the Ninth International Symposium on Theory and Practice in Transport Economics, Madrid.

Reid, R.B. (1985). 'Organising the railways as a business', *Rail International* (January), pp. 33–7.

Singh, B. (1985). 'Managerial Actions to be Taken so as to Cope with the Future', *Rail International* (January), pp. 39–44.

Sobemap, (1984). *Studie van de financiele toestand van de nationale maatschappij der Belgische spoorwegen.*

Tefra, M. (1984–5). 'La productivité des differents modes de transport de 1970 à nos jours', *Transports*, **298**, 436–42; **299**, 518–21; and **300**, 36–41.

Transport and Road Research Laboratory (1980). *The Demand for Public Transport. Report of the International Collaborative Study of the Factors Affecting Public Transport Patronage.* Crowthorne, Berks: TRRL.

Vázquez Cábezas, G. (1982). 'Railways'. Paper presented to the Ninth International Symposium on Theory and Practice in Transport Economics, Madrid.

Webster, F.V. (1984). 'Urban transportation: expenditure and effectiveness', *International Colloquium on Financing Urban Transportation.* Lyon: Laboratoire d'Économie des Transports, pp. 39–66.

11 Travel Demand or Need for Access as Future Determinants of Transport Policy-Making

*S. Reichman and I. Salomon**

1. Introduction

The purpose of this paper is to identify some of the main features of the existing frameworks for decision-making in transport policy, and to point out their inadequacy in coping with forseeable changes in the socio-economic and institutional environments of transportation systems. Finally, we shall introduce a rather different concept in the rationale of decision-making in transportation, aiming to bring it more into line with that commonly used in the domain of the provision of public services.

To clarify matters, the existing framework of decision-making is viewed here as a combination of the functions of public officials and of the principles which underlie their actions. In the transportation-system framework, these functions are generally identified as being performed by planners and supervisors (Reichman 1983). Planners are defined here as people trained to follow a certain chain of procedures from the definition of a problem, through the design of alternative solutions, to the selection of a preferred solution on the basis of some policy criteria (Thomson 1974). The role of supervisors in the system, on the other hand, has not been so neatly identified. Generally, they follow the spirit underlying the activities of every civil servant: to implement and monitor transport policies, projects and programmes, as far as this can be done, given the powers vested in the hands of the public administration. To use the analogy of regional policy, we know that such powers may vary considerably, ranging from regulative measures to the use of fiscal expenditure or pricing incentives (Bennett

*The authors thank Alain Bieber and David Derry for their excellent comments.

1980). Another type of decision-maker, to whom planners and administrators have to account, are elected officials.

The behaviour of elected officials differs in some fundamental ways from that of civil servants, two illustrations of which should suffice: first, elected officials are far more sensitive to the issue of consensus and conflict inherent in a given policy; second, they are essentially in charge of the difficult task of policy determination (Bardach 1976; Behn 1978).

2. Prevailing principles of transportation policy and their implementation

It is suggested that current and past planning and policy formulation in transport evolved, in very broad terms, from two basic approaches: the regional and urban economics approach, prevailing up to the end of the 1960s (see, for example, Wilson *et al.* 1966, Owen 1964) and the systems approach which emerged during the 1970s, in parallel with the development of large-scale computers, and a growing belief that large-scale systems can be formalised, understood and manipulated by models.

The regional and urban economics approach rested on a market philosophy. Transport investments were seen as bringing about development effects — that is to say, a utilisation of resources previously inaccessible — and distributional effects, namely a change in the geographical location of economic activity. Both factors, set out by Winfrey and Zellner (1971), seemed to justify public investments in infrastructure, in expectation of the benefits to be accrued by the subsequent entry of private-sector investments. This reasoning is usually applied to the development of new territories, but Winfrey and Zellner (1971) extended it to the context of urban expressways developing the urban fringe, in a similar way to a new frontier. The problem to be solved under this approach was underdevelopment, defined in terms of an economic and infrastructural gap or bottle-neck between regions, and transport was consequently viewed by (transport) economists as the opportunity.

With hindsight, the impacts of major capital investments in infrastructure have not necessarily acted in the expected or desired direction. The decrease in the friction of distance was found to induce exit from deprived regions and not just the desired entry into them (Reichman 1983). It was also found that greater exploitation of resources in a given area does not necessarily lead to an improvement in the well-being of the developing area's residents (Cumberland 1973).

Intervention through transport infrastructure as a principal agent for bringing about regional change seemed for a long period a politically feasible and even attractive instrument. The linearity of transport infrastructure made it come to be viewed, mistakenly, as a relatively easy to implement and certainly a very visible policy tool from the policy-maker's perspective. The immediate political gains served as an impetus for implementing the policy, even if its main objective — that of achieving economic development and redistributional effects, which anyway take a very long time to become evident — was not accomplished.

The second approach, known as the systems framework, was applied particularly to urban or metropolitan settings, and focused mainly on short-distance passenger traffic. The systems approach was also embedded in the market approach, but, in the urban environment, the economic justification for transport investments was so obvious that often it was not even noted.

By its nature it was a diagnostic approach. It attempted to identify factors which hamper optimal performance. The problem was for many years defined in terms of level of service: time, financial and energy costs. Thus, it was a problem of the system's performance and the opportunity was seen mainly in the increase of capacity.

An underlying assumption was that mobility is synonymous with motor-car use and that it was only a matter of time until the ultimate symbol of freedom of movement would be universally available. Planners in this period were mostly preoccupied with estimating demand in order to construct sufficient supply to accommodate it. The use of the motor car was viewed as a social choice and hence this approach was not only socially acceptable, but also esteemed. Planners believed that the transport system is, to a great extent, an independent, closed system, and that technology is, if not immediately, at least in the near future, a source of remedies for most ills.

By the end of the 1960s, the transport planning profession had to face the negative externalities that the transport subsystem inflicted on the urban system (see the contribution of Kutter (Chapter 4) in this volume). Efforts were made to improve transit services, not only through infrastructure and technology, but also through improvements in service standards (Tober 1977) and priority treatment, which were intended to attract motor-car passengers to public transport.

During the 1970s, according to Altshuler (1979), perceptions of the problem changed the focus of concern. First air pollution, then energy and later the concern for mobility-deprived groups, took turns in heading the agenda. Towards the end of the decade, the agenda included the issues of the financial drain, first of the public transportation agencies and then of government funding for social services in general.

Thus, a systems approach seemed all the more relevant, as an instrument for dealing with complex, sometimes contradicting factors. The realisation that planning and policy-making cannot be divorced from broader socio-political and economic systems led to a new definition of the challenge of transportation systems analysis: 'to intervene, delicately and deliberately, in the complex fabric of society to use transportation effectively, in coordination with other public and private actions, to achieve the goals of that society' (Manheim 1979, p. 5). This typifies the second phase of the systems approach, which could be labelled the 'social engineering' period (Taebel and Cornehls 1977) though the objective function of transport systems was still defined in terms of performance, subject to a broader set of constraints.

In the social engineering era of transportation-systems analysis, while the problems set on the agenda are largely from outside the transportation system, the universe of solutions at their disposal is still restricted to options within the system.

Despite the broader challenge, the limitations of the systems approach as it stands today stem from the fact that, in the final analysis, transportation policy-makers still evaluate the performance of the system in terms of its own effectiveness, rather than in those of the needs of society, as will be elaborated below. It should be noted that a different situation prevails in the transport of freight. Technological improvements, structural change and the fact that fewer decision-makers and objectives are involved, result in significant improvements in some elements of this sector as reported by Pedersen (in Chapter 5 of this volume). One of the possible explanations for the different evolution between passenger and freight transport lies probably in the specific effects of the increasing institutionalisation of the decision-making process in the former. Indeed, within each of these approaches, decision-making has become increasingly institutionalised, with respect to four main attributes: the definition of the transportation problem; the types of indicators or data used by both types of transportation practitioner; the areas in which the solutions are being sought; and finally, the professional background of the transport analysts.

2.1 Nature of the transportation problem

We may perhaps generalise two different aspects of the suggested institutionalisation. First, the task of identifying a problem area does not necessarily rest within the strictly defined set of transportation planners and supervisors. In many cases, the statements regarding both the problems and the agenda for dealing with them originate from other sources, such as public commissions of inquiry, politicians or academic scholars. Despite the variety of the originating actors, there is still a common factor at work — namely that, more often than not, transport problems are treated separately from other sectors of the economy. A noteworthy exception was the energy crisis with its economy-wide effects. Secondly, the operational definition of the problem areas tends to vary as a function of (a) scale — national, regional or local; (b) the disciplinary background of the actor, the most frequent variations being between engineering *vis-à-vis* the economic background; and (c) the prevailing state of society, which is in turn influenced by fluctuations in economic cycles, between growth and stagnation.

2.2 Indicators

The types of indicators used in the decision-making frameworks currently operating in the transportation system are probably the best example of the relatively high degree of institutionalisation prevailing in the system, as the indicators are mostly institution-dependent. For example, it has been suggested that the choice of indicators (or data sets) is nothing other than an intentional reduction of information regarding the complexity of the social reality for the sake of operationalisation (Hottler 1981). A similar point was made with respect to the built-in biases found in most socio-demographic variables which are customarily provided by the national bureaux of statistics (Matalon 1982).

2.3 Solutions

The areas of solution sought have traditionally tended to remain within the realms of the transportation system, particularly in urban areas (Merlin 1984). Often, they are sought within a mode-specific, area-specific or jurisdiction-specific environment. As for the scope of interventions, the fundamental difference between solutions in the United States and those developed in Western Europe are illustrative. The latter are characterised by a greater interaction between measures on the demand and on the supply sides (Dunn 1981), and seen more as an instrument of urban policy than in the American case.

The definition of the 'Transport Problem' is a useful indicator of the limits of the universe in which policy-making takes place. Over the last three decades, it is possible to identify a gradual change in the definition of the problem. If we accept the definition of a problem in a public policy context as an opportunity for improvement (Dery 1984), then the set of opportunities considered by policy-makers for intervention must correspond to the problem definition. Once the definition is altered, the set of opportunities must also be changed.

2.4 Professionals

Finally, all three aspects noted above are affected by the type of professional, in terms of the unique combination of education, experience and position held by each individual. Traditionally, transport professionals were educated as engineers, economists and planners. An objective of this paper is to demonstrate the need for a new role for the professional, which may not be based on any of these disciplines.

3. Socio-economic and institutional trends inadequately treated in existing approaches

The inadequacies of existing approaches can be viewed from two perspectives: first, a more technical and abstract viewpoint focusing on the existing models, and on some of their characteristic drawbacks in dealing with the real world (discussed by Williams (Chapter 17) in this volume); the second method starts from the opposite end, and asks which trends in the real world can already be discerned, and appear to be of such a nature that they can hardly be incorporated in the existing market or performance approaches.

The main problems in the existing approaches were exposed in a number of recent gatherings which brought together social scientists, transportation analysts and policy-makers (see, for example Part C of this volume). Several main problem areas were identified:

1. The existence of a definite, though unmeasurable element of uncertainty in forecasting future trends. What makes this uncertainty a serious problem is the fact that the models, and the forecasts incorporated within them, are used in a policy-making context, and thus create a well-known dilemma: if the analyst reports explicitly that some uncertainty has to be taken into account, there is a risk that politicians would react negatively towards such information, or, even worse, that this information could be used by opponents of a given plan or policy (Richards 1981). The other alternative, namely omitting any references to uncertainty, is hardly more attractive.
2. The need to accept that there are built-in *time-lags* in both market- and policy-induced processes (see Holtgrefe in Chapter 10 of this volume). For example, new transportation technologies often interact with a land-use pattern which was actually shaped by a

previous transport technology (Moses and Williamson 1967). However, in a recent paper, it was shown that the vast majority of existing transportation/land-use models fail to address themselves to this problem (Wegener in Chapter 14 of this volume).

3. *Capturing the salient processes* existing at any given moment in the socio-economic and institutional setting which transportation models are supposed to represent. This is a central problem in the modelling of travel behaviour, which is sometimes represented by trip rates and sometimes by additional data on activity patterns. Similarly, the unit of analysis in disaggregate models is the individual traveller, rather than the household. This is particularly questionable, given the current and expected increase in the plurality of household forms and lifestyles and particularly the growth in the number of single-parent households (Salomon and Ben-Akiva 1983).
4. The use of *objective measures* of system parameters in forecasting future behaviour may be erroneous or biased, because decisions in the real world are made on the basis of subjective perceptions, and these are not necessarily randomly distributed around the means of objective measures.

In summary, while these inadequacies unquestionably have a real impact on the effectiveness of existing approaches, policy-makers seem to have learned by now from their experience that for certain problems they can rely on information provided by planners, whereas in some problem areas such information may be less forthcoming or could, at the limit, be altogether disregarded as an input in the decision-making process. This apparent co-existence of the main actors of the system can be perturbed by two inter-related factors: first, the emergence of new technologies, social processes or institutional frameworks which might modify the underlying assumptions that the transport sector is an indispensable element for the smooth functioning of the existing economic and social systems. Secondly, an alternative conceptual framework to that currently used in transportation planning, with different goals, target populations and time-spans. Such a framework might conceivably be derived in those instances where it is expected that market approaches are doomed to failure. Holtgrefe's discussion (Chapter 10 of this volume) of the fictions surrounding public transport come to mind in this respect, or when values are being threatened by excessive mobility, as suggested by Hägerstrand (Chapter 2 of this volume).

Let us turn now to some of the changes which seem to be occurring around us, and which might have profound effects on the existing transportation decision-making frameworks.

First there is the appearance of what has been termed an 'urban turnaround' in Europe, characterised by the net decline in the population of the largest agglomerations (and not just of their central cores), to the benefit of middle-sized towns which experience an increase in their populations and economic base (van den Berg *et al.* 1982; Myklebost 1984). If this phenomenon is indeed widespread, as seems to be the case in Europe, then it could result in an increase in the importance of migration decisions, rather than of commuting decisions. Let us also remind ourselves that the migration of labour from overseas to Europe has also been severely curtailed.

Such structural changes might eventually lead to the conclusion that transport investments to enlarge traffic capacity may no longer be needed to ensure the growth of the economy in an existing city region, since such traffic increases are not likely to occur. In fact, in many developed, industrialised regions, the problem will become that of transport over-capacity and its costs, especially since natural deterioration of the existing infrastructure has started to set in. Its proper maintenance and repair are likely to be expensive and not necessarily justifiable on short-term economic grounds (Larson and Rao 1984). Taken to an extreme, this trend may well lead to a situation where the transport sector is perhaps going to be viewed by decision-makers more as a liability than an asset and a fail-safe component of economic growth. If we were to add to this assessment the widespread belief, yet to be substantiated (see Salomon forthcoming), that progress in telecommunications will make it possible to reduce traffic volumes and travel requirements (OECD 1983), then the perception of transportation as a declining industry becomes even more accentuated.

Secondly, large-scale urbanistic choices which have underlain most transport investments in the past decades in most European large urban centres are no longer in fashion. Instead, we turn more and more to land-use solutions designed to overcome transportation problems.

Thirdly, the increasing trend of reduction, by means of privatisation, of formal services previously provided by the Welfare State (Graycar 1983; Rainwater and Rein 1983) and also in transportation (Farrington 1985) has also had unforeseen, but none the less significant effects on the segmentation of mobility levels in welfare societies. While it is probably true to say that income maintenance and other transfer payments have little direct relationship to mobility levels, the same is not the case with the delivery of education and health services. Here we have simply to introduce the notion that these services are delivered through a network of facilities, each with its own jurisdictional space or service area (Honey 1983; Lerman 1984). Given that population densities and income levels are unevenly distributed, a reduction in public expenditure on public services, or their privatisation, will lead to a closure of facilities in low-density regions, and a concomitant increase in the distance that will have to be overcome in order to benefit from the service (Nash 1982). There exists, however, another highly relevant benefit, which is not always included in the welfare economy, although it plays an important role in the distribution of resources in society — namely, employee benefits, otherwise known as occupational welfare. In many countries car or travel allowances are the second most important employee benefit after superannuation (Jamrozik *et al.* 1983). In other words, a working person gets an extra mobility bonus, which facilitates his access to opportunities, whereas an unemployed person is worse off without this bonus, though he may actually spend more resources in search of job opportunities (Vipond 1984).

Now, if we add both the privatisation of services and the incidence of occupational welfare, we may easily envisage an alternative societal system which would distinguish sharply in both the level of and the access to social services it provides between more or less densely populated regions, between employed and unemployed people, and between car-owners and non-car-owners. Such a division of society into mobility categories based on the inequality of opportunities due to differences in population densities, motorisation and earnings (though the needs of health and education are considered as universally distributed) cannot always be accommodated within the logic of prevailing transportation planning models. Instead, it may call for intervention by politicians since such a segmentation into mobility categories could be a factor of social destabilisation.

Finally, we come to the growing importance of temporal accessibility in shaping travel behaviour. A decade ago, the thesis was put forward that urban areas offer themselves to activity patterns almost around the clock, a process which was then termed the 'colonisation of time' (Melbin 1978). While it is probably accurate to say that such a process was observable in large agglomerations at a period of economic growth, it may no longer be operating, particularly in smaller cities and in a period of relative urban decline. Owing to the reduction in public services referred to above, it may well be that the temporal accessibility of a facility providing these services has actually been curtailed, so that we may face a period of 'decolonisation of time', if only in terms of the service hours of public services.

Judging from a longitudinal study of mobility modification brought about by residential relocation from a metropolitan core to a suburban new town (Andan *et al.* 1984), it appears that households tend indeed to employ temporal strategies in order to overcome the increased burden of spatial constraints in the suburbs. Activities such as shopping and entertainment are more and more restricted to non-working days, a solution which is not feasible for access to most public services. Hence individuals are in a greater need of space–time approaches. This issue becomes more relevant in view of the increase in women's participation in the paid labour force, while the fact that they fulfil dual roles puts them under greater time–space pressures (Hanson and Hanson 1981; Fagnani 1983).

4. The need-assessment approach as a complement for future policy-making

We have shown so far that transport policy-making has been motivated primarily by market and performance approaches. However, if we are entering a period where significant parts of the transport sector are declining in importance it may no longer be so, and consequently, serious distributional problems may result from a continuing reliance upon existing approaches. A possible remedy to this problem lies in proposing a complement to the market approach, in the form of the need-assessment approach generally used in the public sector in the determination of the size of goods and services to be delivered to the public. More specifically, we shall discuss four components of transport as if it were part of the social policy:

- how transport services can be redefined in terms of needs;
- what the main instruments that could be used to answer these needs are;
- what the size of the economic resources provided by public institutions should be; and
- through which administrative mechanisms should funds be regulated.

Not surprisingly, we shall find that in many cases present-day transport services are already discussed in these terms, though not necessarily within the framework of the comprehensive approach that we have termed here as need-assessment.

Let us start by redefining transport services in terms of needs. In a modern society, all major actors in the economy, namely households, entrepreneurs and public authorities experience the need for access to materials, markets, labour and services. Let us then redefine mobility in terms of need-to-access by households, while recognising that it tends to vary systematically according to income, life cycle and the nature of the man-made environment of the household, to mention just a few of the factors affecting this need. From a public policy perspective, we may distinguish between needs that are met through the market mechanism, which then become wants regulated by supply and demand relationships, and needs that are not properly regulated by the market. In the latter category we tend to find instances where access standards have been set by administrative regulations. The most explicit cases are the distance-criteria which were established in access to schools. Implicitly, the same principle should apply to access to major health facilities, though this is not always the case. In both instances an essential public service is delivered through jurisdictional space, that is to say that users are allocated to a facility on a territorial basis, rather than by a market mechanism. Viewing access as an integral element of the provision of public services means, in fact, that the need-assessment approach is actually a supply-side rather than a demand mechanism.

The major problem in defining access needs is the justification of the standards or the criteria used. This is not made any easier by the lack of mobility-dependency indicators which might have assisted policy-makers in determining such standards. We do not currently collect data on how many people commute to work for over an hour and a half in each direction (!), nor do we know the distances people have to overcome to reach public services. In another instance, we know that in the United Kingdom 26 per cent of the elderly have no access to a department store within 26 minutes' walk or bus journey (Town 1982). In all these mobility-dependency indicators, some threshold values should be developed, on admittedly normative grounds, so that the policy-makers may refer to them in assessing both the size and the trend of access-needs which have to be met.

Turning now to the main instruments through which the access-needs should be met, we shall ignore, for the sake of simplicity, those which are outside the scope of the transportation system, such as the suitable location of facilities like hospitals to ensure accessibility, as discussed by Alun and Phillips (1984). Within the transportation system, access is of course provided both by infrastructure and by transport services. In the case of infrastructure, most of the investments are justified by market approaches, with the notable exceptions of road construction in remote, low-density regions, such as the mountainous regions of Switzerland (Kaspar 1984). What remains, then, is the supply of public transport as a universal, rather than a selective instrument for meeting the access-needs of households.

The most controversial problem in any need-orientated programme is the determination of the size of economic resources that ought to be allocated for its provision, and more specifically, what the share of public funds in it should be. Here we find great variations across countries: in Denmark it has been estimated that the average participation of the public, or the per-capita contribution in covering the deficit of public transportation (except in Copenhagen) is around US $25 to $35 per annum (Rallis *et al.* 1984), whereas in highly urbanised Israel the current annual size of the public transport subsidy was around US $72 per capita until the recent drastic curtailment of subsidies. The same variation persists when relative figures of recovery rates or depth of subsidy are measured. In the mid-1970s these ranged from around 70 per cent in Belgium and the Netherlands to around 10 per cent in Greece and Finland (Webster and Bly 1979). Since the size of the subsidy is clearly a political issue, it is obviously difficult to suggest guidelines that would satisfy both socialist and liberal orientations. What can be said, however, is that there exist a number of accounting problems: what is commonly considered as a transport cost should in fact be apportioned to another sector. Thus, in reality, to the fixed costs of a central facility delivering public services should be added variable costs that are built in, that is to say, the future stream of access costs to the new location. The question then becomes to what degree the current level of deficits in public transport in effect reflects the hidden savings in other sectors, and should therefore continue to be treated necessarily as an economic burden.

5. The new equilibrium between planning and programme formulation

Finally, let us address the issue of the administrative mechanisms involved in meeting access needs through public service procedures.

In the first place, the need-assessment approach assumes that mobility levels, especially those provided by public transportation, are an item on the public agenda. This has perhaps been shown most clearly in the recent French legislation on the 'right to transport' which puts transport squarely within the realm of public goods (Reichman 1984).

Next, we ought to consider the various means by which transport expenditure should be allocated, particularly when market mechanisms are not feasible alternatives. In general, the following issues are under consideration:

- earmarked *versus* block grants;

- central government funding *versus* local or regional government expense; and
- the share of the inner city *versus* the suburbs in public transport funding (Blum 1984).

A typical example of earmarked funding is the recently introduced payroll tax levied from entrepreneurs in French towns, and designed to cover both capital and operating expenses of public transportation in those areas. In a way, it represents a belief that public transport provides benefits to the economic basis of a city, even if these cannot be measured in strict economic terms. Also of importance are the recent advances reported by Orski (1985) in developers' participation in transport investments in the United States, with particular reference to suburban problems.

Another important issue relates to the size of the administration employed in the provision of public services. In the case of the transportation sector this is not a negligible problem, particularly if railway personnel are State employees.

The main point, though, is that we generally have a large variety of administrative mechanisms which address themselves to the delivery of transport services in the context of public policy. What is still missing is a recognition that the provision of transport services should be considered in terms of a comprehensive need-assessment framework. In the short run this may result in a change in existing levels of interaction between planning and administration in the sense that closer institutional links between the two functions should be initiated, so as to devise new transportation programmes. Such programmes could take different forms, either in terms of novel methods of funding, or in identifying new targets for intervention. In such a framework it is not inconceivable that hitherto untapped resources may be mobilised, instead of relying solely on the quickly diminishing public expenditure funds. By looking at transport services from the viewpoint of social policy, it is not inconceivable that other possible sources for the funding of access needs could be mobilised. Both the corporate and the household sectors can contribute their share, either by enlarging the practice of the payroll tax referred to above, or by a variety of joint development mechanisms, as described by Orski (1985). Another possibility is that of introducing concepts of deferred payments for transportation funding, thus allowing people in their productive stage of the life cycle to contribute towards their access needs during their non-earning stage of life cycle. Similarly, people moving out to low-density suburbs, thereby maximising their personal welfare, may be asked to participate in covering some of the extra costs that were spent in providing public services in such low-density zones, and which resulted in making them so attractive. These hypothetical examples are given solely to indicate that the adoption of a need-assessment approach to complement the existing market and performance approaches is not necessarily concurrent with an increase in public expenditure.

Finally, we suggest that to the existing administrators and planners who deal with transport problems should be added another professional profile: that of the (transport) policy analyst, with a background in public policy (Dror 1968). The relevance of the policy variable is increasingly recognised in transport research, as noted by Farrington (1985), in view of changes toward privatisation of services. This role may parallel Pahl and Vickerman's (1980) concept of a transport facilitator of service-orientated planner. Needless to add, such a professional has to be properly trained in order to communicate with the engineer and the economist who are currently engaged in transportation planning based on market and performance approaches. However, it is felt that such an evolution is both feasible and inevitable, as has been indicated in recent changes in the orientation of the physical planning profession in general towards a greater interaction with policy sciences. On the other hand, it is not clear at this stage to what extent such a profile would enhance or undercut the existing image of the traditional transport planners. This will probably be determined on the basis of the attitudes of elected officials towards the new function. Politicians may find a common language with these transport analysts but they may want to continue to rely on more supply-side options, with a touch of innovative technology, which has proven in the past to be an effective conflict-avoiding strategy.[1]

Note

1. This point is credited to A. Bieber.

References

Altshuler, A. (1979). *The Urban Transportation System*. Cambridge, MA: MIT Press.

Alun, J. and D. Phillips, (1984). *Accessibility and Utilization: Geographical Perspectives of Health Care Delivery*. New York: Harper and Row.

Andan, O. *et al.* (1984). *Mobilité et espace urbain*. Paris: Ministère des Transports, Mission de la Recherche.

Bardach, E.C. (1976). 'Policy Termination as a Political Process', *Policy Sciences*, 7 (2), 123–32.

Behn, R.D. (1978). 'How to Terminate a Public Policy: A Dozen Hints for the Would-be Terminator', *Policy Analysis*, **4**(3), 393–413.

Bennett, R.J. (1980). *The Geography of Public Finance*. London: Methuen.
Blum, F. (1984). 'Spatial Distribution of the Mass Transit Funds in the Chicago Metropolitan Area'. Paper presented at the International Geographical Union Symposium on Transport Geography, Rome (August).
Cumberland J. (1973). 'Regional Development, Resource Allocation and Transportation' in J.S. DeSalvo, ed., *Perspectives on Regional Transportation Planning*. Lexington, Mass: Lexington Books.
Dery, D. (1984). *Problem Definition in Policy Analysis*. Lawrence, KS: University Press of Kansas.
Dror, Y. (1968). 'Policy Analyst: A New Professional Role in Government', *Public Administration Review*, **27** (3), 197–203.
Dunn, J.A. (1981). *Miles to Go: European and American Transportation Policies*, Cambridge, MA: MIT Press.
Fagnani, J. (1984). 'Women's Commuting Patterns in the Paris Region', *Tijdschrift voor Economische en Sociale Geografie*, **74** (1), 12–24.
Farrington, J.H. (1985). 'Transport Geography and Policy: Deregulation and Privatization', *Transactions of the Institute of British Geographers*, **10**, 109–19.
Graycar, A. (1983). 'Retreat from the Welfare State' in A. Graycar, ed., *Retreat from the Welfare State*. Sydney: Allen and Unwin, pp. 1–12.
Hanson, S. and P. Hanson, (1981). 'The Impact of Married Women's Employment on Household Travel Patterns. *Transportation*, **10**, 165–83.
Honey, R.D. (1983). 'Versatility vs. Continuity — The Dilemma of Jurisdictional Change' in N. Kliot and S. Waterman, eds., *Pluralism and Political Geography*. London: Croom Helm, pp. 228–44.
Hottler, R. (1981). 'Some Issues of Policy Sensitivity in Behavioural Travel Models' in P. Stopher, A. Meyburg and W. Brog, eds, *New Horizons in Travel Behaviour Research*. Lexington, Mass: Lexington Books.
Jamrozik *et al.* (1983). 'Occupational Welfare: Supporting the Affluent' in Graycar (1983).
Kaspar, C. (1984). 'Elements scientifiques et politiques des transports envers les regions' in G. Gaudard, ed., *Les transports et la region*, Colloques économiques no. 15. Fribourg, Switzerland: Institut des Sciences Economiques et Sociales, pp. 161–73.
Larson, T.D. and K. Rao, (1984). 'Breaking Out for Transportation Progress: Policy Responses to Investment Stalemate', *Transportation Research A*, **18** (2), 141–9.
Lerman, D. (1984). 'The Economics of Public Schools Closings', *Journal of Urban Economics*, **16** (3), 241–58.
Manheim, M.L. (1979). *Fundamentals of Transportation Systems Analysis*. Cambridge, MA: MIT Press.
Melbin, M. (1978). 'The Colonization of Time' in T. Carlstein, D. Parkes and N. Thrift, eds, *Human Activity and Time Geography*. London: Arnold, pp. 100–13.
Merlin, P. (1984). *La planification des transports urbains*. Paris: Masson.
Moses, L. and H.F. Williamson (1967). 'The Location of Economic Activity in Cities', *American Economic Review* (May), 211–22.
Myklebost, H. (1984). 'The Evidence for Urban Turnaround in Norway', *Geoforum*, **15** (2), 167–76.
Nash, C.A. (1982). *Economics of Public Transportation*. London: Longman.
OECD (1983). *Urban Policies for the 1980's*. Paris.
Orski, K. (1985). 'Suburban Mobility: The Coming Transportation Crisis', *Transportation Quarterly*, **3952**, 283–96.
Owen, W. (1964). *Strategy for Mobility*. Washington DC: Brookings Institute.
Pahl, R. and R. Vickerman (1982). 'Transport in Society' in TRRL (1982).
Rainwater, L. and Rein, M. (1983). 'The Growing Complexity of Economic Claims in Welfare Societies' in S.E. Spiro and Yuchtman-Year, eds, *Evaluating the Welfare State*. New York: Academic Press, pp. 111–29.
Rallis, T. *et al.* (1984). 'The Organization of Public Transport in Denmark', *Trans-*

portation Research A, **18** (2), 163–75.

Reichman, S. (1983). *Les transports: servitude ou liberté*? Paris: PUF.

Reichman, S. (1984). 'Le droit au transport: acte declaratif ou project innovateur?', *Transports*, **298** (November), 413–15.

Richards, M.G. (1981), 'Issues in Policy Sensitivity of Behavioral Models' in P. Stopher, A. Meyburg and W. Brog, eds, *New Horizons on Travel-Behavior Research*, Lexington MA: Lexington Books, pp. 413–22.

Salomon, I. (forthcoming). 'Telecommunications and Travel Interactions: A Review', *Transportation Research A*.

Salomon, I. and M. Ben-Akiva (1983). 'The Use of the Life Style Concept in Travel Demand Models', *Environment and Planning A*, **15**, 623–38.

Taebel, D. and J. Cornehls (1977). *The Political Economy of Urban Transportation*. New York: National University Publications.

Thomson, J.M. (1974). *Modern Transport Economics*. Harmondsworth: Penguin.

Tober, R. (1977). 'Improving Service Quality through the Use of Service Standards', in *Transportation Systems Management*. TRB Special Report 172. Washington DC.

Town, S.W. (1982). 'Transport Problems and Social Structure' in TRRL (1982), pp. 115–31.

TRRL (1982). *Social Aspects of Transport*. Supplementary Report No. 689, Crowthorne, Berks.

Van den Berg, L. *et al.* (1982). *Urban Europe: A Study in Growth and Decline*. Oxford: Pergamon.

Vipond, J. (1984). 'The Intra-Urban Unemployment Gradient: The Influence of Location on Unemployment', *Urban Studies*, **21**, 377–88.

Walker, A., ed. (1982). *Public Expenditure and Social Policy*. London: Heinemann.

Webster, F.V. and P.H. Bly (1979). 'Financing: Subsidisation of Urban Public Transport' in OECD–CEMT. *Urban Transport and the Environment*. Paris.

Wegener, M. (1984). 'Transport and Location in Integrated Spatial Models'. Paper presented at the ESF Workshop on Mobility, Vienna (October).

Wilson, G.W. *et al.* (1966). *The Impacts of Highway Investments in Development*. Washington DC: Brookings Institute.

Winfrey, R. and C. Zellner (1971). *Summary and Evaluation of Economic Consequences of Highway Improvements*. Washington DC: NCHRP-122.

PART C: METHODS AND MODELS

12 Travel-Demand Modelling: A State-of-the-Art Review

*M.M. Fischer**

1. Introduction

Transportation planning as a discipline is rooted in the tradition of engineering problem-solving and had its beginnings in the 1950s as an extension of highway design and traffic engineering. The primary concern of early transportation planning was the planning and provision of transportation facilities for the motor car in order to ensure maximum mobility for the anticipated increase in traffic. Problems of investment planning and resource allocation were approached mainly from a mechanistic and non-behavioural perspective. In general, transportation problems were viewed in relative isolation from the more general socio-economic problems and aspects of society. Models, methods and techniques were adopted, developed and applied because of their descriptive usefulness and without the justification of predictive validity or behavioural content (Anas 1982, p. 4).

Since the early 1970s, the emphasis in transportation planning and policy has shifted from the ideal of individual motorised mobility for all to a combination of motor-car restraint and public transport priority. In many metropolitan areas serious attempts have been made to regulate and restrain the use of motor cars in general and peak-hour commuter travel in particular, to develop and improve public transport alternatives to the motor car as well as to co-ordinate the existing transport systems (see Holtgrefe (Chapter 10) in this volume). This change in emphasis was fortified by facing serious environmental, social and economic effects of urban traffic problems such as traffic

*The author wishes to thank Peter M. Jones (Transportation Studies Unit, Oxford University) and Huw C.W.L. Williams (Institute for Transport Studies, University of Leeds) for their useful comments on an earlier draft.

congestion, increasing air and noise pollution levels, and so on. As energy and resource constraints became significant issues of public policy, more attention began to be paid to the potential energy and environmental effects of the construction and operation of transportation facilities. Evidently, transportation planning and policy is increasingly being viewed in a much broader context than in the past. Examples for this broadening view of the role of transportation are the use of transportation controls to improve air quality, transportation investments to catalyse economic and urban revitalisation and improvements to the quality of life through transportation actions such as vehicle-restricted zones (see Meyer 1983, p. 145). But transportation not only affects many aspects of community life. It is itself affected by changes of economic, social and political factors of society. Thus, there is an obvious need to deal with the interrelationships between transportation and other subsystems of the societal system. Linked models of land-use–transportation interactions are reviewed in Snickars (Chapter 15 of this volume).

The subject of transportation planning is concerned with the movement of people and goods as well as with the supply of and demand for transportation facilities. This paper focuses on passenger or travel demand analysis. The primary objective of travel-demand analysis is to provide an understanding of why people travel, to identify the essential factors influencing their travel decisions and to provide information for the evaluation of alternative transportation policies by predicting the travel consequences of alternative policies or planning. The past decade has witnessed strong research efforts in travel-demand analysis and several new avenues of qualitative research have opened up. Without claiming to be exhaustive, this paper attempts to review current knowledge of travel demand modelling in conceptual rather than technical terms. First, it provides an insight into the evolution of the field (see Section 2). Second, it describes the random utility travel choice model approach which has been brought to the attention of the transportation community in the early 1970s and has gradually gained credibility since that time (see Section 3). In Section 4, a variety of issues important in the application of this travel-demand framework are discussed, such as the definition and representation of choice sets, the incorporation of aspects of complex and constrained travel behaviour, alternative decision structures, sampling and estimation, model evaluation and model transferability. Concluding comments point to efforts in seeking new approaches to travel behaviour such as the introduction of the household rather than the individual as the decision-making unit and the activity-travel approach.

2. The development of travel-demand models: an historical perspective

Travel-demand analysis owes its beginnings to the pioneering Detroit, Washington and Chicago large-scale transportation studies which provided comprehensive information for the development, evaluation and implementation of future transportation planning proposals. A very large number of travel-demand models have been proposed and implemented in various transportation studies since that time. In order to compare and contrast these models, several categorisations using various criteria have been put forward (see, for example, Brand 1973; Manheim 1973; Domencich and McFadden 1975; Williams 1981). In these typologies the development of travel forecasting models is basically viewed in terms of a divide between two different generations, the first involving the so-called classical aggregate travel-demand models, and the second, the disaggregate perspective based on the probabilistic choice theoretic paradigm.

First-generation models emphasise the aggregate movement patterns of mode-specific trips within a travel network. They were developed as a process conducted with aggregates of individuals — termed traffic zones — within urban areas and are based on data representing zonal aggregates of socio-economic, land-use and transportation system variables. The traffic zones are considered as the basic 'behavioural' units in the travel forecasting process. The most well-known prototype of the first generation models is the aggregate urban transportation model system approach (UTMS) widely used in the United States during the 1960s and associated with the very broad macro-planning objectives of large urban transportation studies. The travel-demand forecasting process consists of the well-known sequence of trip generation, trip distribution, modal split and route assignment (see Figure 12.1). The trip-generation submodel forecasts the number of trips produced by each traffic zone as well as the number of trips attracted to each zone. The trip-distribution submodel uses the zonal trip productions and trip attractions predicted in the trip generation stage as input and yields the volume of trips between each pair of traffic zones as result. The modal-split submodel assigns proportions of each trip-interchange volume of trips to the various alternative modes of travel available. Finally, the route-assignment submodel allocates the trip bundles for each mode to routes on the modal network (see, for example, Wilson 1974, p. 129; Stopher and Meyburg 1976). The absence of any feedback between the various stages of the travel-demand forecasting process is a major weakness of this model approach. The submodels are applied in a unidirectional way. Thus, errors in submodels are compounded in any forward linkage.

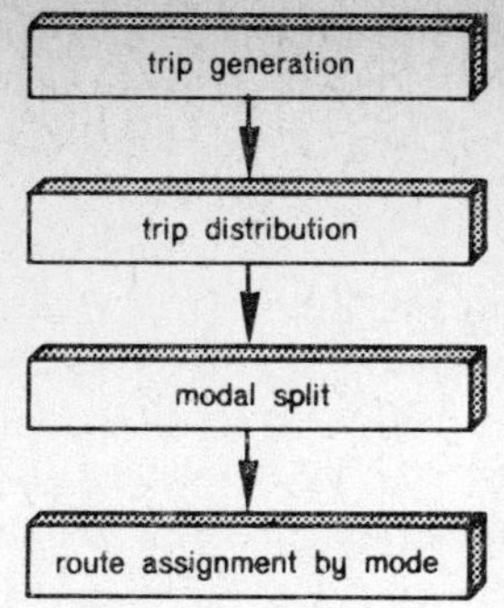

Figure 12.1 Sequence of submodels typically involved in the classical aggregate travel-demand model prototype

In the early 1970s, first-generation travel-demand models were heavily criticised, mainly because of their descriptive rather than causal nature of travel-demand relationships, their lack of a behavioural rationale and their lack of policy responsiveness in the context of new policy issues such as car-pooling schemes and bus schedules. A major area of dissatisfaction which was identified early on was the prediction of choices among modes of travel. The dissatisfaction with this particular aspect of the travel-demand forecasting process led directly to an emphasis on greater disaggregation in travel-demand analysis.

Considerable progress has been made with the development of the second generation or disaggregate travel-choice models within the framework of probabilistic discrete choice theory. This approach was brought to the attention of transportation scientists and planners in the early 1970s and has gradually gained credibility within the transportation community, especially through a series of four biennial international conferences on travel behaviour, held in South Berwick (Maine, USA) in 1973, in Asheville (North Carolina, USA) in 1975, in Tanunda (South Australia) in 1977 and in Grainau (FRG) in 1979. The disaggregate travel-choice models show several conceptual and practical advantages over the first-generation models. First, they are formulated and estimated at the level of the individual travellers and founded on an explicit principle of human behaviour (the principle of utility maximisation) rather than merely on statistically derived correlations in aggregate analysis. Secondly, they have the potential of increased policy sensitivity. In particular, they are capable of providing valuable insights into the likely implications of various transportation-system management strategies by making it possible to trace the behavioural outcomes of changes in transportation networks. Thirdly, they have the potential for greater statistical efficiency. And finally, they are highly flexible in that they can be applied at any level of aggregate prediction.

It is worth mentioning that at the same time aggregate models have been improved considerably by introducing household- and individual-based category analysis for trip generation, incorporating the generalised cost concept (with micro-parameters) within the entropy-maximising methodology and interrelating the stages of the travel-demand forecasting process. The SELNEC transportation model (see Wilson *et al.* 1969) and its descendants belong to the first aggregate models which anticipated elements of the new disaggregate modelling philosophy and are free from some of the criticisms directed against the classical aggregate model approaches. Thus, in many respects the distinctions between aggregate or first-generation and disaggregate or second-generation models are becoming blurred (see Williams and Ortuzar 1982b). It is possible to develop aggregate travel-demand models derived from a realistic representation of decision-making at the micro-level. There is no doubt now that travel-demand models, whether aggregate or disaggregate, should be based on a well-specified behavioural representation of the decision process. Thus, the clearest remaining distinction between the two classes of travel-demand models is the level of data analysis. Disaggregate choice models cannot be considered any more as a direct substitute for aggregate models. Each model type has a distinct role to play in transportation planning and policy (see Jones 1983, p. 90).

3. The random utility discrete choice approach: basic concepts and range of applications

The disaggregate model approach based upon the hypothesis of utility-maximising discrete choice behaviour has yielded the most important progress in travel demand research over the past 15 years. In random utility travel-choice models it is assumed that individuals' evaluation of available travel-choice options such as frequencies, destinations, modes and routes of travel, can be conceptually described by utility functions and that travel decisions are made on the basis of the utility-maximising principle. The utility of an alternative is represented as the sum of two components: a deterministic and a random one. The deterministic component accounts for the effects of the average tastes of the population and the observed alternative- and individual-specific attributes. The random element enters the utility function because certain choice-relevant attributes are unobserved and because the perception of observed attributes may vary from individual to individual. Random utility travel-choice models forecast the probability that an individual will choose a particular travel-choice option as a function of the observed attributes of the individual and the available alternatives. The functional specification of such a model involves three fundamental steps: specifying the probability distribution of the random terms, specifying the functional form of the deterministic component of utility and specifying the set of travel alternatives an individual is facing. If an error is made in one of these steps the resulting model may produce highly erroneous forecasts (see Horowitz 1982).

The models are usually classified according to the functional form of the probability distribution of the random terms. The multinomial logit model widely used in a variety of travel-choice contexts assumes that the random terms are independently and identically distributed (IID) across individuals and alternatives. It has been widely recognised that the independence of irrelevant alternatives (IIA) property — a property which implies that the relative choice probability of any two alternatives depends exclusively on their systematic components — can cause problems and lead to counterintuitive predictions when the alternatives are close substitutes for each other. Thus, the search for alternatives to the IIA-based multinomial logit model has been a major concern in discrete choice analysis. For more details on this issue see Fischer and Nijkamp (1985).

Many alternatives have been suggested in recent years to accommodate varying degrees of similarity between alternatives. The most general one is the multinomial probit model which can handle arbitrary correlation expressed in the form of a general variance - covariance matrix (see Hausman and Wise 1978). This model allows random taste variation across individuals with identical attributes. But it is rather intractable in practice, even though quite recently progress has been made in developing more efficient and accurate procedures, such as direct numerical integration methods (see Hausman and Wise 1978), the simulated frequency method (see Lerman and Manski 1981) and iterative approximation procedures (see Daganzo *et al.* 1977).

At an intermediate level between the two extremes of the multinomial logit and probit models lies the nested or hierarchical multinomial logit model, the most practical special case of the family of generalised extreme-value models which are generalisations of the multinomial logit models (see, for example, McFadden 1979; Fischer and Nijkamp 1985). Nested logit models take for granted a recursive sequential choice structure (for example, a 4-stage nested structure with the trip-frequency choice, the destination choice, the modal choice and the route choice forming the lowest level) where results of decisions on lower decision levels feed into those of higher levels. Inclusive values representing expectations of the outcomes of lower-level choices serve as the feedback linking mechanisms. This implies that the systematic part of utility has to be additively separable. Because partitioning of choices may affect the model results it is necessary to determine the correct sequence of choices. A sufficient condition for the nested multinomial logit models to be consistent with random maximisation is that the inclusive value parameters lie in the unit interval (see McFadden 1979). Since nested models are able to provide good approximations to true simultaneous decision structures where no choice hierarchy exists, they may also be used to simplify greatly the magnitude and computations of the demand estimation task in a simultaneous situation, especially when the set of travel options becomes unmanageably large (see Fischer and Maier 1986). Thus, nested logit modelling provides a convenient methodological framework for treating subsets of choices within a general model by relaxing the IIA assumption. It is important to distinguish the principles of the nested model from the classical aggregate four-stage sequential model approach where the stages of trip generation, trip distribution, modal split and route assignment are carried out in an unidirectional manner, possibly with iteration, but not with other interactions between the levels (see Daly 1979, p. 322).

Random utility discrete choice models have been very widely applied in travel-demand analysis in recent years. They have been used simply to replace the forecasting components of aggregate models. But often inflexibility in the large-scale aggregate framework has restricted the benefits obtained. Most success has been found in specialised policy analysis. For example, car pooling has been studied by Ben-Akiva and Atherton (1977) and the elasticity of petrol taxes, parking taxes, transit fares and housing taxes to finance public transit by Anas (1982). Travel choices modelled by means of the random utility travel-choice approach include choices of travel mode (see, for example, Charles River Associates 1967; Domencich and McFadden 1975; Sobel 1980), choices of travel destination and trip chaining (see, for example, Horowitz 1979; 1980b; Adler and Ben-Akiva 1979), choices of time of day of travel (see, for example, Abkowitz 1981). Random utility discrete-choice models have also been applied to multi-dimensional choice contexts, such as mode, destination and frequency (see Domencich and McFadden 1975; Horowitz 1979), mode, destination and trip chaining (see Horowitz 1980b), frequency, mode, destination and time of day of travel (see Charles River Associates 1967).

Changes in the transportation system are likely to have significant effects not only on travel decisions, but also on travel-related choices such as car-ownership, employment and residential location, and so on. In turn, these decisions may have a significant impact on travel demand, since, for example, travel decisions of an individual are constrained by fixed employment and residential location as well as by fixed car-ownership or availability. Thus, a fully successful travel-demand model has to take into account the structural relationships between these decisions which directly or indirectly influence trip-making behaviour (see Domencich and McFadden 1975, p. 9). There are good reasons why the longer-run travel-related choices are assumed to be intertwined with the short-run travel choices made conditional to the travel-related choices whereas within each of the two bundles of decisions a simultaneous structure may be assumed. Figure 12.2 illustrates one possible choice hierarchy in a travel and travel-related context. Until the nature of the interactions between transportation services, travel and travel-related decisions is better understood, there is little hope that travel-demand models will provide reliable tools for long-term policy analysis.

4. Specific problems and recent advances

Research on random utility travel-demand models has been going on now for over 15 years. During this time significant progress has been achieved. This section attempts to summarise some major advances which have been made in the following main research areas: model representation, sampling and estimation, model assessment and model transferability.

4.1 Model representation issues

Substantial research efforts have been devoted to issues such as the definition and representation of choice sets, the incorporation of aspects of complex and constrained travel behaviour and alternative decision structures.

A crucial problem area in formulating a travel-choice model lies in defining the choice set available to each traveller. In current practice, a universal choice-set faced by all individuals in the population is assumed. This assumption is very likely to break down, especially in the case of destination sets for non-work trips. Even though the set of potential non-work destinations may be very large in principle, the size of the choice set is severely limited in practice by a variety of perceptual filters, by household travel resources and space–time, contextual and institutional constraints on behaviour. Decision-makers

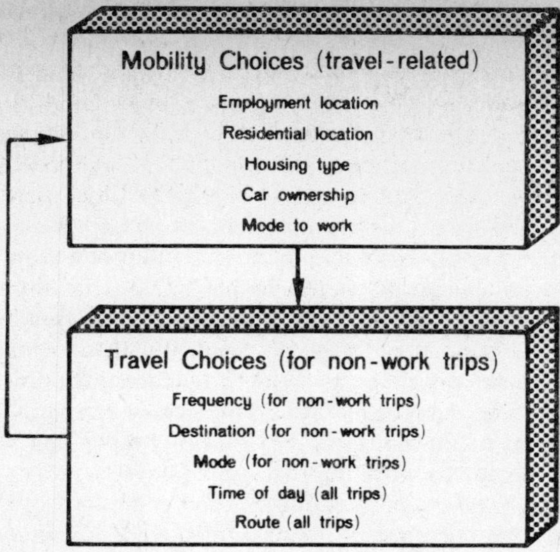

Source: Ben-Akiva and Lerman 1979, p. 669

Figure 12.2 A simple hierarchy of travel and travel-related choices

act under restricted knowledge of alternatives in accordance with individual search and information spaces. In order to accommodate such aspects of constrained behaviour it is necessary to divide the set of potential alternatives into feasible and non-feasible subsets. Then choices can be modelled within these restricted subsets in accordance with the random utility methodology. The feasible choice alternatives may be viewed as an outcome of the choice-set formation process. In principle, there are two possibilities to model the choice-set generation process as an integral part of the travel-choice framework. Exogenous choice set generation models proposed by Burnett and Hanson (1982) and Williams and Ortuzar (1982a) among others consider choice-set formation as a forerunner to the final choice, whereas endogenous choice-set formation emphasises that the final composition of the feasible choice alternatives is not known until the final choice is determined. This latter type of choice-set generation modelling has recently been suggested by Richardson (1982). The choice-set problem which is extremely important to make the travel-choice models more realistic certainly continues to be an area of future concern.

Applications of models of travel choice have generally assumed that the information about travel options available to the decision-maker is exogenous and subject to systematic inaccuracies. This classic assumption, however, is unrealistic. Individuals' information about travel options is not only imperfect, but also depends on observations made in the course of experience with the transport system and on information-gathering activities conducted in order to learn more about the system (see Manski 1981b). The integration of the dynamic relation between information and travel choice moves one away from the current cross-sectional to a dynamic framework where effects of experience, time-discounted preferences, learning processes, habit persistence, and so on, become central issues. In recent years, there has been an increased interest in developing panel data discrete choice models to examine dynamic aspects of travel behaviour. Heckman's (1981) pioneering work, although not implicitly including information concerns, may be considered as an important starting point for future research activities and opens up a whole new range of important methodological issues central to the process of modelling behavioural response in anticipation of improved predictive capability.

Current probabilistic models of travel choice embody compensatory decision rules. In such models it is assumed that individuals trade off attributes of the travel options in the decision process. Only little transportation research, however, has been conducted to verify the correspondence between travel choice processes and the linear additive utility formulations of these compensatory models. Recent empirical research has pointed to the notion that transport-system attributes are not compensatory and that response to attribute changes is discontinuous (see Stopher, Meyburg and Brög 1981). Especially in reasonably complex decision contexts a compensatory representation of the travel-choice process seems to be highly unrealistic. Discontinuous evaluation and choice processes may be captured basically by non-compensatory discrete choice models. Such models are based on dominance, conjunctive, disjunctive, lexicographic, satislex, minimax regret, elimination by aspect or similar decision rules in which changes in one attribute cannot be compensated by opposite changes in other attributes (see Foerster 1979; Timmermans 1984). Up to now, only the elimination by aspect models suggested by Tversky (1972a; 1972b) have received significant attention in the transportation community. Transportation researchers should consider the possibility of non-compensatory decision processes and test a broad range of compensatory and non-compensatory choice models before adopting any one model as an explanation of travel choice behaviour. Moreover, future research should focus on information processing and evaluation mechanisms involved in travel-choice behaviour.

Finally, the treatment of multi-purpose and multi-stop trips deserves at least a short note (for more details, see Hensher 1976; Hanson 1979; 1980; Hanson and Burnett 1981; Burnett and Hanson 1982). Only quite recently, some efforts have been undertaken to tackle this problem within the random utility discrete choice framework. A travel-pattern model has been suggested by Adler and Ben-Akiva (1976). This model is an important achievement in travel-demand modelling because it provides a framework to deal with trip chaining and to treat policy questions such as whether households are more likely to react to increases in petrol prices by increasing multi-stop, non-work travel rather than by reducing their frequency of travel to non-work locations. A major problem of this model approach, however, is that travel patterns are taken as the basic units of travel whereas the set of travel patterns available to households is in principle virtually infinite (Horowitz 1980a, p. 129). This problem may be avoided by a trip-based approach or non-work travel-demand approach suggested by Horowitz (1979, 1980b). In this framework the daily activity period is decomposed into a series of sufficiently small discrete time intervals, and travel demand over a day is obtained by simply summing up the individual demands of the time intervals. This approach, however, has difficulty in accommodating the interactions between past, current and future travel. There is no doubt that further work needs to be done to extend the travel-demand models in order to touch issues such as interactive decisions involving the whole household, the cyclical nature of travel demand for a given non-work purpose, and so on.

4.2 Sampling and estimation issues

The traditional sampling process in travel-demand modelling is exogenous stratified sampling (exemplified by the home interview survey). In exogenous sampling the population is classified on the basis of stratification criteria exogenous to the selected choice alternatives and then a random sample is drawn from each stratum where different strata may have different sample sizes. Under certain regularity conditions, maximum likelihood estimation from exogenous samples does not present any new problems in comparison with estimation from random samples.

Quite recently, choice-based sampling (exemplified by transit-on-board surveys) has been suggested as an important alternative to exogenous sampling, and significant progress has been achieved in developing appropriate maximum likelihood and related statistically sound estimators. In choice-based or endogenous stratified sampling the classification of the decision-maker population into subsets is based on the observed chosen travel options and for each and within each subset the required number of individuals is drawn at random. For example, in a study of travel-mode choice one may choose 300 individuals using each travel mode — bus, car, train, and so on. Choice-based sampling has a cost advantage and is especially appropriate when some choice alternatives are infrequently chosen.

Conventional maximum likelihood estimators will be inconsistent and, thus, asymptotically biased in choice-based sampling. This fact has not infrequently been overlooked in empirical applications. But in the recent past significant progress has been made in developing a variety of computationally tractable and statistically appealing choice-based sampling estimation procedures (see Manski and Lerman 1977; Manski and McFadden 1981; Cosslett 1981). Manski (1981b) describes three alternative approaches for obtaining statistically sound estimators. The first approach assumes that the attribute density function can be a priori restricted to a parametric family of density functions. This approach has been applied in practice only infrequently because computation is rather costly and theory does not give strong guidance about the parametric restriction on the attribute density function. The second approach, which does not involve the attribute density, leads for example, to the 'weighted exogenous sampling maximum likelihood' estimator (see also Manski and McFadden 1981, pp. 17–18). Use of this estimator assumes that the proportions of the population choosing each choice alternative are known. This assumption is quite often satisfied in applications. The third approach suggested by Cosslett (1981) involves the use of joint maximum likelihood estimation of model parameters and the attribute density function.

It is worth mentioning that a properly designed choice-based sample may provide more precise estimators at lower costs than a random sample of the same total size. Because of lack of information about the choices and independent variables in the population one may be forced to consider hybrid sampling procedures in which endogenous sampling is linked with additional survey data or statistics taken from a random sample of the entire population. Maximum likelihood estimators for a series of hybrid sampling procedures are provided by Cosslett (1981).

4.3 Model performance issues

Probabilistic choice models are highly sensitive to a large number of specification errors such as mis-specification of the choice set, incorrect specification of the probability distribution of the random component and incorrect functional form of the deterministic component of the utility function. Models with specification errors can cause large errors in the choice probabilities. Thus, the identification of specification errors is of central importance in travel-demand modelling.

Two types of formal statistical specification tests have been developed. The first type refers to comparisons of models with different specifications and includes likelihood ratio tests, Lagrangian multiplier tests and tests of non-tested hypotheses suggested by Horowitz (1982; 1983). These procedures, however, do not identify specific causes of specification errors. Furthermore, they involve testing logit formulations against parametric generalisations of themselves and are thus only of limited use for comparing entirely different model representations. Further research is needed on developing methods for testing non-logit choice models. The heuristic procedure suggested by Halperin *et al.* (1984) might be a starting point in this direction. The second type of procedure is based on testing the statistical significance of the differences between predictions and observations. For example, Horowitz (1984) suggests formal statistical tests for comparing predicted and observed aggregate shares in population strata.

The utility-maximising principle is, without doubt, extremely useful for travel-demand modelling activities. But its validity as a principle of travel behaviour is uncertain. Thus, there is a need to encourage empirical research on this fundamental question. Moreover, it is necessary to evaluate the utility-maximisation principle in terms of alternative decision rules such as simultaneous versus (recursive) sequential, compensatory versus non-compensatory, constrained versus unconstrained ones.

4.4 Model transferability

Since the development of a travel-choice model is relatively expensive in terms of the time and cost associated with data collection and analysis, the issue of model transferability is of central importance in practice. Temporal transferability is usually assumed when a model is used for predictive purposes. Also, spatial transferability has often been assumed and exploited rather widely in current practice.

In a strict sense, the term 'transferability' has a rigorous scientific meaning. For a model to be transferable over space and time it must represent a mathematical structure whose coefficients are independent of any specific spatio-temporal structure. Thus, the issue of transferability is one of parameter invariance over space and time. Most of the available evidence, however, suggests that there is no parameter invariance (Louviere 1981). But it is not known whether the lack of agreement between the parameter values is due to the differential influence of specification and other sources of error or due to real differences in travel-choice behaviour observed to occur in time and space. Thus, the transferability issue can only be completely resolved if considerable progress is made in separating the biases owing to specification and data from the real differences in the estimated model parameters (see Anas 1982, p. 126).

As a consequence, it is now widely accepted that the idea of accepting or rejecting a model transfer is inappropriate and that a more pragmatic perspective of viewing model transferability in a partial sense should be adopted in order to aim at a balance between the analysis resources and the accuracy of predictions within the constraints of time, money, data and professional capabilities (Ben-Akiva 1981, p. 670). From this pragmatic point of view it is important to determine which components of a model can be transferred to a new choice context and which components have to be adjusted. Formal test procedures have been suggested for this purpose. Koppelman and Wilmot (1982) show that the alternative-specific constants in the utility function which represent the average effect of excluded variables are least likely to be transferable. A model's transferability can be improved by using data from the new space–time context and re-estimating the values of these constants. Additional improvements may generally be achieved by rescaling the remaining utility function parameters with the use of space–time specific information. Further work is necessary to specify more clearly the limits of transferability in the context of complex travel-demand models.

5. Outlook: new approaches to travel behaviour

The current generation of random utility travel-choice models represents an important advance over other operational modelling approaches and reflects a widening of policy problems as well as an increasing awareness of the need to understand a wide range of travel and travel-related decisions. Nevertheless, the advances achieved in the recent past have been predominantly methodological rather than theoretical in nature.

The lack of the dynamics of adaptation response in the current cross-sectional travel-choice models was notable in provoking the call for new approaches to studying human activities within a space–time framework as suggested by Hägerstrand (see, for example, Jones 1979; 1983; Clarke *et al.* 1981; Hanson and Burnett 1981). Notions such as social roles, lifestyles and life cycles are important themes. The household rather than the individual is introduced as the decision-making unit. The activity-travel approach is the most prominent example of these new approaches to travel behaviour. This approach, being useful to provide deeper insights into the derived nature of travel and the structure of multi-purpose and multi-stop trips, emphasises the way individuals form and reinforce behavioural patterns of travel and other activities in space and time. Travel is considered as an integral component of the activity pattern. Spatial and temporal constraints as well as the linkages between household members deserve an explicit and more comprehensive treatment. Even though the studies adopting the activity-travel approach are valuable contributions to an important and highly neglected area, they are more exploratory and descriptive than explanatory and predictive in nature. Time will show how these new approaches will affect travel-demand modelling practice.

References

Abkowitz, M.D. (1981). 'Understanding the Effect of Transit Service Reliability on Work-Travel Behavior', *Transportation Research Record*, **794**, 33–41.

Adler, T.J. and M. Ben-Akiva (1976). 'Joint-Choice Model for Frequency, Destination and Travel Mode for Shopping Trips', *Transportation Research Record*, **569**, 136–50.

Adler, T.J. and M. Ben-Akiva (1979). 'A Theoretical and Empirical Model for Trip Chaining Behavior', *Transportation Research*, **13B**, 143–257.

Anas, A. (1982). *Residential Location Markets and Urban Transportation. Economic Theory, Econometrics, and Policy Analysis with Discrete Choice Models*. New York: Academic Press.

Ben-Akiva, M. (1974). 'Structure of Passenger Travel Demand Models', *Transportation Research*, **526**, 26–42.

Ben-Akiva, M. (1981). 'Issues in Transferring and Updating Travel-Behavior Models' in P.R. Stopher, A.H. Meyburg and W. Brög, eds, *New Horizons in Travel-Behavior Research*. Lexington, MA and Toronto: Lexington Books, pp. 665–86.

Ben-Akiva, M. and T.J. Atherton (1977). 'Methodology for Short-Range Travel Demand Predictions: Analysis of Carpooling Incentives', *Journal of Transport Economics and Policy*, **11**, 224–61.

Ben-Akiva, M. and S.R. Lerman (1979). 'Disaggregate Travel and Mobility Choice Models and Measures of Accessibility' in D.A. Hensher and P.R. Stopher, eds, *Behavioural Travel Modelling*. London: Croom Helm, pp. 654–79.

Brand, D. (1973). 'Travel Demand Forecasting: Some Foundations and a Review', *Highway Research Record*, Special Report 143, 239–82.

Burnett, K.P. and S.M. Hanson (1982). 'The Analysis of Travel as an Example of Complex Human Behavior in Spatially-Constrained Situations: Definition and Measurement Issues', *Transportation Research*, **16A**, 87–102.

Charles River Associates (1967). 'Disaggregate Travel Demand Models', vol. 2. Report prepared for the National Cooperative Highway Research Program, Transportation Research Board, Washington, DC.

Clarke, M.I., M.C. Dix, P.M. Jones and I.G. Heggie (1981). 'Some Recent Developments in Activity-Travel Analysis and Modeling', *Transportation Research Record*, **794**, 1–8.

Cosslett, S.R. (1981). 'Efficient Estimation of Discrete-Choice Models' in C.F. Manski and D. McFadden, eds, *Analysis of Discrete Data with Econometric Applications*. Cambridge, MA and London: MIT Press, pp. 51–111.

Daganzo, C., F. Bouthelier and Y. Sheffi (1977). 'Multinomial Probit and Qualitative Choice: A Computationally Efficient Algorithm', *Transportation Science*, **11**, 338–58.
Daly, A.J. (1979). 'Some Developments in Transport Demand Modelling' in D.A. Hensher and P.R. Stopher, eds, *Behavioural Travel Modelling*. London: Croom Helm, pp. 319–54.
Daly, A.J. (1982). 'Applicability of Disaggregate Models of Behaviour: A Question of Methodology', *Transportation Research*, **16A**, 363–70.
Domencich, T.A. and D. McFadden (1975). *Urban Travel Demand: A Behavioral Analysis*: Amsterdam: North Holland Publishing Co.
Fischer, M.M. and G. Maier (1986). 'Regional Labour Supply Mobility and the Logit Model: Testing Some Alternative Probability Choice Structures by Means of Monte Carlo Simulation' in M.M. Fischer and F.-J. Kemper, eds, *Modelle für diskrete Daten und raumbezogene Probleme*. Schriftenreihe des Österreichischen Instituts für Raumplannung, Reihe B12. Vienna: ÖIR, pp. 38–75.
Fischer, M.M. and P. Nijkamp (1985). 'Developments in Explanatory Discrete Spatial Data and Choice Analysis', *Progress in Human Geography*, **9**, 515–51.
Foerster, J.F. (1979). 'Mode Choice Decision Process Models: A Comparison of Compensatory and Non-compensatory Structures', *Transportation Research*, **13A**, 17–28.
Halperin, W.C, G.D. Richardson, N. Gale and C.M. Costanzo (1984). 'A Generalized Procedure for Comparing Models of Spatial Choice', *Environment and Planning A*, **16**, 1289–1301.
Hanson, S. (1979). 'Urban-Travel Linkages: A Review' in D.A. Hensher and P.R. Stopher, eds, *Behavioural Travel Modelling*. London: Croom Helm, pp. 81–100.
Hanson, S. (1980). 'Spatial Diversification and Multipurpose Travel: Implications for Choice Theory', *Geographical Analysis*, **12**, 245–57.
Hanson, S. and K.P. Burnett (1981). 'Understanding Complex Travel Behavior: Measurement Issues' in P.R. Stopher, A.H. Meyburg and W. Brög, eds, *New Horizons in Travel-Behavior Research*. Lexington, MA and Toronto: Lexington Books, pp. 207–30.
Hausman, J.A. and D.A. Wise (1978). 'A Conditional Probit Model for Qualitative Choice: Discrete Decisions Recognizing Interdependence and Heterogeneous Preferences', *Econometrica*, **46**, 403–26.
Heckman, J.J. (1981). 'Statistical Models for Discrete Panel Data' in C.F. Manski and D. McFadden, eds, *Structural Analysis of Discrete Data with Econometric Applications*. Cambridge, MA and London: MIT Press, pp. 114–78.
Hensher, D.A. (1976). 'The Structure of Journeys and Nature of Travel Patterns', *Environment and Planning A*, **8**, 655–72.
Hensher, D.A. (1977). 'Demand for Urban Passenger Transport' in D.A. Hensher, ed., *Urban Transport Economics*. Cambridge: Cambridge University Press, pp. 72–99.
Hensher, D.A. and P.R. Stopher (1979). 'Behavioural Travel Modelling' in D.A. Hensher and P.R. Stopher, eds, *Behavioural Travel Modelling*. London: Croom Helm, pp. 11–51.
Horowitz, J. (1979). 'Disaggregate Demand Model for Non-work Travel', *Transportation Research Record*, **673**, 56–71.
Horowitz, J. (1980a). 'Random Utility Models of Urban Non-work Travel Demand: A Review', *Papers of the Regional Science Association*, **45**, 125–37.
Horowitz, J. (1980b). 'A Utility Maximizing Model of the Demand for Multi-destination Non-work Travel', *Transportation Research*, **14B**, 369–86.
Horowitz, J. (1982). 'Specification Tests for Probabilistic Choice Models', *Transportation Research*, **16A**, 383–94.
Horowitz, J. (1983). 'Statistical Comparison of Non-nested Probabilistic Discrete Choice Models', *Transportation Science*, **17**, 319–50.
Horowitz, J. (1984). 'Testing Probabilistic Discrete Choice Models of Travel Demand by Comparing Predicted and Observed Aggregate Choice Shares'. Dept of Geography, University of Iowa. (Forthcoming in *Transportation Research*.)

Horowitz, J. (1985). 'Random Utility Travel Demand Models' in G.R.M. Jansen, P. Nijkamp and C. Ruijgrok, eds, *Transportation and Mobility in an Era of Transition*. Amsterdam: North Holland Publishing Co.

Jones, P.M. (1979). 'New Approaches to Understanding Travel Behaviour: The Human Activity Approach' in D.A. Hensher and P.R. Stopher, eds, *Behavioural Travel Modelling*. London: Croom Helm, pp. 55–80.

Jones, P.M. (1983). 'A New Approach to Understanding Travel Behaviour and its Implications for Transportation Planning'. Unpublished PhD thesis, University of London.

Koppelman, F.B. and C.G. Wilmot (1982). 'Transferability Analysis of Disaggregate Choice Models', *Transportation Research Record*, **895**, 18–24.

Lerman, S.R. and C.F. Manski (1981). 'On the Use of Simulated Frequencies to Approximate Choice Probabilities' in C.F. Manski and D. McFadden, eds, *Structural Analysis of Discrete Data with Econometric Applications*. Cambridge, MA and London: MIT Press, pp. 305–19.

Louviere, J.J. (1981). 'Some Comments on Premature Expectations Regarding Spatial, Temporal and Cultural Transferability of Travel-Choice Models' in P.R. Stopher, A.H. Meyburg and W. Brög, eds, *New Horizons in Travel-Behavior Research*. Lexington, MA: Lexington Books, pp. 653–66.

McFadden, D. (1979). 'Qualitative Methods for Analysing Travel Behaviour of Individuals: Some Recent Developments' in D.A. Hensher and P.R. Stopher, eds, *Behavioural Travel Modelling*. London: Croom Helm, pp. 279–318.

McFadden, D. (1981). 'Econometric models of Probabilistic Choice' in C.F. Manski and D. McFadden, eds, *Structural Analysis of Discrete Data with Econometric Applications*. Cambridge, MA and London: MIT Press, pp. 198–272.

Manheim, M.L. (1973). 'Practical Implications of Some Fundamental Properties of Travel-Demand Models', *Highway Research Record*, **422**, 21–38.

Manski, C.F. (1981a). 'Recent Advances in and New Directions for Behavioural Travel Modeling' in P.R. Stopher, A.H. Meyburg and W. Brög, eds, *New Horizons in Travel-Behavior Research*. Lexington, MA: Lexington Books, pp. 73–86.

Manski, C.F. (1981b). 'Structural Models for Discrete Data: The Analysis of Discrete Choice' in S. Leinhardt, ed., *Sociological Methodology 1981*. San Francisco: Jossey-Bass, pp. 58–109.

Manski, C.F. and S.R. Lerman (1977). 'The Estimation of Probabilities from Choice Based Samples', *Econometrica*, **45**, 1977–88.

Manski, C.F. and D. McFadden (1981). 'Alternative Estimators and Sample Designs for Discrete Choice Analysis' in C.F. Manski and D. McFadden, eds, *Structural Analysis of Discrete Data with Econometric Applications*. Cambridge, MA and London: MIT Press, pp. 2–50.

Meyer, M. (1983). 'Future Developments in Transportation Planning in the U.S.' in P.H.L. Bovy, ed., *Transportation and Stagnation: Challenges for Planning and Research*.Volume 2. Proceedings of the 10th Transportation Planning Research Colloquium. Delft: CVS, **2**, 143–9.

Richardson, A. (1982). 'Search Models and Choice Set Generation', *Transportation Research*, **16A**, 403–19.

Sobel, K.L. (1980). 'Travel Demand Forecasting by Using the Nested Multinomial Logit Model', *Transportation Research Record*, **775**, 48–55.

Stopher, P.R. (1975). *Urban Transportation Modeling and Planning*. Lexington, MA and Toronto: Lexington Books.

Stopher, P.R. and A.H. Meyburg (1976). 'Behavioral Travel-Demand Models' in P.R. Stopher and A.H. Meyburg, eds, *Behavioral Travel-Demand Models*. Lexington, MA and Toronto: Lexington Books, pp. 73–85.

Stopher, P.R., A.H. Meyburg and W. Brög (1981). 'Travel-Behavior Research: A Perspective' in P.R. Stopher, A.H. Meyburg and W. Brög, eds, *New Horizons in Travel-Behavior Research*. Lexington, MA: Lexington Books, pp. 3–32.

Timmermans, H.J.P. (1984). 'Decision Models for Predicting Preferences among Multiattribute Choice Alternatives' in G. Bahrenberg, M.M. Fischer and P. Nijkamp, eds, *Recent Developments in Spatial Data Analysis: Methodology, Measurement, Models*. Aldershot: Gower, pp. 337–54.

Tversky, A. (1972a). 'Elimination-by-Aspects: A Theory of Choice', *Psychological Review*, **79**, 281–99.

Tversky, A. (1972b). 'Choice-by-Elimination', *Journal of Mathematical Psychology*, **9**, 341–67.

Westin, R.D. and C.F. Manski (1979). 'Theoretical and Conceptual Developments in Demand Modelling' in D.A. Hensher and P.R. Stopher, eds, *Behavioural Travel-Demand Modelling*. London: Croom Helm, pp. 378–92.

Williams, H.C.W.L. (1977). 'On the Formation of Travel Demand Models and Economic Evaluation Measures of User Benefit', *Environment and Planning A*, **9**, 285–344.

Williams, H.C.W.L. (1981). 'Travel Demand Forecasting. An Overview of Theoretical Developments' in D. Banister and P. Hall, eds, *Transport and Public Policy Planning*. London: Mansell Press, pp. 283–306.

Williams, H.C.W.L. and J.D. Ortuzar (1982a). 'Behavioural Theories of Dispersion and the Mis-specification of Travel Demand Models', *Transportation Research*, **16B**, 167–219.

Williams, H.C.W.L. and J.D. Ortuzar (1982b). 'Travel Demand and Response Analysis — Some Integrating Themes', *Transportation Research*, **16A**, 345–62.

Wilson, A.G. (1973). 'Travel Demand Forecasting: Achievements and Problems', *Highway Research Record*, Special Report 143, 283–306.

Wilson, A.G. (1974). *Urban and Regional Models in Geography and Planning*. London: Wiley.

Wilson, A.G., A.F. Hawkins, G.J. Hill and P.J. Wagon (1969). 'Calibrating and Testing the SELNEC Transport Model', *Regional Studies*, **2**, 337–50.

Wrigley, N. and P.A. Longley (1984). 'Discrete Choice Modelling in Urban Analysis' in D.T. Herbert and R.J. Johnston, eds, *Geography and the Urban Environment. Progress in Research and Application*, 6, 45–94.

13 Transport and Mobility Research in a Changing Social and Technological Context

C.J. Ruijgrok

1. Causes of change in mobility

Mobility, no matter how it is defined, is always a consequence of human activities taking place at different locations. The amount of these activities, their location in time and space, the way they arise, determine the indicators from which mobility measures are derived. The number of passenger-kilometres per mode of transport, the total time spent travelling and the number of trips made all depend on the combined actions of individual household members. Research that addresses developments in mobility deals with the functioning of society as a whole. It is clear that such a research item is not easy to handle and that often simplifying assumptions are necessary to be able to analyse developments in a tractable way.

In a period of stable growth such simplifications do not lead to serious mispredictions in developments. No matter what is the real cause of change, time series analysis gives reliable results if the structural trend is described correctly. However, in a period of instability such simplification easily leads to erroneous results. Only if the key variables that cause instability are included in the analysis is an improvement of the explanatory power to be expected. But certainly this is not a sufficient condition. The impact of changes in such key variables may be filtered because of threshold phenomena, public inertia, aggregation bias and the like (Nijkamp *et al.* 1985). Neither time series analysis nor cross-section analysis are able to allocate the impact of restrictions on behaviour that were not topical at the period of measurement. If it is known that such restrictions exist, specific analysis tools are necessary to estimate their influence on behaviour.

The changed circumstances demand changed research subjects and methods. This paper tries to give an overview of these with a focus on sociological and technological changes causing shifts in mobility. A restriction is made regarding the type of mobility that is taken into account: this paper only deals with passenger transport. In Chapter 15 of this book, Snickars takes into account the consequences of technological change on freight transport.

2. Effects of external forces on transportation

In this section the effects of a number of external forces outside the transportation sector upon the level of mobility are discussed. The identification of the main factors that cause change in mobility figures is a necessary condition for predicting changes and describing the required analysis tools. Distinction is made between sociological, technological, economic and spatial developments.

2.1 Demographic developments

Changes in the composition of the population may cause important changes in mobility figures. Many European countries face a growing number of elderly people whose mobility needs are different from young people's. Figure 13.1 shows the expected consequences for mobility of the imminent changes in population developments in the Netherlands, under the assumption that the mobility level (person-mileage per mode per purpose) is constant per age and sex group. This figure shows that these demographic changes can form an important source of change.

The decline of public transport patronage is due in particular to the decrease in the number of schoolchildren using this mode of transport to and from school. The increase in bicycle usage later on is caused by the assumption that population will grow again in the 1990s, leading to a new set of schoolchildren.

It is questionable, of course, whether the assumption of stable mobility levels will be correct for such a long period. For instance, the usage of cars will be dependent on the percentage of people having a car and a driving licence at their disposal. Developments in car-ownership and licence-ownership will certainly influence mobility levels.

The effect of 'age' and 'ageing' is clearly described by Goodwin and Layzell (1983). They distinguish three kinds of influence upon individual or group behaviour: ageing effects, whereby the value of a variable (such as trip rates) is found to vary with the age of the individual; cohort effects, whereby the value of a variable differs systematically between cohorts after ageing effects have been allowed for; and period effects, whereby the value of an independent variable which

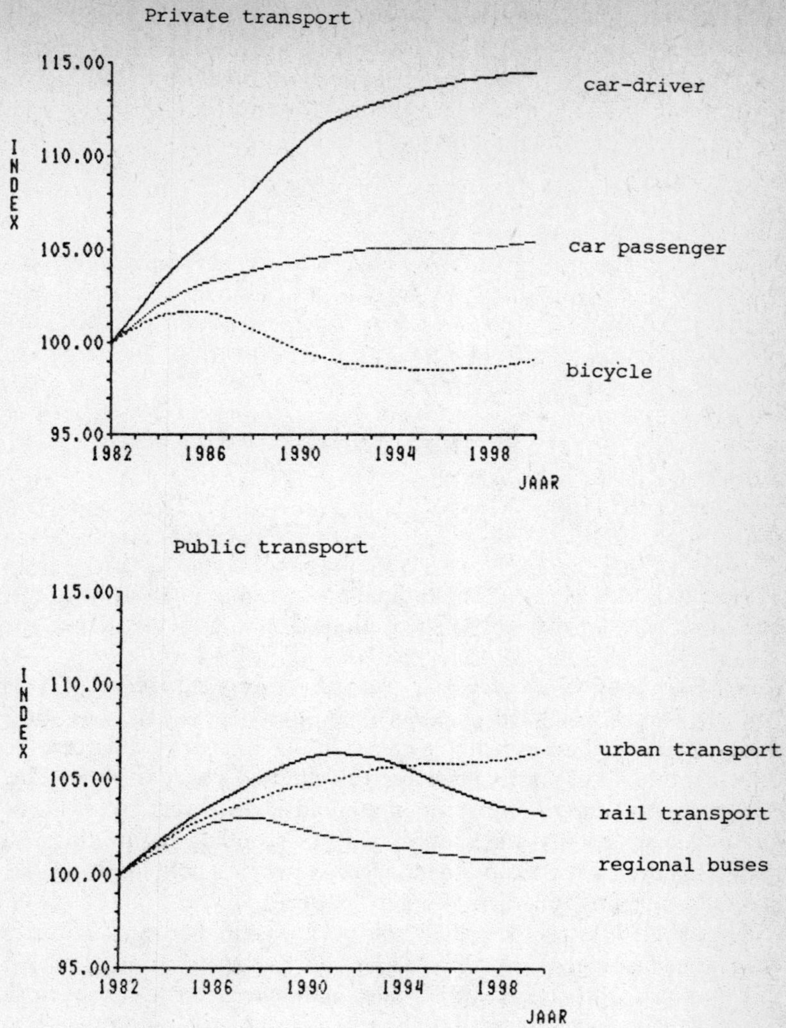

Figure 13.1 Mobility per mode: exclusively demographic effects

changes over time affects all age groups and cohorts uniformly. In their paper Goodwin and Layzell (1983) present an example from Wachs (1979) based on work of Baltes (1968). Here two cohorts ten years apart were surveyed at ten-year intervals. If the ages are grouped into ten-year bands then, at each survey, the younger cohort will occupy the age group which the older cohort has just left.

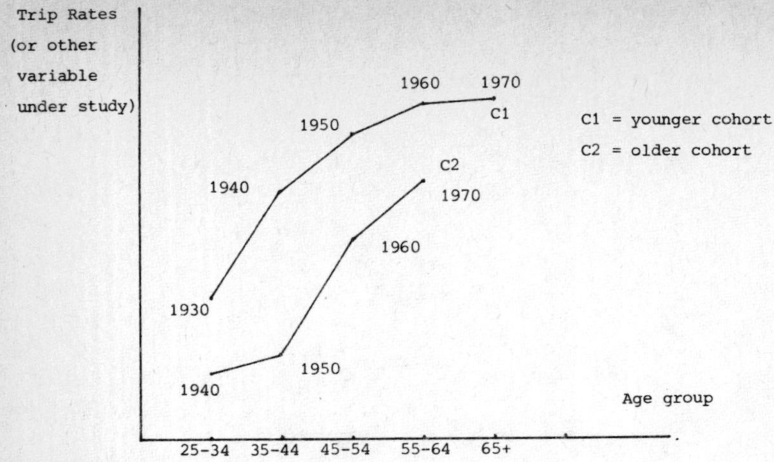

Source: Wachs (1979)

Figure 13.2 Developments of trip rates by age and cohort

Specific problems with longitudinal analysis and analysis of cohort behaviour will be mentioned in Sections 3 and 4 in this paper.

2.2 Emancipatorial development and other lifestyle changes

Not all households have changed their lifestyles as much as some trend-setters do. However, the increase in the number of divorces, the growing number of married women with children and (part-time) jobs, the change in responsibility for household tasks earlier reserved for one of the sexes only, the changed way of spending leisure time, all these are developments causing changes in people's activity behaviour and, through this, on their mobility patterns.

Pickup (1983) has described the relationship between women's travel disadvantages and their gender role in society. It appears that three kinds of restriction explain these differences in travel behaviour between men and women: family role-playing and car availability; family role activity constraints on accessibility (women have more severe time constraints to cope with than men); and the effect of gender roles on travelling conditions, specifically the difficulties of escorting children and the fear of sexual assault. What would the consequences of the removal of these restrictions be on mobility patterns? For instance, is car availability for women likely to increase in the future? Some figures show that this is not unlikely. Licence-holding among women in younger age groups is more than twice that of those in late middle and old age (Pickup 1983). Of course the additional costs of purchasing a second household car certainly forms a threshold, so it depends on agreement between household members whether car-availability for women will increase with increased licence-holding.

Changes in part-time work arrangements are not only likely to affect peak travel distribution but also to have their effects on women's participation in the labour market. Also, better co-ordination of times between work, school and nurseries could improve women's access to jobs. The increase in the number of single-person households could lead to a decrease in car-sharing possibilities and lead either to an increase in car usage or to an increase in public transport patronage, owing to the lower cost per mile per person. Clearly, lifestyle developments can have a huge impact on mobility patterns. They imply new types of activity, new conditions for these activities, changing options in changing choice situations.

2.3 Technological innovations

To-day the functioning of society is more dependent on technological aids then ever before in history. Without means of transport distances could not be covered as quickly as they are now. Without telecommunications information flows would not be as widespread, and without automation production processes would be organised quite differently. All these technological innovations have worked as push-factors in the demand for mobility and these developments have certainly not yet stopped. What will be the effect of increased telecommunications on mobility levels? Will it lead to substitution of travel by telecommunications or will travel be induced by it? Several studies have been devoted to this subject, all addressing the problem that this type of future exploration is of a highly speculative nature (Claisse 1982; Sviden 1983). Most researchers at the moment conclude that, although many organisational and social consequences could be the result of the 'boom' in technological developments, on balance these effects will have minor influences on aggregate mobility figures (Holst 1982; Kakumoto 1983).

Telecommunications can make some travel unnecessary (home–work trips, shopping, business trips) but it might also give rise to more travel for recreational and social purposes. There will also be possibilities for controlling transport flows (in vehicle information and advice, vehicle monitoring and control, automated guidance, automated public transport services). All these developments, if economic prerequisites for introducing them are fulfilled, will have a decreasing effect on traffic congestion, but whether this will lead to further concentration of activities is highly doubtful (Bly 1984). As

Kakumoto has stated: 'all aspects of human life today are constantly under the control of two elements: necessity and possibility'. New technologies can be demanded by the market to solve existing problems. It is also possible that new technologies will create their own demand. This means that the assessment of technological innovations in the transportation sector demands a broad treatment and cannot be studied in isolation. We shall elaborate on this subject in Section 4.

2.4 Economic developments

There is a growing consensus nowadays that the present economic stagnation will have a sizeable influence on the volumes of private and public transport in future years. In the Netherlands, for example, the levelling off and even decline in incomes, the increased unemployment and the decline in the number of jobs seem to have ended the steady growth of car-traffic volumes and the small but persistent decline of public transport patronage. This does not mean, however, that we can now expect a clear downward trend in car use or a steady increase in the use of public transport. In fact, the situation is becoming more and more confused. Some future developments are already visible or may logically be expected, and will influence the volumes of passenger transport in opposite directions. The net effect of these developments is highly uncertain, as is illustrated by overall volumes in the most recent years. Public transport patronage started to grow in 1978 and reached the fairly spectacular rate of about 5 per cent per annum, but this now seems to be levelling off. The steady growth in car traffic on the motorways came to a halt in 1980–1, but some increases have occurred since.

Under present circumstances, the task of researching the various factors that work in opposite directions and their net effect on passenger transport volumes has become even more important than it was in the past. It is certain that one of the most important factors is disposable income.

Although there is clearly a relationship between income and mobility, this is not always straightforward. The income variable correlates with many other variables which have a particular effect on mobility: level of education, age, lifecycle, for example. Mobility is dependent upon activity patterns and upon the availability of transport means, both of which are dependent upon income.

It is not generally possible to analyse the effects of changes on household income in isolation: parallel with changes in income, many other circumstances also change, each interfering with mobility patterns. A study dealing with the effect of a change in income on mobility should ideally give attention to two simultaneous effects:

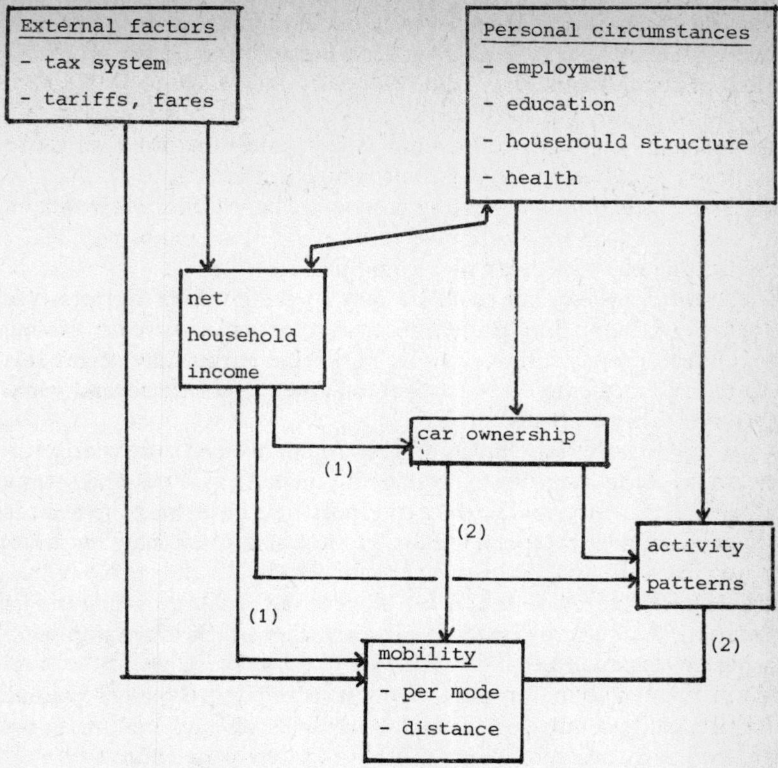

Figure 13.3 Relations between income and mobility

first, the *direct* effect of a change in earned income on the freely disposable budget and through this on expenditure in the transport sector; and second, the *indirect* effect of those circumstances that change simultaneously with income and which lead, via household activity patterns and locational characteristics, to changes in mobility.

In examining the first of these direct effects, the following questions arise: what is the effect of a change in income on the availability of transport means (that is, car-ownership)? and, what is the effect of income change on the usage of the available means of transport? The second indirect effect is of an even more complex nature. It deals with changes in employment, working hours, health, education, household structure, and so on, each of which affects activity patterns of household members as well as their incomes; some of these changes also affect travel opportunities. In a society all these effects occur simultaneously and to try to predict the possible outcome is not an easy task.

From the review of research results and adequate research methods of Baanders *et al.* (1985), some general conclusions are drawn on the effect of income and travel behaviour:

1. Income varies with many other circumstances and it is difficult to measure its effect in isolation from other effects.
2. The effects on travel behaviour attributed to income, derived from data gathered in a period of income increase, cannot be directly translated into effects of income decline.
3. In the short run substitutions may be made which will preserve present behaviour (postponing the replacement of cars, buying cheaper ones); in the long run, relocation effects may occur. It is therefore essential to distinguish between short-term and long-term income effects.
4. The effects of a decline in income do not always cause changes in travel behaviour in the same direction: travel distances may increase or decrease; public transport patronage may increase or decrease. It is therefore important to be able to estimate the effect on balance.
5. Research results so far do not support the expectation that public transport usage will be seen as a means by which to economise on travel expenditure.
6. It is essential to distinguish between different types of income decline; generally low rates for most people and high rates for some will cause different effects on travel behaviour.

Bly (1982; 1985) has reviewed available evidence showing how travel has been affected by the fuel price rises and recurrent economic difficulties in OECD countries which have followed from the initial oil crisis of 1974. He concludes that in the long term the tendency to dependence on the private car and dispersing land-use patterns will probably continue.

2.5 Dynamics in settlement patterns

Clearly the degrees of freedom that still exist depend on the flexibility of society to adapt to changing needs. The design and use of space is one of the most important constraints. In the development of towns different stages can be distinguished, succeeding one another as economic circumstances evolve, each stage showing its own spatial structure and transportation pattern (i.e. van den Berg and Klaassen 1982). This pattern is not predetermined and exogeneously given: in the long run spatial structures and transportation structures become part of an interdependent system in which *inter alia*, urban policies and income are important factors.

In periods of economic growth urban structures tend towards spatial deconcentration; should the present economic recession continue progressive spatial concentration is to be expected, each development having the opposite influence on travel distances. Nijkamp *et al.* (1985) review a number of theories developed to describe the process of structural change in urban dynamics. They distinguish between factors external to the urban system, that is, general economic decline, and factors internal to urban structural change, namely congestion, price developments, housing and environmental preferences, ageing and obsolescence of physical stocks.

3. Developments in transport costs and available means of transport

Apart from external factors as described in the previous section, developments within the transport sector have also played and will play an important role in the demand for transport.

In nominal terms both petrol prices and public transport fares have increased considerably in the last decade in most European countries. In real terms, however, this increase is much less and for certain periods even a decrease can be found.

There appear to be many ways in which car-owners can offset increases in the costs of ownership. The short-term response to higher operating costs such as fuel price rises seem to be a reduction in expenditure on car purchase: cars are retained for longer before replacement, and possibly the replacement car will be cheaper than it would otherwise have been. Also, by improving fuel efficiency the variable costs of driving can be reduced significantly, either by changing driving habits or by acquiring more fuel-efficient vehicles. Mogridge (1983) shows that in the period following 1974 there was a shift towards smaller-engined vehicles; and when the fuel price rises were eroded rapidly by inflation, the tendency towards buying larger-engined cars reappeared. Obviously there are limits to the extent to which the cost of car-ownership and use can be adjusted in the face of higher fuel prices and/or reductions in disposable income. Only about 10 per cent of the vehicle fleet is replaced each year. In countries with high car-ownership levels and a correspondingly high proportion of multiple-car-owning households a greater opportunity exists for reducing car use by combining trips that were earlier made separately.

It seems that reductions in car use are more often the result of reductions in trip rate and trip distance rather than of higher occupancy rates and change of mode (Bly 1985). Apparently, for a large number of trips no realistic alternative exists. High public transport patronage exists only in areas where the level of service is good and accessibility by car rather bad (inner cities, congested areas).

The rise in public transport patronage in many countries after the oil crisis and higher petrol prices is not the result of a substitution from car traffic but of increased subsidies leading to better and cheaper services. The cheaper fares have meant that it has been possible for people to make more use of public transport without increasing the fraction of budget devoted to this travel (Bly 1985). In many countries this trend has been altered by cuts in government subsidies for public transport. For instance in the Netherlands last year a plan was adopted which resulted in real fare increases of 10 per cent per annum on average for a number of consecutive years. Preliminary figures show that public transport patronage has decreased by 6 per cent since then. From the point of view of minimising deficits this loss is not serious because the increased revenues outweigh the losses, but from a social and environmental point of view it can be doubted whether the macro-economic cost–benefit ratio is still less than one. Cuts in public transport services which will be the result of a demand decrease will cause deprivation of people in isolated areas captive to public transport. Some argue that traffic safety and environmental quality will also suffer from this tendency towards cutting public transport services.

Planners responsible for allocation funds to investments in either car infrastructure or public transport infrastructure are faced with serious problems today: will car usage retain its old growth rate as the economy picks up again? Is the slowing down of the increase in public transport patronage incidental or structural? Is new car infrastructure necessary or should present facilities be maintained as well as possible? Has disurbanisation come to an end and will there be a trend towards the city centre, leading to an increase in demand for public transport facilities?

4. Intermediate conclusions and research questions

The uncertainties concerning future developments in mobility patterns are disturbingly great. Social as well as economic developments relevant to the transport sector are highly uncertain even for the near future, technological innovations are not likely to have a large impact in the short run, but in the long run estimates of their impact are very speculative, but can be substantial. Almost none of the key variables addressed above can be analysed in isolation. The economic situation is inter-related with social changes in our society, prices of commodities and funds available for new investments. The spatial organisation of society is also dependent on economic and social developments. Activity behaviour, car usage, car-ownership, public transport patronage are the result of numerous tendencies working in opposite directions. What will the outcome be on balance? The answer to this question is highly relevant for the planners and policy-makers responsible for allocating funds in the transportation sector.

Examples of research questions that arise at different levels of aggregation are:

- What changes in the composition of the population are likely to occur in terms of number of persons, households, composition of those households, demand for labour and education?
- What changes in (aspired) activity behaviour are likely to occur in terms of (part-time) employment rates, location of houses and jobs, emancipatorial changes, scheduling of activities, shopping behaviour, leisure activities?
- What will be the consequence of macro-economic developments in investment decisions of firms, disposable income of households, (aspired) consumption levels, economising behaviour, (un)employment rates?
- What developments will occur in car- and licence-ownership?
- What will be the development of commodity prices, especially petrol prices and public transport fares?
- What are the likely developments in car usage, public transport patronage, car-sharing, usage of slow modes?
- What are the consequences of changed mobility levels on the quality of the environment?

Questions of this kind are not topical at this time. In earlier years, planners have asked researchers the same kinds of question; however, the problem is that research methods and research assumptions that seemed to be adequate then are certainly not adequate now because of instability and interdependency of exogeneous variables and relationships.

5. Research methods adequate for today's needs

The research questions posed at the end of the previous section were tackled in periods of stable growth by making aggregate models of travel demand. The complexity of the underlying processes was simplified by making sequential submodels each dealing with an isolated element of activity behaviour, ultimately resulting in traffic flows on transportation networks. Trip production, trip distribution, modal split, assignment and car-ownership were analysed separately, assuming a given distribution of households and activities over space, and assuming that the differences in households living in a specific zone were negligible. Models of this type became popular in the early 1960s in the United States and were useful tools in order to make plans for long-run infrastructural projects in situations where stable economic growth existed. Most of these models were mainly car-orientated.

In the 1970s, owing to economic stagnation, limits to growth, increased congestion and opposition to environmental damage, more attention was focused on the possibilities for increasing the use of public transport. This required a more disaggregate approach, taking variation in individual circumstances in travel decisions into account. Especially the variation in access and egress distances and the differences in valuation of alternatives for different market segments required a lot of attention. Certainly these disaggregate travel-demand models have meant a big step forward in the understanding of travel behaviour and possibilities to formulate policies to restrict car travel and to promote public transport (Horowitz 1985).

The weakness of these models, which they share with their predecessors, is that they are constituted (calibrated) on cross-sectional data, which means that their explanatory power is derived from the variation between different spatial situations at a specific point in time. For analysing car-ownership, aggregate time series analysis techniques were used. Both these techniques fail as the *ceteris paribus* conditions that existed at the time of analysis are violated. Changing circumstances, like economic recession instead of economic growth, changes in restrictions on behaviour, changing evaluation of alternatives, require changes in the structure of these models and the value of their parameters. It is shown, for instance, that the reaction to an increase in income can be quite different from a decrease in income.

Furthermore, the reason for the origination of disaggregate travel-demand models, although it has not disappeared, seems to be less important in comparison with the other problems planners have to face. Experience in practice and analysis results shows that the possibilities for achieving considerable change in modal split are rather limited. What is topical now is the exploration of the possibilities of cutting down public transport deficits, making optimal use of existing facilities, minimising the risks of incorrect investment decisions. This calls for a different kind of research. This research should:

- incorporate uncertainty in input variables and parameters;

- be able to address the influence of changing restrictions to choice processes of individuals;
- make the evaluation of policy choices possible; and
- pay attention to the optimisation of usage of infrastructure and allocation of funds.

In the following paragraphs we mention some types of analysis that, partially, try to cope with these objectives.

5.1 Uncertainty analysis on an aggregate level

Normally, transport-demand forecasts based on transport models, whether aggregate or disaggregate, are presented as 'end-state' projections. Uncertainty in input variables, such as population, income, employment are either neglected or dealt with by making 'sensitivity tests'. In these tests alternative scenarios for input variables are translated into forecasts without assigning probabilities to the likeliness of each forecast.

In practice, errors in forecasts are attributable to two factors — the suitability of the model, and the accuracy of the input variables. The subject of model errors is a complex one, and there are a number of ways of approaching it, but for the sake of simplicity we will divide it into two areas — calibration error and specification error. If we have some confidence in the specification of the model, then the calibration error can be determined by standard statistical procedures.

Unfortunately, in models of human behaviour at any rate, we are very rarely in the position of having such a degree of confidence in the form of the underlying relationships, and if our specification is to any marked degree incorrect, we are no longer able to make such a simple deduction about calibration error. Thus the two sources of model error are often in practice difficult to separate.

If it is possible to quantify all these various errors by means of probability distributions, and if information is available about the dependence among random variables, techniques such as the Monte Carlo simulation can be used to identify probability distributions of output variables. Such a procedure is applied in a number of cases but to perform it for a complex transport model certainly is a complex task. MVA (1979) has proposed such a procedure and in fact has shown its applicability, using simplifying assumptions on the number of error sources and the probability distribution concerned.

This exercise could be much simplified if it were possible to make transport-demand models without taking spatial variation into account. In fact such a procedure was chosen for a study undertaken by our group under contract to the Dutch Ministry of Transport

(Ruijgrok and van Maarseveen 1984).

In this study the level of mobility, measured in terms of passenger-kilometres, is related to various indicators of economic and demographic development by means of direct elasticities and cross elasticities. This model is used as the basis for the Monte Carlo simulation.

The value of this model exercise is above all that it addresses the relative influence of the different sources of uncertainty and that it is able to allocate mobility categories that are highly sensitive to change. This procedure has two main weaknesses: the assumption of stable mobility patterns in each age and sex group will only be valid for a short period of time, because of all kinds of moral and cultural changes; and the assumption that mobility patterns can be modelled ignoring changes in the spatial distribution and spatial circumstances can also be made only for relatively short periods and on a very aggregate scale. The advantages and disadvantages of this method should therefore be weighed up. Certainly such a method is not able to help policy decisions only relevant for a specific region, like the construction of a road or the improvement of a transit line.

If the policy questions are rather general and the uncertainties on mobility developments are mainly due to factors outside the transportation sector that are assumed to influence mobility in a general way, such a procedure might help to give a rough estimate of the reliability of aggregate forecasts.

In fact the problem is often whether to undertake a long-lasting in-depth survey which gives the correct answers far too late, or a short, coarse type of analysis giving biased estimates fairly quickly. If possible, one should undertake both exercises: preliminary calculations on a coarse level can help the design of the analysis on a finer level.

5.2 Analysing changing behaviour over time

Classically, there are three types of analysis designed to measure changes over time, with increasing complexity: time series analysis; repeated cross-sections; and longitudinal panels.

In time series analysis, one or more variables are measured over a given period of time at a number of time intervals. Models are constructed in which the behaviour over time of one variable is related to that of others. Typically these time series data are not concerned with the individual level but use existing aggregate-level data. Although many (econometrical) types of research are based on this type of analysis, it has some fundamental weaknesses: it does not take into account the variability of behaviour between members of the population; nor does it not take into account which parts of the population change and to what extent. In time series analysis it is not possible to distinguish between the different circumstances that exist in the population and the consequences of changed circumstances on behaviour. Therefore this type of analysis could disguise causal relationships.

In repeated cross-section analysis a number of research units (not necessarily the same) are observed during a number of time periods (points). In this type of analysis the first weak point of time series analysis is counteracted but the second remains. This type of analysis is generally of a more complex nature than time series analysis, because the pooling of different sources of variation leads to statistical problems which have to be solved. The differences in circumstances that influence behaviour (car-ownership, income, distance to the station) can be taken into account, thus allowing a much more detailed level of analysis. By performing repeated analysis of cross-sectional data also the unstability of model parameters over time can be established. In general, however, it is not possible to identify changes in behaviour of specific (types of) individuals.

In longitudinal analysis this identification of changing behaviour is possible, ideally, if the data set is complete. This completeness of the data set is one of the severest problems with longitudinal data analysis. Owing to non-response and other causes it is very hard to establish the same sample more than once. Also there exists the problem of bias because the behaviour of the individuals may be changed because of being a member of a panel (see, for example, Baanders *et al.* 1982). If these problems can be solved a rich variety of analysing possibilities exists, which are able to address the changing composition of the population and the causes of their changed behaviour.

Goodwin and Layzell (1983) have recently given an excellent review of the research alternatives one has in trying to address changing behaviour, postulating that behaviour 'sticks to people', and hence their sensitivity to stimuli is related to their age. His research shows the importance of taking into account changing conditions in analysing changing behaviour.

In addressing the research questions mentioned in the previous chapter it is clear that longitudinal analysis can provide the best answers if enough data are available, especially for analysing behaviour that is related to changed circumstances. Time series analysis is valuable in particular when one wishes merely to monitor the changes in the output indicators. Repeated cross-section analysis makes the changes in the mobility structure visible. The value for planning purposes depends on the translation of these research results into predictions of trends and structural changes. Here the evaluation of the usefulness of the analysis tools mentioned above gives just an opposite ordering. Models derived by time series analysis can in general easily be applied in making predictions, models based on repeated cross-section give more problems whereas in general it is very difficult to derive forecasting models from longitudinal analysis methods. This analysis technique gives information on the causes of change and this information can be used qualitatively for making predictions, but interpreting such predictions quantitatively is far more problematical for the most part.

5.3 Analysing restrictions on behaviour

Research concerning choice behaviour pays more and more attention to the inclusion of the information of restrictions on the availability of alternatives. Brög and Erl (1981) were among the first to identify the importance of the incorporation of information on choice restrictions analysing activity behaviour. More recently this line of thought has been adopted by a number of researchers working in different fields of transport research. Restrictions that are taken into account are the time and money budgets and the means of transport that are available in particular. These restrictions influence the set of alternatives travellers have at their disposal and therefore play an important role in describing mobility behaviour. MVA (1981) has proposed this line of thought for the application of a model designed specifically for long-distance trips, and such ideas can also be found in activity-based travel analysis (Recker and Kitamura 1985).

Different kinds of mechanism are used to restrict the choice set to realistic proportions, such as maximum, conjunctive and disjunctive choice strategies. This area of research is not yet well developed and much research has still to be done.

A specific way of treating changing restrictions on behaviour has recently got increased attention. Several researchers (such as Louviere *et al.* 1981) have proposed the use of stated preference techniques instead of revealed preference methods. Using this type of analysis, choice situations can be created that do not exist in reality. By controlling the design of such experiments carefully, it is possible to analyse the expected effect of changed circumstances on behaviour. Critics of this method argue that intentions to behave are not equivalent to real choice behaviour, but some examples show that this method can be very effective and even in some cases is to be preferred to revealed preference techniques. This type of research can be highly relevant for policy-making because the effectiveness of proposed planning options that do not yet exist can be tested. However, as empirical evidence on the method is still very limited, one must be careful in assuming this is the panacea for many research questions.

6. Research directions

In this section we shall mention very briefly research subjects that will deserve further attention in the near future. The subjects are derived by comparing the topical questions of today with existing research methods. From this comparison it appears that there is a lack of understanding of the way the transport sector functions, internally as well as externally. A better understanding is required in the way exogenous as well as endogenous developments influence levels of mobility and in the way transportation planning can play a role in guiding mobility in a desired way. Allport and Gwilliam (1982) conclude by means of an investigation of the state of the art on a European level that a large research effort is necessary.

The research questions mentioned in Section 4 can partly be tackled by the research methods mentioned in Section 5. Each of the types of analysis described (uncertainty analysis, longitudinal analysis, cognitive choice analysis) will have to play its role in this. Specific attention is to be given to the following subjects:

1. Aggregation. The translation of analysis results of very detailed activity behaviour analysis into aggregate terms is still very hard to make. What is necessary here is a sound method of aggregating disaggregate data. This involves measurement of (changing) choice situations in society, the interdependency between explanatory variables and the development of simulation techniques that can take care of the aggregation problem.
2. Data availability. The setting up of an extensive longitudinal data base that enables us to research changing behaviour more accurately and to show the changing of structural relationships in society.
3. Simultation. The further investigation of the usefulness of stated preference techniques and other laboratory simulation experiments.
4. Social change. The extension of research dealing with the consequences of social changes in society as information in this subject is rather limited. This research can address the consequences of emancipatorial processes, unemployment and the like.
5. Interaction. Studies that deal with the interactions between the urban development and developments in the transportation sector are necessary.
6. Uncertainty in planning. Methods need to be developed that aid planners to make decisions in uncertain circumstances. Risk analysis, flexible planning methods, adding of additional data that reduce uncertainty and so on.

It is clear that this list can be enlarged further if specific research questions are taken into account.

References

Allport, R. and K. Gwilliam (1982). 'Long Term Options and Forecasts for Transport in Europe'. Leeds: Institute of Transport Studies, FAST occasional papers no. 25.

Baanders, A., J.M. Garden and W. Brög, (1982). 'Panels: Attractions and Pitfalls'. Paper presented to the PTRC Annual Conference, Warwick, July.

Baanders, A., J. Kremer-Nass and C.J. Ruijgrok (1985). 'Income decline and Travel Behaviour: Some Recent Dutch Findings and Research Orientations' in Jansen *et al.* (1985).

Baltes, P.R. (1968). 'Longitudinal and Cross-sectional Influences in the Study of Generation Effects', *Human Development*, **2**.

Bly, P.H. (1982; 1985). 'The Effect of the Recession on Travel Expenditure and Travel Patterns', in OECD-proceedings of the workshop on The Impact of the Economic Situation on Travel and Urban Areas, Paris. (An updated version of this paper is published in Jansen *et al.* (1985).

Bly, P. (1984). 'Surface Transport' in J. Brotchie, *et al.*, eds, 'Technological Change and Urban Form. London: Croom Helm.

Brög, W. and E. Erl (1981). 'Application of a Model of Individual Behaviour (Situational Approach) to Explain Household Activity Patterns in an Urban Area and to Forecast Behavioural Changes'. Paper presented to the TSU Conference on Travel-Demand Analysis, July.

Claisse, G. (1982). 'Transport and Telecommunications'. Report of the 59th Round Table on Transport Economics, European Conference of Ministers of Transport, Paris.

Goodwin, P.B. and A.D. Layzell (1983). 'The Differences between "Age" and "Ageing" for Public Transport Policy: An Application of Longitudinal Analysis' in P.H.L. Bovy, ed., *Transportation and Stagnation: Challenges for Planning and Research*. Proceedings of the 10th Transportation Planning Research Colloquium. Delft: CVS.

Hall, P. (1985). 'Urban Transport Planning: Paradoxes for the 1980s', in Jansen *et al.* (1985), 367–76.

Holst, O. (1982). 'European Transport: Crucial Problems and Research Needs, a Long Term Analysis'. FAST (Forecasting and Assessment in the Field of Science and Technology) series, no. 3. Brussels: Commission of the European Communities.

Jansen, G.R.M., C.J. Ruijgrok and P. Nijkamp, eds (1985). *Transportation and Mobility in an Era of Transition*. Amsterdam: North Holland Publishing Co.

Kakumoto, R. (1983). 'Dream and Reality in New Technologies', *IATTS Research*, **8**, 102–10.

Louviere, J.J. *et al.* (1981). 'Laboratory-Simulation versus Revealed-Preference Methods for Estimating Travel Demand Models', *Transportation Research Record*, **794**.

Mogridge, M.J.H. (1983). *The Car-Market: A Study of the Statistics and Dynamics of Supply–Demand Equilibrium*. London: Pion.

MVA—Martin & Voorhees Associates and Van den Broecke Social Research BV (1981). 'Long Distance Travel Study, Phase 1'. Study prepared for Projectbureau Integrale Verkeers- en Vervoerstudies. Den Haag.

Nijkamp, P., A. Rima and L. van Wissen (1985). 'Structural Changes in Urban Dynamic Models' in Jansen *et al.* (1985).

Pickup, L. (1983). 'Travel Issues in Women's Job Choice — an Activity Based Approach'. Unpublished PhD thesis, University of Reading.

Recker, W. and R. Kitamura (1985). 'Activity-Based Travel Analysis' in Jansen, *et al.* (1985).

Ruijgrok, C.J. and M.F.A.M. van Maarseveen (1984). 'A Method for Making Short Term Predictions of Passenger Transport'. Paper presented at the 11th Transport Planning Research Colloquium, The Hague.

Sviden, O. (1983). 'Automobile Usage in a Future Information Society', *Futures* (December).

Tacken, M. and C.J. Koman (1983). 'Impacts of Changing Employment States on Household Travel Mobility' in P.H.L. Bovy, ed., *Transportation and Stagnation: Challenges for Planning and Research.* Proceedings of the 10th Transportation Planning Research Colloquium. Delft: CVS, 1 225.

Van den Berg, L. and L.H. Klaassen (1982). 'Interrelationships between Car Use and Changing Space–Time Patterns' in: *The Future of the Use of the Car*. Paris: OECD.

Wachs, M. (1979). *Transportation for the Elderly*. Berkeley: University of California Press.

14 Transport and Location in Integrated Spatial Models

M. Wegener

1. Introduction

That transport opportunities codetermine location decisions is one of the fundamentals of regional science. Human settlements, commerce and industry first developed and prospered at river crossings, natural harbours or along important trade routes, later along railway lines or canals and still more recently near motorways and international airports. The contributions by von Thünen, Weber, Lösch and others introduced space (that is to say, transport costs) into economics and thus paved the way for new disciplines like urban or regional economics. In the 1950s the notion that transport was also a major force behind the internal spatial structure of regions became generally recognised. It was obvious that the urban sprawl observed in American metropolitan areas could not have occurred without the mass diffusion of the private motor car. Empirical investigations followed, and Hansen (1959) could demonstrate 'how accessibility shapes land use'. It was soon recognised that transport and location decisions are mutually dependent, and so the 'land-use transportation feedback cycle' became a widely used stereotype in the planning literature.

However, it took more than a decade to develop tools to deal effectively with this kind of two-way interaction in analytical models. For virtually all urban and regional models of the 1960s the transport–location interface was a one-way street: transport affected location via fixed travel times or costs, and no impacts of land use on transport were modelled. This was particularly true for the broad stream of modelling approaches following Lowry's (1964) model, including many of its later extensions and refinements. Even the 'land-use transportation studies' conducted in large American cities, despite their name, applied separate models for land use and transport and nowhere achieved their integration (Boyce *et al.* 1970).

It was only when Putman developed the first version of his ITLUP model package in the early 1970s that land-use transport interaction modelling really began (for a retrospective see Putman 1983). Now the transport cost matrix itself became part of the model and reflected the impacts of location on transport in terms of congestion, capacity bottle-necks and cost differentials, which again would have their impact on location in the next round.

From there on the number and variety of approaches to tackle the transport–location interaction problem increased tremendously. It is impossible to review all of them in a short paper. There exist a number of excellent reviews of the area (see, for instance, Senior 1973; 1974; Los 1979; Berechman and Gordon 1986). So the review undertaken here does not aim to be complete, but focuses on a few aspects thought to be of particular relevance to the ongoing discussion about new theoretical developments in the modelling of spatial dynamics.

The paper proceeds as follows. First, are spelt out what is understood by integrated spatial models, and what are the major links leading from the transport sector to other subsystems of the urban or regional system and vice versa. Next, current model approaches addressing the transport–location interface are reviewed in terms of kind of interaction, dynamic structure and underlying causality assumptions. It is demonstrated that virtually all current land-use transport models are based on the work–home relationship and that most of them are expressed in the form of the singly constrained spatial-interaction location model. Starting from a critique of that model, it is argued that future land-use–transport models should be based on a more balanced consideration of spatial and aspatial locational factors.

2. Integrated spatial models

Models are simplified representations of objects of scientific investigation designed in order to gain insight into their behaviour under changing conditions. Simplification is the essence of model-building, and the success of the modelling exercise depends on the skill with which it is done. Basically there are two ways of simplification: reduction in scope or in detail.

In regional science, model builders have predominantly opted for reduction in scope. In their search to understand the complex behaviour of urban or regional systems, regional scientists have tried to identify groups of actors behaving in similar, regular and predictable ways, such as travellers, shoppers, workers, households, firms or organisations. Next they have tried to separate the decision fields in which these actors pursue their specific activities such as travel, shopping, finding a job or residence, establishing a business, investing, producing or shipping commodities. Such decision fields are commonly called markets: the transport market, the labour market, the retail market, the housing market, the construction market, the land market, and other less visible markets like the ones for knowledge and capital. Finally they have constructed models of these markets: transport, retail, employment, housing or land-use models.

Characteristically, such models focused only on one, at most two, of the decision fields or markets at a time and thus comprised only a small section of the activities relevant for regional development at large. However, the markets interact and these interactions cannot be ignored without missing essential feedback information. This was the motivation for building more comprehensive, multi-activity urban and regional models that explicitly addressed the interconnectedness of the various urban and regional markets.

Such models are called 'integrated' spatial models in this paper. In particular, the term is used for empirically orientated, spatially disaggregated, multi-activity mathematical models built for the purpose of forecasting the spatio-temporal development of urban and regional systems, where 'multi-activity' indicates that the model includes more than one sector or field of human activity such as employment, population, housing and transport, and 'urban and regional systems' may be anything from a town to a system of regions in a nation.

To fix ideas, an 'ideal-type' multi-activity urban/regional model will now be sketched out. Figure 14.1 represents one possible realisation of such a model, with each box standing for a group of variables and adjacent boxes being closely interrelated by causal links. The arrows indicate the direction of the most important links; however, at this level of aggregation most links are bidirectional.

It is noted that the model in Figure 14.1 is only part of a multi-level model system, as information flows enter it from above and leave it from below. The model can be considered as representing the 'urban' level in a two-level spatial system where the top level represents the larger region or a system of regions within the nation, for example, a state or province or any larger spatial entity for which aggregate economic and demographic forecasts exist (for a discussion of the two-level system model see Wegener 1984). The 'urban' level is subdivided into geographical sub-units called zones.

It can also be seen that the model is organised by markets. Four markets are distinguished: the urban transport market; the urban

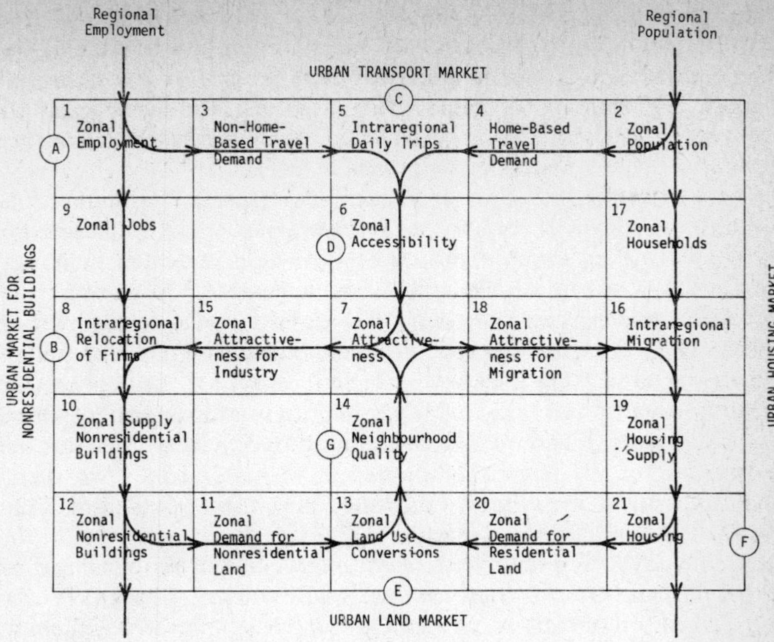

Figure 14.1 An integrated spatial model

market for non-residential buildings; the urban housing market; and the urban land market. These four markets form the four sides of the model diagram linking the corner boxes or major stock variables of the urban system: zonal employment; zonal population; zonal non-residential buildings; and zonal housing. Of these, the two on the left-hand side refer to the production or employment sphere, the two on the right to the population or household sphere. Each market is represented by two other boxes identifying demand and/or supply and a central box containing the relevant transactions occurring in each market: intraregional daily trips; intraregional relocation of firms; intraregional migration; and zonal land-use conversions. The four markets are interconnected by the central boxes of the diagram representing attractiveness indicators, each composed partly of spatial, or accessibility, and partly of aspatial, or place utility, attributes.

One possible way of tracing the most important causal links and feedbacks in this paradigmatic model is to follow the numbers in the boxes: in a top-down perspective, total regional employment and total regional population are disaggregated to zonal employment (1) and zonal population (2). These are the causes of non-home-based (3) and home-based (4) travel demand which, in conjunction with transport supply, results in intraregional daily trips (5). The accessibility (6) derived from such trips represents an essential component of the locational attractiveness of the zones (7).

For predicting intraregional relocations of firms (8), employment needs to be converted into jobs or work-places (9). They represent the demand for floor-space in the market for non-residential buildings, where new or vacant such buildings represent supply (10). New factory or office buildings consume land (11) and are added to the existing stock (12), which also changes through degradation, rehabilitation or displacement. Changes in land use (13) affect the neighbourhood quality of a zone (14), the other important component of zonal attractiveness (7), and as such are an input to relocation decisions of firms (15).

For predicting intraregional migration (16), zonal population has to be aged and converted into households (17), the demand side of the housing market. The supply side of the housing market is represented by zonal attractiveness for migration (18) and housing supply (19). The latter may be new housing competing with non-residential buildings in the land market (20), or vacant existing stock (21). Also residential buildings change through degradation, rehabilitation or displacement.

The letters in the circles on the edges of boxes of Figure 14.1 indicate local government policy instruments. Economic policies include direct subsidies (A) or relocation assistance (B) given to individual firms. Policies to improve the residential quality of the region may include upgrading of the public transport system (C), new road construction (D), land-use controls (E), public housing programmes (F) or neighbourhood improvement schemes or new public facilities (G).

Of course, no existing model can be expected to contain all the subsystems, causal links and policies listed in this section. However, the ideal-type model may serve as a useful bench-mark to evaluate current model approaches in terms of their claim to represent the relevant aspects and interactions of the modelled system. This will now be done for some land-use transport models.

3. Models of transport and location

With the above comprehensive model framework in mind, the 'land-use transportation feedback cycle' can be represented as in Figure 14.2.

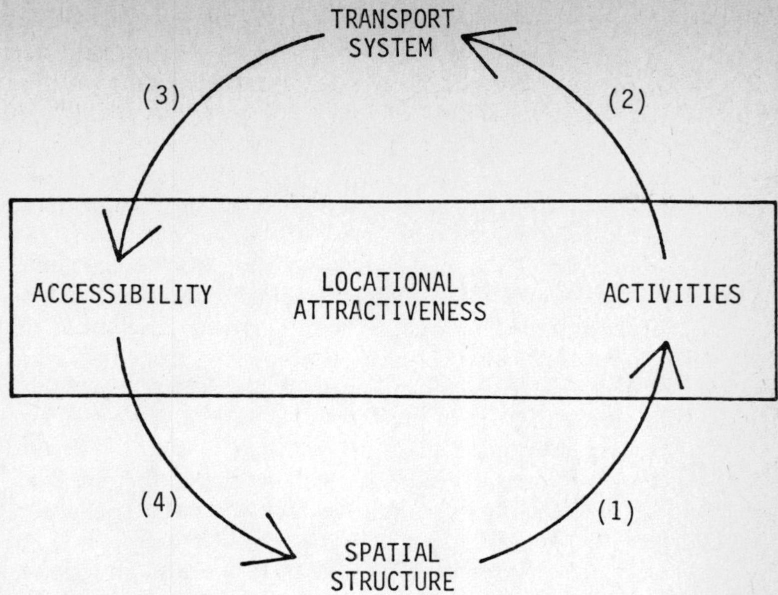

Figure 14.2 The land-use transportation feedback cycle

1. The *spatial structure* of the region determines the distribution of *activities* in space.
2. *Activities* generate traffic in the *transport system.*
3. The response of the *transport system* affects the *accessibility* of locations.
4. Locations with high accessibility attract more development than less accessible ones thus changing the *spatial structure*.

Hence a location is characterised by the activities it accommodates and by its accessibility. Activities *and* accessibility together constitute the locational attractiveness of a location.

If that is a valid description of the interaction between transport and location, it may be asked how they are represented in models claiming to address the transport-location interface. For this purpose, a sample of 20 urban models documented in the literature have been selected for this review. Although most of them are fairly well known, they will be briefly commented on in chronological order.

3.1 The sample of models

The sample starts with two historical examples. The first one is the

Herbert and Stevens (1960) residential location model using linear programming to allocate households and housing in a region, the other the celebrated 'Model of Metropolis' by Lowry (1964), later put into matrix form by Garin (1966). Lowry for the first time used the singly constrained gravity or spatial-interaction location model to allocate households to residential locations as a function of workplace locations and work-to-home travel costs. In addition he introduced feedback between household and service locations by nesting two spatial-interaction models into each other. Wilson (1970) generalised the gravity model subject to marginal constraints to produce a 'family of spatial interaction models', and replaced its power function by the negative exponential or entropy function, which later turned out to be consistent with various concepts of utility (Williams 1977) and choice theory (Anas 1983).

As indicated earlier, modelling the transport–location interface really began with Putman (1973, 1983) who developed the first land-use–transport model explicitly taking account of traffic congestion. Nearly in parallel, the POLIS model was applied to the cities of Cologne and Vienna (Wegener 1973, 1974). It was also congestion-sensitive, but differed from the Lowry model in that it used the original Hansen (1959) accessibility to drive its location models rather than the spatial interaction model.

With the work of Anas (1975; 1982) and the NBER model (Kain *et al.* 1976) micro-economic theory was introduced into residential location modelling. Now for the first time land and housing prices and rents figured in the models not as exogenous data, but as endogenous indicators of the supply–demand relationship. The NBER model also demonstrated that micro simulation, nearly forgotten since Chapin and Weiss (1968), was a powerful tool for simulating event-based processes too intricate to be modelled analytically.

The next three models deal with the problem of simultaneous equilibrium of transport and location. Berechman (1976, 1980) showed that previous transport–location models with endogenous travel costs were inconsistent because the travel costs used to drive the location model were not normally the same as the ones that resulted from the activity pattern so derived. He as well as Boyce (1977) and Los (1978, 1979) suggested model frameworks to derive a general equilibrium of transport and location based on network equilibrium techniques known from transport engineering. Later, Boyce *et al.* (1981) generalised these ideas into a comprehensive scheme of transport–location equilibrium models including location, destination, mode and route choice. With less sophisticated assignment techniques, the same was achieved by the Bilbao version of the ARC model by

Echenique (Geraldes *et al.* 1979), which in addition contained a floor-space price adjustment mechanism similar to the micro-economic NBER and Anas models.

TRANSLOC (Lundqvist 1978) and TOPAZ (Brotchie *et al.* 1980) are different from the other models in that they are optimisation models. Both seek to find a distribution of activities in the urban region that minimises the objective function containing both location and interaction costs; however, in the TOPAZ model the interaction component of the objective function may also contain entropy terms to account for the dispersion of travel choices by private actors. In that respect, TOPAZ is close to the multi-activity location model proposed by Leonardi (1981), in which the spatial interaction location model is embedded into a non-linear optimisation model allowing choice dispersion. The Leonardi model is also important because it takes account of capacity constraints at the destinations.

The LILT model (Mackett 1980) and the Toronto model (Said and Hutchinson 1980) are both highly disaggregated multi-activity spatial-interaction location models in the Wilson tradition. However, the LILT model stands out by its explicit distinction between physical structure (jobs, houses) and activities (workers, households), which makes it possible to model phenomena such as vacant jobs and unemployment, housing vacancies and overcrowding.

The last group of models is characterised by an interest in dynamics — these models do not suppose that the urban system comes close to equilibrium at any point in time. The Turin model (Bertuglia *et al.* 1980) is in essence an incremental multi-activity Lowry model, in which the levels of activity in each zone are progressively altered through time by the variation of the attraction of the zone. The 'Brussels' model (Allen *et al.* 1981) and the model by Wilson and his colleagues (Beaumont *et al.* 1981), while derived from different theoretical positions, are very similar: they both interpret the difference between a spatial-interaction demand model and supply at the trip ends as unsatisfied demand or excess supply, depending on its sign, and their convergence as an adjustment process over time, thus arriving at a fully dynamic model. The Dortmund model (Wegener 1982) is a multi-level, multi-activity composite model containing various types of submodel, among them an equilibrium-type transport model, accessibility-based location models, and a micro-analytic housing market and migration submodel, linked together in a recursive fashion.

3.2 Model classification

There are innumerable ways of categorising models of this kind.

Earlier reviews (such as Berechman and Gordon, 1984) have concentrated on technical aspects such as the solution method used. This one will proceed in a much simpler way by first asking three basic, substantive questions. How are the subsystems of transport and land use represented in the models? Are transport and location costs endogenous in them? What is their dynamic structure?

The answer to the first question is given in Table 14.1. In the case of transport, the question means whether the transport system is represented in network (or some equivalent) form which permits transport policies as well as congestion effects to be investigated. It can be seen that eight of the 20 models do not contain a representation of the network. With respect to the location side, it is asked if the location submodels include some notion of land and physical stock such as housing or non-residential buildings, or if they just locate activities. The latter is true for 11 of the 20 models, and this means that with these models no land scarcity can be modelled.

Table 14.1 Representation of transport and land use

		Representation of transport	
		Network not represented	Network represented
Representation of land use	Physical stock not represented	Lowry Wilson Leonardi Allen *et al.* Beaumont *et al.*	ITLUP Berechman Boyce Los TRANSLOC Toronto
	Physical stock represented	Herbert–Stevens NBER TOPAZ	POLIS Anas ARC LILT Turin Dortmund

The second question extends the last point. How are costs (prices) determined in the models? Are they exogenous or endogenous? This question is crucial because with fixed prices no supply–demand interaction, no market behaviour, no congestion, no capacity bottlenecks can be expected to be exposed by the models. Table 14.2 displays the result of this analysis. It is disappointing to see that seven out of the 20 models have no price mechanism, either on the transport or on the location side. Seven models endogenously generate transport costs as a function of congestion, but have no price signals on the location side, four models do have endogenous land or housing prices, but have exogenous transport costs, and only two models have both endogenous transport and location costs.

Table 14.2 Transport and location costs

		Transport costs	
		exogenous	endogenous
Location costs	exogenous	Herbert–Stevens Lowry Wilson TRANSLOC TOPAZ Turin Beaumont *et al.*	ITLUP POLIS Berechman Boyce Los LILT Toronto
	endogenous	NBER Anas Leonardi Allen *et al.*	ARC Dortmund

The third question is concerned with the dynamics of the transport–location interaction built into the models. Table 14.3 shows that the majority of models are equilibrium models assuming that transport and location are always in equilibrium, that is, that the pattern of activity locations and spatial interactions at all times reflects the current transport cost structure, and vice versa. This statement needs to be qualified. A transport network equilibrium in the strict sense of user equilibrium (Wardrop 1952) is achieved only in the models by Boyce and by Los and in the Toronto and Dortmund models. Other models use more traditional techniques to approach transport equilibrium such as incremental assignment (Putman, POLIS, Berechman). Obviously, in the models that do not calculate endogenous transport costs, travel demand is always in equilibrium by definition. In six models the response of the land-use system to changes in transport costs is lagged in a recursive fashion, with instantaneous adjustment to changes in activity location assumed on the transport side. There are only two models which assume a delayed response also on the transport side.

Table 14.3 Transport and location dynamics

		Transport dynamics	
		Network equilibrium	Lagged response
Location dynamics	Land-use equilibrium	Herbert–Stevens Lowry Wilson Anas NBER Berechman Boyce Los TRANSLOC TOPAZ Toronto Leonardi	
	Lagged response	ITLUP POLIS ARC Turin Allen *et al.* Beaumont *et al.*	LILT Dortmund

3.3 Types of location models

The preceding analysis has demonstrated that only very few of the current urban models claiming to address the transport–location interface are able to do so because the majority of the models either fail adequately to represent the transport and/or land-use systems, or treat crucial variables such as transport and/or location costs as exogenous, or are equilibrium models that ignore the time dimension of the adjustment processes they postulate. In a final step of the analysis, it will be shown that, on top of these deficiencies, these models are victims of a confusion about what is cause and what is effect in the relationship between transport and location.

To illuminate this point, a few remarks about the temporal characteristics or urban change processes need to be made. Following Snickars *et al.* (1982), urban change processes can be classified with respect to their temporal characteristics as in Table 14.4 (Wegener *et al.* 1983). It can be seen from Table 14.4 that the average response time of urban change processes ranges from less than a year to a human lifetime, and the duration of the response can be even longer. The implications of this for the design of urban models are straightforward: urban change processes are slow in relation to human life and planning perspectives, and therefore urban models intended for planning should take account of the retarding forces, frictions and delays responsible for that inertia.

Table 14.4 Urban change processes

Level	Change process	Stock affected	Response time (years)	Response duration (years)
1 Slow	industrial construction	industrial buildings	3–5	50–100
	residential construction	residential buildings	2–3	60–80
	transport construction	transport system	5–10	>100
2 Medium speed	economic change	employment/ unemployment	2–5	10–20
	demographic change	population/ households	0–70	0–70
	technological change	transport equipment	3–5	10–15
3 Fast	labour mobility	work-place occupancy	<1	5–10
	residential mobility	housing occupancy	<1	5–10
	daily mobility	traffic	<1	2–5

However, this seemingly simple and common-sense conclusion is disregarded by most existing urban models. With few exceptions, they are based on the concept of the spatial-interaction location model. The spatial-interaction model itself, first developed in transport planning, predicts traffic flows in equilibrium, subject to given activity locations — a reasonable proposition given the fast adjustment of travel patterns. The problems start when this model is used to predict activity locations by interpreting the trip destinations of the traffic model as residences, work-places and the like, rather than taking them as given. The spatial-interaction model used as a location model, as pioneered by Lowry (1964) and later systematised by Wilson (1970), assumes that there exists in urban areas an equilibrium between traffic flows and activity locations. In reality, however, as Table 14.4 has attempted to show, changes of location, due to contractual or habitual constraints and long planning and construction times, are many times slower than changes of travel behaviour. In fact, the spatial-interaction location model predicts a slow and inert process — location — from a volatile and flexible process — travel — and this exchange of cause and effect is a common feature of current mainstream urban modelling.

This can be demonstrated by looking at Table 14.5, which lists nine types of spatial choice models differing by the choice process represented. For each model it is indicated which variables are predicted and which are taken to be known. In addition, the models are classified as 'doubly constrained', 'singly constrained', or 'unconstrained' depending on the number of constraints (or 'known' entries) in each row.

The first three models in Table 14.5 are doubly constrained. In doubly constrained models, both the decision-makers and the choices made are known, while the pattern of choices linking decision-makers to choices (the 'choice matrix') is to be predicted. The most widely known doubly constrained spatial choice models are traffic models in which the decision makers are, say, workers at their place of residence (the 'origins'), the choice set are jobs at places of employment (the 'destinations'), and the choice matrix to be predicted is the matrix of work-trips. In migration models, households willing to move from their old residence are the origins, new or vacant dwellings the destinations, and the choices to be predicted are migrations. Similarly, in employment-change models, labour mobility is predicted as spatial interactions between old and new jobs.

The next three models are singly constrained, that is to say, constrained only in their origins. Residential location models are models predicting residence locations from a known distribution of employment as destinations, or column totals, of the work-trip matrix. Similarly, in employment-location models, household-serving (or 'non-basic') employment is predicted from residential locations as destinations of shopping and service trips. Residential locations are also predicted by housing-market models, but here the decision-makers are households at their old place of residence and the spatial interactions modelled are migrations.

Table 14.5 Types of spatial choice models

Model type	Constraints	Residence		Work-place		Interactions			Number of models
		old	new	old	new	trips	migration	labour mobility	
Traffic models	doubly constrained	known	—	known	—	predicted	—	—	3
Migration models	doubly constrained	known	known	—	—	—	predicted	—	1
Employment change models	doubly constrained	—	—	known	known	—	—	predicted	1
Residential location models	singly constrained	—	predicted	known	—	predicted	—	—	17
Employment location models	singly constrained	known	—	—	predicted	predicted	—	—	14
Housing market models	singly constrained	known	predicted	—	—	(known)	predicted	—	2
Housing location models	singly constrained	—	predicted	(known)	—	—	—	—	3
Job location models	singly constrained	(known)	—	(known)	predicted	—	—	—	1
Resid./empl. location models	unconstrained	—	predicted	—	predicted	predicted	—	—	2

There are two more singly constrained models in Table 14.5, although their origins are not shown in the table. In housing-location models, the decision-makers are housing investors looking for sites for new dwellings, while in job-location models they are firms deciding on new firm locations. In both cases vacant land by zoning type, possibly weighted by attractiveness indicators, constitutes the choice of destinations, and no spatial interactions are involved.

Finally, there are residential and employment-location models, in which residential and employment locations are simultaneously determined by an unconstrained spatial-interaction location model. This type of model is typically applied in an optimisation framework.

The last column of Table 14.5 shows how many times each model type is represented among the 20 models of the sample or any of their sub-models. It can be seen that indeed nearly all models of the sample contain a residential location model of the singly constrained spatial-interaction type simultaneously predicting residential locations and work trips, and that most contain an employment-location model constructed along the same lines. In other words, most of the models examined in their core submodels are founded on the reversal of cause and effect between transport and location discussed above. Such models are unable to take account of the frictions and delays slowing down the response of the location system to transport changes, and hence are likely to overestimate the impacts of such changes. In contrast, only very few models of the sample explicitly predict longer-term changes of the location system such as household or labour mobility or changes of the physical stock of the city through industrial or housing construction.

4. Conclusions

In summary, if the sample of models investigated is only nearly representative, the art of modelling the transport–location interface is not nearly as well developed as one might believe, considering the high degree of sophistication achieved in terms of mathematical theory and modelling technique. The main deficiencies of most current modelling approaches can be identified as: (a) incomplete representation of the subsystems affected; (b) lack of endogenous cost or capacity variables; (c) neglect of the specific dynamics of the transport–location interaction; and (d) inappropriate preoccupation with one particular model type.

The conclusions to be drawn from this analysis are very simple and straightforward. It has to be realised that location decisions are different from transport decisions and are made in a decision environment where transport considerations tend to become less important in the face of changing work and leisure patterns and new communication technologies. What is necessary then is to free location modelling from its transport fix and bring it back to a more balanced view where spatial and aspatial locational factors play an equal role. This would mean investing more effort and talent in designing and empirically testing housing market models or models of job choice or work-place location rather than spatial-interaction models.

References

Allen, P.M., M. Sanglier, F. Boon, J.L. Deneubourg and A. de Palma (1981). *Models of Urban Settlement and Structure as Dynamic Self-Organizing Systems*. Washington, DC: Department of Transportation.

Anas, A. (1975). 'The Empirical Calibration and Testing of a Simulation Model of Residential Location', *Environment and Planning A*, **7**, 899–920.

Anas, A. (1982). *Residential Location Markets and Urban Transportation*. New York: Academic Press.

Anas, A. (1983). 'Discrete Choice Theory, Information Theory, and the Multinomial Logit and Gravity Models', *Transportation Research*, **17B**, 13–23.

Beaumont, J.R., M. Clarke and A.G. Wilson (1981). 'The Dynamics of Urban Spatial Structure: Some Exploratory Results Using Difference Equations and Bifucation Theory', *Environment and Planning A*, **13**, 1473–83.

Berechman, J. (1976). 'Interfacing the Urban Land-Use Activity System and the Transportation System', *Journal of Regional Science*, **16**, 183–94.

Berechman, J. (1980). 'A General Framework for the Integration of the Land-Use Model with a Transportation Model Component', *Journal of Regional Science*, **20**, 58–69.

Berechman, J. and P. Gordon (1986). 'Linked Models of Land-Use Transport Interactions' in B.G. Hutchinson and M. Batty, eds, *Advances in Urban Systems*. Amsterdam: North Holland Publishing Co.

Bertuglia, C.S., S. Occelli, G. Rabino and R. Tadei (1980). 'A Model of Urban Structure and Development of Turin: Theoretical Aspects', *Sistemi Urbani*, **1**, 59–90.

Boyce, D.E. (1977). *Equilibrium Solutions to Combined Urban Residential Location, Modal Choice, and Trip Assignment Models*. RSRI. Discussion Paper 98. Philadelphia: Regional Science Research Institute.

Boyce, D.E., N.D. Day and C. McDonald (1970). *Metropolitan Plan Making*. Philadelphia: Regional Science Research Institute.

Boyce, D.E., L.J. LeBlanc, K.S. Chon, Y.J. Lee and K.T. Lin (1981). *Combined Models of Location, Destination, Mode and Route Choice: An Unified Approach Using Nested Entropy Constraints*. Publication no. 3. Transportation Planning Group, Department of Civil Engineering. Urbana, IL: University of Illinois.

Brotchie, J.F., J.W. Dickey and R. Sharpe (1980). *TOPAZ — General Planning Technique and its Applications at the Regional, Urban, and Facility Planning Levels*. Berlin/Heidelberg/New York: Springer Verlag.

Chapin, F.S. and S.F. Weiss (1968). 'A Probabilistic Model for Residential Growth', *Transportation Research*, **2**, 375–90.

Garin, R.A. (1966). 'A Matrix Formulation of the Lowry Model for Intra-Metropolitan Activity Location', *Journal of the American Institute of Planners*, **32**, 361–4.

Geraldes, P., M.H. Echenique and I.N. Williams (1979). *A Spatial Economic Model for Bilbao*. PTRC Summer Annual Meeting 1979, Warwick.

Hansen, W.G. (1959). 'How Accessibility Shapes Land Use', *Journal of the American Institute of Planners*, **25**, 31–5.

Herbert, D.J. and B.H. Stevens (1960). 'A Model for the Distribution of Residential Activity in Urban Areas', *Journal of Regional Science*, **2**, 21–6.

Kain, J.F., W.C. Apgar, Jr. and J.R. Ginn (1976). *Simulation of Market Effects of Housing Allowances. Vol. I: Description of the NBER Urban Simulation Model.* Research Report R77-2. Cambridge, MA: Department of City and Regional Planning, Harvard University.

Leonardi, G. (1981). 'A General Accessibility and Congestion-Sensitive Multi-Activity Spatial Interaction Model'. *Papers of the Regional Science Association*, **47**, 3–17.

Los, M. (1978). 'Simultaneous Optimization of Land Use and Transportation', *Regional Science and Urban Economics*, **8**, 21–42.

Los, M. (1979). 'Combined Residential Location and Transportation Models'. *Environment and Planning A*, **11**, 1241–65.

Lowry, I.S. (1964). *A Model of Metropolis*. RM-4035-RC. Santa Monica, CA: Rand Corporation.

Lundqvist, L. (1978). 'Urban Planning of Locational Structures with Due Regard to User Behaviour', *Environment and Planning A*, **10**, 1413–29.

Mackett, R.L. (1980). *The Mathematical Representation of a Model of the Relationships between Transport and Land Use*. Working Paper 123. Leeds: Institute for Transport Studies, University of Leeds.

Putman, S.H. (1973). *The Interrelationships of Transport Development and Land Development*. Final Report. Washington, DC: Federal Highway Administration, US Department of Transportation.

Putman, S.H. (1983). *Integrated Urban Models*. London: Pion.

Said, G.M. and B.G. Hutchinson (1980). *An Urban Systems Model for the Toronto Region: 1. Model Structure*. Working Paper. Waterloo, Ontario: Department of Civil Engineering, University of Waterloo.

Senior, M.L. (1973). 'Approaches to Residential Location Modelling 1: Urban Ecological and Spatial Interaction Models (A Review)', *Environment and Planning A*, **5**, 165–97.

Senior, M.L. (1974). 'Approaches to Residential Location Modelling 2: Urban Economic Models and Some Recent Developments (A Review)', *Environment and Planning A*, **6**, 369–409.

Snickars, F., B. Johansson and G. Leonardi (1982). *Nested Dynamics of Metropolitan Processes and Policies*. Draft Project Description. Laxenburg: International Institute for Applied Systems Analysis.

Wardrop, J.G. (1952). 'Some Theoretical Aspects of Road Traffic Research', *Proceedings of the Institution of Civil Engineers* (London), **2** (1), 325–78.

Wegener, M. (1973). *POLIS Wien: Anwendung des Simulationsmodells POLIS für die Stadtentwicklungsplanung Wiens*. Frankfurt: Battelle Institute e.V.

Wegener, M. (1974). *Network Design as an Iterative Process of Urban Simulation and Evaluation: Some Applications of the POLIS Simulation Model.* PTRC Summer Annual Meeting, University of Warwick.

Wegener, M. (1982). 'Modeling Urban Decline: A Multilevel Economic-Demographic Model of the Dortmund Region', *International Regional Science Review*, **7**, 21–42.

Wegener, M. (1984). *Integrated Forecasting Models of Urban and Regional Systems*. Working Paper 15. Dortmund: Institute of Spatial Planning, University of Dortmund.

Wegener, M., F. Gnad and M. Vannahme (1983). *The Time Scale of Urban Change*. Working Paper 11. Dortmund: Institute of Spatial Planning, University of Dortmund.

Williams, H.C.W.L. (1977). 'On the Formulation of Travel Demand Models and Economic Evaluation Measures of User Benefit', *Environment and Planning A*, **9**, 285–344.

Wilson, A.G. (1970). *Entropy in Urban and Regional Modelling*. London: Pion.

15 The Transportation Sector in the Communications Society — Some Analytical Observations

F. Snickars

1. Introduction

Economists who during the 1960s investigated the share of transport costs in the total production costs of most industrial sectors came to the conclusion that it was generally very low. For most industries those costs made up less than 5 per cent of the total cost. It was then argued that production costs were insensitive to the choice of location of production establishments. However, the other conclusion which would have been warranted was generally not drawn. Since unit costs of transportation were low, firms could increase the volume of transport while saving on other cost items in the production process. With the increase in the value content of industrial products in general, this overlooked tendency became even more obvious. Technical change entailed a large increase in the demand for freight transport. This type of transport connected nation-wide or global production systems where components were integrated into products which were themselves systems, such as cars, consumer durables or computers. International business travel boomed as a consequence in view of the necessity to keep the production systems together, and to reach the ever more distant expansive markets. One of the results of this development has been increased international competition (see also Wandel 1985).

Western Europe today is basically one integrated transport system. Two-thirds of world trade still takes place within Europe. The effectiveness of the transport system is one factor where continental Europe has a comparative advantage over many other economic regions of the world. The economic conurbations are so closely connected by land transport networks, both road and rail, that air transport is not overwhelmingly competitive, even for personal traffic.

The communications society is often thought of in terms of employment structures. The number of persons engaged in the primary sector is very low and the share of persons employed in commodity production is also declining. More importantly, the share of the labour force engaged in service production is staggering, while employment in information-handling and communication activities is gathering an ever increasing share of the work-force. It may be more important to understand the economic forces which drive the work-force resources into the communications area.

Highly productive economic sectors have traditionally had a high propensity to make capital investment. This no longer seems to be the case. The most expansive parts of industry are not extremely capital-intensive but must rather be associated with large immaterial investments and dynamic competition.

For large segments of Swedish manufacturing industry, for instance, the intensity of immaterial investment is higher than that of material investment. This does not imply that the investment types are substitutes. New and modern capital equipment will demand human skill in production, logistics and marketing to maintain the dynamic competitive advantages so typical of modern industrial development. In the mode of dynamic competition, firms will look for local and temporal monopoly situations in expansive markets. They will protect themselves through patents, licensing and service agreements for a period of time. After that, the niche is left and other dynamic monopolies are established (Snickars and Strömqvist 1985).

The transportation sector has a role in the communications society different from its role in the former more stable and locally orientated economic environment. The properties of modern information technology play an important role in this context. In the first generation computers were, for instance, used to solve computational problems of product composition and product design. The second generation of computers were primarily used as information storage and database handling devices. In the third generation the role of computers as tools of communication is stressed. In industry, this has meant that information technology was first used to rationalise production in a given organisational context. Now the marginal benefit from that activity may be decreasing. The interest is then directed towards using computers and information technology to reorganise production systems (see also Perez 1983). It may well be that this restructuring will have profound effects on regional development and on development in the transportation sector itself.

The aim of this paper is to provide some analytical observations concerning the interplay between the transportation sector and the economic and social processes that are typical of the communications society. Indirectly, then, the paper will point to the need to reassess carefully the role of transport planning in this new economic and social context. It may well be that current methods and models used in transport planning are not flexible enough to be useful in such a new planning environment. The intention here is not to make a definite statement in this regard, but to point out that economic and technical development has entered a stage in which such questions will have to be addressed by future interdisciplinary research on transport and mobility.

2. Transport and economic change

The transport sector has a strategic position in the modern post-industrial economy. Goods and services are channelled via that sector from buyer to seller. It also serves as an active agent in the provision of mobility to individuals, households, organisations and firms. Different goods and services make different demands on transport systems and the pressure on transport supply therefore takes on a variety of forms, involving a broad spectrum of means of transport. The inner structure of the transport sector is complicated. There is an intertwined network structure of roads, railway lines, air corridors, harbours and other transport terminals serving as some of the physical infrastructure. The claim on the sector to provide transport services of the proper type at the proper place and at the proper time introduces a multitude of dependencies between system components that extend far beyond the physical properties of the network infrastructures themselves.

In terms of Figure 15.1 the arguments above may be reformulated as follows. The economic development process will affect development in the transport sector since the demand for transport is a derived one. It is the demand for other goods and services, and the geographical separation of supply sources and demand sinks which drive development in the transport sector. To a certain extent changes in the level of economic activity can be accommodated within a given transport supply capacity. This can be done by changing the choice of transport means, the choice of chain of transport links and the transport time.

In energy systems it is common to make a distinction between energy flow and instantaneous effect. The effect is the claim on instantaneous delivery response that the system or system component should match. The energy flow constitutes the total path of service that the system should yield during a fixed period of time. The effect claim determines the total level of installed capacity. The difficulty in storing

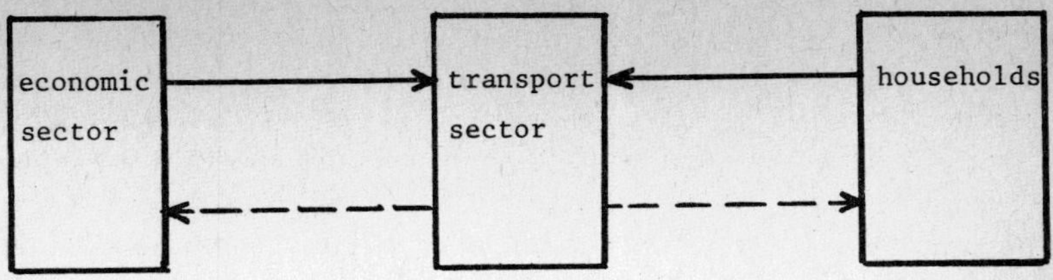

Figure 15.1 Flows of impact between the transport sector and other sectors of the economy

electricity or heat or cold determines the relationship between peak capacity and average flow. The situation is somewhat similar in transport systems, although not as binding. There are storage possibilities, but as is quite clear from recent development trends, inventories are being brought down considerably in size in many sectors of the economy. This is a strong trend in the impact of economic development on the transport sector which will be of considerable importance in the future.

The influence of the transport sector on economic development is more difficult to pinpoint. Of course, low transport costs are beneficial to the economic performance of a firm in comparison with other firms. Low and diminishing specific costs of goods transport have allowed other costs to influence in a major way the optimal scale and location of production. At the same time, these cost declines have entailed that companies are now willing to spend more on transportation to reduce other costs of production. Thus, the transport sector layout at a certain point in time will have an effect on the organisation of production systems. The clearest example of this tendency is the above-mentioned increasing geographical scope of intermediary shipments in the ripe post-industrial economy. A complex technical system such as a car will have components produced in a mesh of large-scale component factories all over the world. Low specific transport costs are not the only factors behind this development. High inventory costs are especially important besides transport costs. Other factors lie in the increased speed and regularity of international connections made possible by modern communications technology (see also Andersson and Johansson 1984).

There is also another way in which the transport sector influences economic development. Transport systems are some of the most important infrastructures of the modern communications society. Transport infrastructures are public in nature; the use of them by one economic agent does not normally influence the access of other agents to them. Economic research is divided when it comes to assessing the importance of these infrastructures to economic productivity and growth. There is some consensus concerning the presence of threshold effects. Also the publicness of the transport networks tends to incur insufficient service provision in pure market economies. A further discussion relates to the role of accessibility to input and output markets in the location decisions of different types of firm.

We have now elaborated on the relationships between the transport sector and the economy. Of course, some profound changes in consumer behaviour and household welfare have also been incurred by properties of the transport sector. Even though interregional mobility has been quite stable, at least in Sweden, over a period of several decades, the same cannot be said about local mobility. The private car has put substantially more of the local and regional resources into the access range of many households. Increased commuting has had a double effect in industrialised economies. It has enabled households to choose among a wider supply of work-places with a fixed dwelling location. It has also brought a larger supply of specialised labour within reach of more metropolitan firms.

Therefore developments in the transport sector have had considerable effects on the level and distribution of consumer welfare. Consumers also have influenced the transport sector substantially. The behaviour of urban commuters in their choice of causing external effects to each other in terms of peak-hour congestion has been one of the most vivid examples of this reverse interaction between consumers and transport. The indirect effect of increased accessibility on urban sprawl is a subsequent reaction from consumers to the freeway investment strategy adopted by planners in many metropolitan regions to alleviate congestion problems.

3. From commodity to knowledge transports

The discussion presented above points out the need to adopt a double perspective when analysing relationships both between the transport sector and firms and between the transport sector and private households. The main argument is that the starting point of the analysis should be the demand perspective, since transport is not a means in itself, but rather a sacrifice necessary to achieve other goals. The presentation in this section is tentative and proceeds by way of example. The idea is to analyse some trends in economic development which may be of importance to the transport planners of the future. The presentation is based mainly on recent Swedish studies, eg. Snickars and Strömqvist (1985).

Since all Western European economies are becoming more internationally orientated, there should be quite a strong relationship between the growth of GNP and various indicators of output in the goods transport sector. At least for a geographically extended economy like that of Sweden, one may expect that this is definitely the case. In 1960 Swedish foreign trade amounted to 40 per cent of GNP. During the 15-year period to 1985 this share has increased to 70 per cent and it is expected to increase even further. Western Europe has been the most important market for Swedish foreign trade throughout the period, its share remaining steadily around two-thirds.

Figure 15.2 provides an illustration of the relationship between the volume growth of goods transports and the Swedish GNP. A very stable pattern was broken in the middle of the 1970s and has not re-emerged since then. During most of the post-war period total transport work has grown more rapidly than GNP. The elasticity of the transport work with respect to GNP was 1.1 during the 1970s. It has currently a falling tendency and is expected to diminish to around 0.7 during the coming decade. There are several reasons for this decline. As indicated above, one would expect the volume of commodity transports to increase faster than GNP even in the future in view of the growth in foreign trade. The reason why this may not happen is the structural change in the economy. That change takes two forms. The most rapid economic growth will take place in economic sectors the production of which has a higher value content in its commodities than the average. This is one reflection of entry into the communications society. The second change factor is that even within economic sectors there is an expansion of the production of commodities with a high value–volume ratio.

These tendencies have had a profound effect on the development of different kinds of freight submarket. There has been a rapid expansion of national and international shipments of high-value commodities. The expansion has been even more pronounced if one considers the market development in terms of the value of the products shipped rather than weight. Figure 15.3 gives a revealing picture of the competitiveness of different transport modes, using Swedish data for 1980. The relationships may possibly be peculiar to Sweden in view of the geographical properties of the country. However, the data for a small nation should even more clearly favour truck and air freight transport. The figure gives a powerful picture of the superiority of truck and air transport in the high-value commodity segments of the market. It is only among the last 20 per cent of the value transported by road and air vehicles that rail transport is competitive. Another way to phrase this is that the willingness to pay for commodity transport is highest

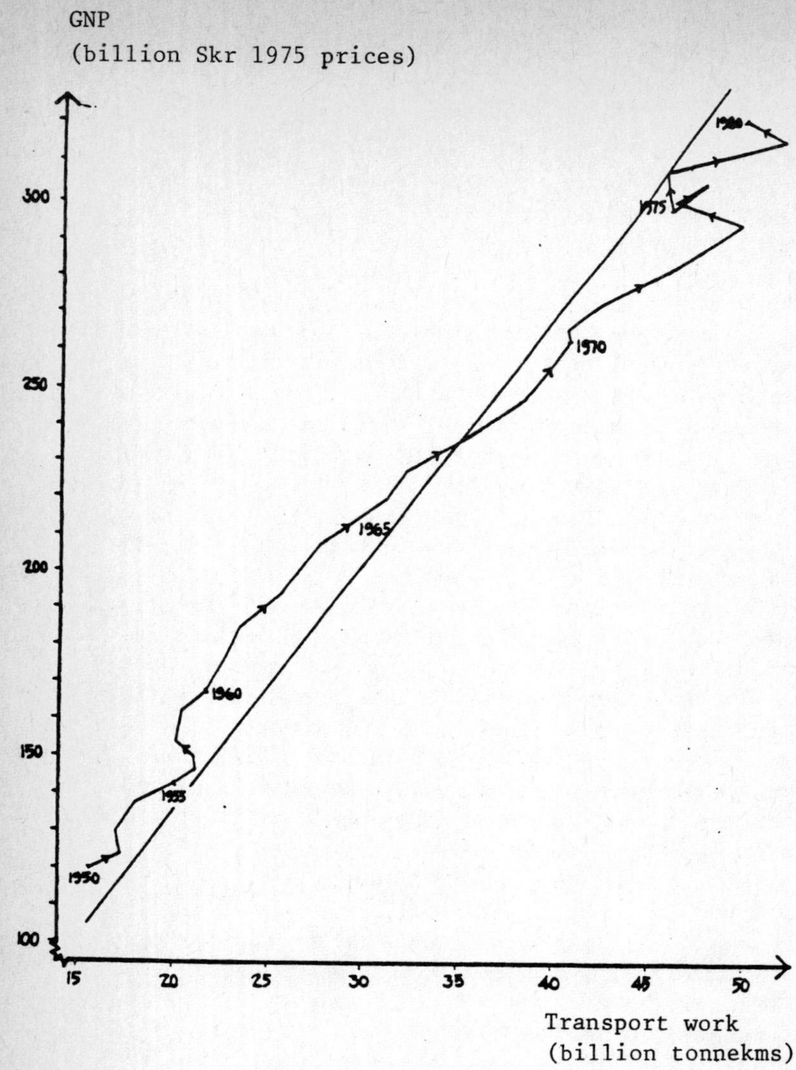

Figure 15.2 The long-term development paths of Sweden's GNP and domestic transport work for goods transport. Straight line indicates uniform growth starting from 1968

for vehicle transport up to 80 per cent of the total goods volume transported.

Figure 15.4 gives a further clear illustration of the long-term

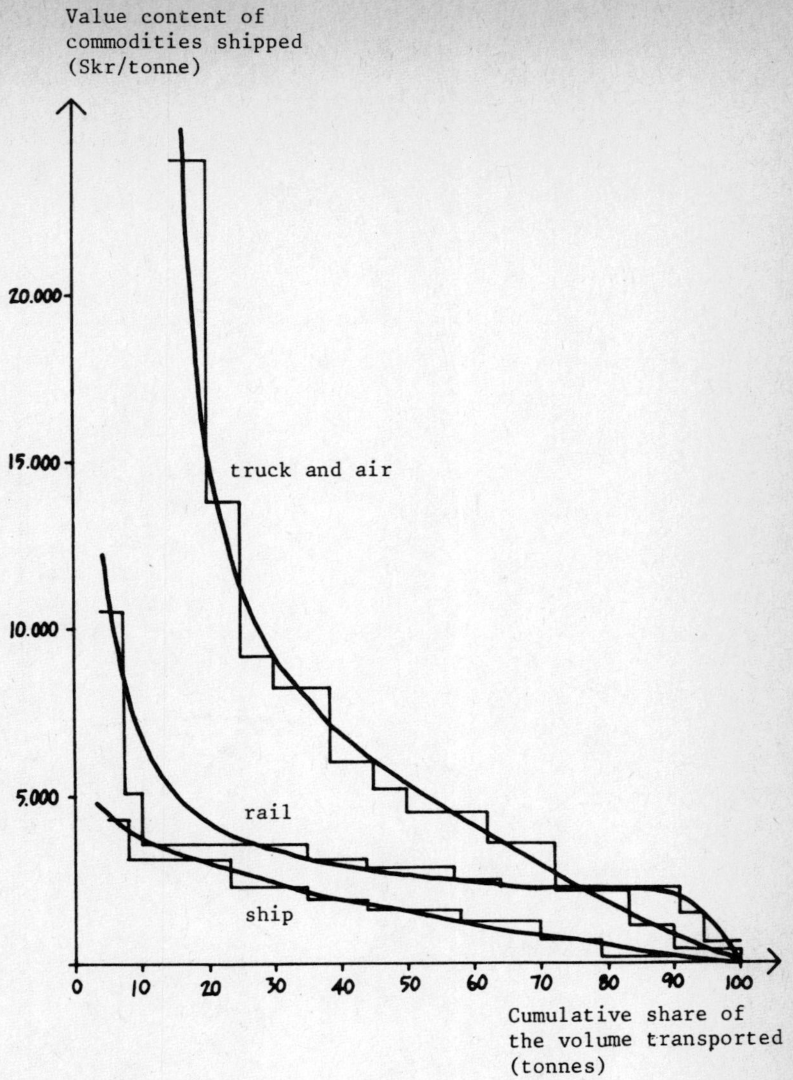

Figure 15.3 Value content of commodity shipments by three different modes of transport. Swedish data 1980

tendencies of substitution among modes of freight transport. It shows how different transport modes have substituted one another in the export of electrical machinery and related products. The trends are surprisingly clear. Even for such a relatively homogeneous product group there is a strong substitution going on. Evidently, firms in this market segment have shifted towards air transport as product values have increased, even at the expense of road transport. A so-called logistic trend forecast to the year 2000 indicates that truck and air transport might be equally significant if current tendencies continue to prevail.

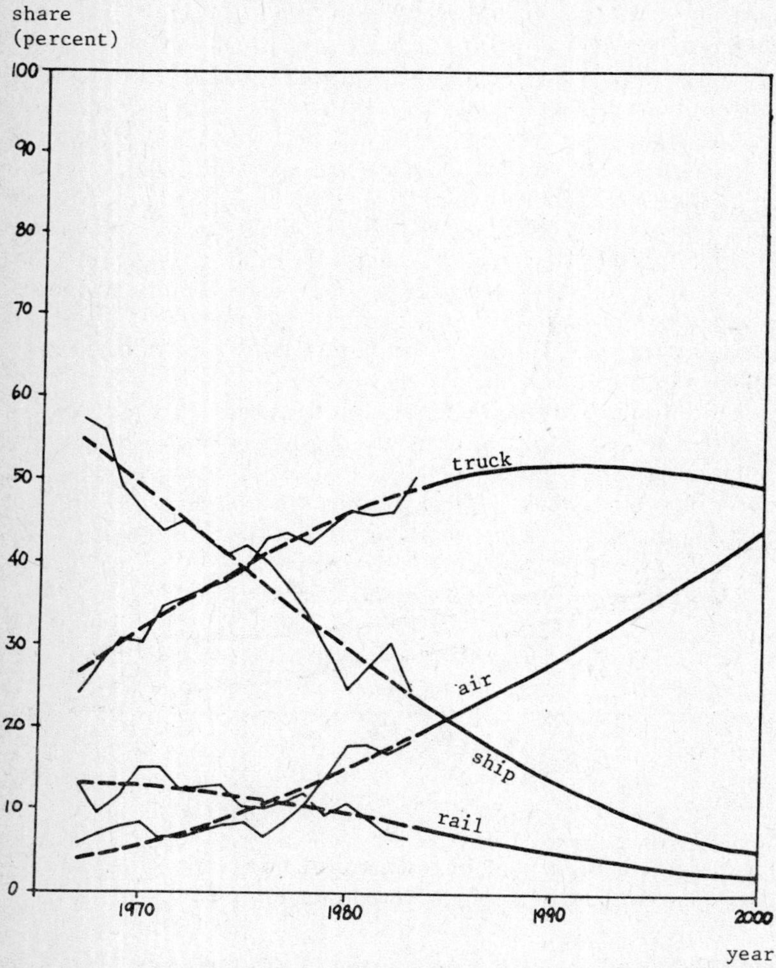

Figure 15.4 Distribution of the export value for electrical machinery, tools and materials 1965–1984. Logistic trend forecast to the year 2000

The substitution among means of transport will depend on the position of the firms involved in the economic system. In Swedish industry there is a clear tendency for exports to have a higher value content than imports. Thus, exports are more likely to leave Sweden by air. What happens on the input side will depend on the prevalence of one of two opposite tendencies present in the interfaces between industrial sectors and transport sectors.

In some sectors transport is currently looked upon as an integral part of the production process. There is a shift away from space-localised inventories to time-localised ones. To shorten lead times at all levels in the manufacturing process production networks are tightened both in space and time. The result is an ever increasing mutual dependency between transport and production.

In other sectors of the economy the trend is rather towards a complete separation of production processes and transport. High-value commodities produced by footloose industries are handed over to multiregional and multinational forwarding companies which operate large logistic systems according to strict optimisation criteria. Shippers become separated from carriers. And carriers do not actually perform the physical shipments but rather operate as managers of the transport system at hand.

It is difficult to say which of these tendencies will become dominant in future freight transport markets. The outcome may be that they continue to co-exist. It is important to note, however, that firms operating under either of these regimes are likely to look quite differently upon the regional distribution of their production systems.

4. Business trips versus telecommunications

In view of the above remarks on the freight-transport sector one could expect a rapid increase in the total number of business trips in the economy. In a way it could be argued that the value content of person-to-person contacts is even higher than most of the value contents of goods shipments. Those personal contacts normally bring about non-routine information exchange which cannot be transferred via any telecommunications system. In view of the importance of personal contacts for the service and information economy it is surprising how little knowledge is systematically gathered about business trips.

The rapid growth of total person transport work in Sweden during the last 30 years is due to the expansion of travel by private motor car. The interesting fact is that this long-established trend was broken at the end of the 1970s. The recent expansion of public transport in relative terms is primarily related to the increased share of commuting by public transport even in less urbanised areas. Also, car-ownership and use is less frequent in metropolitan areas. The proceeding urbanisation has therefore reinforced the trend towards stagnation in the transport work done by car. Of course, the overwhelming factor in this context is the increased relative cost of private car transport.

A special problem in this context which may be peculiar to Sweden is the fare structure of public transport. It is kept very low so that costs are not covered directly but are partly met indirectly, through taxation. In the longer term such a situation may not continue. A fare structure such that the supply of public transport breaks even its revenues and costs might cause a shift back to private car transport. Such a development may also have repercussions in the area of land-use–transport interactions both in urban and in rural districts.

A very characteristic trait of Swedish person transport during the 1970s is the expansion of longer-distance commuting. Typically, such an increase in home-to-work travel reflects the expansion of urban areas. In Sweden commuting has also become a major means of balancing regional labour markets among lower levels of the settlement system. Increased commuting is also a direct reflection of the fact that residential building activity has taken place in peripheral or even rural locations around established settlements. The urbanised countryside typical of such continental regions as the Tuscany region in Italy has thus become a concept of relevance even in a Swedish context.

Behind every goods shipment or person-to-person contact in the modern communications society there is a prior contact established through telecommunications. Distributed computer systems make it possible to work on a main-frame computer in a metropolitan region even though one's own firm is located elsewhere. In one sense, therefore, telecommunications and transport flows are complementary: one cannot, or rather does not, grow unless the other does. In a temporal sense the interactions are substitutes. After an initial contact has been made between persons, that contact can be followed up by telecommunications contacts. There is no need to travel to maintain routine contacts.

Swedish research (Törnqvist 1978) has shown that the most common form of telecommunications, telephone contacts, will yield a pattern of intra- and interregional flows of information very reminiscent of the patterns produced by goods shipments or person-to-person trips. This is a verification of the observation that any substantial physical flow nowadays is preceded by an information flow. Table 15.1 shows an example of telephone contacts from the metropolitan region of Malmö in south Sweden to the rest of Sweden. The local calls are dominant. Thereafter calls to the Stockholm region with its important decision and market points are among the most dominant ones.

Table 15.1 Contact patterns from the Malmö region to other regions in 1978

	Goods		Services		Personal contacts	Telephone contacts
	Sales	Purchases	Sales	Purchases		
Malmö	25	24	59	62	56	65
Neighbour regions	8	11	11	3	10	4
Gothenburg	7	4	3	1	2	3
Stockholm	20	9	10	13	10	10
Rest of Sweden	14	26	15	15	18	16
Denmark	1	3	1	1	1	1
Rest of world	25	23	1	5	3	1
Total	100	100	100	100	100	100

This example shows that at a superficial level there seems to be no major difference between goods shipments, business trips and telecommunications contact patterns. Yet it is quite obvious that these different kinds of interaction put different pressures on the transport sector. The freight and person transport subsystems for any mode of transport are almost completely separated. While commodity shipments can take place at any time of the day or during the week, the business trips are very much more concentrated. The organisation of working life will lead to peak-hour problems also in the air transport market as it has caused metropolitan road and rail transport systems to become congested. It is indeed surprising that so little research has been devoted to furthering the understanding of how person transport systems will develop.

A classic example of infrastructure effects on regional development concerns the connection of a mainland and an island via a bridge. It is generally argued that the connection of an economically strong region to an economically weak one will be to the detriment of the latter. In the long run concentration to the strong region will occur. This example may be rephrased in another context which is of more relevance to person-to-person contacts in the communications society. The opening of a domestic airline between a metropolitan area and a peripheral region might generate a similar pattern of development. What may have been intended as a point of exit from the peripheral region to the core might turn out to be a point of entry for competition in the service- and knowledge-based industries in the peripheral region. The result might be a cumulative process of concentration which might well occur at a faster rate in this case than in the example of the bridge connection.

There is thus a need for a better understanding of those aspects of the information society which may change the conditions for the transport sector. One fundamental question concerns whether the structural change towards service industries and knowledge-based industries will increase or decrease the demand for transport. A shift towards further information processing as an underpinning of goods and service production would tend to increase the demand for business trips. So would a continued expansion of international trade, both of goods and services. On the other hand modern computer and telecommunications technology might reduce the need for transport to establish and maintain world-wide production systems.

Telecommunications can only replace certain of the functions that the creation and spread of information and knowledge will play in future economic development. However, information may be too wide a concept to be useful in this context. The massive supply of information in modern society is in a way spurious. The output of information is not the same as the input of knowledge useful for various productive processes. The crucial problem is how to be able to discern the relevant pieces of information for a particular situation. It demands uncommon skill and competence to select proper pieces of information and to combine these into new creative patterns.

Figure 15.5 represents a simple summary of some of the arguments above. The more creative contacts or communications need to be, the more likely is it that person-to-person contacts cannot be substituted by telecommunications interactions. The promotion of R&D as a major avenue to continued economic growth in post-industrial nations therefore would entail a less pronounced substitution of telecommunications for transports. Thus, for instance, locations advantageous from a person transport viewpoint might become more and more attractive to large portions of the high-technology industry.

The discussion above has concerned the interaction between the transport sector and the economy. Much research and future-orientated study has also been devoted to the effect of telecommunications on the contacts between consumers and the transport sector (see, for example, Andersson *et al.* 1984). Different views have been expressed about the future of commuting as a labour-market balancing mechanism. The organisation of the provision of private and public services to future consumers has been debated. There are reasons to believe in a stagnating need for local trips, that is to say, that telecommunications will act as substitutes for transport. How-

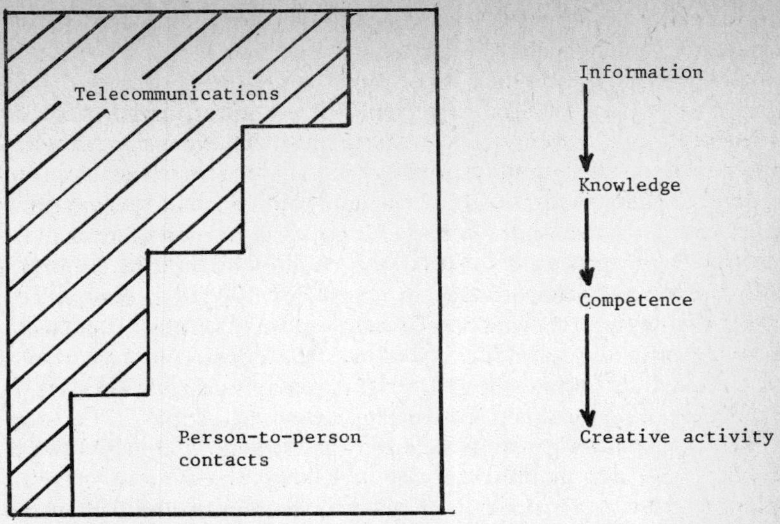

Figure 15.5 Forms of contact relevant to different economic activities in the information society

ever, the better possibilities of finding good alternatives in a region- or even nation-wide supply of services might work in the other direction. Therefore, the outcomes of the impact on land-use–transport interactions, for example in a metropolitan context, are also indeterminate.

5. Some claims on transport modelling

We have stressed the need for a better understanding of how the demands put on the transport sector are influenced by future economic and consumer activity. Future technological change will proceed towards removing even further local, regional, national and global barriers to communications. How will the transport sector react to these structural changes? How should it react so as not to cause conflicts between welfare goals and goals of economic efficiency and growth? In which segments of the economy will the reactions be most important and occur earlier than in other segments?

Since modern economic activity involves more than before a mixture of goods, person and information shipments there is a need to analyse these three modes of interaction in a common framework. Otherwise, the complementarity, or substitutability, of issues will be assumed away by definition. It is necessary to let a qualitative analysis of these processes precede, and complement, any modelling exercise. Hypotheses need to be formulated concerning which interactions are most important, that is, on which signals from the transport sector will economic activity react most strongly, and vice versa.

Let us illustrate this with an example of major importance. It concerns the choice of an interregional or an intraregional, basically metropolitan, perspective. We know that the expansion of interregional and international trade of goods and services will call for forecasts and policy analyses of how demands on freight and person transport systems will develop. Aspects of spatial separation other than the cost of shipments, such as speed and regularity, might be important enough to effect changes also in interregional location patterns. To model this future we would need more information than is currently available about modern location factors for industry, and the role of storage and inventories in their production and distribution systems.

The other regional perspective which might be adopted is the intraregional one. It is generally believed that structural change towards services and information handling will incur a new wave of metropolitan growth. This may not always occur in established metropolitan regions at least if their economies are deeply connected with stagnating segments of manufacturing industry. The metropolitan problem is multidimensional in these respects. The dynamics of a large number of economic and social processes determine the patterns of land-use–transport interaction. The inner differentiation of the metropolitan region in terms of economy and demography exhibits cyclical phenomena. Earlier strategies of infrastructure development are not viable in the future for financial reasons. From a research perspective, therefore, we would argue that the metropolitan land-use–transport interactions are more difficult to analyse than the interregional ones. It is the dominance of short-distance shipments and trips in transport work which makes such a research task necessary in the framework we have delineated.

It is interesting to note that in spite of the complexity of the interactions between different economic and social processes in metropolitan regions the state of the art of transport modelling seems to be more advanced there than in freight transport. The models available are based on explicit behavioural theories among which the ones pertaining to the class of random utility models seem to be the most powerful ones for the time being. There is wide experience in estimating these models, and in applying them to complex problems in metropolitan transport planning.

The level of sophistication and completeness is not as high in freight transport modelling (see Nelldal 1984). There exist examples of partial approaches to modelling freight shipments as well as business trips. Some of these are founded on production theory, whereas others rest on similar theoretical foundations as the random utility models of households' choice of travel behaviour in metropolitan regions. Very few models pay anything other than lip-service to the concept of transport demand as a derived one. The common procedure is to treat economic development as an exogenous process and to perform transport sector analysis in technical terms.

A model system to accommodate some of the factors of reality discussed above must be given a two-level structure in two dimensions. There should be an economic level and a transport-sector level. These levels should interact with one another. A macro-economic model operating at both a national and a regional level might drive the transport sector submodel. The regional detail in the transport sector submodel might be different from the one in the economic model. There may also be a need to provide a means for bridging the gap between economic variables and transport-sector variables. The reason for the double regional perspective might be the need to consider properly the network aspects of transport supply.

It should be clear from the above exposition that it is indeed well known how one could go about modelling the interregional transport sector development. The reasons why this has not been done (see, however, Los 1980 and Snickars, Strömqvist and Eriksson 1983) are various. No bottle-neck phenomena such as the congestion issue in metropolitan areas have urged planners to increase their understanding of mechanisms and policy effects. The responsibility for research in this field has been scattered among several parties. Operations researchers have mostly been occupied with technical subproblems using optimisation methods. There has been a lack of reliable data on a large enough scale. The resolution of some of these problems is long overdue. The presentation above has indicated that planners and policymakers have every reason to watch the development of the transport sector in the communications society quite carefully.

Operations researchers have traditionally adopted a bottom-up perspective in modelling. The ideas underlying many model attempts have been aimed at simplification by segmentation. A subproblem has been identified which seems to be tractable by the methodology at hand, at least after some ingenious reformulation. Strangely enough from this simplifications perspective, the theorists in the field have always strived for generality. Theorems proved for subclasses of models have been extended to ever more general sets of circumstances by various continuation theorems. Thus general theories have been applied to partial problems. Partial problem solutions have then been generalised by superposition principles.

Model validation is a good example. Validation is normally done for a model system component by component, using statistical goodness-of-fit measures. Once high correlations have been obtained for the parts, the system is joined together and expected to perform well in forecasting and policy analysis also as a whole when interdependencies are taken into account.

In the current paper a top-down perspective to modelling of system interaction has been suggested. In validation less recourse is then made to econometric techniques for model components. Instead methods allowing for consistency between model parts should be utilised. Once system interactions are modelled under simple behavioural or other submodels, disaggregation may be performed. This may be done in a hierarchical fashion always keeping track of the level of consistency already achieved. Such a view on modelling of interactions between economic and transport sector development is compatible with the development of future transport markets as we have described them earlier in this chapter. Only when this approach is adopted may a proper balance be obtained between the modelling of transport demand and the analysis of different channels of supply.

References

Andersson, Å.E. and B. Johansson (1984). 'Industrial Dynamics, Product Cycles, and Employment Structure'. WP-84-9. Laxenburg, Austria: IIASA.

Andersson, Å.E., G. Törnqvist, F. Snickars and S. Öberg (1984). *The National Benefit of Regional Variety*. Stockholm: Liber (in Swedish).

Issaev, B., P. Nijkamp, P. Rietveld and F. Snickars (1982). *Multiregional Economic Modelling: Practice and Prospect*. Amsterdam: North Holland Publishing Co.

Los, M. (1980). 'A Transportation-oriented Multiregional Economic Model for Canada'. Publication 178. Centre de Recherche sur les Transports, University of Montreal.

Nelldal, B.L. (1984). 'The Role of the Transport Sector in the Future Regional Development' in F. Snickars, ed., *Decisions for Regional Renewal*. Stockholm: Liber (in Swedish).

Perez, C. (1983). 'Structural Change and Assimilation of New Technologies in the Economic and Social Systems', *Futures* (October), 357–73.

Snickars, F. and U. Strömqvist (1985). *A Way Out for Bergslagen. A Study of the Potential for Making the Örebro Region a Communications Node in a Revived Regional Economy*. Örebro County Research Council (in Swedish).

Snickars, F., U. Strömqvist and J. Eriksson (1983). 'Economic Development and Transport Demand — A Top-down Method for Interregional Freight Transport Forecasting'. Mimeo, Stockholm (in Swedish).

Törnqvist, G. (1978). *Connections over the Öresund Strait*. Stockholm: Liber (in Swedish).

Wandel, S. (1985). 'IIASA Study of the Evaluation of the World Transport System'. Department of Management and Economics, University of Linköping.

16 Integrated Transportation Planning: Physical Expansion versus Economic Constraints

A. La Bella

1. Introduction

Transportation consists of the transfer of persons and/or goods between geographically separate places. The resulting benefits arise from the linking of human settlements and activities distributed over space. So it is obvious that there will exist a close relationship between transportation and spatial structure.

Thus transportation planning is a relevant component of the design of a regional or national development policy. Transportation planning should therefore be treated together with physical and economic planning, but it is clear that this is not an easy task. For a comprehensive treatment of integrated modelling of transportation and location see Wegener (Chapter 14) in this volume.

In this paper, we shall try to formulate the problem of the comprehensive evaluation of transportation plans, considering the wide range of effects of non-marginal changes in the provision of transportation infrastructure. Generally speaking, transportation improvement generates productivity gains, increases the level of economic activities and influences the location process modifying existing accessibility patterns. However, decreasing returns to scale pose the problem of finding the spending point beyond which improved transport becomes a luxury afforded out of economic growth and not a productive investment (Hart 1983).

The bulk of the literature on the evaluation of investment in transportation is quite recent. However, the analysis of the economic impact of transportation activities can be traced back to the early work of Dupuit (1844), Pigou (1912) and Samuelson (1954), at least as far as infrastructures as pure public goods are concerned. The productive role of public goods has been further described by Negishi (1973), and Mera

(1984) provides an analysis of the contribution of infrastructure to economic development. Tinbergen (1957) first dealt with the economic appraisal of road investment, while more recently Kanemoto and Mera (1983) provided a general equilibrium analysis of the benefits of large transportation improvements.

The theory of public goods has been integrated with analysis of spatial general equilibrium and the theory of economic planning by Tulkens and Kabantu (1983), providing a very formal and comprehensive treatment of the problem of efficient allocation of resources to transportation infrastructure. This model, however, only accounts for commodity transportation; moreover, the model operates without recourse to a price system.

Another approach to evaluating the economic impact of a transportation system, based on input–output modelling, is presented in three papers by Liew and Liew (1984a; 1984b; 1985). The model differs from traditional multiregional input–output models (Isard 1951, Leontief and Strout 1963, Amano and Fujita 1970) by being price- and cost-sensitive. The model is static and, even being multimodal in its more recent extension (Liew and Liew 1985), does not allow for explicit consideration of passenger transport.

The evaluation of transportation system change from the viewpoint of the consumer is dealt with by Sasaki (1983). His model is based on an application of the household production function approach (see Becker 1965). This approach needs strong assumptions, but can prove very useful in the evaluation of transportation plans. However, its application other than to passenger transport as well as its multiregional extension would prove to be extremely difficult.

Practically all the papers we have made reference to deal with an analysis of the effects of a given change in the transportation system. Very little attention is paid to the costs of the transformation, which should be seriously considered if the evaluation of competing plans is based on comparing alternative economic states. This would also require the translation of all the forecasted effects in a homogeneous measure of benefit and disbenefit (externalities), which is usually not an easy task. Moreover, little attention has been given to demand functions, which, in general, should have among their arguments the characteristics of supply (see Gartner 1980a). Our aim here is to introduce a formulation of the evaluation problem general enough to allow for a full economic appraisal of transportation plans, taking into account both elastic demand functions and the two main classes of instrument variables available to planning authorities — changes in the transport networks, and the pricing system.

Our discussion will not concern a further evaluation model, but rather a micro-economic approach to comparing alternative economic states involving individuals, firms and different goods and services among them transportation. It should therefore be considered as an attempt to establish a unifying framework in order to link and put to use the results of the available models. Treatment will be given explicitly in terms of urban passenger transport. However, it will be easy to recognise the simplicity of generalisation.

2. The planning goal

Investment in transportation has system-wide implications which can be assessed at several levels, and so the modelling of a transportation network and its links with the overall socio-economic system cannot leave out of consideration the planning goals and the geographical scale which they refer to.

At the national or interregional scale, planning goals are usually related to macro-economic variables. Transportation is therefore included in the models at a low level of detail, usually in the form of aggregated transportation costs and trade coefficients, even when much emphasis is placed on multisectoral and multiregional modelling, as in the papers by Liew and Liew (1984a; 1984b; 1985).

At the regional scale (see for instance Blum 1982) some indicators of transportation supply are often related to regional growth via econometric modelling. At the urban scale more explicit evidence is given to transportation networks, including users' behavioural models about choice and routing (see Boyce 1984). The costs (and benefits) are more directly related and measured in terms of the users' welfare, and therefore the use of traffic assignment algorithms becomes part of the evaluation procedure. At the intraregional and intraurban scale (Anas 1984) the emphasis shifts to the relationships among transportation supply, accessibility, residential and locational choice.

Very few models allow for the treatment of multimodal transportation networks (Liew and Liew 1984b), and there is no evaluation model able to handle simultaneously freight and passenger transport in a multimodal framework.

The difficulty of simultaneous treatment stems from the need to consider transportation as an intermediate service in the production process in the case of freight and as a final consumption in the case of passenger. In practice, substantial improvements of the supply of transportation infrastructure are likely to affect both passengers and freight. However, the practical relevance of the simultaneous consideration of passenger and freight changes with scale. At the urban level, for instance, the main problem is related to the movement of people, while freight gains importance at the interregional and national scale.

The most common treatment of passenger transportation is that of considering labour as an input commodity in production processes (Tulkens and Kabantu 1983). This obviously leaves out of consideration trips other than those from home to work. On the contrary, Sasaki (1983) deals only with passenger transportation, but changes in interregional commodity flows are considered in that they affect individual users, altering the income distribution.

A similar approach is followed here: our main assumption is that transport is not desirable in itself, but only as a necessary complement to the fruition or production of other goods and services. It is because of the complementary nature of transport that variations in its pattern can produce redistributive effects which must be taken into account in the evaluation of investments.

Given the complexity of the issue, we shall start our analysis with the simplifying assumption that the user's benefit is equal to his ability to pay. To give a simple geometric illustration, and with no loss of generality, we consider here a simple transportation system consisting of one link and a single origin-destination pair (i, k). In Figure 16.1 the cost incurred to the user is depicted, as a function of flow, against the inverse demand curve (interchange travel cost as a function of trip rate W_{ik} (g_{ik}). Subscripts are omitted since there is no risk of ambiguity. Under the condition of Figure 16.1, the equilibrium is reached with a flow f, and the cost incurred to the user is c. The dashed area indicated as US represents the user's surplus.

It is interesting to inquire the meaning in this framework of the shaded area Q. In the case of Marshallian equilibrium this would be the supplier's surplus. Here, this paradigm does not apply directly, since $c(f)$ is more a travel performance function rather than a supply function. It is easy to see that Q is exactly the integral of marginal social costs (that is, the increment in transportation cost occasioned by users) which are not charged to the users, and therefore represent a surplus from their standpoint. In other words, in the case of transportation, all system surplus is retained by users. Then, Q must be added to the conventional user surplus in order to get the total users' benefit (system surplus):

$$\text{System surplus} = US + Q$$

It can be shown (Beckmann *et al.* 1956) that system surplus is maximised when each trip-maker strives to minimise his own travel costs, leading to an equilibrium state in which travel costs on all

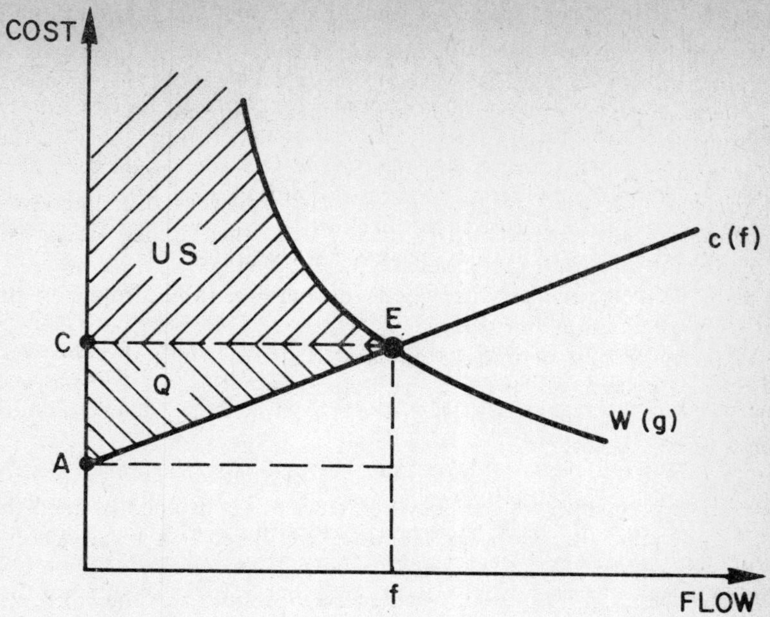

Figure 16.1 Equilibrium in a transportation system

utilised routes between any origin–destination pair are equal to or less than those on non-utilised routes (Wardrop 1952). The resulting flow pattern is termed 'user-optimised'.

It should be noted that, since the user does not perceive social costs, the above traffic pattern will not be the most efficient. Excluding here a normative approach, to induce an efficient use of the available capacity every user should be charged a toll which is equal to his marginal social cost. It can be shown (Gartner 1980a) that this policy increases the system surplus. The resulting flow pattern is termed 'system-optimised'.

3. Comprehensive evaluation

In the previous section we have mainly dealt with the direct effects of transportation policies, that is, with benefits and costs to trip-makers. In this section we shall introduce the micro-economic tools utilised to represent the behaviour of the operators and trip-makers and to analyse the effects of a transportation plan on the entire economic system.

We shall limit our analysis to refer to purely static and fully deterministic conceptual schemes. Furthermore, we will assume a unique and constant price system (different from transport), disregarding possible effects on the land revenue.

Let us consider an economic system characterised by

- produced and traded goods and services;
- persons that allocate their income according to different consumption patterns derived rationally from their utility functions, and that constitute potential labour suppliers;
- firms that use and produce goods and services in accordance with given production functions;
- a given amount of initial resources; and
- a price system, equal for every individual.

Now let

q^k_i be the quantity of the goods or services *i* consumed by the *k*th individual (the supply of labour is considered as a negative consumption), $i = 1, 2, \ldots, n$; $k = 1, 2, \ldots, m$

q_{ih} be the quantity of goods or services *i* produced by the *h*th firm; the quantities produced or used are conventionally considered respectively positive and negative: $h = 1, 2, \ldots, v$

q_{io} be the quantity of goods *i* assigned as initial resource

p_i be the price system

r_k be the individual's income.

Since in this study we deal mainly with the transport system, it is appropriate to separate this sector from the others, aggregating all operators in a single $(v + 1)$th firm producing transport services, and using as inputs quantity $q_{i,v+1}$ of the other goods and services. We will then indicate with

T_k the quantity of transport service consumed by every individual (expressed in some homogenous unity, for example, kilometres per day)

p the unit price of transportation

t the time spent by each individual in consuming a unit of transport

T total transport consumption, $T = \Sigma_k T_k$

With the explicit introduction of transport as a complementary service we must consider the time directly involved with the consumption of goods or services. This allows us to compare transport time with the time strictly necessary for consumption. We will then let

t_i^k be the time spent by individual k in consuming the unit of goods or services i.

In the above system, every individual will be characterised by a utility function, depending only on consumption quantities:

$$S_k = S_k(q_i^k, T_k)$$

We shall assume here that individuals rationally allocate their income and time to their maximum satisfaction, that is, according to the solution of the following optimum problem:

$$\max S_k\,(q_i^k, T_k) \qquad (1)$$

$$q_i^k p_i + pT_k = r_k \qquad (2)$$

$$q_i^k t_i^k + tT_k = \tau \qquad (3)$$

$$q_i^k \geqslant 0 \;\forall\; i,\; T_k \geqslant 0 \qquad (4)$$

where τ is the total available time.

We shall assume also that a social utility function of the Samuelson–Bergson type may be defined, depending on the individual utility functions:

$$U = U(S_1, S_2, \ldots, S_m) \qquad (5)$$

Without entering into the difficulties connected with the characterisation of this function in comparing two alternative economic states, henceforth we consider as socially preferable the one with the highest U value.

Finally, to simplify our treatment, we introduce a closedness hypothesis for the economic system:

$$\sum_k q_i^k = \sum_h q_{ih} + q_{io} + q_{i,v+1} \quad \forall i \qquad (6)$$

The initial equilibrium state can be calculated by solving problems (1–4). Forming the Lagrangean and writing the first order conditions, it is easy to see that the multiplier associated with the time constraints gives the marginal utility of time to individual k.

4. Economic effects of changing transportation patterns

Investment in transportation not only changes a component of the overall socio-economic system, but also causes substantial redistributive effects and/or alterations in consumption patterns. In this section we discuss the effects of changes in transportation-related variables as $\{T_k, t, p,\}$.

Differentiating the social utility function and letting $U_k = \partial U / \partial S_k$, after calculation we get:

$$dU = \sum_k \sum_i \frac{U_k}{\lambda_k}(p_i + f_k t_i^k) dq_i^k + \sum \frac{U_k}{\lambda_k}(p + f_k t) dT_k \tag{7}$$

where λ_k is the marginal utility of income to individual k (Lagrange multiplier associated with constraint (2)) and f_k is the monetary value of kth individual's time.

Let us now introduce a transformation in the transport system, which, with constant prices, changes the time spent in consuming the service unit. Since the total available time obviously remains constant, by differentiating the relative constraint (3) we have:

$$\sum_i t_i^k dq_i^k + T_k dt + t dT_k = 0 \quad \forall k \tag{8}$$

Multiplying (8) by $\frac{U_K}{\lambda_k} f_k$, summing over k and subtracting from (7) we have

$$dU = \sum_k \sum_i \frac{U_k}{\lambda_k} p_i dq_i^k + \sum_k \frac{U_k}{\lambda_k} p dT_k - \sum_k \frac{U_k}{\lambda_k} f_k T_k dt \tag{9}$$

The first term of (9) is a weighted average of monetary variations in consumption and represents the redistributive monetary effect; the second term is analogous to the first, but deals with monetary variations in the consumption of transport services; finally, the third term is the weighted average of individual time savings, properly monetised.

We can easily deduce from (7) that weights U_k/λ_k represent the marginal social utility of the kth individual income. This implies the exact definition, at least in ordinal terms, of a social preference scale with respect to individuals' or groups' income increase. Moreover, the third term is not only weighted with respect to the social utility of income for the various categories, but also with respect to the possible different monetary evaluations of time resulting from different values assigned to f_k.

Equation (9) can be interpreted from another point of view, utilising the hypothesis of a closed system with full use of resources. From (6) we have:

$$\sum_k p_i dq_i^k = \sum_h p_i dq_{ih} + p_i dq_{i,v+1} \tag{10}$$

and letting

$$\sum_k \frac{U_k}{\lambda_k} p_i \, dq_i^k = z(r) \sum_k p_i dq_i^k$$

where $z\ (r)$ is a function expressing the social preference for a given distribution of income, we have

$$dU = z(r)\{\sum_i \sum_h p_i dq_{ih} + \sum_i p_i dq_{i,v+1}\}$$

$$+ \sum_k \frac{U_k}{\lambda_k}\{pdT_k + T_k dp\} \quad - \sum_k \frac{U_k}{\lambda_k}\{T_k\,(dp + f_k dt) \tag{11}$$

where the first term represents profit variation; the second, cost variations for the transportation operator; the third, revenue variation for the transport operator; and the fourth, consumer surplus as regards transport. Assigning a numerical value to these four terms is an extremely difficult task. However, equation (11) shows that a comprehensive evaluation of transportation planning schemes must be based on the following elements:

- the social preference of the various possible distributions of income, here indicated by $z(r)$;
- the firm's profit variations;
- the cost variations for the transport operator;
- the changes in the consumption of transport; and
- the variations in efficiency of the transport system.

5. Conclusion

In this chapter a comprehensive model has been introduced for the evaluation of investment in transportation. With respect to the many existing models for measuring the social, economic and environmental impact of a transportation system change, our aim has been to provide a common micro-economic framework for the comparison of alternative economic states resulting from different investment patterns in transportation.

Several models should be used in order to get estimates for the elements listed at the end of the previous section as the main ingredients of the evaluation process.

As for the indicator of social preference for income distributions, unless we think its derivation from an assigned utility function possible, we can try to assess the implicit preferences of decision-makers. Nevertheless, a neutral attitude towards the various classes of income corresponds to assuming that the current income distribution is also the optimal one.

It is also useful to point out that the evaluation should be based on the integral of equation (11) calculated between the initial and final states. An obvious implication is therefore that the choice process regards not only the comparison of those two economic states, but also the various possible paths in between. It is possible to demonstrate that total change in U is independent of the particular evolution of the system only when the evolution takes place through an infinite sequence of equilibrium states. The building and use of dynamic transportation models should therefore receive more attention.

References

Amano, K. and M. Fujita (1970). 'A Long-Run Economic Effect Analysis of Alternative Transportation Facility Plan: Regional and National', *Journal of Regional Science*, **10**, 297–323.

Anas, A (1984). 'Discrete Choice Theory and the General Equilibrium of Employment, Housing, and Travel Networks in a Lowry-type Model of the Urban Economy', *Environment and Planning A*, **16**, 1489–1502.

Becker, G.S. (1965). 'A Theory of the Allocation of Time', *Economic Journal*, **75**, 493–517.

Beckmann, M.J., C.B. McGuire and C.B. Winsten (1956). *Studies in the Economics of Transportation*. New Haven, CT: Yale University Press.

Blum, U. (1982). 'Effects of Transportation Investments on Regional Growth: A Theoretical and Empirical Investigation'. *Papers RSA*, **49**, 169–84.

Boyce, D.E. (1984). 'Urban Transportation Network. Equilibrium and Design Model: Recent Achievements and Future Prospects', *Environment and Planning A*, **16**, 1445–74.

Dupuit, J. (1844). 'On the measurement of the Utility of Public Works'. Reprinted in D. Munby, ed., *Transport*. Harmondsworth: Penguin (1968), pp.19–57.

Fernandez, J.E. (1981). 'Influence of Demand-quality Interrelationships of Optimal Policies for Stage Construction of Transportation Facilities', *Transportation Science*, **15**, 16–31.

Gartner, N.H. (1980a). 'Optimal Traffic Assignment with Elastic Demands: A Review. Part I. Analysis Framework', *Transportation Science*, **14**, 174–91.
Gartner, N.H. (1980b). 'Optimal Traffic Assignment with Elastic Demands: A Review. Part II. Algorithmic approaches', Transportation Science, **14**, 192–208.
Hart, T. (1983). 'Transport and the Economic Development: The Historical Dimension' in K.J. Button and D. Gillingwater, eds, *Transportation, Location and Spatial Policy*. Aldershot: Gower.
Isard, W. (1951). 'Interregional and Regional Input–Ouput Analysis: A Model of a Space-Economy', *Review of Economics and Statics*, **33**, 318–28.
Kanemoto, Y. and K. Mera (1983). 'General Equilibrium Analysis of the Benefits of Large Transportation Improvements'. Discussion Paper. Institute of Socio-Economic Planning, University of Tsukuba. Mimeo.
Leontief, W. and A. Strout (1963). 'Multiregional Input–Output Analysis' in T. Barna, ed., *Structural Interdependence and Economic Development*. London: Macmillan.
Lesourne, J. (1975). *Cost–Benefit Analysis and Economic Theory*. Amsterdam: North Holland.
Liew, C.K. and C.J. Liew (1984a). 'Measuring the Development Impact of a Proposed Transportation System', *Regional Science and Urban Economics*, **14**, 175–98.
Liew, C.K. and C.J. Liew (1984b). 'Multi-Modal, Multi-Output, Multiregional Variable Input–Output Model', *Regional Science and Urban Economics*, **14**, 265–81.
Liew, C.K. and C.J. Liew (1985). 'Measuring the Development Impact of a Transportation System: A Simplified Approach, *Journal of Regional Science*, **25**, 241–58.
Mera, K. (1984). 'Measuring Economic Contributions of Infrastructure in Cities of Developing Countries'. Paper presented at the *Second World Congress of Art and Sciences*, Rotterdam.
Negishi, T. (1973). 'The Excess of Public Expenditures on Industries', *Journal of Public Economics*, **2**, 231–40.
Pigou, A.C. (1912). *Wealth and Welfare*. London: Macmillan.
Samuelson, P.A. (1954). 'The Pure Theory of Public Expenditure', *Review of Economics and Statistics*, **36**, 387–9.
Sasaki, K. (1983). 'A Household Production Approach to the Evaluation of Transportation System Change', *Regional Science and Urban Economics*, **13**, 363–82.
Tinbergen, J. (1957). 'The Appraisal of Road Construction: Two Calculation Schemes', *Review of Economics and Statistics*, **39**, 241–9.
Tulkens, H. and K. Kabantu (1983). 'A Planning Process for the Efficient Allocation of Resources to Transportation Infrastructure' in J.F. Thisse and H.G. Zoller, eds, *Locational Analysis of Public Facilities*. Amsterdam: North Holland.
Wardrop J.G. (1952). 'Some Theoretical Aspects of Road Traffic Research', *Proc. Inst. Civil Eng.* (Part II), **1**, 325–78.

17 Some Reflections on Transportation Models

H.C.W.L. Williams

1. Introduction

In this chapter I propose to discuss various aspects relating to the development of transportation models, and offer some views on outstanding research issues. Although primarily concerned with passenger-demand models and particularly those applied within an urban context, the common heritage, theoretical frameworks and statistical methods render many of the remarks relevant to a range of activity-travel contexts including the study of logistics and commodity transportation.

Because I shall only be able to touch on the following aspects in a superficial way, it is worth emphasising at the start that model developments seldom have an *absolute* significance, but are relevant to a set of *comparative* issues and questions. Are the alternative approaches for the generation of required information in any particular planning context? How are appropriate competitors characterised in terms of the use of data, specification of models, and estimation procedures? How should they be judged in terms of statistical accuracy, theoretical integrity, and practical considerations — including the economics of development and application? In what contexts and to what questions are specific developments important? How significant in any situation are approximations, errors and uncertainty, which are inevitably present in a variety of forms?

Thus, while the interrelationship between the nature of the information to be derived, the model specification, and the context of development (be it in a projective, policy-testing, or plan-design context; in short-, medium-, or long-term analyses; sketch planning or system evaluation; local or area-wide studies; etc.) are often acknowledged in discussions on model design, the quantitative implications of these relations are not in fact well understood in practice, and their specific relevance to the assessment of different models is seldom fully acknowledged.

For more than a decade these comparisons and critiques have been associated with the development of discrete choice models and their implications for more traditional styles. These are considered in Section 2, while in Section 3 more recent theoretical issues and research requirements relating to the 'micro-behavioural' approach are examined. Various aspects concerned with the development of supply models and the interaction between the demand for and supply of transportation services are introduced in Section 4. The interrelationship between demand analysis and evaluation frameworks is then considered in Section 5, and in a short conclusion some further general research requirements are emphasised.

In a paper of this length and scope it would be invidious to present but a few selected references. Their omission reflects the general level of the discussion, and the broad-ranging but inevitably selective nature of the views expressed. As such the chapter is intended to be complementary to others in this part of the book.

2. Econometric analysis of discrete choice behaviour

One of the most significant developments in travel research during the 1970s was the establishment of demand analysis within the framework of discrete choice theory. The formulation of demand functions through the specification, estimation and aggregation of probabilistic choice models was thus placed on a sound econometric footing. The dispersion in, and explanation of, aggregate behaviour were related directly to the distribution of unobserved and observed attributes associated with individuals and their travel-related options, and accommodated through a random utility calculus.

The contribution of theory was essentially found in the generation of new model forms — notably the probit and logit family — consistent with utility maximisation, in suggesting variables to be incorporated in preference relations, and in the provision of restrictions on model parameters. By focusing on what were presumed to be the 'behavioural invariants' of individual choice processes, hope was expressed that such models would be transferable in a spatial and temporal sense, and much empirical analysis has been, and continues to be, directed towards this issue. In terms of statistical considerations there were important insights into appropriate sample designs, associated properties of estimation methods, and the characteristics of aggregation schemes. As such, the 'first principles' approach proved a tremendous stimulus to research in a wide variety of travel-related contexts.

A particular emphasis in the development of the micro-econometric approach which was appropriate and desirable was a focus on specification and aggregation errors accompanying more traditional model applications. Without wishing to detract from these contributions, it is perhaps unfortunate that its promotion was sometimes at the expense of rather poor competitors, notably the UTPS models in the United States in the late 1960s, which did not reflect the state of the art. The coarser characteristics of the old regime would inevitably compare unfavourably with 'good' examples of the disaggregate approach, even though the latter had been tried and tested predominantly in short-term policy testing contexts based essentially on modal choice models, and not subject to the same terms of reference as strategic transport studies.

But even in those days hybrid model forms were developing in the context of urban transportation studies which anticipated some of the emphases of the new approach, and this was not perhaps surprising as a rudimentary behavioural theory did underpin traditional forms. Thus, for example in the United Kingdom since the SELNEC study, there emerged model systems which included: household- and individual-based category analyses for trip generation; 'embedded' micro-models based on (compensatory) generalised costs; and nested model structures in which decisions were interrelated by composite costs (later to become known as 'inclusive costs' in the jargon of the nested-logit model). Elements of discrete choice theory were later invoked in the mid-1970s to give some belated respectability to the sequential structuring of models in which choices were ordered according to the values of elasticity parameters indicating the propensity to respond to policy variables in the various 'dimensions' of choice.

It is now recognised that, when subject to the same ends, conventional aggregate and disaggregate styles (which were always rather unfortunate descriptors in view of the capacity for and practice of stratifying demand variables in the former, and the requirement to aggregate micro-relations in the latter) have moved closer together, the former anticipating and absorbing characteristics of the micro-econometric approach, and the latter subject to the compromises of practical developments, notably in the treatment of spatial interaction, and in the representation and interface with supply-side variables (level-of-service variables in the transport sector and stock variables in the activity system). This supports the view of an evolutionary rather than revolutionary development of travel forecasting models, based on the common strategy of cross-sectional revealed preference analysis.

The discrete choice framework, implemented through random utility models continues to prove an extremely fertile area for development, and significant advances both in *method* and *application* are currently evident. Among the former are: the specification of models and their estimation with longitudinal data sets, a comparison of revealed and stated preference methods, the further incorporation of attitudinal variables, the inclusion of constraints and limited information, the use of simulation for the formation and aggregation of choice models. The latter embraces a wide range of applications over many different travel and location decisions, with extensions to the study of logistics as a basis for policy sensitive commodity transportation models. However, the full practical implications of the development of the micro-econometric approach for a range of situations, including models for locational choices and discretionary travel, are still to be fully explored.

3. Some theoretical issues and developments

The characteristics of activity-travel frameworks, with emphases on the time-structuring of activities and associated travel, linked trips (tours), the interdependence between the activities and travel capabilities of different household members, the variety of constraints to which each is subject, and so on, are now familiar. These developments, in which European researchers took a prominent role, have had important implications for the description and explanation of travel behaviour, but hitherto a relatively small impact on traditional forecasting contexts (which were not particularly prominent in the outlook of the researchers concerned).

In recent years the distinctions between constraint-orientated and choice/preference-orientated approaches to the analysis of travel behaviour have been emphasised. Although the former have hitherto had relatively little to say of preferences, and the latter accommodate constraints incompletely and often implicitly through a variety of devices (market segmentation, proxy variables, random residuals and, occasionally, choice-set specifications) it is important that artificial distinctions between conceptual approaches are not created, for both necessarily fall within integrated decision models accompanying the activity-travel framework. In the design of improved models it will be important to establish for which decisions, and for which groups, significant degrees of choice are evident, and who is at the margin in policy-testing contexts. While in a forecasting operation the latter is clearly an output of the modelling process, the importance of appropriate experimental designs for testing hypotheses on response is evident.

Among the more important features to emerge from empirical studies founded upon the activity-travel representation is in fact evidence of rich and often subtle forms of adaptation available to individuals and households in response to policies, compared to more traditional conceptions, and this is particularly true of discretionary trip-making. (It is important to explore the corresponding issues of organisational choice in relation to logistics and the transport-related decisions of firms.) To date, however, few quantitative insights into the potential mis-specification of more traditional probabilistic choice models have emerged, for although there now exist a more sophisticated view of appropriate forms of market segmentation and available choice/response sets, alternative general decision rules based on compensatory and non-compensatory constructs and alternative means of exploring behaviour through revealed and stated preferences (including transfer-pricing), the establishment and testing of substantive hypotheses relating to behavioural response still requires much research effort.

Of particular interest in this respect is a better understanding of the relationship between 'strategic' and 'tactical' decisions of households and firms and their significance over different time-scales, not only for improving the structures of cross-sectional models, but also for the specification of longitudinal models and appropriate interpretation of the results from aggregate time series data. (This is currently a topic of some interest in the analysis of public transport demand, and specifically in disentangling the effects of external factors from the longer-term effects of policy measures under the control of local operators.)

The establishment and reconciliation of demand models at different levels of commodity aggregation remains a challenging aggregation in the two-stage budgeting process of consumer theory, there is a requirement to relate the discrete choice models to continuous demand models whose independent variables are the expenditure on time and/or money pertaining to trips or journey groups for individuals or households, so that empirical regularities in time and money budgets can be sensibly accommodated within a hierarchical travel-demand theory and the implications for forecasting and policy analysis assessed. Some early and fruitful work on this topic which married ideas from entropy and utility theories is still to be fully developed.

4. Supply models and equilibrium analysis

There have been frequent calls in recent years for an improved understanding of the supply side of the transportation equation. This has been interpreted in different ways by the various disciplines whose interests converge on the analysis of transportation and activity systems, although three areas may immediately be identified. Firstly, there are the engineering characteristics of level-of-service expressions for transport modes, regarded as functions of volume or flow, technological parameters and the regulation and organisational determinants of system behaviour. Secondly, there are the familiar economic concerns for the production characteristics of firms in regulated and deregulated contexts; and thirdly, there are the determinants of spatial organisation, and more specifically the availability of opportunities and activities in planned and unplanned urban and regional systems. In all these contexts the representation and resolution of the interaction between the supply of and demand for transportation services are important theoretical and practical focuses of attention.

The recent introduction in applied network models of junction characteristics as the prime determinant of traffic delay in road systems constitutes a major advance for the analysis of local and area-wide transportation schemes. However, the expression and computation of network equilibria in multi-user systems with realistic interdependent (junction-based) cost functions still prove problematic, although there is no shortage of theoretical research in this area. A substantive problem is the determination of the mis-specification implications, for both the analysis and evaluation of schemes, of the more traditional link-based time-volume relations applied at different spatial scales.

The specification and estimation of service characteristics for public transport systems — notably the waiting times, boarding times and reliability — still pose significant theoretical and practical problems, particularly in the progression from detailed corridor studies to area-wide network analyses. Because poor and/or declining reliability is known to be a very important determinant of passenger loss, further work on the dependence of this service factor (expressed, for example, through the variability in waiting time) on patronage, congestion, crew organisation and availability, fare-collection systems and current service levels, is well justified.

The establishment and reconciliation of demand and supply models at different levels of aggregation remains a challenging research topic. An important example in public transport planning concerns the consistent representation of the service functions in different policy studies. In network-design contexts service changes are reflected in a set of (disaggregate) local spatial variables and incorporated in generalised cost models in the usual way. On the other hand, for financial analyses and a determination of the balance between fares and services, area-wide models have been developed in terms of the total output of an operation which is presumed to incorporate the effects of changes in frequencies and route coverage on demand. It is widely recognised that there may well be substantial specification and aggregation biases associated with this formulation, and the establishment of a consistent hierarchical planning framework for financial analysis, fare and service planning and network design requires early consideration, both to improve the methods for expressing and estimating service elasticities, and to explore more fully the implications and potential errors associated with current practice.

With regard to multimodal systems, there are still a number of issues unresolved concerning the determination (both conceptually and numerically) of the equilibrium conditions which resolve modal supply functions and capacity restrictions, with demand models which embrace a range of choices over routes, time periods, modes, locations and frequencies. This general issue subsumes the difficulties associated with the establishment of the demand functions themselves. For non-work trips and commodity flows the (unrealistic) assumption of a fixed trip matrix is widely invoked in scheme appraisal, and there is little evidence available to date of the relative contributions in benefit assessment of the satisfactory treatment of congestion, on the one hand, and of an improved representation of demand response, on the other.

In the second supply category are included the empirical investigations and associated model development for multi-product firms in regulated and deregulated systems. In the case of public transport systems which involve the operation of services of different types over different routes at different times of day, the classical problems associated with the establishment of short- and long-run cost models at different levels of resolution remain of considerable interest and importance. In particular, this includes the empirical investigation of the incremental costs associated with service changes. In this context, the establishment, for different crew-scheduling arrangements, of appropriate conventions for allocating costs to routes and time periods, in the presence of substantial overheads and cost interdependencies (arising from scheduling arrangements) poses significant research issues. This is important for monitoring and predicting internal cross-subsidisation (measured through incremental or fully allocated costs and revenues) between units of output on different routes at various periods of the day and week.

In this context there has been rather little research on the likely network implications of operators acting (more) commercially, and the generation of systems characterised by low degrees of external subsidy and internal cross-subsidy. This is currently of particular interest in Britain in the light of proposed legislation to deregulate the stage carriage services. Indeed, much debate surrounds the characteristics of the end-states associated with deregulated and partially regulated systems and in particular whether stable outcomes will be achieved. Limited results from gaming-simulation models of the different forms of competition suggest, not surprisingly, that results will depend on the starting conditions, individual behaviour expressed through demand models associated with the different carriers, the cost characteristics of the existing operator(s) and potential entrants, together with the nature and extent of any intervention.

Allied to this issue is that of identifying, in the case of deregulated systems, an appropriate role for planning itself and of the establishment of associated information systems by different agencies and local authorities. This is of particular concern for the support of unremunerative but worthy services not provided by the market. Of immediate interest is a determination of the means by which different needy groups should be served, and confronting the problem of co-ordinating transportation supply over different local services, including health, education, the social services, and the voluntary sector. From a modelling viewpoint this may well involve extensions of the traditional operational research methods involving detailed routing and scheduling exercises under demand-responsive conditions.

With regard to the availability of transportation opportunities, it does therefore seem likely that in the near future unconventional forms of supply will emerge, or become more widely available, in both urban and rural contexts. The demand for such options is, of course, either absent or poorly reflected in the current situation. With the limitation of revealed preference methods evident, a great reliance on stated intention and market-research methods for short-range forecasting seems inevitable.

In the third category are included the determinants of the spatial (and temporal) organisation of the opportunities in the *activity/land-use system* at different spatial scales. While some progress has been made over the last ten years in extending economic and systems approaches to the industrial, housing and retail sectors, a further elaboration of the *behavioural approach* is called for in order to explore more fully the types of spatial organisation which may emerge under different processes and policies. This is, of course, a substantial research area, and would seem to call in the first instance for the development of *qualitative* and *semi-qualitative methods*, to assess the implications of alternative hypotheses underpinning dynamic *processes* (relating to the detailed working and role of transportation variables in the various markets, and in the location of discrete public service facilities) and the response of the system to various policy measures.

In the short term there appears a need to consider current developments in travel and locational research to improve the representation of both transportation demand and supply in *integrated land-use–transport models* (for example, in the level of *market segmentation* associated with residential and retail location models to incorporate captivity and choice appropriately, in a more careful characterisation of transport–supply opportunities at different levels of spatial resolution, and in incorporating more realistic *elasticity measures* for transport policy assessment).

More generally, the above considerations must be subject to the study of *approximations* and *mis-specification* in the various application contexts. This is particularly important in determining the degree of detail to be incorporated on the demand and supply sides, and the treatment of their interaction in dynamic or more simple comparative static forms.

5. Evaluation issues

Demand analyses are seldom ends in themselves, and some of the most interesting and arguably most important questions concern the interrelationship between measures of demand and performance/evaluation indices which relate to the objectives of the planning system.

The integration of user-benefit analysis and response prediction is now well established within the random utility theory of discrete choice, and for a wide range of models including different members of the logit family (which are the stock-in-trade of the demand analyst) exact benefit (consumer-surplus) measures have been derived. In a locational context the notion of accessibility has been interpreted in terms of preferences over spatial opportunities, and exploited in the evaluation and design of land-use plans. Random utility theory has thus provided a unification between the analysis and evaluation of activity and transportation systems founded upon the derived demand for travel.

One immediate consequence of these advances — that is, the explicit derivation of expected surplus values from discrete choice theory — is that the evaluation measures themselves are vulnerable to precisely the same criticisms as the choice models with which they are compatible (if the latter are deemed to be mis-specified). In spite of the potential importance of these issues, and their wide recognition, in, for example, modal choice/value-of-time contexts, there has been relatively little work on the development of measures which incorporate intra-household interactions and constraints, captivity and choice-set variation over samples, the ranking of preferences according to alternative (for example, non-compensatory) decision rules, information limitations and thresholds in decision-making (and the old problem of adding up small benefits), and so on. The problems are even more severe for decisions involving complex forms of adaptation, and this is as evident in the study of firm logistics as it is of personal travel behaviour. In principle, these issues may be accommodated in the random utility theory of discrete choice, by making appropriate adjustments to current assumptions, and efforts should be made to follow them through at least to determine order-of-magnitude estimates of different elaborations. Again, it is the comparative implications of different evaluation measures which is of significance, and whether such measures are applied in the ranking or the detailed assessment of particular plans.

Activity-travel analysts, through their emphasis on constraints rather than preferences, have had much more to say on the distributional rather than the efficiency aspects of transport-policy appraisal, and emphasis has typically centred on the characteristics of choice sets available to individuals (variously characterised) undertaking different activities, and the general effects of transport policy, including the status quo, on such choice sets and levels of travel service available. Over the last decade much social research has been conducted into needs, both revealed and latent, and various forms of comparison and priorities have been discussed, including those involving different activity-travel categories for specific groups of individual or household, those between specific activity-travel categories for different individuals, and comparisons between groups within and between communities. This work has been largely descriptive with few clear implications for or relationships to the distributional and efficiency objectives of transport planning, and the formation of practical evaluative frameworks (whether these involve a conventional benefit-cost framework, or the adoption of specific criteria such as 'pounds per needs met', with their explicit weighting systems or standards).

Few comparisons are available between sophisticated needs-assessment methods, conceived within activity-travel frameworks, and those methods currently applied by local planning authorities, which in Britain employ a variety of demand and supply proxy variables to reflect relative disadvantage. If both efficiency and distributional objectives are to be appropriately embraced in the design and evaluation of schemes, both preferences and constraints must be incorporated within an integrated activity-travel framework. However, simplifications will have to be invoked if the methods are the be useful to transport operators and local authorities. Much remains to be done in this area of research, and its importance is clear with the prospect of substantial changes in the transportation environments of urban and particularly rural areas.

6. Conclusion

There is a continuing and pressing need for behavioural research on travel and, more generally, urban systems, which embraces the effects of demographic, economic, social and technological processes on relevant 'decision units'. To be effective the inevitable compromises of practical forecasting, (in the specification, estimation and aggregation of models) whether in a projective or policy-testing context, should be recognised at the start. The claims of competing models and methods which generate comparable information should be carefully scrutinised. Further, while there is a need to emphasise contemporary problems and policy issues, let us not turn our backs on the traditional strategic and longer-term concerns associated with network analysis and infrastructure planning, whether primarily associated with urban, inter-urban, or international studies, passenger or freight transportation, in developed or developing countries. A sophisticated view of the problems associated with strategic planning models has emerged which needs to be matched by a vigorous approach to their improvement.

In the light of rather rapid social, technological and organisational changes, the use of present behaviour as a basis for long- and medium-term projections is notably suspect. The increasing practice of incorporating errors, uncertainty and scenario developments in forecasts, together with the more general investigations of behaviour through stated intentions, would appear to be justified, in what has always been an awkward dilemma.

Predictably, in any conclusion on forecasting methods for policy assessment, whether these pertain to the short, medium or long term, the need for more attention to be paid to the validation of models must be cited. While this will always be a problematic area, the strong emphasis on cross-sectional methods and the dominance of statistical fitting as a criterion for acceptability do give some cause for concern, particularly because experience has shown that severely mis-specified projective and response models have passed through the net in many practical studies. Both theoretical and empirical analyses must become more response-orientated, in the former case through the formulation of alternative hypotheses relating to the changes likely to be induced by processes or policies, and in the latter case through the accumulation and assessment of more out-turn evidence, so that response models (based on stated and/or revealed preferences) may be validated in a more meaningful sense. It is sobering to think that knowledge of elasticities in stratified markets, even for rather mundane policies such as parking or public transport service strategies, is still very limited.

Finally, let us recognise and explore more fully the duality between demand and evaluation frameworks. Improvements, limitations or errors, either in general conception or detail, associated with the former will have (possibly very significant) implications for policy evaluation and plan design.

PART D: POLICY-MAKING

18 Configurating Change: Reflections on Transport Policy Processes

D. Starkie

1. Introduction

Crucial to the understanding of public policy is a conception of why and how government policies change. Why, for example, do certain issues get raised in the first place, why do some issues get on to the political agenda and, having done so, how are they analysed and how do governments finally react? The chief concern of this paper is with the last of these questions in a transport context and particularly with the form or pattern of the political response (or what Heclo (1976) dubbed the 'configurations of change').

My overall approach is set in a pluralist framework of interest-group competition and a general acceptance of democratic values. Consequently, I do not discuss transport policy in terms of political power and who exercises such power. Those interested in these issues are referred to Blowers (1980) or, for an application of class-dialectic models to transport policy, to Whitt (1982). My initial treatment of the subject is prescriptive and broadly based but, as the argument is developed, it becomes focused more sharply on the empirics of transport policy with a British emphasis. I start with a brief examination of the difficult question of issues, how they arise and how they become political and, therefore, have policy relevance.

2. Issue cycles

For policies to change, their subjects must become 'political', they must each become an issue.[1] Becoming an issue, however, does not guarantee that policies will change; it is a necessary but not sufficient condition.

How or why issues reach the political agenda is far from clear. At any one time competition between 'potential' issues seeking attention is considerable. Some float to the surface, others remain submerged. We can specify two interrelated factors which, it is most likely, provide powerful currents within the sea of issues. One factor is the increasing material well-being of society which leads to a satisfaction of basic needs and the respecification of these. The other factor is an evolving set of social values, with the effect that certain concerns move up and down in the list of social priorities.

Not all commentators would share this view. Gunningham (1974), for instance, rejects the idea of change in society's fundamental values and, instead, attributes the projection of certain issues to the machinations of the communications media. Nevertheless Gunningham's views still beg the question as to why newspapers, radio and television should react in the way they do, if not to reflect the underlying views of society.

On occasions an issue is projected to the fore because of a dramatic development. One example is the issue of whether lighting systems should be installed throughout the British motorway system. It becomes an issue each time there is a large-scale accident caused by fog or bad weather. The bigger the accident, the stronger the issue becomes. This kind of 'dramatic' issue is the exception rather than the rule, but it does illustrate a point emphasised by Downs (1972) that public attention rarely remains focused upon any one issue for very long. Downs refers to this waxing and waning as the 'issues attention cycle'. Downs's cycle has five stages which may vary in duration depending upon the issue, but 'which almost always occur in the following sequence':

- the pre-problem stage (e.g. an awareness that bad accidents can happen during winter fog on motorways);
- alarmed discovery and euphoric enthusiasm (e.g. serious crash, demands for action);
- realising the cost of significant progress (e.g. cost of lighting when public expenditure is constrained);
- gradual decline of interest (e.g. UK weather improves with the onset of spring — sometimes!); and
- post-problem stage — prolonged limbo (e.g. summer holidays arrive).

In this scenario, interest groups clearly play an important role. The better organised and the larger they are, the greater the opportunity for keeping an issue alive before the down-cycle sets in.

Such cycles can be subject to systematic analysis with a view to measuring the intensity of an issue at various times, thus giving shape or form to the cycle. One approach would be to measure the frequency with which an issue is raised in parliamentary questions and debate. However, at this stage, an issue will be close to, or will have arrived on, the political agenda. An alternative and more fruitful approach would be to examine the content of news media, especially newspapers. Such a measure might provide suitable early warning of an issue's political significance.

Table 18.1 illustrates the only substantive content analysis focused specifically upon transport issues that I am aware of. In this case the focus is Sydney, Australia, and we are presented with a snapshot of issues at three dates — 1930, 1955 and 1975 — culled from the pages of Sydney newspapers. There are the obvious difficulties in classifying material and, in this example, the infrequency of the snapshot prevents firm or even tentative conclusion regarding cycles. But it does provide a lead for future research.

Table 18.1 An analysis of transport issues in Sydney

	Newspaper content					
Mode	Entries per cent*			Leaders no.		
	1930	1955	1975	1930	1955	1975
Ferries	3	2	19	0	0	4
Parking	1	10	12	0	3	1
Railways	50	22	0	7	9	0
North Shore Bridge	21	4	10	2	1	1
Trams/buses	13	35	2	0	12	0
Traffic/roads	13	26	31	1	3	2
Non-specific	—	1	25	—	1	5
Total	100 (353)	100 (418)	100 (232)	10	29	13

*Rounding errors apply.
Source: Adapted from Black *et al.* (1983)

The idea of an issue cycle raises the question of the length of the cycle. If, in the Sydney case, the content analysis had been conducted on a monthly or even annual basis, it might have been possible to express a view regarding the length of issue cycles in Sydney. Some issues, because of their dramatic nature (like motorway accidents) have short cycle times, but how long are cycles related to more basic issues such as public transport services, parking problems, and so on? More especially, do we get recurring cycles or waves, and are certain issues subject to Kondratieff[2] long waves? For example, if we consider the fundamental issue of whether and to what extent transport systems should be subject to economic regulation, one finds at least a hint of a long wave. The late-nineteenth-century concern with such an issue in relation to the railways was repeated in the 1920s and 1930s, this time in the context of road transport. In this post-war world, the same issue has gained attention again, but now largely with an inverted emphasis — deregulation (see for example Bauchet and Masset (Chapter 19) in this volume).

3. Modes of change

How governments react to issue cycles and why policies change when they do is an even more testing question; I would suggest this is best approached by analysing and classifying patterns of change on the assumption that the patterns revealed provide clues to the factors involved.

Figures 18.1 shows the configurations of change for two polar cases, labelled A and B. The trajectory labelled A indicates a pattern of discontinuous or discrete change. Change in this instance emanates in such a way that there are distinct breaks in policy, with new programmes replacing (rather than modifying) existing policies. The trajectory labelled B emphasises, on the other hand, the idea that policies essentially evolve or metamorphose over time.

At this initial stage it is perhaps useful to clarify further some aspects of the figure. The vertical axis represents a *degree* of change in policy. Such a representation abstracts entirely from the issue of the type or form of policy involved. Consequently, point *x*, for example, although showing trajectories A and B to have converged, is not meant to signify that the respective paths of change have resulted in the same policies but a similar degree of change. It needs to be stressed also that the concern here is with policies *per se* and not with the style of analysis used for resolving problems. Analysis may take one of several styles or forms without the degree of change being necessarily predetermined. Nevertheless, the former may influence the latter and consequently there has been a tendency to link a pattern of change to a particular analytical style.

One such example is the pairing of discontinuous change and the 'rational' or 'scientific' model of policy analysis. There are a number of variants of this model but in essence the approach focuses on four particular activities. The first is a survey or information stage which

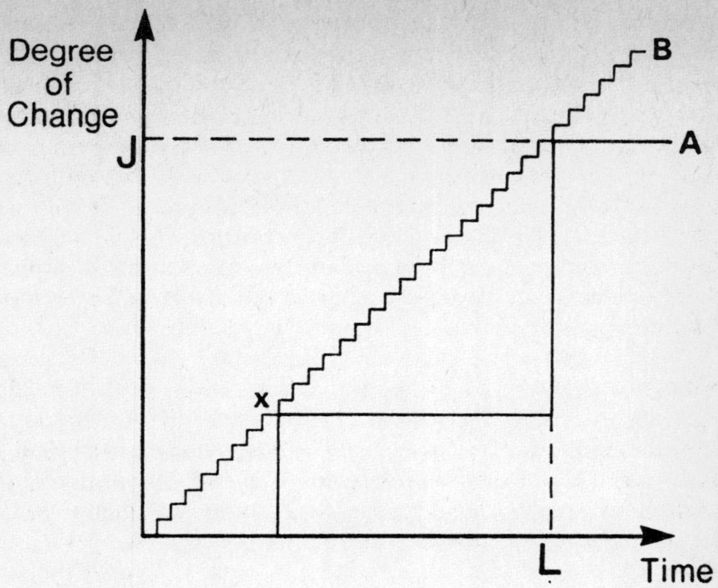

Figure 18.1 Policy change, polar cases

attempts to interpret policy issues and synthesise the problems involved. A second stage clarifies values and objectives and then, if necessary, orders or ranks these to establish a hierarchy. In a third stage, the analyst develops a comprehensive list of ways of achieving these objectives. This list of solutions is then evaluated against sharply focused criteria and scored according to the extent to which each achieves the objectives. Emphasis, therefore, is placed upon explicitness, comprehensiveness and, where possible, quantification (modelling).

The idea was influential during the 1950s and 1960s. Its initial advocates were operational researchers and systems analysts who advocated it as a rational basis for formulating policies.[3] Such advocacy received further support from modern welfare economics and its practical arm of cost–benefit analysis. In this form the rational model was applied widely to public sector projects. Transport specialists will recognise in this scientific paradigm the methodology of the metropolitan transportation study. Indeed, I think it fair to say that the early transport modeller presumed that his findings would carry over (automatically?) and become *the* transport policy for many cities. This heroic model was, in a manner of speaking, a child of its time. It suited well the ethos of the space-age 1960s and the optimism of the Kennedy era.

In spite of the appeal of the rational model, Lindblom (1979) suggested that Western democracies have structures that limit their ability to solve problems in accordance with these prescriptions. Limitations arise particularly because of dispersion of veto powers throughout the political system. These veto powers are manifest in the distribution of so-called 'property rights', and these rights in turn limit the relevance of decision criteria frequently used in applications of the rational model. The practised rationality of cost–benefit analysis, for example, is based on counting individual preferences, weighing them, in effect, by purchasing power and calculating whether the gainers secure sufficient by way of net benefits to be able to compensate (hypothetically) the net losers and still enjoy a residual gain.[4] But, with poorly developed mechanisms for compensating those who lose from changes of policy and with the distribution of political votes differing from the distribution of money votes, rational analyses are not guaranteed to lead to other than incremental changes of policy.

An appreciation of this situation led Lindblom (1959a; 1959b; and 1979) to suggest a style of policy analysis consistent with (or as he expressed the point, 'nicely suited to') the trajectory of change B in Figure 18.1. Lindblom argued that, in contradistinction to the assumptions of the rational model, administrators and politicians often were reduced to deciding upon a policy without first clarifying objectives. Quite apart from politicians not necessarily wishing to reveal their objectives, the more fundamental point made by Lindblom was that in many circumstances objectives and policies are inexplicably linked. Frequently, objectives are expressed meaningfully only by describing the policy chosen to achieve them: decision-makers simultaneously choose a policy to obtain certain objectives and choose the objectives themselves. A second, but related, point made was that the policy analyst focuses attention on marginal or incremental values and consequently makes marginal or incremental comparisons. This, in turn, places stress on valuing change by reference to existing circumstances, 'continually building out from the current situation, step-by-step and by small degree'. Lindblom not only argued that this is what does tend to happen, but added a normative touch by regarding it, with some qualification, as a superior way of making policy. By proceeding through a succession of incremental changes to policy the policy-maker can avoid 'serious lasting mistakes'.

Since this incremented model was first propounded, a number of commentators have challenged its claims either to be a better prescriptive tool or to be a better representation of reality. Dror (1964), for example, argued that change will tend to be discontinuous rather than incremental unless three conditions are fulfilled. First, existing policies should at least be reasonably successful; second, the problems which policies address should continue in similar form; and third, the technology available for dealing with problems should exhibit continuity. He went on to argue that even in stable societies, many important areas of policy are associated with rapid changes in levels of aspiration, in the nature of issues and in the availability of the means for tackling problems; therefore, discontinuous changes of policy will occur.

Lindblom's (1979) response to this implication that incremental analysis was slow-moving was to argue that a fast-moving sequence of small changes can speedily accomplish a drastic alteration in the status quo. Speed of change is the product of size of step and frequency of step, and is not merely a matter of size alone. This is illustrated in Figure 18.1. Over the period of time *OL*, incrementation achieves a degree of change equivalent to that achieved by the discontinuous mode and, for a number of discrete periods of shorter duration, achieves a greater degree of change. Lindblom argued that, in practice, incremental change outpaces discontinuous change because 'incremental steps can be made quickly because they are incremental. They do not rock the boat, do not stir up the great antagonisms and paralyzing schisms as do proposals for more drastic change.' In short, 'incremental politics is also a way of "smuggling" changes into the political system'.

Another analytical style — mixed scanning — has been suggested as a 'third' approach. It incorporates features of both the rational and the incremental models. Its chief proponent, Etzioni (1967), concurred with the incrementalists' view that rationalistic models were unrealistic but was critical also of the incrementalists' philosophy. He argued that the consensus-seeking implied by incrementalism served the interests of the powerful at the expense of the underprivileged and politically unorganised. But his more important criticism was that 'while an accumulation of small steps could lead to a significant change, there is nothing in this approach to guide the accumulation'. He suggested, therefore, a nesting of incremental decisions within a broader framework provided by high-order, fundamental policy-making processes. These set basic directions and 'are made by exploring the main alternatives the actor sees in view of his conception of his goals, but — unlike what rationalism would indicate — details and specification are omitted so that an overview is feasible'.

Like incrementalists, Etzioni claimed his problem-solving style was both an effective strategy and also a realistic description of approaches used in a variety of fields. In the latter, descriptive context, he went on to argue that what are observed as incremental changes 'are often the unfolding of trends initiated at critical turning points at which fundamental decisions are made' and added that the number and role of these latter are significantly greater than the incrementalists state. Etzioni, therefore, was really drawing an important distinction between the decision to change and the implementation of that decision. In terms of the decision itself, Etzioni, in effect, returns the spotlight to the large-scale, discontinuous change of trajectory A in Figure 18.1.

Trajectories A and B in Figure 18.1 illustrate alternative modes of change by deliberately emphasising the respective polar cases. In practice, configurations of change are likely to exhibit hybrid or compound patterns. For example, the degree of policy change *OJ* might have been achieved by any combination and degree of discontinuous and incremental change. One plausible pattern of development would be a period of incremental 'creep' followed by a sudden change when existing policies are no longer sustainable by modification alone.

This, I believe, is a pattern most likely to be found in practice in pluralist societies. Rose (1981) has stressed the importance of secular trends in economic and social environments (what he calls 'force of circumstances') in bringing about a continually changing consensus regarding appropriate policies. Such trends are of a fairly smooth nature and we might expect a 'creeping' response; an incremental pattern of change. On the other hand, there will be groups in society with an interest in maintaining the status quo who will resist change however incremental. The inclinations of such groups will be reinforced by the cautious nature of the executive, its frequent commitment to existing policy, and by administrative inertia. When conservative groups are weak or poorly organised, incremental change is to be expected.

At the same time it is to be expected that when strong conservative elements see a tactical advantage in accommodating pressures for change within the basic framework of existing policy. But, if secular trends continue to emphasise a need for change, we might expect the weak groups to mobilise and the strong groups to draw the line. The result will be a build up on a pressure point (no longer released by an incremental response). In these circumstances, change will come suddenly if and when lobbyists, capitalising on favourable pressures from economic, social and intellectual forces, have developed a sufficient head of steam to 'collapse' existing policy (Starkie 1982, Chapter 14).

4. Configurating British policy

Is this idea, that policies have a resilience but change suddenly in response to a build-up of pressure, supported by events? There have been few studies directed to answer this type of question and few with data suitable for interpretation in this way. To throw more light on the question let me review briefly two quite distinct areas of UK transport policy — the trunk-road programme and bus licensing.

In relation to trunk roads a detailed account of the events analysed will be found in Levin (1979), Painter (1980) and Starkie (1982). However, we can note the following salient features. The basic outlines of a trunk-road policy with its focus on a national network of motorways was sketched out immediately after World War II. Construction commenced in the mid-1950s and the programme gathered pace during the following decade. By the early 1970s a large annual programme had become well established. This had been achieved in a number of ways, not least by the creation of a substantial road bureaucracy. Increasingly, this stable environment was challenged especially in the late 1960s and early 1970s by the growth of opposition to road building, particularly by the environment movement. In an attempt to ease these pressures the government announced palliatives such as improved compensation to affected households and revised procedures for public participation in road planning. These measures were unsuccessful in reducing opposition, which grew more militant. The culminant of the anti-roads campaign was the physical disruption of a number of enquiries in the mid-1970s. By this stage there were indications that the basic policy was subject to review. In the February 1976 public expenditure White Paper (Cmnd. 6393), a decline in trunk-road construction expenditure was proposed and further reductions in the programme were announced later that year. By mid-1977 these changes were codified in a White Paper (Cmnd. 6836) which formally announced a more selective approach to road schemes with an emphasis on bypasses rather than motorway networks.

Bus licensing is an area of British policy currently subject to change. In 1930 a rigorous system of licensing bus services was established. Its effect, if not its aim, was to reduce competition, thus enabling bus operators to cross-subsidise within a network, to provide a socially adequate level of service and to break even financially, taking groups of services as a whole. At the time, this regulatory policy was supported by a powerful concensus; 'all the strongest interests were agreed on the need for the new system' (Dudley and Richardson 1983) and support in Parliament was bipartisan. For 25 years the position remained unaltered. But in the 1950s, first rural services and then city services came under pressure from various 'forces of circumstance': rising car-ownership, fewer cinema visits, and so on. This placed increasing strain on the symbiotic relationship between protection, cross-subsidy and financial viability. The response in the late 1960s and early 1970s was that government supported the third prop via subsidy. But this, in turn, conflicted with policies aiming to curtail public expenditure. This placed increasing pressure on the fundamentals — the licensing system. Existing operators and especially employee representatives were strongly opposed to change. In spite of this, change did occur but it was at first 'ordered and incremental' (Dudley and Richardson 1983) and was concerned with licensing peripheral areas and activities (school buses and voluntary organisations with a rural focus). But the subsidy burden continued to mount and this encouraged those in favour of radically new policies. The dam of 'conservatism' was fractured, but not finally broken, by the 1980 Transport Act; this abolished road-service licensing for services in excess of 30 miles and led to the *de facto* deregulation of fares generally. The Transport Act 1985 is intended to 'collapse' the 1930 policy completely.

These potted histories suggest that, at least in the two areas reviewed, British transport policies did change in a manner which tends to support the idea that policies collapse under pressure. In both cases policies, in a fundamental sense, were long-lasting; both incremental and discrete patterns of change were evident, but it was discrete or sudden change that dominated. This was not easily explained by ideology and succession. Dudley and Richardson (1983) noted, for example, that although the Conservative government had a more ideological approach on the licensing issue, nevertheless the 'Labour government realised that deregulation represented a possible means of saving public expenditure and, despite the basic opposition of operators and unions, pushed ahead with its plans'. Similarly with respect to trunk roads, the Conservative government of 1971 adopted the revitalisation strategy fashioned in the dying days of the previous Labour administration while the fundamentals of the 1977–8 reappraisal were adopted by Mrs Thatcher's first government. This lends support to the idea that it is the underlying forces, both encouraging and resisting change, that are the important factors and that inquiry should concentrate upon the articulation of these.

5. Policies and catastrophes

The tendency, apparent in areas of British transport policy, for fundamental change to emerge, not from a continuous process of incrementalism, but from clear-cut revision associated with the collapse of existing policies, suggests that such cases may be susceptible to more rigorous analysis using techniques of catastrophe theory.

Catastrophe theory is a new branch of mathematics concerned particularly with discontinuous change in what are referred to as 'state' variables brought about by continuous changes in 'control' variables where the 'state' of the system analysed is governed by an 'energy function'. The theory's originator, René Thom (1975) concluded that in cases of up to four control variables most discontinuities fall into one of only seven elementary types, which he called elementary catastrophes. For example, Thom showed that a model with two control variables and one state variable, if it generates catastrophic behaviour, will in general exhibit the topographical form shown in Figure 18.2: the surface of possible equilibrium values is likely to have overlaps. These, if projected onto the *u* (or control) plane, give the cusp shape which in turn gives this particular catastrophe its name.[5]

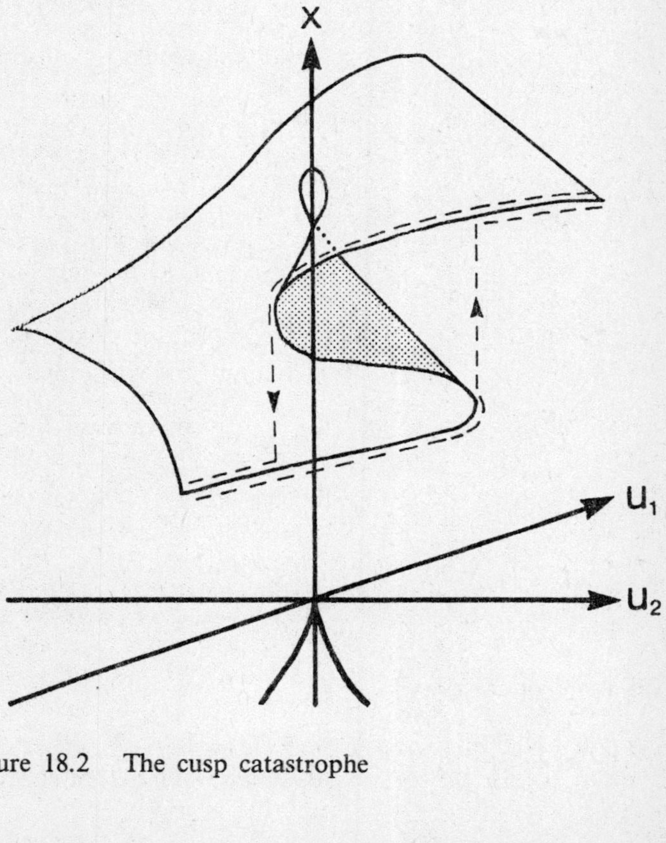

Figure 18.2 The cusp catastrophe

The existence of overlaps in the cusp catastrophe produces unusual behaviour in the state of the system examined. For example, suppose that one of the control variables is decreased steadily from an initially high value (whilst the other is held constant). In terms of Figure 18.2 we will be moving leftwards from the right-hand edge of the control plane. This will correspond to a similar leftward movement across the upper surface of equilibrium values. Providing this movement results in the path of the control variable cutting across the *V* or area of overlap, the state of the system will collapse (to the lower surface in Figure 18.2). On the other hand, if we reverse this process (steadily increasing the control variable from an initially low value), again with provisos, there will be a 'jump' in the state of the system. However, the paths of the two catastrophes will diverge.[6] This divergence is on account of the hysteresis (or delay) effect, and it is this effect that *may* have particular significance in the policy context if, as hypothesised, administrative and political inertia act as a sheet-anchor to change. Thus, if pressure which led to a collapse of policy A (and the adoption of policy B) were reversed we would not necessarily expect a sudden jump back to policy A at the same critical threshold. Pressure might have to be maintained beyond the original threshold of collapse to achieve a (catastrophic) reversal of policy.

Catastrophe theory has been applied in relation to urban and regional systems (Wilson 1981) including a more limited application to transport. In this latter context Goodwin (1977) and Blase (1979) focused upon the hysteresis effect; the underlying behaviour represented was habit. In Goodwin's case, it was habit with respect to choice of transport mode, whilst Blase examined the response to changes in petrol prices and was able to attach a quantitative value to a habit threshold. Elliot and Wright (1982), in contrast, discussed both discontinuities in behaviour and threshold effects. Their subject was parking enforcement in London. This, they showed, was prone to collapse (because non-compliance with the regulations was a function of enforcement pressure which itself depended upon the degree of compliance) and to return the system to normal after this had happened the enforcement effect had to be increased well beyond the level at the point of collapse.

To apply these concepts in the policy field we need first to interpret policy in the form of an energy function; we need, for example, to view the political system as a vote-maximising or popularity-maximising system. Second, we need to be able to give policy, as a 'state' variable subject to discontinuities, quantitative significance. Policies, however, are not always explicit, or if they are, are not easily measured. As a consequence, we might have to interpret the 'outputs' of the policy process as indicative of a policy 'level' (and the difference between these levels as a measure of policy change).[7] In the case of road policies, for example, we might choose to measure the kilometres of freeway planned for, or the kilometres of freeway under construction or the proportion of a transport budget spent on roads, and so on.

Similarly, we need also to measure the 'control' variables. The 'control' variables selected would depend upon the precise hypothesis under examination. However, in the roads context plausible ones might include a factor measuring the pressure to construct roads (the rate of economic growth or vehicles per mile of road or membership of motoring organisations) and a factor, or its proxy, measuring the resistance to road-building policies (membership of environmental groups). We might also wish to add a factor to reflect Painter's (1980) idea that sectors of government under stress have their budgets raided by rival departments; perhaps we can represent this by the rate of growth in public expenditure, the higher the rate the less incentive to 'raid'.

Thus, there are various possibilities for introducing the policy variables in measured form suitable for the application of catastrophe theory. Consequently, where transport policies are subject to discontinuities (and the state of the system prone to catastrophic behaviour) catastrophe theory might provide a useful means for giving the discontinuities both definition and form.[8]

6. Conclusion

To conclude, I would like to suggest a number of possible research topics based on the preceding reflections. I have grouped these to reflect the three basic lines of thought:

- Is transport policy prone to issue cycles and, if so, can we classify these by length? Can we use content analysis in a predictive role? Is there a 'critical mass' before issues impact and, therefore, can we monitor news content, parliamentary questions, and so on, for warning signs?
- Which model of change — incremental, discontinuous or hybrid — prevails? Is there a variation between countries with different styles of government. For example, does the federal German system produce results different from those of the centralised French and British system? Is there a tendency for areas of transport policy — road, public transport, aviation, and so on — to reveal different configurations? (Changes to British aviation policy, for example, appear to have been less discontinuous and more incremental than

road policies — why?) Is there a secular trend in the modes of change? Olsen (1982) suggests that societies become more burdened with interest groups as they mature economically; is this reflected in modes of policy change?

- If transport policies are subject to discontinuities (and if the state of the system is prone to catastrophic behaviour) can one describe these dynamics using catastrophe theory? How far is it possible to develop, refine and measure 'state' and 'control' variables? What type of catastrophe is likely to emerge? And can we use this approach not only as a descriptive device but also to predict the likelihood of a change of policy?

Notes

1. This statement ignores changes introduced by administrative discretion, and so on; it remains accurate for any change of substance.
2. Kondratieff was a Russian economist who analysed long-term trends in selected economic indicators and suggested (in 1925) that the existence of long waves was at least very probable. Subsequent work has indicated that the identified waves may have been due to the statistical techniques Kondratieff used.
3. For example, McKean (1958).
4. Pearce and Nash (1981) provide one of the better discussions of the value system forming the basis of the economist's rational model.
5. The equilibrium states correspond to stationary values of the energy function and these might be stable or unstable equilibria depending upon whether the energy function is at a maximum or minimum. Within the folded region, multiple equilibria are possible. The energy function for the cusp catastrophe is given by:

   $$\tfrac{1}{4}X^4 + \tfrac{1}{2}U_1X^2 + U_2X$$

   where X and U are the state and control values respectively. An elementary account of catastrophe theory will be found in Stewart (1975).
6. Figure 18.2 presumes that the catastrophic change is triggered by a fall over the edge of the fold. An alternative view is that the critical values are reached immediately the upper and lower surfaces overlap. In this case the directional paths will be reversed.
7. A problem with using measured, final outputs is that there may be a considerable difference from planned outputs owing to various factors frustrating government intentions. See Barrett and Fudge (1981).
8. Starkie (1984) illustrates the application of these ideas in the context of British road policies.

References

Barrett, S. and C. Fudge (1981). *Policy and Action: Essays on the Implementation of Public Policy*. London: Methuen.

Black, J. *et al.* (1983). 'Transport–Land Use Issues, Problems and Policy Implications: Sydney since the Thirties, *Proceedings*, 8th Australian Transport Forum, AGPS, Canberra.

Blase, J.H. (1979). Hysteresis and Catastrophe Theory: Empirical Identification in Transportation Modelling, *Environment and Planning A*, **11**, 675–88.
Blowers, A. (1980) *The Limits of Power*, Oxford: Pergamon Press.
Downs, A. (1972) 'Up and Down with Ecology — the "Issue-Attention" Cycle'. *Public Interest*, **28**, 38–50.
Dror, Y. (1964). 'Muddling through — "science" or inertia?', *Public Administration Review*, **24**, 153–7.
Dudley, G.F. and J.J. Richardson (1983). 'Regulation and De-regulation in the Bus Industry', *Public Administration Bulletin*, **42**, 26–43.
Elliot, J.R. and C. Wright (1982). 'The Collapse of Parking Enforcement in Large Towns: Some Causes and Solutions', *Traffic Engineering and Control* (June), 304–10.
Etzioni, A. (1967). 'Mixed-Scanning: A "Third" Approach to Decision-Making', *Public Administration Review* (December), 385–92.
Goodwin, P. (1977). 'Habit and Hysteresis in Mode Choice', *Urban Studies*, **14**, 95–8.
Gunningham, N. (1974). *Pollution, Social Interest and the Law*. London: Martin Robertson.
Heclo, H. (1976), in R. Rose, ed., *The Dynamics of Public Policy: A Comparative Analysis*, Beverly Hills: Sage, Chapter 9.
Levin, P.H. (1979). 'Highway Inquiries: A Study in Government Responsiveness', *Public Administration*, **57**, 21–49.
Lindblom, C.E. (1959a). 'Policy Analysis', *American Economic Review*, **48**, 298.
Lindblom, C.E. (1959b). 'The Science of "Muddling Through"', *Public Administration Review*, **19**, 79–88.
Lindblom, C.E. (1979). 'Still Muddling, Not Yet Through', *Public Administration Review*, 517–26.
McKean, R. (1958). *Efficiency in Government Through Systems Analysis*. New York: Wiley.
Olsen, M. (1982). *The Rise and Decline of Nations*. New Haven: Yale University Press.
Painter, M. (1980). 'Whitehall and Roads: A Case Study in Sectoral Policies', *Policy and Politics*, **8**, 163–86.
Pearce, D. and C. Nash (1981). *The Social Appraisal of Projects: A Text in Cost Benefit Analysis*. London: Macmillan.
Rose, R. (1981). *Do Parties Make a Difference*. London: Macmillan.
Starkie, D.N.M. (1982). *The Motorway Age: Road and Traffic Policies in Post-War Britain*. Oxford: Pergamon.
Starkie, D.N.M. (1984). 'Policy Changes, Configurations and Catastrophes', *Policy and Politics*, **12**, 71–84.
Stewart, T. (1975) 'The Seven Elementary Catastrophes', *New Scientist*, **68**, 447–54.
Thom, R. (1975). *Structural Stability and Morphogenesis*. Benjamin, MA.
Whitt, J.A. (1982). *Urban Elites and Mass Transportation*. Princeton, NJ: Princeton University Press.
Wilson, A.G. (1981). *Catastrophe Theory and Bifurcation: Applications to Urban and Regional Systems*. London: Croom Helm.

19 European Transport Policy: Need for Deregulation *à l'américaine*

P. Bauchet and V. Masset

In this discussion of the deregulation of transport we draw attention to the various factors that must be considered in advance of any action. In the United States, deregulation has been applied to date in specific areas only. It has been in operation for eight years and we can now analyse some of its effects and ask ourselves whether it would lead to the same results in Europe. Before examining this further, however, it is necessary to recall the history and the background to deregulation in the United States, and then see its effects.

1. Deregulation in the United States

1.1 Criticism of former regulations

Regulations covering transport had met with sharp criticism as being contrary to public interest and lacking effectiveness.[1] Regulatory activities by government had tended to retard economic growth, increase costs and encourage inflation. In air transport, existing companies were reluctant to admit newcomers to the market; this protected their position while stifling innovation and depriving air travellers of the choice between price and quality. G. Graf explained the consequences of the regulations thus: 'if a firm's position is not directly threatened by the innovative or imitative competition of others, that firm will not see any need to innovate in view of the greater or lesser risks innovation always entails.'[2]

Competition developed in fields other than that of price, such as the type of aircraft used, flight frequencies or service on board. Prices seem, therefore, to have been higher than they would have been under deregulation. Further, the absence of competition with regard to fares seemed to allow a high level of social costs, restrictive rules on working conditions with a consequent worsening of productivity.

'Thus, when competition is not allowed or allowed to a limited extent only, what we sometimes see is competition in quality over and above the level justified at a macro-economic level'.[3]

1.2 Some historical aspects of deregulation

The deregulation movement began under the Nixon administration when the value of the US dollar was made independent of gold. In transport, deregulation was initiated under the Carter presidency, then carried on by Ronald Reagan. The first sector in which the question of deregulation arose was that of civil aviation, where the regulatory level had always been particularly high. Generally, in this field anything not authorised is forbidden, in contrast to maritime transport where anything not forbidden is authorised. It is therefore not surprising that deregulation should have first begun where there was the greatest number of regulations.

In air transport, this consisted of the removal of controls exercised over company administration, capacity and fares by Federal Boards (such as the Civil Aeronautics Board or CAB) and the liberalisation of bilateral agreements concluded between the United States and other countries. For this purpose Congress enacted two laws: the 1978 Airline Deregulation Act which dealt with domestic carriers and provided for the demise, in 1985, of the CAB responsible for price control and market access; and the 1979 International Air Transportation Act (IATCA) which extended the principles of domestic competition to the international field. At the same time the CAB issued a Show Cause Order to IATA (International Air Transport Association) with a view to waiving the anti-trust immunity it had benefited from until then. This procedure failed as a result of manifold negative reactions from IATA itself and many other States, and was postponed.

In maritime transport, the 1948 Shipping Act proposed not so much deregulation as an amendment of the 1916 Act. Based on liberal philosophy, the new Act contains provisions designed to improve the competitiveness of the American flag, which is currently suffering from the world crisis in maritime transport. The Act authorises door-to-door tariffs and thus permits maritime transport companies to concern themselves with terminal land transport which is more productive. Further, various agreements, pools, groupings or even mergers benefit from a greater degree of anti-trust immunity so as to allow a movement towards concentration which would give American companies the advantages of economies of scale. Financial support is also dealt with in the Act, which reorganised the budgetary involvement of the government. The Shipping Act also ensures that sanctions can be taken against companies (foreign or domestic) failing to respect freedom of trade.

In the field of land transport, similar deregulation has followed with the 1980 Rail Deregulation Act and the Motor Carrier Act.

It is a little too early to grasp all the effects of this new general policy; however, we do perceive a trend towards limiting government subsidies with the aim of increasing competition. We shall take a closer look at the effects of deregulation on civil aviation since its effects on other modes of transport are too recent and too few in number to lend themselves to proper analysis.

1.3 Effects of deregulation: case of air transport

Supporters of deregulation foresaw greater competition, increased load factors and productivity, together with a fall in costs and prices to the consumer.

It should not be forgotten that, since 1978, other factors in the economic system have changed: between 1976 and 1981, oil prices went up by 230 per cent and there was rapid growth in GNP in the United States from 1977 to 1979, whereas the period 1979 to 1982 was characterised by recession. These exogenous influences undoubtedly left their mark on air transport; however, it is possible to isolate certain effects of the new aeronautical policy.

Fares and costs. Whereas, before 1978, 20 per cent of travellers flew at reduced fares, their number had increased to 80 per cent in 1985 at an average saving of 50 per cent.[4] This seems to be attributable to the fact that air fares appear to correspond more closely to production costs. After a sharp fall, fares tended to increase in the years following the introduction of deregulation, but this increase would appear to have been less than it would have been on a regulated market, on account of increased productivity and falling costs; for example, aircraft operated at higher load factors. Former CAB chairman Alfred Kahn states that, between 1977 and 1982, the average load factor was 60 per cent as compared with only 53 per cent between 1971 and 1976.[5] New companies cut their costs by reducing trade-union influence, salaries and welfare benefits, which prompted many existing carriers to follow suit by invoking Section 11 of the Bankruptcy Act which permits company reorganisation, including the rescinding of existing welfare agreements and the employment of non-union labour.[6]

Network development. Companies selected longer routes than those they had operated on hitherto and services to the larger cities, at the expense of the smaller, were improved. The network is now better integrated and better adapted to the desired traffic flow, although the increase in 'hub-and-spoke' operations is less attractive to travellers than non-stop services.[7]

One problem, however, has not been resolved: congestion at peak hours at major airports. Paradoxically, this might lead the government to introduce new controls, especially on air-traffic safety grounds.

Air safety. Some commentators have argued that deregulation would mean lower standards of air safety. The figures have been comparatively good, although there is no proof that certain companies are not cutting aircraft-maintenance costs in order to be more competitive.[8]

Concentration. Of all the changes in civil aviation the most significant has been concentration. Whereas until 1978 access to the market had been relaxed so as to promote genuine competition among a larger number of companies, it would seem that in this sector of the economy the number of large companies is on the decrease, towards perhaps half a dozen. Were they able to cut their costs, the larger companies would benefit from their size and various advantages such as their wide and extended networks and control of the Computer Reservation System (CRS), which is becoming more important on account of the growing complexity of new air fares. Clients are in fact shopping around for the best buy among travel agents, and in the system of agency distribution American and United have emerged as occupying a dominant position in CRS. (The smaller companies have complained that this dominance distorts healthy and fair competition, which might mean — if the government agrees with them — that regulation could be introduced in an area where it did not exist before 1978.)

Alfred Kahn has voiced the fear that this trend might 'end up by producing a radically transformed and highly concentrated industry, infinitely less competitive in its behaviour in the matter of prices'.[9] J. Thackray for his part claims that 'these oligopolies (with their high costs and their inefficiency) will end up by being transformed into monsters created by deregulation'.[10] This concentration is also apparent in the many company mergers that have taken place.

The new policy may thus seem contradictory: it was introduced in the belief that there were no longer diminishing costs in air transport, that yields were constant, since there was no relation between a company's size and its unit production cost.[11]

If the bigger companies are now more successful than the smaller ones, this is said to show that diminishing costs do exist in multi-line companies. Thus, Jacques Pavaux contends: 'economies of scale following growth in traffic, and economies of scope linked to the size of the network do exist in air transport'.[12]

This theoretical setback to supporters of deregulation may be only an apparent weakness, since, internationally, American companies have become infinitely more competitive as a result of the reorganisation of their lines, the low level of salaries, their equipment strength and general improved productivity.

It is noteworthy that the same phenomenon is currently observable in other modes of transport. Thus, subsequent to the Motor Carrier Act there has been an upheaval in road transport through a collapse in prices, which has led to the elimination of smaller firms to the benefit of the larger. In maritime transport, the Shipping Act has been conducive to a certain concentration by granting a greater degree of anti-trust immunity to inter-company agreements and by concentrating Operating Beneficial Subsidies (OBS) on a few companies. This is a mode of transport requiring tremendous amounts of investment capital — the Evergreen Company from Taiwan has invested US1,000 million for its 'tour du monde' — and only the big companies can afford them. Thanks to prospects of liberalisation and immunity from anti-trust legislation, US maritime shipping companies should be able to achieve a size which will put them in a stronger position in terms of international competition.

2. Deregulation in Europe?

Is deregulation a policy that could be adopted on the market of the European Community? This is the question facing Europe since 1978.

2.1 Towards the creation of a European Common Transport Policy

On 22 May 1985, the Council of Justice of the European Communities handed down a judgement on an application lodged by the European Parliament against the Council of Ministers in the field of Community transport policy. In the Parliament's view, the Council had not fulfilled the obligation placed on it by the Treaty of Rome to define such a policy. The Council held that there had been no breach of the Treaty of Rome since the latter granted discretionary power to the Council in the area concerned.

This example brings out the delays and difficulties the Twelve are confronted with when it comes to achieving a consensus in this field in order to apply the general principles of the Treaty such as the liberalisation and harmonisation of the economic policies of member States. However, it is thought that this judicial ruling will have positive effects on future developments in Community transport.

In the past, many proposals — sometimes leading to Council

decisions — have been put forward with a view to co-ordinating certain specific aspects of transport. Then three common policy documents with a more global approach to a common transport market were drawn up by the Commission at the request of the European Parliament. These were memoranda concerning land transport (February 1983), civil aviation (March 1984) and maritime transport (March 1985). The texts propose the drawing up of a common policy based on the principles of liberalisation and harmonisation.

Air transport. Memorandum no. 2 Com. (84) 72 Final of the Commission was used as orientations for the High-Level Group at the request of the Commission. These orientations were eventually adopted by the group as a basis for an intra-Community air transport policy. This text is now being assessed by various Community authorities.

As far as competition is concerned, what is involved is not so much deregulation proper as a weakening of the inflexible organisation of air transport in Europe. States will no longer be able to lay down a 50:50 ratio for their airlines' capacity and revenue. Inter-company consultations on fares are permitted but not mandatory as was earlier the case. A system of 'fare zones' could be introduced and allow for more flexible forms of governmental approval. The thrust of these orientations is rather towards a gradual but limited liberalisation in 'regulatory' framework.

Maritime transport. Memorandum Com. (85) 90 Final of the Commission entitled 'Towards a Common Policy in Maritime Transport' proposed a general framework for the maritime policy of the EC. It presents new measures designed to promote Community maritime and commercial interests.

The idea first of all is to eliminate distortions in competition between member countries and third countries as well as within the Community. The text proposes to combat protectionist measures by third countries (reservation of part cargoes) which are detrimental to Community interests, since such practices create difficulties for the operation of a system of commercial competition. This community action is to be accompanied by equal treatment for Community shipowners; the Commission thus proposes, subject to certain exemptions,[13] unrestricted passenger and freight transport services between the ports of a member State, overseas territories included. With respect to ports, the text proposes to eliminate unfair competition existing between Community ports as a consequence, *inter alia*, of disparities between national regulations concerning traffic with the hinterland. The Commission will also look into State aid to ports and maritime companies with a view to liberalisation and harmonisation.

Since the EC has ratified the Code of Conduct of the UN Conferences, the Community bodies have proposed that bilateral treaties between member countries and third countries should be denounced on the grounds that the term 'national company' should be construed to mean a company within the Community and not only a company of the individual Community member party to a bilateral treaty.

In addition to its action on unfair competition, the Memorandum proposes to improve the competitiveness of Community firms. In order to improve productivity (through a lowering of production costs), ship-owners should be allowed a less restrictive use of free registration flags, provided of course that their fleets continue to observe international conventions on safety at sea and working conditions.

In 1982, this Memorandum was supplemented by a further Memorandum concerning control of ships by the State of the port, in order to ensure compliance with safety rules and regulations. This system should be extended to neighbouring countries so as to provide for fairer competition between European ports.[14]

Land transport. The Council made in 1982 a decision conferring a certain authority on public railway companies *vis-à-vis* the system of State control, with a view to making them more productive. It has also adopted various rules on road transport.

2.2 Characteristics of the European Market

The European transport market differs from the American for reasons that are both directly and indirectly related to transport. Deregulation in Europe is therefore difficult to bring about. A 'Common Market' in transport does not exist. Each member country has its own regulations. In this field the EC is multinational in character and does not constitute an integrated political and economic system. Any policy such as deregulation has to be agreed by each individual sovereign State, whereas in the United States, even if it has to go through a manner of consultation with the federated States, a single government is able to select the desired policy, and the fact is that there is no unity of view on deregulation in the EC.

In air transport, the biggest companies are State-owned (with 50 per cent of the equity) with the exception of UTA (France) and British Caledonian. These public companies enjoy a certain monopoly on individual lines on national territory and may receive aid or subsidies from their governments. Similarly, the status and financing of airports vary from country to country.

In maritime transport, financial support from public funds is also very widespread, but the degree to which this support is harmonised for companies, ports and shipyards is very low.[15] In addition, each government has its own protectionist policy which is a mixture of quotas, customs, duties, commercial rules and subsidies for the export of services.

The railways are publicly owned, enjoy a monopoly in every State and receive subsidies, *inter alia*, on account of the public service obligation which is placed upon them. In the United States, the various railroad companies are in private ownership.

In order to create a common transport market the Community countries need to co-ordinate several aspects of their economy which indirectly affect transport such as tax legislation, subsidies, labour and social security.[16] The Greek merchant fleet, for example, has 66 per cent of its ships under free flags as compared with France's 2 per cent. In addition, direct subsidies for shipping seem comparatively low in the United Kingdom, but since social security is budgeted the result is lower wage levels for sailors. In the United Kingdom, welfare accounts for 19 per cent of wages as compared with 42 per cent in France. The disparity between the nationalities of crews is just as great; France and Italy are very strict and employ only their own nationals, whereas British legislation is much more flexible.

Competition already exists among the various modes of transport such as air and rail. Competition between these two modes of transport seems to be more intense in Europe than in the United States because of the importance of railways in Europe, where they enjoy the advantages of shorter distances and a high-quality service. Air transport costs per mile are greater over shorter distances (more energy required) and railways also deliver the passenger to the city centre. The TGV is thus a keen rival of Air Inter in France.

In addition, competition exists within the same mode of transport, for example, between charter flights and schedule services by airlines belonging to several States, or between ports of different European countries such as Dunkirk, Rotterdam and Hamburg. The competition so dear to supporters of deregulation is thus present as a result of competing national interests.

The adoption of deregulation gives rise to political problems. First of all, there is certainly political resistance on the part of States to a common transport market via deregulation, as this would mean losing a part of their powers to the Community authorities; a measured dose of liberalisation allows them to preserve some degree of control over this sector of the economy. Further, to varying degrees, European governments carry historical, political and economic responsibilities towards certain African companies, and it is difficult to imagine the EC adopting deregulation which could be detrimental to structurally fragile African companies in need of protection.[17]

Given the obstacles inherent to the Common Market, it is not surprising that the Council should not have been able to reach many more concrete decisions than it has. Had more precise studies been carried out, the Commission might have been more circumspect, bearing in mind the position of transport in Europe. True, the proposals concerning air transport are moderate, perhaps even excessively so; they are confined to intra-Community traffic and seek to ease government controls over prices and quantities in bilateral agreements.

However, it appears impossible to bring all the proposals in the Memorandum on maritime transport to a successful conclusion. As was the case in air transport, it might be necessary — at least as a first stage — to contemplate a second, more limited memorandum. Indeed, disparities in structures and regulatory provisions currently obtaining in all production factors related to transport are such that to allow them to compete at a stroke of the pen would have catastrophic consequences. A gradual approach is essential.

Conversely, Europe should not be over-timid in its decision-making. European companies that are too small, largely unrestructured, operating at excessively high costs, would no longer be competitive with their reorganised and concentrated American and Asian counterparts. When it adopted the Klinkenborg Report on air transport, the European Parliament, as has been pointed out by Paul Holubowicz, Secretary General of EURACA,[18] 'no doubt recommended no change in the *status quo* as air tariffs were low enough, there was no need for additional competition between airlines; the masses don't need to fly any more than they are flying now'.

For every mode of transport it is necessary to set as the final and priority objective the gradual creation of a genuine common market without which any deregulation would be unrealistic. This means harmonisation of conditions of competition and free access to the common market. Such is not the purpose of deregulation *à l'americaine* since it already has its single market — the United States.

Notes

1. G.W. Douglas and J.C. Miller, *Economic Regulation of Domestic Air Transport:*

Theory and Practice. Washington, DC: Brookings Institution, 1974. T.E. Keller, 'Domestic Trunk Airline Regulation: An Economic Evaluation', *Study on Federal Regulation*, **6**, 1978.

2. G. Graf quoted in *Transport Review*, **305** (June 1985).
3. H. Seidenfus, L'évaluation rétrospective et prospective des mesures de politique des transports', *Transport Review*, **305** (June 1985), 326–36.
4. 'Turbulence in the Skies', *Time*, 21 February 1983.
5. A.E. Kahn, 'Deregulation and Vested Interests: The Case of Airlines' in R.G. Noll and B.M. Owen, eds, *The Political Economy of Deregulation*. Washington, DC: American Enterprise Institute, pp. 132–51.
6. Cf. the example of TWA in *Lloyd's Aviation Economist*, October 1985, p. 2. There is scope for a study on European and American fares on lines flying similar distances with aircraft of the same capacity and at the same frequency.
7. An analysis of the geography of air transport in the United States before and after 1978 as compared with the European network would yield significant data.
8. The FAA, responsible, *inter alia*, for air-safety problems, has recently imposed a severe penalty (US $1.5 million) on American airlines for failure to observe certain standards: 'FAA Chief Says Public Is Confident', *Herald Tribune*, 13 October 1985.
9. Quoted in 'US Deregulation: Patterns and Prospects', *IATA Review*, July–September 1985, p. 11.
10. Quoted in *Problèmes économiques*, 26 June 1985, from *Management Today*, May 1985.
11. Douglas and Miller, *Economic Regulation*.
12. J. Pavaux, 'L'économie du transport aérien: la concurrence impracticable', *Economica*, 1984, p. 302.
13. An analysis of the situation of coastal shipping in Europe with a break-down by flags and a comparison of company costs would be very useful.
14. It would be useful to look into the effects of deregulation (or liberalisation) on the competitive position of non-EC countries with market economies with respect to airports or seaports.
15. A useful study could be devoted to a comparative analysis of subsidies granted to EC airports and seaports by the States, regions and municipalities.
16. A prior study of cost disparities owing to structural disparities should be undertaken for each mode of transport.
17. A comparison of cases of African and European or American air and maritime lines could bring out the fragility of African companies confronted with deregulation.
18. Quoted in 'The Road to Liberation', *Lloyd's Aviation Economist*, October 1985, p. 19.

20 Economic, Political and Legal Aspects of Regulation and Deregulation in European Transport Policy

E. Fanara

1. Preliminary remarks

In recent years, the term 'deregulation' has taken on the meaning of a distinct political-economic choice, by emphasising principles and laws of the free market through an increasing suppression of the State's intervention in a specific field. In this framework it should be printed out that we are not concerned with a rediscovery of an abstract principle or with the reconfirmation of a value judgement in the legal system, introduced by a new set of laws that could eliminate every presence of government intervention in the economy; in such a case we would face a significant and considerable turning point, which could deeply affect the State's structure, so that it would be necessary to analyse and study the system with the help of constitutionalists and experts in public law in general.

The aim of deregulation in transport, however, is the enhancement of the efficiency of the market: it should be noted that for every type of transport a policy of administrative intervention limits the free supply of services, while it also imposes fixed prices. In other words, the purpose of deregulation is to obtain the maximum of efficiency and to facilitate the process of adjustment and reconversion of transport enterprises.

Bearing this in mind, it seems that our topic is more concerned with the field of economists and experts in administration than that of lawyers. Only when technical-economic choices (through political mediation) become normative principles and criteria does deregulation become the lawyer's concern. Therefore the lawyer's analysis cannot be concerned with the subject of 'deregulation' in general, but with the legal rules, that is to say, the specific rules that determine public intervention in a specific economic sector.

Transport is one of these sectors; in fact, air transport is indeed the field where deregulation was first introduced in the United States with the Airline Deregulation Act 1978. The deregulation of the American air-transport market has had many impacts on various countries, where a lively and articulate discussion continues.

The different theses regarding the regulation–deregulation debate are known. Even at the level of the European Communities (EC) perplexity and resistance are still registered. The EC Commission has long since submitted to the EC Council's three requests for a 'directive' gradually to introduce the process of liberalisation in air transport, even though the Council itself seems to be orientated towards maintaining the present system.

The economic and social reasons for and against deregulation of Community air transport, which are numerous and articulate, have been widely explained in several studies. It is therefore not necessary to look at different authors' positions, but briefly to re-examine the fundamental reasons that induce a State or the European Economic Community (EEC) to impose a legal code which liberalises a sector regulated by public administration. The deregulation of air transport could certainly be the prototype model for other types of transport, and could also be used for other sectors of the economy that are at present influenced by government action.

The lawyer's duty is to make it clear that a discussion concerning the deregulation of transport policies (with the purpose of examining the validity of the system, the effectiveness and the efficiency of the legal techniques of non-intervention in a sector that is already strongly controlled) can indicate the beginning of a wider process of reflection and of a critical overhaul of the whole public presence in the economic market.

It does not seem that today the discussion on deregulation has come to this point, in spite of the liberal economic measures adopted with some success in Western democracies. In effect, the starting point for a revision of the transport system is the pragmatic answer to problems of a recession following the oil crises in the 1970s. To the above historical reason has to be added probably the will to limit the public deficit, which is particularly serious in the transport sector.

However one cannot deny that, in so far as deregulation, instead of being a modest answer to the problems of a specific sector, is transformed into a general strategic solution to every problem of the State's economy, interventions for and against will lose the character of technical evaluation (namely a function of the reduction in costs and of an increase in the profits of the enterprises of a single sector) and become political debates on the pros and cons of solutions of state intervention in the economy on purely ideological bases.

We cannot exclude the fact that this basic concern for a possible extension of deregulation as a possible general address for a political-economic choice is an implicit obstacle in various states of the EEC, limiting not only an 'integral' deregulation, but even a courageous modification of transport regulation with the purpose of rationalising the normative in a much more liberal way based on the 'cost–profit' principle.

We may affirm that an analysis of the economic and social motivations of the legal choices for the regulation or deregulation of the transport market has its origins in the political position of each country of the EEC.

The political choices, either as defence of corporative interests in this sector or as aiming at other military, strategic, industrial, etc., objectives, condition the analysis of both the economist and the lawyer, who cannot work *in vitro*, but should address themselves to pragmatic and delimited sectors. In our contribution we will discuss road, sea and air transport.

2. Road transport

It is clear that the answer to the question of 'regulation or deregulation' in European transport should result from an analysis of the policies of the individual countries and of the Community in relation to the many types of land, sea and air transport. Looking at the facts, one should take into consideration the fact that an indistinct 'common market of transport' does not exist, but that there are different markets, more or less common, in relation to different types of transport. From this clear observation, it follows that various systems and forms of regulation of the same sector exist (in the various European countries) with different motivations, which complicate the start of a deregulation process in European transport.

In such a context one should observe that the term 'European transport' is merely descriptive for the whole of transport flows within the countries of Western Europe and — in turn — with the rest of the world. European transport in the sense of an integrated system, is today the aim of all countries within the EEC. In any case it is realistic to say that the integration of the organisation and administration of transport 'at an European level' proceeds slowly, step by step, together with the integration of the whole economy of the individual countries.

Finally, even the policies which control and guide transport in Europe are the effects of a compromise among the positions of individual states, which are imbued sometimes with principles which are diametrically opposed; and so different legal systems, based on different national economies and politics, co-exist inside the community.

If we take a look at road transport, we observe that the following policy principles co-exist:

1. the regime of the fixed quota authorisation and a system of liberalisation, more or less large, depending on bilateral agreements even with European countries that are not members of the EC; and
2. a regime of compulsory minimum and maximum freight rates and a more liberal system of reference tariffs.

The examples are many and generally reflect the more liberal position of England, while France and Italy are more conservative about the present system of national intervention.

It is evident, however, that at a European transport level — referring to the Community transport system yet to be built — the first knot to untie in order to resolve the problem of regulation or deregulation is not of a legal and economic nature, but of a political nature. In other words, is it the aim of the Commission of the European Communities to realise only a zone of free trade, where public and private transport enterprises liberally operate according to the free market laws and respecting free competition? Or has it a more ambitious goal, namely the economic integration of the countries of the Community that want to constitute a real Community organisation of European transport? In other words the question of regulation or deregulation is not one that can be settled exclusively on the basis of the economic aspects of the transport problem. It is meaningless to point out, in a 'distortion of the market', the negative economic effects of regulation when it is just this 'distortion' (or 'rationalisation', as far as the models of regulation are adopted) which they intend in the general, social and economic interests of every nation. For instance — in theory — charging the user of a certain profitable transport line with the financial deficits of other less profitable lines does not correspond to the principles of a fair fiscal system based on 'direct' and rising 'taxation' on income. In fact, there is no doubt that the costs of social services have to be borne by the entire community, that is the state, and not only out of the pocket of some users of a certain service. This principle, though in abstract valid and right, cannot, however, find enforcement in a country (like Italy), which, due to the enormous deficit of the national balance of payments and the inefficiency of the fiscal governmental revenue organisation, is unable to eliminate tax evasion. In such circumstances, the choice is between covering with an increased fee on profitable lines the deficts of non-profitable lines, or abrogating those lines, with certainly more disastrous economic and social costs.

Another common argument against government regulation is that monopoly is not advantageous to the consumer, whereas free competition reduces costs, while it gives better demand and supply conditions. Even this economic controversy does not prove anything: regulation is always needed in the free market, to avoid the substitution of free competition by the private monopoly. The inefficiency of State monopoly cannot rise to the presumption *iuris et de iure*, the proof of which, in some sectors of economic activity, is possible.

In other words, the problem is not so much the *quantity* of public intervention, as the *quality* of government action, so that the regulation–deregulation problem boils down to political choices and the validity of the legal instruments adopted. It is dangerous to contrast, on the one hand, the free and efficient economy and, on the other, the law as an authority which restrains the free economy and eliminates, for political aims, the efficiency of the mark(t. This basic opposition dominates much of the discussion on deregulation.

Getting to the nub of the discussion, we can say that when we refer to the quality of intervention and to the quality of regulation of an economic sector, we have to look at the organisation and the legal regulation of this sector. The problem of regulation–deregulation is focused then — in legal terms — on the efficiency of the administrative sector, as it addresses public and private economic activity for the collective good.

In other words, in order to achieve the maximum general well-being, how and how much do the administrative agencies have to influence the transport market? A single answer to this question cannot be given in terms of efficiency of the public administration organisation and of the validity of the legal rules. The picture which results from an analysis of the legal system of transport in the countries of the EC is perhaps for some sectors more of an 'organised disorder', than of a restrained market distorted by over-severe regulation.

Let us now briefly consider road transport with reference to the regulations of a single country (Italy) and to community control.

Land transport includes two modes of transport: road and rail. Each mode is divided into goods and passenger transport. For goods there is the possibility of combined transport between the two modes, and the possibility of the integration of land transport with sea, river and air transport.

At present both Community and national regulation are considerably out of date. The techniques of combined transport are hampered by a railway management originally reserved to the State and regulated by legal rules that do not take into consideration the need to compete with transport by road, which is managed entirely by the private sector. In the first regulation concerning transport by road, in 1935, deregulation in fact intervened, giving rise to a myriad of self-employed drivers in road transport. The new regulation (law no. 298 of 1974 and DPR no. 783 of 1977) recomposes a minimal number of enterprises to improve services and reduce costs.

At a Community level, the system of licence quotas or the more favourable system originating from bilateral conventions limits the development and the integration of transport, not only at an international level but also at a regional level within bordering countries. In fact, liberalisation of road transport does not only presuppose a system of deregulation of authorisations but also of removing customs barriers. It appears then, even in pure economic terms, that regulation and deregulation are both necessary in the different realities of the same mode of transport.

Even in passenger road transport one observes both the necessity of a Community-level deregulation and of a more rational and organic domestic and urban transport regulation (in Italy at least).

Finally even the motoring sector, traditionally free and not controlled by regulations, is still governed indirectly and effectively by national rules, through fiscal measures on petrol prices, on road tax, on motorway tolls and on the regulation of circulation and traffic.

Passenger and goods railway transport is a sector run for the most part by the State: the concession of railway lines to private persons has not been widespread in Italy, the sector being managed as a government monopoly. It is clear that the poor service on Italian railways will not be resolved by deregulation. It is not the form of public administration through a special enterprise which has destroyed the market position of railway transport in Italy, but the way in which transport policy has run it, giving privilege to road over rail: in other European countries, rail transport sometimes appears to be efficient even though it may be managed by a State monopoly.

In general the railway fares less well than road transport, even though the costs of transporting goods and passengers by road are economically higher. As for the Italian experience (even if in less strong terms, this is also valid for other countries), we can observe a strange deregulation of land transport: competition between rail and road, the first managed by a national monopoly, the second mainly managed by the private sector, but with a regulation system erected as protection for the national management. The outcome of this competitive policy puts the burden on the State carrier and reserves the profit for the private carrier. Given this competition, a twist in the national transport economy is now observed, so that goods are preferably carried by road, while passengers utilise the train. In fact, the market tendency should be the reverse if we consider the high social costs.

3. Maritime transport

Even for maritime transport, the freedom of the seas in the actual international context appears to be more a very general and abstract principle than an attainable target. In a few words we cannot even try to outline the organisation of intra-Community maritime transport and of that with respect to the rest of the world. No doubt transport by sea has great importance for all European countries in the present Community import–export system. From the motivations contained in a recent regulation project of the EC Council, which was meant to protect free access to maritime transport in ocean-traffic, one can observe that

1. an ever increasing number of countries resort to protectionist measures with regard to their mercantile fleets, through unilateral regulation or administrative measures or through bilateral agreements with other countries;
2. third nations which are bound by the UN convention to the code of conduct for maritime conferences (which came into force on 6 October 1983) interpret the dispositions in such a way as to extend considerably the rights granted by the same convention to their own main companies, at the expense of the EC's main companies or of those countries belonging to the OECD — whether they are conference members or not;
3. in maritime traffic where the convention cannot be applied, unilaterally reserved allotments of cargo or bilateral agreements threaten to limit free access to line transport beyond the convention's principles and of the international agreements;
4. as for loads in bulk, an even greater tendency exists in Third World countries to delimit the admission of loads in bulk, which causes a great threat to the free competition that widely prevails in this sector;
5. restrictions on access to loads in bulk would have negative repercussions on the mercantile fleet of the EEC members and would also enormously increase the transport cost of such a

cargo, and would therefore weigh heavily on the Community's commercial interests.

For this purpose, we observe that the Community should have the possibility to proceed with co-ordinated action on behalf of its members in those cases in which the competitive position of the mercantile fleet of a member will undergo negative repercussions following reserves of cargo in favour of shipping companies of third nations.

As for cabotage, as some members reserve coasting trade to ships which fly their own flag, the EEC Committee, although having considered the particular social and security reasons which hinder the opening (in the individual States) of the respective national maritime trade to the competition of ships which fly flags of other members, has recently foreseen the abolition of such restrictions and has proposed the issue of a Council regulation (in accordance with Article 84 of the Treaty of Rome, and in application of Articles 58, 60 and 66 of the same treaty). These few hints are enough to show how in the present intra-European economic and legal context, the problem of deregulation for maritime transport is not even considered. On the contrary, there exists another problem: more efficient and rational regulation at a Community level.

4. Air transport

The 'regulation–deregulation' debate in Community transport started in air transport, but even in this sector this is not an abstract debate. It is not a principle of freedom, but a precise political choice to place the consumer's interests before other economic and social interests.

One may doubt, however, whether fares, as a ratio of the real cost of each line, are for the customary air passenger preferable to equalised fares on all networks. For instance, after deregulation a Milan business person pays more to get to Rome, but the same passenger will pay less to get to Palermo or Lampedusa. Thus operating commercially on two markets (approximately 2,000 kilometres apart) will not be prohibitive. It is not true, however, that all costs are exclusively borne by the customer, since the deficit of the national companies, in one way or another, falls on the State budget (at least in Italy).

No valid objective reasons exist to sustain deregulation in air transport as a natural law principle of a free market in preference to a regulation made by the State.

The problem then appears in more dramatic terms: what answer must be given to the deregulation which is unilaterally imposed by American companies on international air transport? Is an EC answer to the fare war possible? The answers at this stage depend on political and economic aspects, not on the law.

At a Community level the experience of the last few years has shown that ministers of many Community countries are orientated towards maintaining — for as long as possible — the structure which protects the national airline companies from competition.

It was in fact neither possible to introduce an intraregional air transport liberalisation of a third level among Community countries, nor to approve the Community regulation that allocates to the Committee the right to intervene in order to prevent abuses of power, nor to revoke the rules which prevent the system of 'country-of-origin pricing' for the fare on the intra-European route.

The maintenance of the status quo does not mean, however, that the previous balance has remained unchanged. Tensions still remain strong and the positions of the various countries are different. The most liberal position is the British one. In 1977 the CAA, in establishing air fares on European routes, affirmed that competition is preferable where such a policy is held to be practicable. On the other routes, the fares should not be discriminating, allowing an efficient company to cover the cost. The Netherlands, for instance, is a supporter of free trade, as its national company has much interest in entering the traffic basin of its neighbouring countries. The French, Italian and German positions are more protectionist.

Moreover, the pressures coming from the same market owing to the users' action and to the prolonged stagnation of demand are to be considered, which could make it extremely difficult to keep the trust, the pools on the European routes, and the same IATA fare agreements.

Finally, it may be recalled that (during a public hearing of the EEC Transport Commission held in Brussels on 21–22 February 1985) the necessity for effective deregulation was pointed out, with greater fare flexibility and the entry of new companies in the civil airline section.

Two different tendencies have arisen on this subject. The Union of European Consumers and independent airlines have suggested the adoption in EC countries of the 'deregulation' system already experimented with in the United States, where it has caused a slight reduction in domestic air fares. On the other hand, the ECAC and the Union of Transport Workers, even considering the actual fragmentation of the European market system (with more than 2,000 bilateral agreements among States), and on seeing the negative consequences of the American experiment on a security and occupational level for employees, have suggested the necessity for a precise regulating plan for airline competition.

5. Conclusion

Clearly it is not possible today to predict future market positions and therefore it is wise to ask oneself what will be or should be the organisation and the new institutional market regulation. It must be observed that the regulation–deregulation discussion is not a debate on fundamental principles — free market or controlled market — of today's institutional system. The principle whether or not the market should be controlled by the public administration is not under discussion.

The problem is only concerned with the *quality* of regulation; there exists a problem on a State and on a Community level to convert transport policy from a regulation form that is exclusively protectionist, to new forms of competitive regulation, which allow public and private enterprises, which control transport, and which are a prompt and efficient response to the sudden changes in the complicated reality of international, Community, regional and local markets.

21 Policy Research for Transport Planning: A Synthesis

I. Masser

1. Introduction

The previous chapters in this section highlight the need for more attention to be given by those involved in transportation research to the issues involved in transport planning and policy analysis. When giving greater emphasis to these questions transport planners and decision-makers are able to draw on the experience that has been built up in other policy fields and utilise the methods and models that have come into existence over the last 20 years as a result of the efforts of social scientists in a wide variety of decision areas in both the public and private sectors.

Broadly speaking, these efforts can be grouped into two categories according to the stance that is adopted by the researcher and the level of generalisation that is involved. The first category concerns research which is usually carried out at a relatively high level of generalisation with a view to making broad statements about the issues involved. In most cases the researcher adopts a stance which is relatively detached from a day-to-day involvement in events. The findings of research studies of this kind are usually concerned more with the interpretation of events than with the outcomes themselves. A key theme in this kind of research in recent years has been the critical interpretation of activities in various policy fields in terms of the changing role of the State in relation to the continuing struggles between capital and labour. Other recurring themes include the way in which issues get on to and off the political agenda and the efforts of planning agencies to establish their legitimacy in the eyes of the rest of society that are considered in Starkie's contribution (Chapter 18) to this volume.

The second category of efforts is more limited in focus than the first. It is largely concerned with the application of general methods of solving concrete problems in specific instances. In this case the researcher does not take up a detached position but is directly and intimately involved in the day-to-day events that take place. It is not unusual for the findings of this kind of research to be judged largely in terms of the contribution that has been made to improving the quality of the outcomes, as can be seen in Reichman and Salomon's paper in this volume. Key themes in practice-orientated research such as this include the development of appropriate instruments and methodologies for strategic planning and policy analysis. Because of the extent to which planning agencies in different countries see themselves as responding to similar problems in different institutional settings, issues associated with the evaluation and transfer of planning experience at the cross-national level play an important role in this category.

The following discussion is concerned with the latter category of efforts. It attempts to bring together some of the specific issues raised in other contributions and, in particular, to identify a number of generalised themes for further discussion that emerge from these papers. It concentrates on three specific areas where it is felt that transport planners can draw on the experience that has been built up in other policy fields. These concern strategic planning methodology, evaluation research and cross-national comparison respectively.

Strategic planning methodology has been selected because of its vital role in forming opinion. There is a need for broad scenarios to be developed which embody views as to the likely outcomes of current trends and suggest ways in which transport planning can play a more positive role in urban development. An important objective of these efforts is to stimulate public debate and encourage the mobilisation of resources for transport planning.

Evaluation research has been chosen because it is felt that there is a need for a different kind of emphasis in policy analysis within the transport-planning field if planning is seen not as an end in itself but more as a means of achieving broader social and economic objectives. With these considerations in mind, the processes involved and the instruments that are being employed need to be evaluated. In addition, the outcomes of transportation planning efforts need to be mapped in terms of their consequences for different groups within society. Activities such as these require broad-scale evaluation efforts that take account of the unintended as well as the intended consequences of policies. In the process it will be necessary to consider the extent to which there has been a shift in resources between the different groups within society.

Cross-national comparisons inevitably occupy a central place whenever the experience of several countries is being considered. The critical question that has to be resolved in this case is what each country can learn from the experience of others. This involves not only identifying possible topics for transfer but also developing research strategies that facilitate the transfer process. This is particularly important in relation to the current debate on deregulation where there is a great deal of conflicting evidence and an overall lack of comparability between national political stances and institutional systems, as can be seen from the contributions of Bauchet and Masset (Chapter 19) and Fanara (Chapter 20) to this volume.

2. Strategic planning methodology

In the past most transport-planning research has been demand-led in that the task of the analyst has been basically to forecast travel demand. Although the range of variables included in the forecast varies from study to study, the primary purpose of such exercises is generally limited to providing input to the policy formulation process.

This kind of approach can be criticised on two grounds. Firstly, it can be argued that it fails to take adequate account of the wide range of uncertainties that surround transport planning. Because of this there is often a spurious air of precision in the forecasts which conceals the very large range of errors that must be attached to them. Secondly, forecasts of this kind tend to underestimate the extent to which fundamental changes may occur within society during the plan period. For example, there was a general failure in the transportation planning efforts of the late 1960s to anticipate the effects of the world energy crisis of 1973. Because of this, most demand-led forecasts tend to be conservative in character and are easily rendered obsolete as time passes.

Given these criticisms, there is a need to adopt a different style of forecasting to stimulate public debate about transport-planning options. The basic objective of this kind of forecasting is not so much to provide direct inputs to plan-making processes but to stimulate discussion and utilise expert knowledge of all kinds. This requires the systematic collection and collation of opinions about future developments (Fowles 1976). It must be stressed that the question of what constitutes expert opinion is a controversial one in the social science field. However, although it can be claimed that experts are not capable of forecasting the future much better than non-experts, their views are of considerable importance because of the degree to which they represent perceptions about the future that are embodied in current decisions.

The issues that are involved in this kind of forecasting can best be illustrated by reference to two of the most widely utilised techniques, scenario construction and the Delphi method. Scenario construction involves the preparation of multifaceted pictures of the future (Wilson 1978). These pictures are broad in scope and developmental in character, in that they attempt to reflect in a systematic way a large number of speculative interpretations based on the information that is currently available. For this reason, scenarios are rarely produced in isolation. Usually several contrasting scenarios are developed in relation to particular themes and these are often contrasted with trend scenarios based simply on extrapolation. A good example of this kind of approach can be found in the work carried out by the Dutch National Physical Planning Agency (1976 a; b) in connection with the formulation of its national urbanisation policy. Four distinct scenarios were developed for this purpose, a surprise-free scenario which served as a reference point, an optimistic scenario in which urban development is restricted by policies designed to promote energy and environmental conservation, a pessimistic scenario involving urban sprawl with few constraints, and a variant of this scenario with enhanced constraints.

The Delphi approach, as its name suggests, is directly concerned with gathering expert or 'oracular' opinions about the likelihood of future events. It is particularly useful with reference to questions relating to technological innovation and change but it is also of value for exploring current perceptions regarding future developments (Linstone and Turoff 1975). Three elements are common to most Delphi applications: the assembly of a panel of experts chosen to cover as wide a range of viewpoints as possible, the use of questionnaire interrogation to gather information from these experts, and the controlled feedback of the information collected by these means to the experts with a request for them to reconsider their initial views in the light of other people's perceptions. The basic objective of exercises of this kind is to indicate the entire range of possibilities that is forecast by the experts and to identify points where there is a convergence or divergence of viewpoints. A good example of the use of the Delphi method can be found in Foley *et al.*'s (1984) investigation of Sheffield's prospects following the collapse of the local steel industry during a national economic recession.

3. Evaluation research

A great deal of current evaluation research in the transport planning field can be criticised on two main counts: its concern with efficiency rather than equity criteria (see, for example, Reichman and Salomon (Chapter 11) in this volume), and the emphasis that is given to performance as against strategic policy monitoring. The former criticism is of particular importance in the light of discussion of transport policy as a means of achieving broader objectives where the latter can be regarded as a further facet of the discussion in Part C of this book on the need to improve strategic planning methodology in the transport field.

A greater emphasis on equity as against efficiency considerations brings with it a number of practical problems. Firstly, it is necessary to devise new units of measurement to replace the economic cost measures that are used in most current evaluation research (Voogd 1983). In this respect it is also necessary to recognise that there may be important differences between the individual evaluations placed on particular items. The problems experienced by the Roskill Commission on the Third London Airport, for example, in trying to put a monetary value on the cost that would be incurred if several Norman churches were destroyed as a result of airport construction, are likely to be increased substantially in evaluations which seek to expose the distributional consequences of particular actions.

Secondly, the increasing scope of the evaluation is likely to bring with it new problems for evaluation researchers (see, for example, Self 1975). So long as transport planning is viewed as an end in itself then evaluation research in this field can be relatively restricted in scope. As soon as it is viewed as a means of achieving broader social objectives, then the scope of evaluation research is increased enormously. Not only is the boundary of the field inherently loosely defined in studies of this kind but also the nature of the trade-offs that must be considered is likely to involve many policy fields other than transport planning.

Some of the practical problems described above can be resolved in practice by adopting an approach to transport-policy monitoring that incorporates strategic as well as performance considerations. It can be argued that strategic monitoring is central to effective transport planning in an uncertain and often rapidly changing environment. As the experience of strategic land-use planning indicates, the basic task of monitoring in this case is not merely to keep track of the progress that has been achieved towards policy implementation but also to assess the continuing validity of the assumptions underlying the policies themselves in the light of the information that has become available since they were formulated (see, for example Floyd *et al.* 1977; and Wedgewood Oppenheim *et al.* 1975). In this respect an important objective for the planner is to keep one step ahead of the game and identify new issues that must be placed on the transport-planning agenda.

In contrast to performance monitoring, which is largely an internal matter for the planning agency, strategic monitoring has an important role to play in forming opinion outside the agency. This is particularly the case as transport planning, like many other public policy fields, is one in which the majority of institutional and individual decisions that affect the demand for transport facilities lie essentially outside the control of the transport-planning agencies.

4. Cross-national comparison

Wherever a large number of countries is involved there is a tendency for comparisons to take the form of league tables of national performance relative to a limited number of criteria, such as the level of car-ownership or the unit costs of public transport facilities. Although interesting in themselves, statistics such as these are of only limited value to those concerned with transport planning in that they reveal very little about the factors underlying travel behaviour in individual countries or the extent to which this has been influenced by the adoption of particular transport policies. To consider questions such as these, in-depth case studies are required of particular countries within a tightly defined framework which enables a comparative evaluation of individual national experiences at the cross-national level. To be of any value from the standpoint of comparative analysis these case studies must take into account not only travel behaviour and transport planning in these countries but also the social, political and institutional context within which this takes place. Through the analysis of the phenomenon of transport planning in its national context, the analyst is able to distinguish between those elements of practice that reflect unique configurations of national and local circumstances and those that can be regarded as universal in character where the transfer of experience from one country to another can be contemplated.

For practitioners, the main objective of cross-national comparison is to identify possible topics for transfer so that planners and decision-makers in one country can build upon the experience of others (Masser 1984). In drawing upon this experience, however, national policy-makers will inevitably have to adapt and modify it to take account of their own circumstances. Consequently, an important prerequisite for successful transfer is that national policy-makers have a clear idea of their own requirements from the outset so that they are able systematically to evaluate the experience of other countries

(Masser 1985). If this is not the case, there is a real danger that inappropriate policies, which were originally formulated in response to entirely different social, economic or institutional circumstances, may be imposed upon a particular country as a result of the transfer process. This is particularly likely to occur wherever the relationship between the importing and the exporting country is unequal in nature, as is the case with many of the technical aid projects that have been carried out in the transportation- and mobility-planning field in the less developed countries.

5. Conclusions

Three specific areas where it is felt that transport planners can draw upon the experience that has been built up in other policy fields have been discussed in this chapter. Inevitably the level of discussion has been very general in character, in that it has been primarily concerned with identifying topics for further consideration. The next step is to examine each of these topics in greater detail with reference to the substantial amount of material that is already available from other policy fields with a view to identifying more detailed policy research priorities in the transport-planning field.

References

Floyd, M., A. Sutton, J. Friend and L. King (1977). *Monitoring for Development Planning*. Research Report 23, London: Department of the Environment.

Foley, P.D., D.H. Green and I. Masser (1984). 'The Future of the Sheffield Economy: An Investigation Using the Delphi Method'. TRP 49, Department of Town and Regional Planning, University of Sheffield.

Fowles, J. (1976). 'An Overview of Social Forecasting Procedures', *Jour. AIP.*, **42**, 253–63

Linstone, H.A. and M. Turoff, eds (1975). *The Delphi Method: Techniques and Applications*. Reading, MA: Addison Wesley.

Masser, I. (1984). 'Cross-national Comparative Planning Studies: A Review', *Town Planning Review*, **55**, 137–60.

Masser, I. (1985). 'The Transfer of Planning Experience Between Countries Current Trends and Future Prospects' in D. Massey, ed., *The Role of International Agencies in Promoting Cross National Research*. Department of Civic Design, University of Liverpool.

National Physical Planning Agency (1976a). *Scenarios ten behoeve van de Verstedelijkingsnota*. The Hague.

National Physical Planning Agency (1976b). *Summary of the Report on Urbanisation in the Netherlands*. The Hague.

Self, P. (1975). *Econocrats and the Policy Process: the Political and Philosophy of Cost Benefit Analysis*. London: Macmillan.

Voogd, J. H. (1983). *Multicriteria Evaluation of Urban and Regional Planning*. London: Pion.

Wedgewood Oppenheim F., D. Hart and B. Cobley (1975). 'An Exploratory Study in Strategic Monitoring', *Progress in Planning*, **5**, 1–58.
Wilson, I.H. (1978). 'Scenarios' in J. Fowles, ed., *Handbook of Futures Research* Westport, CT: Greenwood Press.

22 Mobility and Transportation Planning Revisited

P. Nijkamp and S. Reichman

1. Transport: a changing role rather than a decline in importance

In this chapter a retrospective view on transportation and mobility will be given. The interest in mobility and transportation issues has shown a wave-like pattern in the post-war period. Until the end of the 1960s massive investments were made in many countries in order to expand and improve (private and public) transportation, as this sector was regarded as one of the necessary conditions or driving forces for economic progress. Since the 1970s the transportation sector has been regarded from a more critical viewpoint, especially because of the many negative externalities involved in large-scale mobility (environmental degradation, high energy consumption, and increasing traffic-accident rates). This has had two consequences for transportation planning and policy.

The first was the attempt to reduce (the growth in) mobility, especially as far as private transportation is concerned. New investments in road infrastructure were postponed or cancelled, private car use was discouraged by means of fiscal measures, and physical planning was orientated towards a territorial organisation marked by less intensive car use. In various countries (like Denmark and the Netherlands) a (slight) reduction in car mobility could indeed be observed by the end of the 1970s. Needless to say, the economic situation also played a decisive role in the changes in mobility patterns in our society.

In the second place, public transport received a clear stimulus in many countries from the middle of the 1970s onwards. Consequently, the rate of use of public transport (especially trains) was increasing in these countries. However, the increase in budgets for investment in (public) transport infrastructure led inevitably to increasing deficits, a situation which was worsened by the economic stagnation which caused the need to reduce public expenditure in many sectors.

In the 1980s the mobility processes have tended to become more stable. Despite stagnation, the transportation sector is not significantly declining, although in some respects it is facing serious problems. For instance, in many countries regional public transport (such as buses) has become problematic. The same holds true for urban transportation in many countries, especially as cities exhibit a phase of structural decline. However, such problems, though serious, do not lead to the conclusion that the transportation sector as a whole is in decline.

In this context, three remarks have to made which indicate the relevance of the transportation sector in the second half of the 1980s. First, transportation is necessarily linked to the production system; it is an important input for many productive activities. Although the production system is at the moment going through a phase of structural transition, it has not become evident that future production systems will tend to be less transport-intensive. On the contrary, future production systems may be expected to exhibit closely interwoven interactions, in which communications and transportation play a key role.

In the second place, the impact of new technologies has to be mentioned. Although from a technical viewpoint the modern telecommunications sector may be a substitute for many physical interactions, it is increasingly realised that this modern technology has become necessary in order to compensate for the rapid increase in physical and human interactions in our modern society, but by no means may be considered to be a competitive substitute for physical interactions themselves. In any case, we have incomplete evidence in this respect, especially because the developments in the field of transportation logistics and telecommunications are exhibiting a rapid growth.

Finally, it has to be observed that modern settlement systems (at both the urban and metropolitan level) exhibit a contrasting impact on the transportation sector. Transportation used to be a major stimulus for the development of new urban centres, while at the same time transportation was endangering a balanced urban development. Positive and negative externalities appear to play an ambiguous role in the spatial evolution of our modern societies.

The trends exhibited by modern transportation systems are — to a large extent — somewhat puzzling. From the point of view of both transportation analysis and transportation policy, it is no doubt true that — due to the multidimensional contribution of transportation to the evolution of modern societies — a profound interest in the transportation sector is certainly warranted. Transportation analysis and planning have a clear role to fulfil, as will be shown below.

Whilst transportation analysis and planning have emerged mainly from the engineering world, it has to be recognised at the same time that — despite this engineering bias — there has been an ongoing shift from conventional engineering to social science approaches, a major reason for this shift being the inadequacy of conventional analytical techniques. These techniques appeared to suffer from two limitations, namely an orientation towards more technically and less behaviourally rooted methods and techniques, and an orientation towards past experience and *not* towards future mobility in its broadest sense. This inertia implies that, for instance, the impact of information technology remains almost completely outside our collective range of experience. Furthermore, this approach also implies that the use of conventional techniques restricts the range of options considered in mobility and transportation behaviour.

The current state of the art in the field of mobility and transportation planning is increasingly covering a wide range of methodologies, research directions and issues from the social sciences. Despite the great diversity in transportation and mobility analysis, the research directions and views thereon are less divergent than is often assumed. For instance, it is an almost commonly accepted standpoint that there is a need for a more profound analysis of the effects of current (and future) developments in communications and information technology on settlement structures and transportation systems. In addition, there is a growing demand to place transportation planning and policy responses within the broad framework of policy analysis and evaluation research in the social sciences. Such recent developments illustrate the shift from traditional transport engineering thinking and demonstrate the departure from past practice.

At least six major new directions can be identified that reflect our view that conventional engineering approaches tend to be definitely substituted by behavioural social science approaches. These new directions are presented here as six statements on the current common views on transportation and mobility analysis.

1. Transportation planning is regarded as a special case of a more general set of planning issues in a socio-economic, political and technological environment (see also Section 3). In other words, there can be no separate transportation planning in that transportation planning is only a means to serve more general social and economic objectives. Consequently, discussions regard-

ing transport mobility must be related more generally to increased levels of personal mobility and the greater awareness of the public regarding disparities in life-styles. The implications of the 'tiptoe' effect, or the keeping up with the Jones's syndrome, in an increasingly aware populace, is leading to growing demands for access to services of all kinds, services which are also offered by modern technology.

2. In the case of these demands, most transport planners and decision makers find themselves in a dilemma because of the extent to which their freedom of action is becoming increasingly restricted by a number of constraints of various kinds. The most important of these concern the constraints that are being imposed by most countries on public expenditure and the extent to which these have led to a re-evaluation of service provision as a whole. The current debates on deregulation provide a good example of the consequences of these constraints on transport policy. The second set of constraints concerns the extent to which the activities of opposition and environmental groups have effectively limited the ability of transport planners and decision makers to carry out large-scale projects in many places. The degree to which the objectors have been willing to go, for example in some of the recent road enquiries in Greater London, illustrates the intensity of feelings on these questions. Thus planning objectives are changing and wider issues are perceived as being important, so that additional components are to be included in the original set of objectives. Finally, it is also necessary to take account of the extent to which conventional notions of efficiency as a policy goal have been supplemented or replaced by the need to stress equity and distributional considerations. The introduction of equity constraints further restricts the freedom of action of transport planners and decision makers.
3. In the face of this dilemma, transport planners and decision makers are being compelled to change the style of transport planning in many countries. Transportation planning used to be demand-following, but the awareness of the limits to growth has led to a reorientation. Saturation phenomena, economic recession and negative spillover effects have evoked the need for a more active 'demand-steering' planning in transportation and mobility behaviour. A more effective interference with and control of the supply and demand side of transportation and mobility have been the logical results of the need for market control in the field of spatial interactions. This is a marked departure from past practice in which traditionally transport planning was largely a response to

present and perceived future demands for transport facilities. As a public good, transportation and mobility are regarded now more as a means of providing access to basic services such as schools and hospitals (the concept of a 'potential'; see also Section 3) and it is arguable that the goal of transportation planning should be to ensure that minimum levels of access are guaranteed to all segments of the community. This implies a basic need and a potentiality approach to transport planning rather than the travel-demand approach adopted in most past and current practices.

4. It is also increasingly realised that public transport will face difficult problems in the future because of an ongoing trend towards deconcentration, rigid budget mechanisms, unsatisfactory achievement indicators and inefficient management structures. There is also a growing awareness that governments will fail to reach their goals in physical planning if public transport is regarded as the major field of intervention from the side of public policy. The need for a coherent and more integrated policy, however, is in contrast with current deregulation goals, so that the position of public transport is likely to remain a problematic one, unless (modern and future) (tele)communications technology induces policy-makers to harmonise the conflicting objectives of private and public transport. In this respect, new and flexible institutional frameworks for decision-making on communications and transportation systems may be necessary.
5. Because of the extent to which transport planning and mobility in different countries vary according to the institutional, social, economic and developmental circumstances of each country, it is necessary to distinguish between *general* issues that are common to more than one country and where consequently experience can be transferred, and *unique* issues that reflect the impact of a set of specific contextual factors in that country. These issues are not limited to the discussion of transportation planning policies but also apply to the interpretation of trends and the kinds of model that have been developed to examine spatial mobility processes.
6. It is likely that current developments in the field of information and communications technology will have a major effect on both settlement structures and transportation systems, as well as on our lifestyles. The extent to which their consequences will complement existing transport systems or lead to alternative forms of provision which replace them are still to be worked out, as have their likely distributional effects on different sections of the population.

The foregoing six observations point out the need for evolutionary analysis of mobility behaviour and of long-term structural changes in transportation systems.

2. Relevance of behavioural analysis

Mobility has become a key concept in the modern Welfare State, so that it is almost regarded as a basic value in a modern society. Consequently, mobility rates are sometimes taken as one of the performance indicators of an economic system.

In contrast to mobility as a positive welfare indicator, it is also worth mentioning that negative spill-overs are caused by the increase in geographical movement. For instance, increased mobility causes intolerable consequences for the urban environment; it results in formidable fuel consumption, it leads to unacceptable changes in the physical environment, while especially car mobility conflicts strongly with other physical planning criteria (such as a pleasant residential quality of life).

Clearly, it has to be realised that in an industrialised society (marked by labour division and specialisation) mobility is a necessary component, which also requires a satisfactory infrastructure system. The basic question is, however, what type of mobility is desirable and compatible with the urban, environmental and residential system? It is evident that mobility based on the private car use is by no means the only option. But as in our society (private) car mobility is a dominating trend, the question may be raised: what are the effects (in terms of costs and benefits) of increasing car mobility? In this respect, the following critical remarks are to be made.

First, car mobility is very much dependent on decisions to move made by one car user (very often the head of the household), so that the actual mobility pattern is very much determined by one single person. This also implies that urban sprawl (and its impact on the urban quality of life) is usually the result of the decision of a single person in a household, who externalises the cost of transport to a large set of individuals and groups in a society. Consequently, there is a gap between individual and social costs of spatial mobility.

In addition, the present rate of car mobility has altered the human settlement pattern in our society, not only in urban, but also in rural areas. The mobility trend, however, has caused enormous distributional conflicts, as the costs and benefits of geographical dispersion are unequally distributed among socio-economic groups, while the potential accessibility and the actual use of specific transport modes is also contingent upon a person's socio-economic position. In this respect, it is regrettable that often in the past transportation planners have been inclined to accept present mobility trends as a datum without any regard to distributional issues.

Next, it is worth noting that future mobility patterns may also lead to conflicting results. On the one hand, one could argue that preservation of environmental quality would require a lifestyle which is modest in terms of spatial mobility. On the other hand, it is clear that the demand for an upswing of economic activities will put heavy demands on a communications and transportation infrastructure which would fulfil the needs of a dynamic society. Unfortunately, little attention has so far been given to the question of thresholds of mobility levels which would be prohibitive for a further socio-economic development and to the question whether alternative settlement patterns might be better favoured by alternative mobility patterns or mobility modes.

Another point which is worth mentioning is the increasingly manifest conflict between implied levels of mobility and the economy of scale of public facilities (like schools, health centres, homes for the aged, and so on). This divergence between individual behavioural choice regarding desired mobility and social compulsory choice implied by large-scale (cost-saving) facilities is a source of primary conflict in the field of mobility planning. Theoretically, one may argue that the externalities of such forced mobility patterns are to be attributed to the social costs of such facilities (instead of being externalised to the members of society).

Finally, there is an urgent need for new accounting frameworks which would spell out the pros and cons (in terms of efficiency and equity) of alternative mobility patterns. Special attention would have to be given to an evaluation of a dual mobility development in which there is an increase in the relative share of people who are either below a lower threshold of mobility (mobility-deprived) or above a tolerable ceiling of mobility (excess mobility). In this context, sufficient attention has to be given to the ineffectiveness of self-regulating processes in mobility behaviour (the prevalence of the so-called 'tiptoe' effect).

In order to allow for a fair choice between a wide range of conflicting options, it would be necessary to generate new alternative configurations of mobility patterns (based on temporal strategies, heterogeneous land uses, job decentralisation, etc.). A minimum prerequisite for a more comprehensive social choice situation would be a monitoring of mobility behaviour modification (based, *inter alia*, on longitudinal panels or a closer analysis of changes in lifestyles and mobility decision). In this framework, special attention would be necessary for structural changes in economic conditions, in environmental and energy constraints and in the potential offered by new communications-based technologies.

3. Need for contextual analysis

The context (or the 'environment' in a systems-analytic framework) of mobility and transportation is a major determinant of the spatial behaviour of mankind. Two notions are important in this context, *possibilism* and *restrictionism*. Possibilism (first introduced by the French geographer Vidal de la Blanche) studies the external conditions which allow a specific kind of behaviour. In the framework of mobility behaviour, possibilism refers to contextual variables that extend the living and working space of people, such as the rise in general welfare, the increased labour division and female participation in the labour force, the supply of new transportation techniques, and so on. Restrictionism, on the other hand, concerns all thresholds and bottle-necks which prevent people from being mobile, such as membership of specific age and income classes or lack of a satisfactory transportation infrastructure. Possibilism is essentially concerned with why people are mobile, whereas restrictionism deals with why people are *not* mobile.

Clearly, in this respect a clear distinction has to be made between private and professional mobility. In a business context, communication and interaction costs are always disutilities, so that an improvement of mobility (leading to lower communication and interaction costs) is always a benefit from an entrepreneurial viewpoint. In a private (for example, household) context, this may also be the case, but this is not necessarily true, as various spatial interactions may be postponed and/or combined with other trips. In this respect, the perception of distance and communication is of decisive importance. The freedom of individual choice does not necessarily imply that more mobility implies by definition an increase in welfare; this is only the case if mobility leads to a rise in the potential to enjoy more welfare, but it may be equally true that the same potential can be reached by using alternative communications technologies (such as telecommunications or video systems). In any case, it has to be realised that there is an increasing tendency towards more social interaction and spatial communication, so that the question may be raised whether the increased demand for mobility in a spatial context does not lead to increasing marginal disutilities of a further rise in mobility. Clearly, the basic question here is whether modern technology can be a proper substitute for the need for physical mobility and whether mobility needs have to be fulfilled in an individual or a collective way. Transportation planning has to be aware of these complicated trade-offs.

It is worth noting that most mobility trends are almost world-wide. The same universal pattern holds almost true of recent development in transportation planning (for example, deregulation), so that it is justifiable to make a plea for a cross-national comparison of mobility patterns and related planning issues in various countries. This is once more justified, as in many countries similar issues are raised and similar analytical tools are developed to assess the long-term impacts of transportation and mobility on the future of our society (for example, settlement patterns), and *vice versa*. For instance, telecommunications issues are studied in almost all countries, and similar analytical tools are also being used (in particular, scenario analysis).

Figure 22.1 offers a concise overview of some basic linkages between the context of mobility behaviour (the inner circle) and mobility patterns themselves. It relates to both persons and commodities/services transportation and may cover geographical scales ranging from urban to (inter)national levels. Apart from the role of technological change (in production, logistics, networks and management), the scheme also points out the links between changes in location patterns, changes in mobility patterns and changes in communication infrastructure (in a broad sense). It is also worth noting that the upper block (the communication infrastructure) refers to *slow* dynamics in adjustment patterns, while the left-hand and right-hand blocks (spatial mobility and settlement patterns, respectively) refer to *fast* dynamics and *medium* dynamics in adjustment patterns.

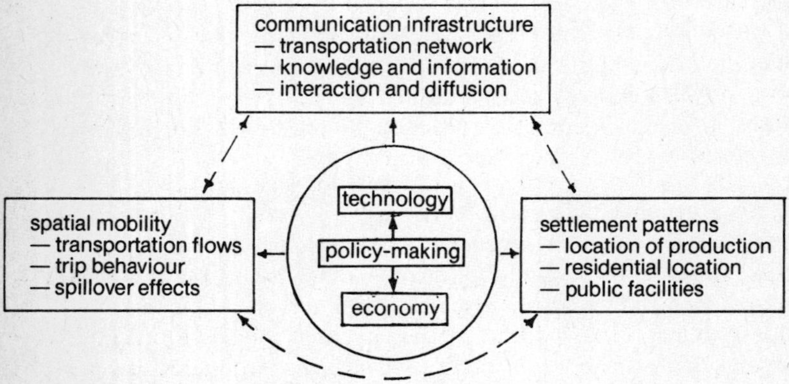

Figure 22.1 Contextual analysis of mobility patterns

In Figure 22.1 policy-making plays a prominent role, not only as a purely transportation- and mobility-orientated activity, but as a consistent set of activities focusing on man's position in land-use activities, environmental systems, socio-economic developments and new technologies. The explosive post-war rise in car-ownership which made transportation an almost autonomous sector of our society has exerted drastic influences on the physical, environmental and social conditions of Western countries. In the light of the large number of negative externalities of this development and in view of the great many alternative choice options offered by modern technologies, the question may be raised whether the original costs of functional segregation in our countries need not be carefully re-examined, for instance by developing new analytical concepts linking societal, technological and spatial dimensions, by seeking appropriate assessment criteria for mobility and transportation investments that do justice to a broad range of social priorities, and by designing an analysis and planning framework that is not mainly characterised by 'planning for transport and mobility' (as an end in itself), but by 'transportation planning for favouring a society's development potential' (being an instrumental activity).

Such issues are not only of academic interest, but of direct relevance for transportation planning and physical planning. For example, in many countries the larger agglomerations are showing signs of decline in terms of decreasing numbers of population, jobs and facilities. Jobs tend to become more spatially dispersed, so that public transport networks are likely to become less effective in the future. An increase in overcapacity in public transport — and hence in costs — is then inevitable, which may lead to a reduction in the service level or an increase in the privatisation of transport services (implying a higher dependence on private car use). Taking car mobility uncritically as a major starting point in transportation planning would no doubt lead to serious social, environmental and spatial distributional problems. Thus, a reassessment of the context of transportation and mobility developments is of the utmost importance.

4. A research agenda

It has repeatedly been emphasised that the transportation sector is part of a highly dynamic 'space-society', so that current theoretical and analytical tools have great difficulties in keeping pace with rapid (r)evolutions in the infrastructure and suprastructure of our society. Consequently, our analytical box of tools is almost permanently lagging behind.

From a *theoretical* point of view, we need to improve our understanding of the complexity of the behavioural response of individuals and groups to contextual variables and policy issues. The rationality paradigm, which makes up the heart of conventional utility analysis, has to be extended with notions from 'satisfying' and 'justifying' behaviour, especially because there is no real 'market' for all categories of the transport sector.

From a *technical* (modelling or statistical) perspective, there is a clear need not so much to advocate the use of a specific type of model or statistical tool, but to choose a methodology on the basis of its appropriateness for the problem under consideration. Special attention has to be given to the analysis of institutional response at the supply side as well as of uncertainty in the medium and long run (for example, demographic shifts, socio-economic changes, locational shifts and technological progress).

Finally, from an *operational* viewpoint the gap between theories and tools, on the one hand, and planning and policy implementation, on the other, has to be bridged. Comprehensible analyses of the effects of mobility and transportation behaviour (for example, regarding acid rain or noise annoyance) have to be designed, in such a way that they have at least a minimum credibility in a policy arena.

These three aspects have also been used to identify a set of items for a research agenda on transportation and mobility planning in a social context. The following main components based on the main structure of the present book are distinguished for this agenda: general research directions, planning issues, analytical tools and policy aspects.

4.1 General research directions

- Generation of ideas for alternative patterns of living that would alleviate problems currently associated with mobility (temporal strategies, heterogeneous land uses, walk- or cycle-orientated policies, use of telecommunications, job redefinition, and so on).
- A programme of monitoring studies, both to establish prevailing trends and to understand how mobility decisions are taken; the latter will require longitudinal studies that follow respondents' life paths and examine major life and mobility choices.
- Development of analytical and theoretical frameworks able to incorporate the breadth and depth of mobility, at least in a qualitative way. One approach for such a comprehensive framework would be the design of a systems-theoretic 'satellite' model, with mobility at the centre.
- Further investigation of measures of mobility and the levels required by people to sustain a given lifestyle or achieve a standard

of well-being. Also critical here is a measure of the value which people place on aspects of their environment and life.

4.2 Planning issues

- Examination of operational possibilities for measuring the socio-economic meaning and achievements of public transport, given the limited budgets of the current deficits in many sectors of public transport, by focusing on both efficiency and equity issues.
- Analysis of substitution effects between private and public transport on markets where both transportation modes are operating (for example, competition between rapid rail lines and airlines on a nation-wide scale, as in France).
- Studies on the integration of transport planning in urban and regional development planning, not only in rapidly expanding areas (such as boom towns), but also under conditions of geographical contraction (as in various European countries).
- Investigation of the effects of economic conditions (growth or decline) on locational and transport behaviour of individuals, households and firms on a local, regional or national scale.
- Studies of the effects of demographic processes and changing patterns of household formation, changing lifestyles, changing work conditions and shifts in consumption and leisure patterns on the locational and transport behaviour of individuals, households and firms (including the extent to which policy measures may exert an influence on such changes).

4.3 Analytical tools

- Introduction of accounting frameworks that incorporate the wide range of costs and benefits of mobility patterns in society. These should be able both to identify direct and secondary effects and to trace the distributional effects across the population.
- Improvements to our existing transport and land-use forecasting models and the construction of new micro-behaviourally orientated kinds of model to take account of developments in our understanding of mobility, and to meet the requirements of the types of framework proposed above.
- Systematic cross-national comparisons of mobility patterns between countries with different systems of regulations, to identify key factors affecting mobility.
- Analysis of the economics of private and institutional actors with regard to the effects of their budgets for various purposes (including transport) and their elasticities, in monetary terms, in terms of time or in terms of qualitative perceptions.

- Research on the future effects of new information and communications technologies on local, regional or (inter)national transport systems (including production activities, logistics and transport infrastructure).
- Design of evaluation and survey frameworks for transport policies on different geographical scales (including methods reconciling micro, meso and macro studies of mobility and transportation and methods for panel, longitudinal and stated preference data techniques).

4.4 Policy aspects

- Research into the changing role of governments over time at all levels through the analysis of policy and planning life cycles.
- Exploration of the potential of a strategic reflection and a development of policy scenarios to stimulate debate and mobilise resources for transport and mobility planning.
- Development of evaluation research to assess the impacts of policy and to identify the costs and benefits of technological change in distributional terms.
- Research into ways of financing deficits in public transport policy by enhancing its efficiency (by means of more appropriate management structures, a closer market orientation such as deregulation, or a better integration with other physical planning measures).
- Examination of a proper integration of transport policy with urban, environmental and regional policy in order to arrive at a meaningful balance between urban sprawl and compact city design.
- Analysis of conflicts brought about by the failure of our welfare society to guarantee a sustained level of economic prospects and by the need to reduce budget deficits in a situation of a historically subsidised mobility.

4.5 New trends in transportation planning

The four categories mentioned above reflect the structure of the present publication, namely actual trends (for example, spatial changes in settlement patterns, structural changes in transportation systems), planning problems (for example, substitution possibilities, integrated spatial impact analysis), analytical methods (for example, performance measures, accounting frameworks, models) and policy issues (for example, institutional aspects, policy instruments).

In the past the main emphasis has mainly been on the analysis of trends (in either a descriptive or a predictive sense) and the development of methods in association with this analysis. In this framework, a behavioural micro-economic orientation has increasingly been stressed and accepted. In view of the changes that are expected in the scope and nature of mobility and transportation planning in the future, an increasing emphasis must be placed on the relationship between spatial behaviour and spatial planning. This once more involves a shift in emphasis from an engineering approach to a stronger social science orientation. Analogously, policy issues are increasingly coming to the fore, witness recent discussions on (de)regulation, organisation and financing of public transport, and so on.

Debates on mobility and transportation planning often centre on two major issues: *internal* analysis focusing on mobility and transportation in a strict sense (for example, changing demands for travel, trends in settlement evolution, models of (dis)aggregate choice, transportation policy analysis) and *external* analysis focusing on the significance of mobility and transportation in a broad social context (for example, transportation as a means of achieving socio-economic goals rather than as an end in itself — the 'potentiality' view — the basic needs approach to mobility, the effects of changing information and communications technology).

Generally speaking, internal transportation and mobility analysis appears to be relatively well developed although there are important gaps in detail. For instance, in the case of actual trends there is considerable scope for further work in connection with the urbanisation/suburbanisation debate and its consequences for public transport usage. Similarly, in the field of methods there is an urgent need to expand existing accounting frameworks to make them more comprehensive in nature, and to develop and strengthen operational methodologies relating to the use of soft rather than hard data.

External research in the field of transport and mobility is in general much less well developed than that relating to internal research. Nevertheless, in general, the position with respect to the analysis of trends is relatively good by comparison with that in connection with the development of proper methods. Much more attention needs to be given, *inter alia*, to the analysis of non-cost factors and of indicators which incorporate social equity as well as cost-efficiency criteria. There is a particular need to bring in policy analysis and evaluation research thinking into the transport-planning field. A similar conclusion can be drawn with respect to the impact that developments in information and communications technology will have on settlement structures and transport systems. Given that a major shift in emphasis in research is needed to develop a broader perspective of such trends, it is plausible to state that the state of the art in current research is not well developed. However, a distinction can be made here between trends and methods, in that more attention has been given to trends than methods in the work that has been carried out so far. Consequently, one may draw the conclusion that there is an urgent need to expand the scope of transport- and mobility-planning research to place more emphasis on policy analysis and the broader consequences of developments in information and communications technology.

A related remark is still in order here. There is a clear need to develop methods for transport policy evaluation within an explicitly comparative perspective. In this framework, particular attention should then be given to a comparative analysis of different policy instruments and institutions in various countries and the likely effects of deregulation and privatisation on the future of public services and the use of private transport modes.

Finally, the inevitable conclusion to be drawn from all previous reflections is that — despite the changing role of transport — there is much scope for further analysis of the important position that will continuously be taken by the transport sector in our changing society.

Subject Index

Author Index

OXFORD
POLYTECHNIC
LIBRARY
WITHDRAWN